Springer Texts in Business and Economics

Springer Texts in Business and Economics (STBE) delivers high-quality instructional content for undergraduates and graduates in all areas of Business/Management Science and Economics. The series is comprised of self-contained books with a broad and comprehensive coverage that are suitable for class as well as for individual self-study. All texts are authored by established experts in their fields and offer a solid methodological background, often accompanied by problems and exercises.

Mehtap Aldogan Eklund •
Gabrielle Wanzenried
Editors

Academic and Educational Entrepreneurship

Foundations in Theory and Lessons from Practice

Springer

Editors
Mehtap Aldogan Eklund
Department of CBA - Accountancy
University of Wisconsin–La Crosse
La Crosse, WI, USA

Gabrielle Wanzenried
School of Management and Engineering Vaud
University of Applied Sciences and
Arts Western Switzerland HES-SO
Yverdon-les-Bains, Switzerland

ISSN 2192-4333 ISSN 2192-4341 (electronic)
Springer Texts in Business and Economics
ISBN 978-3-031-10954-6 ISBN 978-3-031-10952-2 (eBook)
https://doi.org/10.1007/978-3-031-10952-2

This Springer imprint is published by the registered company Springer Nature Switzerland AG
The registered company address is: Gewerbestrasse 11, 6330 Cham, Switzerland

This book is dedicated to Mehtap Aldogan Eklund's father, Ahmet Aldogan, and daughter, Minnie Aldogan Eklund who passed away before this book was published.

Acknowledgment

This book has only been made possible thanks to the collaboration of various people, to all of whom we owe a great debt of gratitude. First of all, we would like to thank all the authors who have contributed. The book lives from the richness of the different perspectives, the valuable experiences, the advice, and the documentation of facts on the topic of academic and educational entrepreneurship. We would also like to thank Springer Verlag and the absolutely professional editors who made our project possible in the first place and who recognized the importance of this seminal topic and actively supported us on the way to the finished book. We received great support from Yashka Huggenberger, a Ph.D. student, who helped us finalize the document. We are also indebted to our excellent Language Editor Chris Engert, who did such a wonderful job from a linguistic point of view. We would also like to thank our leaders and universities, the University of Wisconsin-La Crosse (UWL), USA, and the University of Applied Sciences and Arts Western Switzerland HES-SO, who gave us the necessary time to realize this work.

Publishing a book is a time-consuming process. Accordingly, our families often had to do without us. Mehtap thanks her family—Andreas, Feriha, and Ahmet—for their patience and her fur babies—Minnie, Maya, and Mikmik for making this process easier with their cuddles. Moreover, Mehtap is grateful to Emily Radke for her assistance in the article search related to Chap. 6. Gabrielle thanks her husband Tony, her son Alexander and the Labradoodle boy Chilli for the many hours she could not spend with them. Also, Gabrielle thanks very much Mehtap who initiated and developed the project and also did most of the work related to the guest contributions, and for being such a great co-editor and friend. We hope that this book will inspire as many people as possible and contribute to a more entrepreneurial world.

Contents

Introduction to Holistic Academic and Educational Entrepreneurship

Mehtap Aldogan Eklund

The editors of this book have noticed that the stream of research on corporate entrepreneurship and entrepreneurship education is abundant. However, the research on educational entrepreneurship ("edupreneurship") and academic entrepreneurship ("acapreneurship" or "academicpreneurship") is relatively scarce and has been largely overlooked in entrepreneurship (e-ship) literature (Cuervo et al., 2007; Low & MacMillan, 2007; Papadopoulos et al., 2017; Wartiovaara et al., 2018). It is also noted that in the literature, there is no conceptual framework that holistically associates theories and concepts with the experiences and insights of educational/ education entrepreneurs ("edupreneurs") and academic entrepreneurs ("acapreneurs" or "academicpreneur"). Thus, this book is aimed to fill the gap in the literature and practice.

"Educational entrepreneurship" should not be confused with "entrepreneurship education" because they are two different concepts. Entrepreneurship education research focuses on entrepreneurship education in higher education institutions, and it analyzes why and how entrepreneurship education is a force to solve the social, environmental, and economic problems in the world (Berglund & Verduyn, 2018; Papadopoulos et al., 2017; Smith & Petersen, 2006). On the other hand, educational entrepreneurship concerns the startups of the education businesses, either for-profit or non-profit, to catalyze massive improvement in education (Papadopoulos et al., 2017; Smith & Petersen, 2006; Hess & McShane, 2016). Furthermore, Hess (2006) has defined educational entrepreneurship "as a process of purposeful innovation directed toward improving educational productivity, efficiency, and quality." Edupreneur is defined "as a visionary thinker who creates new for-profit or nonprofit educational organizations from scratch that redefine our sense of what is possible" by Smith and Petersen (2006). On the other hand, academic

M. Aldogan Eklund (✉)
University of Wisconsin-La Crosse, La Crosse, WI, USA
e-mail: meklund@uwlax.edu

M. Aldogan Eklund, G. Wanzenried (eds.), *Academic and Educational Entrepreneurship*, Springer Texts in Business and Economics,
https://doi.org/10.1007/978-3-031-10952-2_1

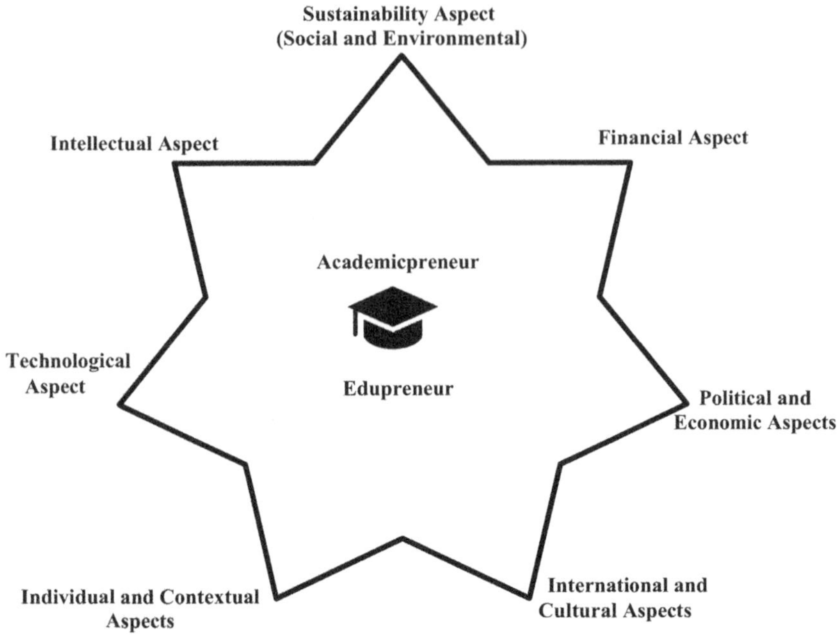

Fig. 1 The seven aspects of academic and educational entrepreneurship (Academic and Edu E-Ship Framework). Source: Created by the editors, derived from the concepts in the literature

entrepreneurship is "an umbrella term that refers to the efforts and activities that universities and their industry partners undertake in hopes of commercializing the outcomes of faculty research" (Wood, 2011). An acapreneur is a person who is a university faculty and establishes a new company or institution based on technologies derived from the university research or who commercializes his/her research project with an expectation of high revenue (Hayter et al., 2017; Lacetera, 2009).

The purpose of this edited book is to introduce foundational knowledge, concepts, and theories of entrepreneurship from the tenet of the "holistic academic and educational entrepreneurship framework" (from further on: "academic and edu e-ship framework") that was scientifically developed by the editors. The cases in Parts II and III link the theoretical concepts discussed in Part I to the real-life context to be successful academic and educational entrepreneurs by using the holistic academic and edu e-ship framework. Moreover, this book illustrates the differences between business, academic, and educational entrepreneurship.

As depicted in Fig. 1, academic and edu e-ship framework has seven aspects: (1) sustainability, (2) financial, (3) political and economic, (4) international and cultural, (5) individual and contextual, (6) technology, and (7) intellectual aspects.

The sustainability aspect is broken into the social and environmental vantage points and it elaborates why sustainability is a salient attribute to the success of edupreneurs and acapreneurs (Praszkier & Nowak, 2012). The financial aspect is about entrepreneurial finance, e.g., the source of entrepreneurial financing and entrepreneurial financial planning (Kuratho & Hodgetts, 2007; Stokes et al., 2010), which is explained from the perspective of academic and educational entrepreneurs. The political and economic aspect discusses the necessity for edupreneurs and acapreneurs to understand the political economy approach because the political and economic systems of the countries shape the institutional setup and offer an opportunity or put-up barriers to entrepreneurs (Nasiri & Hamelin, 2018; Stokes et al., 2010). The nature of the relationship between entrepreneurship, economy, and politics is explained by factor-, efficiency-, and innovation-driven economies (Lambing & Kuehl, 2000; Stokes et al., 2010). The favorable and unfavorable circumstances of economic and political systems in developed and developing countries are exemplified from the perspective of academic and educational entrepreneurship under this aspect. The international and cultural aspect focuses on the international and cultural settings that either support or hinder entrepreneurs. What kind of cultural factors must be taken into consideration in the international arena is explained when academic and educational entrepreneurs are starting up their international businesses (Patricia & Oviatt, 2000; Peiris et al., 2012; Styles et al., 2006; Castaño et al., 2015; Chakraborty et al., 2016). The fifth facet is about the individual and contextual aspects that are addressed from the sociopsychological approach. The distinctive human characteristics, personality traits, entrepreneurial, social, networking, managerial, technical skills, and contextual factors of edupreneurs and acapreneurs are discussed. Besides, whether having a higher education degree contributes to the entrepreneurial skills of edupreneurs and acapreneurs is elaborated (Cuervo, 2005; Littunen, 2000; Marvel et al., 2016; Dvoulety & Orel, 2020). The technology aspect introduces new forms of digital and technology entrepreneurship. How edu- and aca-preneurs can benefit from digital technologies is exemplified (Fossen & Sorgner, 2021; Geissinger et al., 2018; Giones & Brem, 2017). Finally, the intellectual aspect is about is harnessing, integrating, and productively utilizing intellectual energy and talent wherever it is located in order to promote academic, cultural, political, social, and economic changes. The mission of intellectual entrepreneurship is to help students discover their discipline, celebrate the value of their expertise and become successful academic professionals (Cherwitz & Sullivan, 2002; Cutcliffe, 2003; Cherwitz, 2016). Why edupreneurs and acapreneurs should also be intellectual entrepreneurs is discussed in this aspect.

References

Berglund, K., & Verduyn, K. (2018). *Revitalizing entrepreneurship education*. Routledge.

Castaño, M.-S., Méndez, M.-T., & Galindo, M.-Á. (2015). The effect of social, cultural, and economic factors on entrepreneurship. *Journal of Business Research, 68*(7), 1496–1500.

Chakraborty, S., Thompson, J. C., & Yehoue, E. B. (2016). The culture of entrepreneurship. *Journal of Economic Theory, 163*, 288–317.

Cherwitz, R. A. (2016). Diversifying graduate education: The promise of intellectual entrepreneurship. *Journal of Hispanic Higher Education, 4*(1), 19–33.

Cherwitz, R. A., & Sullivan, C. A. (2002). Intellectual entrepreneurship: A vision for graduate education. *Change: The Magazine of Higher Learning, 34*(6), 22–27.

Cuervo, A. (2005). Individual and environmental determinants of entrepreneurship. *International Entrepreneurship and Management Journal, 1*(3), 293–311. https://doi.org/10.1007/s11365-005-2591-7

Cuervo, A., Riberio, D., & Roig, S. (2007). Entrepreneurship: Concepts, theory, and perspective: Introduction. In A. Cuervo, D. Riberio, & S. Roig (Eds.), *Entrepreneurship: Concepts, theory, and perspective* (pp. 1–20). Springer.

Cutcliffe, J. R. (2003). Reconsidering reflexivity: Introducing the case for intellectual entrepreneurship. *Qualitative Health Research, 13*(1), 136–148.

Dvoulety, O., & Orel, M. (2020). Individual determinants of entrepreneurship in Visegrád countries: Reflection on GEM data from the Czech Republic, Hungary, Poland, and Slovakia. *Entrepreneurial Business and Economics Review, 8*(4), 123–137. https://doi.org/10.15678/EBER.2020.080407.

Fossen, F. M., & Sorgner, A. (2021). Digitalization of work and entry into entrepreneurship. *Journal of Business Research, 125*, 548–563. https://doi.org/10.1016/j.jbusres.2019.09.019

Geissinger, A., Laurell, C., Sandström, C., Eriksson, K., & Nykvist, R. (2018). Digital entrepreneurship and field conditions for institutional change– Investigating the enabling role of cities. *Technological Forecasting and Social Change.*

Giones, F., & Brem, A. (2017). Digital technology entrepreneurship: A definition and research agenda. *Technology Innovation Management Review, 7*(5), 44–51.

Hayter, C. S., Lubynsky, R., & Maroulis, S. (2017). Who is the academic entrepreneur? The role of graduate students in the development of university spinoffs. *The Journal of Technology Transfer, 42*(6), 1237–1254.

Hess, F. M. (Ed.). (2006). *Educational entrepreneurship: Realities, challenges, possibilities.* Harvard Education Press.

Hess, F. M., & McShane, M. Q. (Eds.). (2016). *Educational entrepreneurship today*. Harvard Education Press.

Kuratho, D. F., & Hodgetts, R. M. (2007). *Entrepreneurship: Theory, process, and practice* (7th ed.).

Lacetera, N. (2009). Academic entrepreneurship. *Managerial and Decision Economics, 30*(7), 443–464.

Lambing, P. A., & Kuehl, C. R. (2000). *Entrepreneurship* (2nd ed.). Prentice Hall.

Littunen, H. (2000). Entrepreneurship and the characteristics of the entrepreneurial personality. *International Journal of Entrepreneurial Behavior & Research, 6*(6), 295–310.

Low, M. B., & MacMillan, I. C. (2007). Entrepreneurship: Past research and future challenges. In A. Cuervo, D. Riberio, & S. Roig (Eds.), *Entrepreneurship: Concepts, theory, and perspective* (pp. 131–154). Springer.

Marvel, M. R., Davis, J. L., & Sproul, C. R. (2016). Human capital and entrepreneurship research: A critical review and future directions. *Entrepreneurship Theory and Practice, 40*(3), 599–626.

Nasiri, N., & Hamelin, N. (2018). Entrepreneurship driven by opportunity and necessity: Effects of educations, gender and occupation in MENA. *Asian Journal of Business Research, 8*(2), 57–71.

Papadopoulos, P. M., Burger, R., & Faria, A. (Eds.). (2017). *Innovation and entrepreneurship in education*. Emerald.

Patricia, P. M., & Oviatt, B. M. (2000). International entrepreneurship: The intersection of two research paths. *Academy of Management Journal, 43*(5), 902–906.

Peiris, I. K., Akoorie, M. E. M., & Sinha, P. (2012). International entrepreneurship: A critical analysis of studies in the past two decades and future directions for research. *Journal of International Entrepreneurship, 10*(4), 279–324.

Praszkier, R., & Nowak, A. (2012). *Social entrepreneurship: Theory and practice*. Cambridge University Press.

Smith, K., & Petersen, J. L. (2006). What is educational entrepreneurship? In F. M. Hess (Ed.), *Educational entrepreneurship: Realities, challenges, possibilities*. Harvard Education Press.

Stokes, D., Wilson, N., & Mador, M. (2010). *Entrepreneurship*. Cengage learning.
Styles, C., Styles, C., & Gray, S. J. (2006). *New perspectives on international entrepreneurship* (Vol. 23, no. 5). Emerald Group.
Wartiovaara, M., Lahti, T., & Wincent, J. (2018). The role of inspiration in entrepreneurship: Theory and the future research agenda. *Journal of Business Research.*
Wood, M. S. (2011). A process model of academic entrepreneurship. *Business Horizons, 54*(2), 153–161.

Mehtap Aldogan Eklund received a PhD at the University of St. Gallen, Switzerland. She is an Assistant Professor in Accounting at the University of Wisconsin-La Crosse, USA. She is currently on the editorial board of the SN Business and Economics journal and is a regional governance partner at Board Foundation (BF). Previously, she worked as an Associate Professor in Norway. Before her PhD, she worked for 7 years as an auditor in two of the Big 4 auditing firms in Europe, the USA, and the Caribbean. She has published articles and a book on corporate governance and accounting.

Part I

Theoretical Framework Related to Academic and Educational Entrepreneurship

Theories Related to Academic and Educational Entrepreneurship

Mehtap Aldogan Eklund and Birgit Leick

This chapter of the book elaborates on the theoretical background of academic and educational entrepreneurship. Entrepreneurship is a multifaceted phenomenon that has both boundaries and overlaps with many disciplines. Hence, as a research field, entrepreneurship is intertwined with various theories which are rooted in the disciplines of strategic management, business economics, ecology, psychology, sociology, and network theories (Cuervo et al., 2007). In this chapter, only the most commonly cited theories in the entrepreneurship literature that relate to the "holistic academic and educational entrepreneurship framework," e.g., resource-based theory (RBT), the personality-based theory of McClelland, network theories in the social sciences, institutional theory from economics, human capital theory, positive theory, and social cognitive theory, are summarized concisely. The aim of this chapter is thus to provide insights from theories that will improve the understanding of the framework mentioned above.

The Resource-Based Theory (RBT) posits that entrepreneurial opportunities arise when different economic actors are equipped with different resources and can transform these resources—as input factors—into outputs (Alvarez & Busenitz, 2001, 2007). The heterogeneity of resources is crucial to this transformation of resources in the entrepreneurial process; both the recognition of opportunities (that is, entrepreneurial behavior as a resource input factor) and the combination of different resources to resource outcomes are characteristic of entrepreneurship from RBT perspective (Alvarez & Busenitz, 2001, 2007). RBT also includes the cognitive ability of individual entrepreneurs, as Alvarez and Busenitz (2007, p. 208)

M. Aldogan Eklund (✉)
University of Wisconsin-La Crosse, La Crosse, WI, USA
e-mail: meklund@uwlax.edu

B. Leick
USN School of Business, University of South-Eastern Norway, Bø, Norway
e-mail: Birgit.Leick@usn.no

M. Aldogan Eklund, G. Wanzenried (eds.), *Academic and Educational Entrepreneurship*, Springer Texts in Business and Economics,
https://doi.org/10.1007/978-3-031-10952-2_2

state as follows: "entrepreneurs have individual specific resources that facilitate recognition of new opportunities and create heterogeneous outputs." The organization of resources in the entrepreneurial process also influences the growth of enterprises (Wright & Stigliani, 2013). Furthermore, an important argument from RBT is that a greater number of agents will provide both newly founded or existing (incumbent) enterprises with a greater rate of strategic alliances (Eisenhardt & Schoonhoven, 1996), which might spur the growth of enterprises. In this context, international entrepreneurship research more generally refers to RBT and stresses notably networks (that is, ties or relationships of entrepreneurs to other economic actors and enterprises) as an important prerequisite to international opportunity recognition and opportunity exploitation (Peiris et al., 2012).

Social network theory has the following perspectives: network content, network governance, and network structure (Hoang & Antoncic, 2003). Network content is about various resources that are provided based on the network relationships, whereas network governance denotes the management and coordination of resource exchanges through the network relationships, and network structure describes the organization of relationships within the network (Slotte-Kock & Coviello, 2010; Hoang & Antoncic, 2003). From this perspective, social network theory is more comprehensive than RBT because it captures resources associated with the social relationships of entrepreneurs and their organizations. In short, this theory postulates that network relations, including their governance, may facilitate the entrepreneurial start-up process and subsequent growth after the start-up phase (Hite, 2005; Huggins & Thompson, 2015). Entrepreneurs spend more time talking to people during the planning phase than in other phases and they access people in their networks to discuss aspects of starting up a business (in the case of corporate entrepreneurship) or an educational institution (in the case of academic and educational entrepreneurship). Entrepreneurs can often complement their resources by accessing their social and professional network ties (Greve & Salaff, 2003; Scott & Cable, 2002). Social capital theories argue that networks matter for the generation of competitive advantage (e.g., Burt, 2000; Dyer & Singh, 1998). However, it is necessary to manage network relationships, for instance, in order to share value that is created based on the relationships (Duschek, 2004).

David McClelland's theory in the discipline of psychology is another central element to the understanding of entrepreneurship from a societal perspective (McClelland, 1961). He believes that entrepreneurs are characterized by their individual need for achievement, which represents a general driver of entrepreneurship. In addition, McClelland had analyzed why some societies, or nations, are more successful in incubating entrepreneurs than others, and he hypothesizes that the need for achievement as a key psychological characteristic of entrepreneurs is culturally influenced (McClelland, 1961; Cuervo et al., 2007). McClelland's research influenced entrepreneurship research in the 1960 and 1970 years in which a psychological perspective was a key research perspective to explain the individual personality traits of entrepreneurs. It was also found that individual characteristics and personality traits have an impact on distinguishing successful entrepreneurs from unsuccessful ones (Brockhaus, 1982; Gasse, 1982).

The institutional theory posits that the institutional factors on the macroeconomic level, such as formal and informal rules, norms, and cultural traditions, influence entrepreneurship and growth (Urbano et al., 2019). Institutional innovations encourage opportunity entrepreneurship (that is, entrepreneurship aiming to exploit opportunities that entrepreneurs identify in a market) to achieve higher rates of economic growth (Aparicio et al., 2016; Fairlie & Fossen, 2018). Institutional theory is concerned with organizational, regulatory, social, and cultural influences that promote entrepreneurial opportunity and activity (Bruton et al., 2010; Su et al., 2017). As Simón-Moya et al. (2014) state, the economic and organizational context is a determining factor that can drive and shape entrepreneurial activities. Furthermore, Castaño et al. (2015) group the institutional factors into three categories: social, economic, and cultural factors; they claim that all these factors foster entrepreneurial pursuit.

The human capital theory was developed to study the value of education and it links human capital attributes to entrepreneurial success (Unger et al., 2011). It argues that "human capital is vital to discovering and creating entrepreneurial opportunity and it aids in exploring opportunities by acquiring financial resources and launching ventures. Besides, human capital assists in the accumulation of new knowledge and the creation of advantages for start-ups" (Marvel et al., 2016, p. 600).

Another theory is related to social entrepreneurship: the positive theory explains entrepreneurship with an embedded social purpose, so that it focuses on social entrepreneurship, instead of commercial, or corporate, entrepreneurship. It highlights the key trade-off between value creation and value capture while suggesting sustainable solutions to neglected problems with positive externalities to society. The positive theory has four propositions: (1) addressing the neglected problems in society involving positive externalities, (2) operating in areas with localized positive externalities that benefit a powerless segment of the population, (3) seeking sustainable solutions than sustainable advantages, and (4) developing a solution built on the logic of empowerment than on the logic of control (Santos, 2012).

Finally, the social cognitive theory postulates that "any interaction between individual and their environments may influence their behaviors and attitudes. Thus, entrepreneurial behavior evolves in response to social-cultural factors, e.g., entrepreneurship education and activity, and psychological and cultural mechanisms. Individuals evaluate behaviors, cognition, and environmental events and respond to them reciprocally while anticipating possible consequences and evaluating entrepreneurial opportunities" (Oo et al., 2018, p. 402). This theory is, again, based on psychology (e.g., Locke & Latham, 2002). For instance, this theory is applied to determine and/or analyze entrepreneurial motivations and intentions (Liguori et al., 2018).

For the edited book, the editors used these theoretical perspectives to develop the "Educational & academic entrepreneurship framework." In the following chapters, each facet or aspect of this framework will be discussed in detail to exemplify how to be a successful educational entrepreneur and academic entrepreneur.

1 Summary

This chapter is elaborating on the theoretical background of academic and educational entrepreneurship. The theories related to the "holistic academic and educational entrepreneurship framework," e.g., resource-based theory (RBT), personality-based McClelland's theory, network (ties) theory, institutional theory, human capital theory, positive theory, and social cognitive theory, are summarized.

Questions

1. Could you please name the theories discussed in this chapter and briefly explain them?
2. Which theory or theories does/do explicitly emphasize the importance of the entrepreneurs' resources and network when they are converted from inputs to outputs?
3. If your research focuses on the need for achievement and key psychological characteristics of an entrepreneur, then what would be the best theory that you can refer to?

References

Alvarez, S. A., & Busenitz, L. W. (2007). The entrepreneurship of resource-based theory. In A. Cuervo, D. Riberio, & S. Roig (Eds.), *Entrepreneurship: Concepts, theory, and perspective* (pp. 207–227). Springer.

Alvarez, S. A., & Busenitz, L. W. (2001). The entrepreneurship of resource-based theory. *Journal of Management, 27*, 755–775.

Aparicio, S., Urbano, D., & Audretsch, D. (2016). Institutional factors, opportunity entrepreneurship, and economic growth: Panel data evidence. *Technological Forecasting and Social Change, 102*, 45–61.

Brockhaus, R. H. (1982). Encyclopedia of entrepreneurship. In C. A. Kent, D. L. Sexton, & K. H. Vesper (Eds.), *The psychology of the entrepreneur* (pp. 39–56). Prentice-Hall.

Bruton, G. D., Ahlstrom, D., & Li, H.-L. (2010). Institutional theory and entrepreneurship: Where are we now and where do we need to move in the future? *Entrepreneurship Theory and Practice, 34*(3), 421–440.

Burt, R. S. (2000). The network entrepreneur. In R. Swedberg (Ed.), *Entrepreneurship: The social science view* (pp. 281–307). Oxford University Press.

Castaño, M.-S., Méndez, M.-T., & Galindo, M.-Á. (2015). The effect of social, cultural, and economic factors on entrepreneurship. *Journal of Business Research, 68*(7), 1496–1500.

Cuervo, A., Riberio, D., & Roig, S. (2007). Entrepreneurship: Concepts, theory, and perspective: Introduction. In A. Cuervo, D. Riberio, & S. Roig (Eds.), *Entrepreneurship: Concepts, theory, and perspective* (pp. 1–20). Springer.

Duschek, S. (2004). Inter-firm resources and sustained competitive advantage. *Management Revue, 15*(1), 53–73.

Dyer, J. H., & Singh, H. (1998). The relational view: Cooperative strategy and sources of Interorganizational competitive advantage. *The Academy of Management Review, 23*(4), 660–679.

Eisenhardt, K. M., & Schoonhoven, C. B. (1996). Resource-based view of strategic alliance formation: Strategic and social effects in entrepreneurial firms. *Organization Science, 7*(2), 136–150.

Fairlie, R. W., & Fossen, F. M. (2018). *Opportunity versus necessity entrepreneurship: Two components of business creation* (January 30, 2018). CESifo Working Paper Series No. 6854, Available at SSRN: https://ssrn.com/abstract=3140340 or https://doi.org/10.2139/ssrn.3140340

Gasse, Y. (1982). Encyclopedia of entrepreneurship. In C. A. Kent, D. L. Sexton, & K. H. Vesper (Eds.), *Elaboration on the psychology of the entrepreneur* (pp. 57–71). Prentice-Hall.

Greve, A., & Salaff, J. W. (2003). Social networks and entrepreneurship. *Entrepreneurship Theory and Practice, 28*(1), 1–22.

Hite, J. M. (2005). Evolutionary processes and paths of relationally embedded network ties in emerging entrepreneurial firms. *Entrepreneurship Theory and Practice, 29*(1), 113–144. https://doi.org/10.1111/j.1540-6520.2005.00072.x

Hoang, H., & Antoncic, B. (2003). Network-based research in entrepreneurship: A critical review. *Journal of Business Venturing, 18*(2), 165–187.

Huggins, R., & Thompson, P. (2015). Entrepreneurship, innovation, and regional growth: A network theory. *Small Business Economics, 45*(1), 103–128.

Liguori, E. W., Bendickson, J. S., & McDowell, W. C. (2018). Revisiting entrepreneurial intentions: A social cognitive career theory approach. *International Entrepreneurship and Management Journal, 14*(1), 67–78.

Locke, E. A., & Latham, G. P. (2002). Building a practically useful theory of goal setting and task motivation. *American Psychologist, 57*(9), 705–717.

Marvel, M. R., Davis, J. L., & Sproul, C. R. (2016). Human capital and entrepreneurship research: A critical review and future directions. *Entrepreneurship Theory and Practice, 40*(3), 599–626.

McClelland, D. (1961). The achieving society. .

Oo, P. P., Sahaym, A., Juasrikul, S., & Lee, S.-Y. (2018). The interplay of entrepreneurship education and national cultures in entrepreneurial activity: A social cognitive perspective. *Journal of International Entrepreneurship, 16*(3), 398–420.

Peiris, I. K., Akoorie, M. E. M., & Sinha, P. (2012). International entrepreneurship: A critical analysis of studies in the past two decades and future directions for research. *Journal of International Entrepreneurship, 10*(4), 279–324.

Santos, F. M. (2012). A positive theory of social entrepreneurship. *Journal of Business Ethics, 111*, 335–351. https://doi.org/10.1007/s10551-012-1413-4

Scott, S., & Cable, D. (2002). Network ties, reputation, and the financing of new ventures. *Management Science, 48*, 364–381.

Simón-Moya, V., Revuelto-Taboada, L., & Guerrero, R. F. (2014). Institutional and economic drivers of entrepreneurship: An international perspective. *Journal of Business Research, 67*(5), 715–721.

Slotte-Kock, S., & Coviello, N. (2010). Entrepreneurship research on network processes: A review and ways forward. *Entrepreneurship Theory and Practice, 34*(1), 31–57.

Su, J., Zhai, Q., & Karlsson, T. (2017). Beyond red tape and fools: Institutional theory in entrepreneurship research, 1992-2014. *Entrepreneurship Theory and Practice, 41*(4), 505–531.

Unger, J. M., Rauch, A., Frese, M., & Rosenbusch, N. (2011). Human capital and entrepreneurial success: A meta-analysis review. *Journal of Business Venturing, 26*(3), 341–358.

Urbano, D., Aparicio, S., & Audretsch, D. (2019). Twenty-five years of research on institutions, entrepreneurship, and economic growth: What has been learned? *Small Business Economics, 53*(1), 21–49.

Wright, M., & Stigliani, I. (2013). Entrepreneurship and growth. *International Small Business Journal, 31*(1), 3–22.

Mehtap Aldogan Eklund received a PhD at the University of St. Gallen, Switzerland. She is an Assistant Professor in Accounting at the University of Wisconsin-La Crosse, USA. She is currently on the editorial board of the SN Business and Economics journal and is a regional governance partner at Board Foundation (BF). Previously, she worked as an Associate Professor in Norway. Before her PhD, she worked for 7 years as an auditor in two of the Big 4 auditing firms in Europe, the USA, and the Caribbean. She has published articles and a book on corporate governance and accounting.

Birgit Leick is a Professor in Innovation and Entrepreneurship and teaches in the bachelor's program in Innovation and Entrepreneurship at the University of South-Eastern Norway. She is specialized in and teaches the foundational course "Entrepreneurship and Society" and "SME Structures and Dynamics." She is also an active researcher in entrepreneurship, SME and business economics, and regional development. Personal webpage: https://sites.google.com/site/birgitleick/home

Sustainability Aspect of Academic and Educational Entrepreneurship

Gerhard Schneider

We cannot separate organic life and mind from physical nature without also separating nature from life and mind. The separation has reached the point where intelligent persons are asking whether the end is to be a catastrophe, the subjection of man to the industrial and military machines he has created.
John Dewey, Experience and Nature, 1929, p. 296.

1 Introduction

Until some decades ago, as described by Hardin (1968) in the Tragedy of the Commons, those individuals who recognize and seize opportunities (in other words, entrepreneurs) are at the root of our environmental dilemma, with "each pursuing his own best interest in a society that believes in the freedom of the commons".

Until recently, the potential of entrepreneurship for transformation in terms of sustainability had been neglected, and the capacity of entrepreneurs to transform society sustainably had not been seen (Klapper & Farber, 2016). Entrepreneurs had, in some ways, been seen as part of the problem, not as a possible solution.

However, there is abundant literature that affirms that entrepreneurs have the potential to exploit sustainable opportunities and thus create economic, social, and

G. Schneider (✉)
University of Applied Sciences and Arts, Western Switzerland (HEIG-VD), Yverdon-les-Bains, Switzerland
e-mail: gerhard.schneider@heig-vd.ch

M. Aldogan Eklund, G. Wanzenried (eds.), *Academic and Educational Entrepreneurship*, Springer Texts in Business and Economics,
https://doi.org/10.1007/978-3-031-10952-2_3

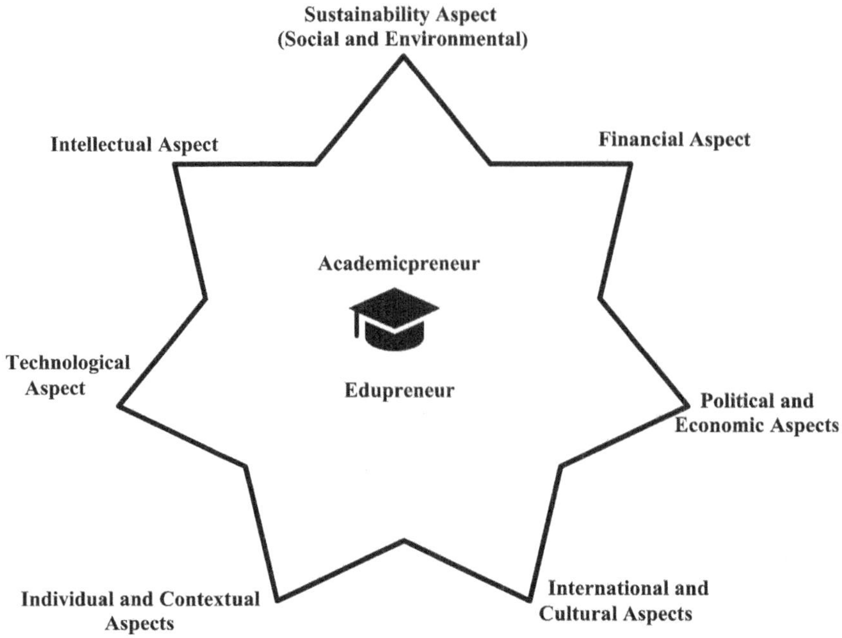

Fig. 1 The holistic conceptual framework of academicpreneurship and edupreneurship, Source: Eklund and Wanzenried (2022)

environmental values. As an example, I want to cite just one recent publication by Farny and Binder (2021). Consequently, environmental, social, and sustainable entrepreneurship can play an important role in the way toward sustainable development. However, the question that must be asked is how sustainable entrepreneurs search for the balance between the economic, environmental, and social objectives, and whether searching for a balance is sufficient.

As we will see, sustainable development is concerned with complex systems; it is a holistic framework itself, with multiple interlinked challenges, to which truly sustainable entrepreneurs have to respond.

That said, sustainable "edupreneurs" are working within two holistic frameworks—the holistic framework of academic entrepreneurs (Fig. 1), and the holistic framework of sustainable development.

The chapter is structured as follows: In the second section, we look at sustainable entrepreneurship, its definitions, and its potential. The third section explores the difficulties and barriers to sustainable entrepreneurship in a profit-oriented world. The fourth section looks at the role of values and the necessary competencies for sustainable entrepreneurship, which leads straight to Sect. 5, which investigates how to teach sustainable entrepreneurship. Section 6 closes with a discussion, some conclusions, and some recommendations, partly based on my own experience.

2 Sustainable Entrepreneurship

Sustainable entrepreneurship is the overarching term for "ecopreneurship", green entrepreneurship, and social entrepreneurship (Strachan, 2018), which is certainly a non-exhaustive list of terms. Sustainable entrepreneurs integrate environmental and social dimensions in their business strategies and perceive opportunities for new products and services that offer not only an economic gain but also noneconomic gains for the environment and society (Joensuu-Salo et al., 2022). There are, of course, more definitions: business circles usually talk of the triple bottom line of social, environmental, and economic goals.

All the above definitions of sustainable entrepreneurship share the notion of a balance between economic, environmental, and social objectives or values. However, no definition describes what this balance should look like. Is it economic value to a high extent, and environmental and social values to a much lesser extent, like some green leaves or foliage used for decoration? Or should it be vice versa?

Entrepreneurs or corporations will determine the balance between the economic, social, and environmental values themselves. As we will see in Sect. 3, the present economic framework or system is not favorable for putting environmental and social values first. It is economic value or profitability that comes first, as any and all nonprofitable companies will fail and disappear. You have to differentiate, however; there really are environmentally or social ventures, just as there are ventures that put profit first, and consider the environment and ethics only when it is accompanied by zero cost.

Markman et al. (2016) argue that a balance between the three values is not enough. They advocate—and I entirely agree—"that the natural environment be the foundation on which society resides and the economy operates. Sustainable, ethical, entrepreneurial (SEE) enterprises are moving in this direction, seeking to regenerate the environment and drive positive societal changes rather than only minimizing harm". This view is supported by Gast et al. (2017), who argues that "truly entrepreneurial enterprises, however, would focus on the discovery of opportunities and proactive strategies guided by the management's commitment to and orientation towards ecological sustainability".

The same is true for mission-driven companies, which Russo (2010) defined as a "for-profit enterprise that seeks to simultaneously meet profit goals and social and environmental goals that reflect the values of their owners". When the values of the owners come into consideration, the company will go as far as it can in its integration of environmental and/or ethical values and will not be satisfied with a minimal engagement or just apply the standards of a label or certification.

Mission-driven companies cannot live without conscious consumerism, because the social and environmental performance of a company becomes a vital competitive asset for consumers who care about the broader attitudes of companies. If a mission-driven company can create a bond with customers on an emotional level, this connection will drive sales.

But nothing on Earth is free—thus, such a bond is highly emotional and relies on the company's attitude to social and environmental values, and the customers believe or trust the company in terms of its engagement toward the environment or with regard to its ethics. For this reason, a mission-driven company may never compromise those values for profit. That would immediately damage or sever the emotional bond with its customers, and sales would fall as a consequence and would eventually put the company at risk. This could pose a dilemma for the company when it is in a financially critical situation—as each decision, be it in favor of much-needed profit, or be it in favor of the environment or ethics, might put the company at risk. Thus, mission-driven companies, as defined by Russo (2010), and sustainable, ethical, entrepreneurial (SEE) enterprises, as defined by Markman et al. (2016), are today's leaders in sustainability by prioritizing social and environmental values both before and above profit. They are, however, limited by the framework of our economic system, in which each company, be it ethical or not, has to be profitable first, as described in chapter "Political and Economic Aspects of Academic and Educational Entrepreneurship".

Nonetheless, sustainable entrepreneurs have the potential to act as agents of change when they make social and environmental values and criteria a part of the core strategy of their ventures, and thus transfer a vision of a sustainable society into their products or services (Ploum et al., 2018). York and Venkataraman (2010) see the social and environmental innovations of sustainable entrepreneurs as an opportunity to disrupt the market and incite large corporations to follow the leaders in sustainability. In these conditions, sustainable entrepreneurs can be considered key actors in the solving of social and environmental problems.

Corporate Social Responsibility, Labels, and Certification

In contrast to sustainable entrepreneurship, corporate social responsibility is a notion that is essentially used by existing companies and does not necessarily involve a new venture. It can be seen as the response of enterprises to the challenges of sustainable development.

Today's formal framework of sustainable development and its definition are given by the United Nations' Agenda 2030, which has, at its heart, the 17 sustainable development goals or SDGs (United Nations, n.d.-a). Social and environmental labels and certifications do not question the purpose of a product, but usually define criteria to make existing products more environmentally friendly or more ethical. As an example, it is generally agreed that cigarettes are harmful products; however, tobacco companies such as British American Tobacco or Philip Morris publish certified ESG (Environmental, Social and Corporate Governance) or sustainability reports according to international criteria, or are certified ISO14001, the environmental ISO norm.

The most well-known certification in terms of corporate social responsibility is ISO26000, which provides guidance on what social responsibility means, and aims to help businesses and organizations to implement the principles of social responsibility. ISO26000 is not certifiable; it encourages enterprises, instead of requiring implementation (International Organization for Standardization, 2014). The advantage of ISO26000 is its holistic approach with seven core subjects: organizational governance, human rights, labour practices, the environment, fair operating practices, consumer issues, and community involvement and development.

By providing guidance, ISO26000 is certainly useful, but, given that it lacks requirements that are independently assessed, it remains toothless. Like other norms, its focus is to minimize harm or impact, which is not enough, as Markman et al. (2016) argue.

3 Difficulties and Barriers to Sustainable Entrepreneurship

As Marius Fuchs states in chapter "Financial Aspect of Academic and Educational Entrepreneurship" of this edited book, "capital, cash and regular cash flow are like oxygen that keeps the blood circulating—they are vital and need a lot of attention", or, more simply, to cite Liza Minelli's metaphor in her famous Broadway show: "Money makes the world go round". Marius Fuchs emphasizes that the financial plan is the basis for every product or service, and forces entrepreneurs to align other aspects of their conceptual frameworks to financial means. Without sufficient funding, entrepreneurs will not be able to create a product or service from their idea(s). However, the difficulty of balancing profitability and environmental and social values will persist throughout the life span of the business. As we have seen before, sustainable entrepreneurs are value based. Focusing on environmental and social value creation will inevitably create tensions with the profitability of the business (Thelken & de Jong, 2020). Thus, sustainable entrepreneurs will constantly have to seek a compromise with profitability, which, in turn, makes their products less green, less social, and less distinguishable from traditional products, which, in turn, makes them less attractive to conscious consumers.

Sustainable entrepreneurs face several barriers in the early phases of their ventures, especially in terms of finance or funding. As Potluri and Phani (2020) bluntly put it: "given the focus of angel investors, venture capitalists and banks to either fund sectors with high growth or shortest exit period, green entrepreneurs figure as the last investment priority for these institutions". Green or sustainable entrepreneurs are perceived to involve a high political risk, low scalability, and long payback times, which discourages investors. Lack of consumer awareness is another major obstacle for green or sustainable products or services, or, as Russo (2010) puts it, conscious consumerism is essential for sustainable products.

This is easier said than done—conscious consumerism involves looking beyond and asking questions such as: "How and where was this product produced? Under what labour conditions? With what environmental impact? Questions that are both difficult and time consuming to answer. Quite often, we only learn that our choice was not a good one, for example, when some thousand needlewomen die in Bangladesh because the building collapsed, and we learn that all the well-known clothing brands were manufactured there. I guess every reader will be able to cite moments when he or she was influenced by glittering labels and wonderful promises. Labels often do not help consumers to make a choice; for example, the well-known OEKO-TEX100 label suggests by its name, that your clothing was produced in an ecological or environmentally friendly manner. In truth, this is not the case: the only requirement of OEKO-TEX100 is that there are no harmful residues, such as pesticides, in your clothing when you buy it (Oeko-Tex). In other words, it had been washed sufficiently to diminish all residues below the requirements before being put on the shelves.

Sustainable entrepreneurs can overcome this problem only by transparency, in order to create a link of confidence and trust with their consumers, which, in turn, leads to loyal and returning customers. Even when customers are aware of the environmental impact of traditional products, this does not mean that greener products will sell more easily. Customer awareness does not mean sales. In 2020, according to the Special Eurobarometer (European Union, 2020), protecting the environment was important for 94% of European citizens. In addition, "changing the way we consume" was considered by the people taking part in the survey as one of the most effective ways of tackling environmental problems. Consequently, we could naïvely expect, for example, a high percentage of customers buying organic food. However, in Germany, the market share of organic food in 2019 was less than 6% (Statista, 2022). Surveys about environmental or ethical values are often misleading. When buying a product, customers usually decide upon the price.

Sustainable products or services are usually more expensive than traditional products. Sustainable entrepreneurs have to sell not only their product(s), but also environmental friendliness, sustainability, and/or ethics to their customers. Sustainable entrepreneurs have to create a discourse around their product(s), one which includes social or environmental issues (Markman et al., 2016), and they need to know about their consumers' level of adherence to the social or environmental welfare logic of the product. If adherence is high, sellers will be more successful in sales, or, as Russo (2010) put it, a strong emotional bond has to be created between a mission-driven company or its products and its customers. In a way, ecological or sustainable entrepreneurs have to educate their future customers about their products and services, as customers do not necessarily recognize the benefits of such products compared to traditional products, as we have seen above. They could use story telling around the product and link their product to "good conscience" or "feeling-well", every time the customer uses the product. Environmental psychologists know the paradox of high environmental awareness, on the one hand, and low environmental behaviour, on the other. The environment, ethics, and sustainability are abstract values and often far away. Climate change is difficult to grasp, one's own contribution is infinitely small, and labour conditions in Asia are far away and rarely visible.

Some Basics About Sustainable Development and Economy

Sustainable development is commonly defined with three dimensions, namely, the environmental or ecological, the social, and the economic dimension, although this contradicts the original definition of the World Commission on Environment and Development, also known as the Brundtland Report of 1987 (United Nations, n.d.-a). As cited and mentioned above, this so-called three-pillar model is better known as the called triple bottom line in business circles.

The three-pillar model gives the impression of three independent elements and does not give priority to any one of the pillars. Nor does it indicate how the unavoidably conflicting objectives between profit, social needs, and environmental impact should be solved. Moreover, it strengthens the idea that the economy can be treated as being detached from the social context and the environmental equilibrium.

Marius Fuchs states, in chapter "Financial Aspect of Academic and Educational Entrepreneurship", that finance is the base. For this reason, the economic pillar will always be prioritized in the end. In terms of sustainability, Markman et al. (2016) question whether searching for a balance between these objectives is sufficient. Indeed, it is necessary to go further. After all, the economy is embedded within society, which itself resides in the natural and physical environment on a planet that is limited (Daly, 1996).

This view is supported by Lehtonen (2004), who supports a concentric circles approach. The three pillars are replaced by three concentric circles, the environment circumscribing the social dimension, which, in turn, circumscribes the economic sphere. This reflects the idea that the economy is embedded in a social context and is at the service of human beings while respecting the biophysical or natural systems.

Daly (1996, pp. 75–76) introduced different forms of capital, essentially man-made capital and natural capital, and departed from the principle that capital must be maintained intact. He showed that each component, i.e., man-made capital and natural capital, has to be maintained individually because they are complements and not substitutes. Man-made capital is essentially a result of the transformation of natural resources into products, infrastructure, and profit.

Parkin et al. (2003) and Freyman (2012) developed this idea further into a five-capital model, which comprised:

- Natural capital: natural resources and services by nature.
- Human capital: health, knowledge, skills, motivation, and spiritual ease.
- Social capital: families, communities, organizations, and the public administration.
- Manufactured capital: infrastructure, products, etc.
- Financial capital.

The model can be adapted to specific entrepreneurial activities in order to find out how activity might increase or decrease the various forms of capital, and it can be adapted so that environmental capital is maximized, or, in other words, so that natural resource consumption can be minimized. If we accept that the natural and physical environment is the base for everything else, we clearly have to prioritize the environment first, society second, and the economy third. Such a prioritization means that organizations have to change the paradigm: away from doing less harm to a do-good paradigm in order to restore the natural environment (Markman et al., 2016).

Recent research by the Stockholm Resilience Centre (2022) showed that our planetary boundaries, in terms of climate change, biosphere integrity, land system change, biogeochemical flows, and novel entities (essentially pollution), have all been vastly exceeded, and thus the choice of the direction in which we have to move is both clear and unequivocal.

However, Does This Fit to Our Economic System?
In short, we can define the existing economic system by the following equation:

$$\text{Financial benefit} = \text{function of (labour} \times \text{capital} \times \text{productivity} \times \text{natural resources)}.$$

Every company is thriving to maximize financial benefit, by adapting the input of labour, capital, productivity, and natural resources. On a national scale, this leads to maximizing gross national product and economic growth, thus using more and more natural resources.

Decoupling economic growth from the use of natural resources is simply not possible. You may become more efficient and produce more products with fewer resources, which is highly valuable, but you cannot produce goods without natural resources. As Daly puts it, "we can surely eat lower on the food chain, but we cannot eat recipes" (Daly, 1996, p. 28).

The contradiction is evident—in terms of sustainability, we need to consider the environment first and consume less natural resources, whereas, in terms of economics and profit, we need to consume more resources.

It becomes evident that sustainable entrepreneurs act in a system that is not favorable for ecological, social, or sustainable products.

Other authors also question whether a capitalist economic system is compatible with humanity and the physical environment. Sahra Wagenknecht (2016, p. 35 ff) correctly points out that humans are primarily social beings who prefer cooperative behaviour to competition, and that the breakthrough of capitalism was only possible with societal and religious legitimation, especially by Calvinism, which turned former vices into virtues, such as money worship and egoism, for example. Binswanger (2019) argues consistently and clearly that a capitalist economic system cannot survive without growth, even if consumers were disposed to consume less.

A way out of this dilemma has to be found, however; we have to ask ourselves whether our actual economic system is compatible with the limits of our planet, with sustainable development, and with cooperative behaviour?

4 The Role of Competences and Values for Sustainable Entrepreneurship

Sustainable entrepreneurship is a concept that is based upon values, and which should contribute to solving environmental and social problems. Motivation, values, and passion for products are key drivers for green or sustainable entrepreneurs. Values also drive the culture and governance of sustainable or mission-driven companies (Russo, 2010).

It is typically the family background that creates or influences the environmental awareness of sustainable entrepreneurs, especially in their youth or childhood

(Schick et al., 2002). This coincides with my own study, which shows that the environmental values of employees who were engaged in the environmental improvement of their company had been formed by their family background in their youth (Schneider, 2018). However, even in companies with an environmental engagement, employees with environmental values tend to become frustrated. In their opinion, the company does not become involved in environmental matters sufficiently and the employees have to live up to their values in private and not in their professional life (Boucher et al., 2018).

As environmental values are formed at a young age, and we all tend to surround ourselves with people with similar values, it becomes understandable that the initial funding of green or sustainable entrepreneurs is often provided by their families or friends, as seen above (in the section on Barriers to Sustainable Entrepreneurship).

Are Social and Environmental Values Linked to Entrepreneurial Intention?

The level of the social and environmental concerns of an individual is not related to entrepreneurial intentions but has a positive relationship with sustainability-oriented opportunities or business ideas. It is an entrepreneurial attitude that is the strongest predictor of who will become an entrepreneur, sustainable or not (Wagner, 2012). The findings of Thelken and de Jong (2020) seem to differ, however, as they show that strong biospheric values (concern for nature and the environment) and strong altruistic values (concern with the welfare of other human beings) had a positive and significant relation toward sustainable entrepreneurship attitudes. However, their sample included 35% of individuals who had followed an entrepreneurship course or had already founded their own company. As the sample was not differentiated into people with and without entrepreneurial desire, the result was almost certainly induced by experimental design.

Only individuals with high sustainable competence and an entrepreneurial desire (Vuorio et al., 2018), or individuals with a high sustainability entrepreneurship competence (Joensuu-Salo et al., 2022), have high intentions to become sustainable entrepreneurs.

We can summarize that social or environmental values are favorable or necessary for sustainable entrepreneurship, but not sufficient. People with such values tend to grasp sustainability-oriented opportunities, but only people with an additional entrepreneurial desire or competence intend to become sustainable entrepreneurs. Vice versa, it is clear that all truly sustainable entrepreneurs are driven by environmental and social values. In Fig. 2, we visualize the different groups. Individuals with social and environmental concerns or competence and entrepreneurship desire or competence become sustainable entrepreneurs (the inner circle). Individuals with only social and environmental concerns or competence tend to seize opportunities, rather than found a sustainable venture.

Entrepreneurial Forms of Behaviour, Values, and Competences

Gibb (2005) defines the typical forms of behaviour, values, competencies, and outcomes that are associated with entrepreneurs. He cites forms of behaviour such as seeking opportunities, taking the initiative, looking beyond, controlling one's own destiny, making intuitive decisions when little information is available, etc. He cites

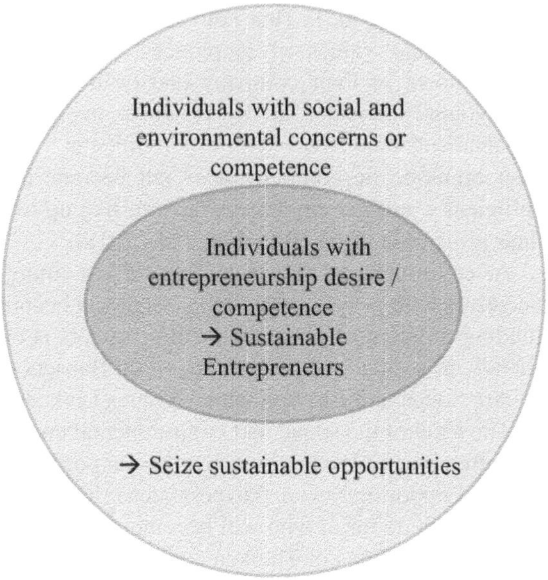

Fig. 2 Social and environmental concerns versus entrepreneur competence. Source: Created by the author

values such as a strong sense of independence as well as belonging, self-sufficiency, the belief that hard work brings rewards, and that everything is possible when one has confidence.

Maybe unexpectedly, intuition is a driver for entrepreneurship intentions; we tend to see entrepreneurs rather as structured, profit-oriented individuals, but it is intuition that helps people to deal with complex systems, insecurities, and risks, in situations where little information is available. Intuitive entrepreneurs are more likely to adopt a holistic and systems approach and use more lateral reasoning and random exploration, instead of a sequential, routinely structured, analytical approach, or adherence to rules. Klapper and Farber (2016) confirm, in their student sample, that those who believed in intuition were more likely to become entrepreneurs.

With regard to competitiveness, we must ask whether competitiveness is a value or competence of entrepreneurship? Usually, we see entrepreneurs as people who are willing to compete in order to gain market shares with their new product(s). Klapper and Farber (2016) showed, however, that competitiveness was negatively correlated with entrepreneurial intention.

This seems plausible, as a holistic and systems approach has nothing in common with competitiveness. In addition, does not entrepreneurship have more to do with creativity and innovation, to make a new, better, more sustainable product? Competitiveness might become involved in the latter phase of the venture, when the new product has to be sold, thus giving the image of competitive entrepreneurs.

Values and forms of behaviour such as intuition, holistic and systems thinking, transversal thinking, looking beyond, and cooperation, rather than competitiveness, are the typical competencies with which to solve complex problems or to find solutions in complex systems, which is equally true for questions relating to sustainability, a transverse and systemic domain which touches almost everything.

The competencies necessary for sustainability and entrepreneurship go hand in hand; actually, you need similar competencies to tackle social and environmental problems or to become an entrepreneur.

It becomes clear why sustainable entrepreneurs are more successful than big corporations in developing new socially- or environmentally-friendly products. Competences such as creativity, taking the initiative, looking beyond, controlling one's own destiny, and making intuitive decisions are limited by the procedures that have to be followed within big corporations. For big corporations, it is easier to follow the path that had been opened by sustainable entrepreneurs.

Competences for Sustainable Entrepreneurship

Competence usually refers to knowledge, attitudes, and skills. Ploum et al. (2018) underline that a successful agent of change for sustainability must have knowledge not only of environmental, economic, and social issues (i.e., knowledge of a complex matter), but also of a value system to support his or her actions (i.e., attitude) and the necessary skills to perform sustainability tasks.

Sustainable entrepreneurship contains two core concepts: entrepreneurship and sustainability, and the relationship between the two.

Let us start with entrepreneurship competence. The literature about entrepreneurial competence is abundant, and Lans et al. (2014) have distilled five generic competencies for entrepreneurship from all those studies:

1. Opportunity competence: this is more than just opportunity recognition, but a systematic development of adequate solutions to problems, thus putting perception, interpretation, and construction at the heart of opportunity identification.
2. Social competence: this builds up and maintains relationships and networks, which play an essential role in the opportunity development process.
3. Business competence: this involves the organization of different internal, external, human, physical, financial, and technological resources, as well as setting, evaluating, and implementing strategies, planning, and controlling.
4. Industry-specific competence: this involves technical knowledge (know-how) and market knowledge (know-what).
5. Entrepreneurial self-efficacy: this broad domain of meta-level competencies such as motivation and psychological constructs, and, above all, the belief in one's own entrepreneurial competence.

Opportunities with regard to sustainability are more complex than business opportunities, which address a one-dimensional problem, such as meeting a significant want or need. As Lans et al. (2014) put it, "sustainability opportunities have more the character of 'wicked' problems that are difficult to pin down, that are highly complex, and that do not have definitive solutions".

During past years, individual competencies for sustainable development have received much attention in the sustainability literature. Lans et al. (2014) describe a framework with seven competencies that are required for sustainability professionals.

1. Systems thinking competence: identify and analyze all relevant (sub-) systems across different domains and disciplines, and understand the interdependency of these (sub-) systems.
2. Embracing diversity and interdisciplinarity: structure relations, recognize the legitimacy of other viewpoints, and involve all stakeholders in order to maximize the exchange of ideas and learning.
3. Foresighted thinking: analyze and evaluate the impact of decisions on environmental, social, and economic domains in the long term.
4. Normative competence: map, apply, and reconcile sustainability values, principles, and targets in order to improve social-ecological systems, according to the normative concept of sustainable development that describes the world as it should be.
5. Action competence: actively involve oneself in responsible actions to improve the sustainability of social-ecological systems.
6. Interpersonal competence: motivate, enable, and facilitate collaborative and participatory sustainability activities or research. This includes skills in communicating, collaborating, negotiating, empathy, and compassion.
7. Strategic management: collectively design projects, implement interventions, transitions, and strategies toward sustainable development practices.

There is significant overlap between the two competence frameworks, entrepreneurship, on the one hand, and sustainability, on the other. According to Lans et al. (2014), they overlap in the centrality of dealing with (complex) problems, the importance of novelty and creativity, the importance of self-involvement, the importance of realizing projects, and the importance of engaging with others.

5 Teaching Sustainable Entrepreneurship

Departing from the competencies required for entrepreneurship, on the one hand, and sustainability, on the other, we now want to answer the question of how the combination of both, to wit, sustainable entrepreneurship, can be taught. The aim should be to form future entrepreneurs as agents of change for sustainable development.

As we saw above, environmental social values and environmental awareness are acquired at an early age, during childhood or youth. This makes it more difficult for higher education to reach this domain. However, as we will see below, entrepreneurship education and education for sustainable development are both transformational processes that induce personal growth which has an impact on the development of personal values.

Higher education plays an important role in laying the foundation for the development of the competencies for sustainable entrepreneurship. Today, institutions focus either on the issue of education for sustainability or on entrepreneurship education. The latter is traditionally located in the business schools, whereas education for sustainable development has its origin frequently either in the natural science faculty, where environmental science or environmental engineering is taught or in the social science faculty, which deals with the social issues of sustainable development.

Similar compartmentalization is true for the teaching of management knowledge, which has its focus and priority on business plans, which is against creativity and innovation and is separated into functional management boxes (such as marketing, finance, operations, and human resources). Entrepreneurial learning, in contrast, is acquired on a how-to and need-to-know basis dominated by doing, solving problems, grasping opportunities, copying from others, making mistakes, and experimenting (Gibb, 2005).

Entrepreneur education can foster entrepreneurial mindsets, forms of behaviour, and capabilities in young people, to enable them to create, lead, and develop new ventures (Gibb, 2005). This has given higher education institutions an important role in encouraging entrepreneurial mindsets. In entrepreneur education, the question is very much how things are taught, and, only in second place, what is taught.

However, the integration of sustainability issues or educational practices in order to raise environmental and social awareness in entrepreneurship education and prepare students for sustainability entrepreneurship remains limited. Even after more than three decades and numerous United Nations summits on sustainable development, the Enterprise and Entrepreneurship Education Guidance for UK Higher Education Providers (QAA, 2018) mentions sustainable entrepreneurship only among the definitions, with no guidance on how to integrate sustainability into entrepreneurship education.

The question which has not yet been definitively answered is how educators should or could integrate sustainable entrepreneurship into their teaching. Traditionally, business schools teach students a profit-first mentality (Lourenço et al., 2012), which corresponds to the logic that enterprises have, first and foremost, to be profitable.

The reason why sustainability and entrepreneurship are usually taught separately is that they originate in different institutions. Educators have, however, called for the integration of sustainability into entrepreneurship courses (Gast et al., 2017) in a way that sustainability or sustainable development is not a burden, but a true opportunity for entrepreneurs. Entrepreneurship courses that integrate sustainability have multiple advantages: they would attract not only students from business schools, who intend to become entrepreneurs, as is the case today but also students with environmental and social concerns and competencies, even from other disciplines, such as the natural or social sciences. In that way, many more students would follow sustainable entrepreneurship courses and become sustainable entrepreneurs and agents of change for a more sustainable world (which corresponds to the inner circle of Fig. 2).

Ideally, sustainable entrepreneurship education should enable individuals to acquire all the competencies described in the competence framework of sustainable entrepreneurship above, i.e., to deal with complex questions, to analyze the impact of decisions, take responsibility, motivate, enable, and facilitate, to name just a few.

Sustainable entrepreneurship contains two elements, entrepreneurship and sustainability: let us look first at entrepreneurship education. According to Lindner (2018), entrepreneur education should:

- Enable individuals to develop and implement their own ideas, not only in the case of a new venture but also in private life.
- Enable an entrepreneurial culture, which focuses on independence, open mindedness, empathy, relationships, and communication.
- Promote a culture of empowerment, autonomy, and responsibility.

Education for sustainable development draws on pedagogies found in environmental education and development education (Strachan, 2018). It aims to contribute to making our society more sustainable, by enabling future professionals to take action for sustainable development. Education for sustainable development is very much value based and can be a transformational process that stimulates personal growth. Effective education for sustainable development needs a whole school approach—the values of the school must reflect the values taught (Strachan, 2018).

There are similarities in terms of pedagogy between entrepreneurship education and education for sustainable development:

- They are transverse topics, which should be embedded across curricula.
- They can be transformational for the individual because they teach holistic approaches that enable individuals to take action and become agents of change not only in their professional lives, but also in their own day-to-day lives and communities.
- They can be effectively taught by experiential education.

The difference between entrepreneurship education and education for sustainable development is essentially the question of economic growth on a national level or profit on a company level, in contradiction to ecological or societal objectives when it comes to decision-making.

Experiential Education

Experiential education is a very effective pedagogy to teach (sustainable) entrepreneurship or sustainable development. It includes several elements:

1. Challenge-based learning or learning by experience fosters basic personal and social issues such as responsibility, autonomy, and cooperation, and should help to develop a culture of solidarity in our society, which has to be coupled with the teaching of the knowledge and skills that are necessary for sustainable entrepreneurship.

   Challenge-based learning is based upon the cycle of challenge—feedback—reflection (Association for Experiential Education). A challenge is a demanding

or complex task, which makes students develop their own solutions, usually in cooperation with others. Feedback can be given by the teachers, peers, or by self-assessment. Reflection provides the opportunity to process the experience from the challenge and feedback phases. Challenge-based learning should be introduced at a young age, which is decisive for the students to acquire the conviction of being able to do what they want to do, what they are doing, or what they are planning to do. It is this conviction that will decide about their success or not in life.
2. Critical and communicative learning (learning in the form of a dialogue between teachers and students).
3. Learning through discourse in order to enhance students' argumentative skills. Arguing in favor of ideas for civil society is essential for democratic societies and cannot be taught in lecture halls and learned by heart but has to be acquired on one's own.
4. Service learning through a commitment to an idea (performing community service that is related to the content that students learn at school), thus assuming responsibility, which is a key element in entrepreneurship education. Students need to be confronted with social issues and become involved if we want them to develop a greater interest in social topics (Lindner, 2018).

Experiential education has proven its worth over many years, and was developed in the 1930s by Kurt Hahn, the first sustainable "edupreneur". The concept of Kurt Hahn included—in particular—challenge-based learning and service learning, as well as dialogue and discourse. Terms were different in the 1930s compared to today; for example, the term "sustainable development" did not even exist.

Kurt Hahn, the First Sustainable "Edupreneur" and the Founder of Experiential Education

Kurt Hahn developed experiential education with all its facets in the 1930s. Ninety years later, his principles and developments are of even greater topicality and even more urgently needed.

Hahn developed experiential education in his time for international peace and social education. His concern was with civic education in order to keep the world whole or to make it whole; today, we would call it sustainability.

At the center of Hahn's educational philosophy was an education for democracy with the vigorous and active individual with humanitarian convictions who felt responsible for the welfare and progress of society (Knoll, 2001). Hahn's model was that of the vigilant citizen who combines in himself or herself the power of thinking with the will to act, which is close to the idea of a sustainable entrepreneur.

He introduced experiential pursuits, by which students come to know their strengths and discover their "grande passion", a powerful, internal motivation to learn and pursue one's true passion, in the journey of life. Service develops the social component: the commitment to others. By participating in rescue, social, or environmental services, students take on responsibility and experience the sublime feeling that "you are needed" (Knoll, 2001). For Hahn, the feeling "you are needed" was central to motivation, and service was the most important part of his pedagogy, a concept that goes well beyond experiential learning. As Hahn himself put it, "There are three ways of trying to win the young. There is persuasion, there is a compulsion, and there is attraction. You can preach at them: that is a hook without a worm. You can say, you must volunteer, and that is of the devil. You can tell them, you are needed. That appeal hardly ever fails".

Hahn put the emotional aspect at the center of his pedagogy, using the term "Erlebnistherapie", which cannot be easily translated. It means that feelings and emotions—not thoughts—are the basis for learning, gaining insights, and changing attitudes (Knoll, 2001). Erlebnistherapie evolved into Erlebnispädagogik or experience and challenge-based learning. Citations and terms from K. Hahn are in italics (Knoll, 1998).

Hahn was a top-class "edupreneur", who realized the need for new pedagogy well before its time; a pedagogy that is, even ninety years later, still not yet accepted in general education. Today's education is essentially based upon knowledge transfer, good marks, and competitiveness—for example, entry to university. Hahn was not a theoretician. He wrote very little literature but he was interested in putting his ideas into practice. He founded or co-founded schools and educational programs all over the world. Examples include the boarding schools of Salem (Germany) and Gordonstoun (Scotland), Outward Bound programs (short-term programs based upon experiential learning, mainly outdoors), or United World Colleges (2-year high schools with an international student body based upon academic and experiential learning, especially service learning).

The challenge for today's sustainable "edupreneurs" is to introduce experiential education into curricula that are often determined by knowledge transfer, and to educate their students in such a way as to foster basic personal and social issues such as responsibility, involvement, autonomy, and cooperation in order to contribute to a more sustainable society and a culture of solidarity.

6 Conclusion

When I look at our society and all the challenges that we should deal with, be it climate change, biodiversity loss, the increase of poor and undernourished people, as well as the increasing difference between the rich and poor, the "haves" and "have nots", the increase in corruption, a world with more weapons, wars, and displaced people than ever before, we could be discouraged and not do anything, or we could set an example and initiate changes in our sphere(s) of influence.

Education is the most powerful tool that we have to initiate change; it will not produce immediate results, but it is very efficient in the long term. I always compare education to the lighting of a candle: once the candle is lit, it will shine for a long time. Let us just imagine how many candles we can light as teachers.

Having had the chance to study in one of the schools founded by Kurt Hahn, I can assure people that those schools do have a lifelong impact in terms of values, engagement, and belief in one's strengths, to name but a few.

During my professional life as a sustainability professional, I have developed several education programs and courses, including environmental science at the university level, environmental education for instructors of alpine associations, and further education in environmental law.

The experience that I wish to share is the following: as a teacher, especially in experiential education, which often starts a transformational process, you are not sure about the outcome. Sometimes, you have the good fortune that your students give completely enthusiastic feedback at the end of the course. At that moment, you know that you have lit a candle—and that the students will carry the light further. Sometimes, you meet former students a couple of years later, and they tell you "we are working in an environmental domain thanks to your course a couple of years ago, even though our salary is miserly". In such a moment, you know that you had done the right thing.

I want to emphasize that it is important for all "edupreneurs" to stay motivated when students leave at the end of the course, and when they might be critical about your course. Especially in business schools, students love to receive "recipes" that they can implement straightaway in companies. This is not the aim, however; a recipe will only work once, and not in a second situation that is different. Only when you succeed in awakening a passion for sustainability will students be motivated to implement their knowledge and competencies in different situations and circumstances.

The question that remains is how to create a passion for sustainability? Experiential-based learning, especially outdoors, permits profound experiences but is not suited for each topic. Environmental law, for example, definitely not. But you can introduce success stories or show videos on environmental crimes which have been solved by barristers, present case studies for students to work on, etc., in your course to introduce experiences and hopefully awake passion. You have to adapt according to the subject and according to your skills and strengths as a teacher. Authenticity is crucial.

Let us close with the famous quotation that is attributed to Antoine de St. Exupéry, which also relies on emotion to motivate people:

> If you want to build a ship, don't drum up the men to gather wood, divide the work, and give orders. Instead, teach them to yearn for the vast and endless sea.

7 Summary

Sustainable entrepreneurship appeared in the 1970s and 1980s, one famous example of which can be found in Yvon Chouinard and Tom Frost of Chouinard Equipment, who developed chockstones, called Hexentrics, instead of pitons to do less harm to rocks when mountaineering. Yvon Chouinard later founded the company Patagonia in California, one of the first companies to design its products to respect the environment. At the same time, in Europe, several environmentally friendly companies were founded in the cosmetics sector, including, for example, Lorien

Goods in 1978, which became Logona in 1984, which developed cosmetics based on natural ingredients. In those years, it was essentially environmental entrepreneurs or green entrepreneurs, especially in the health and food sector, who dominated; social questions were still of lesser importance in Europe and the USA. The term sustainable development was introduced only later, in 1987 by the Brundtland Report. However, sustainable behaviour had existed before, even in its strict sense, which says take only the harvest and not the stock. One example of this can be found in the different laws about the forests in Austria (Habsburg), Switzerland, or Bavaria at the end of the nineteenth century, which essentially said that, for each tree that was cut down, another one had to be planted. The reason behind this was essentially the high number of avalanches which caused many deaths and much damage, and which needed to be reduced.

Sustainable entrepreneurship contains two core terms—sustainable and entrepreneur. Genuinely sustainable entrepreneurs go far beyond obtaining mere labels or certifications, or searching for a simple balance between environmental, social, and economic goals—they prioritize the environment and society as long as their companies remain financially viable.

For me, sustainable academic entrepreneurship is both a philosophy and a vision of education, one which views academics as teachers who enable their students to discover the values and the passion for a sustainable world, in the hope that they will, in the future, take on the responsibility of becoming agents of change with a focus on the capacity to provide real solutions to the environmental and social problems of our world, and the needs of our society. Values, interpersonal competencies, and motivation can best be taught by experiential learning, which was a pedagogic technique founded by Kurt Hahn in the 1930s. He developed it in his time for international peace and social education. Besides academics, it was composed of experiences and challenges outdoors, which had to be solved in groups, project work, and, most importantly, in services, be it the rescue, social, or environmental service. Involvement in services permits people to experience the feeling that "you are needed", an educational principle that rarely fails to motivate people.

Questions

- What are the two core values of sustainable entrepreneurship?
- What are the main difficulties and barriers for sustainable entrepreneurs?
- Explain why searching for a balance between environmental, social, and economic objectives is not enough for a truly sustainable entrepreneur?
- Explain the different forms of capitals, as seen by Daly, Parkin, and Freyman. Why do they prioritize natural capital? Which capital is prioritized by the present economic system? What would be the solution?
- Is having social and environmental concerns sufficient to become a sustainable entrepreneur?
- Which competencies are needed for a sustainable entrepreneur? Why?
- Why is service learning for Kurt Hahn the most important part of experiential learning?

References

Association for Experiential Education. Available at: https://www.aee.org/what-is-experiential-education

Binswanger, M. (2019). *Der Wachstumszwang. Warum die Volkswirtschaft immer weiterwachsen muss, selbst wenn wir genug haben*. Wiley.

Boucher, J., Jenny, C., Plummer, Z., & Schneider, G. (2018). How to avoid pigeonholing the environmental manager? *Sustainability, 10*, 2538.

Daly, H. E. (1996). *Beyond growth. The economics of sustainable development*. Beacon Press.

Dewey, J. (1929). *Experience and nature*. George Allan & Unwin Ltd.

European Union. (2020). *Special Eurobarometer 501 attitudes of the Europeans towards the environment*.

Eklund, M., & Wanzenried, G. (2022). *Academic and educational entrepreneurship: Foundations in theory and lessons from practice*. Springer.

Farny, S., & Binder, J. (2021). Sustainable entrepreneurship. In L. P. Dana (Ed.), *World encyclopedia of entrepreneurship* (2nd ed., pp. 605–611). Edward Elgar Publishing.

Freyman, M. (2012). *An exploration of sustainability and its application to corporate reporting*. Harvard University. IRI Working Paper.

Gast, J., Gundolf, K., & Cesinger, B. (2017). Doing business in a green way: A systematic review of the ecological sustainability entrepreneurship literature and future research directions. *Journal of Cleaner Production, 147*, 44–56.

Gibb, A. A. (2005). *Towards the entrepreneurial university entrepreneurship education as a lever for change*. Policy Paper No. 003. Birmingham: National Council for Graduate Entrepreneurship (NCGE).

Hardin, G. (1968). The tragedy of the commons. The population problem has no technical solution; it requires a fundamental extension in morality. *Science, 162*(3859), 1243–1248.

International Organization for Standardization. (2014). Discovering ISO 26000.

Joensuu-Salo, S., Viljamaa, A., & Varamäki, E. (2022). Sustainable entrepreneurs of the future: The interplay between educational context, sustainable entrepreneurship competence, and entrepreneurial intentions. *Administrative Sciences, 12*, 23.

Klapper, R. G., & Farber, V. A. (2016). In Alain Gibb's footsteps: Evaluating alternative approaches to sustainable Enterprise education (SEE). *The International Journal of Management Education, 14*, 422–439.

Knoll, M. (Ed.). (1998). *Kurt Hahn: Reform mit Augenmaß. Ausgewählte Schiften eines Politikers und Pädagogen* (389 S). Klett-Cotta.

Knoll, M. (2001). Schulreform durch "Erlebnistherapie" Kurt Hahn – ein wirkungsmächtiger Pädagoge. *Pädagogisches Handeln. Wissenschaft und Praxis im Dialog 5*, Heft 2, S. 65–76.

Lans, T., Blok, V., & Wesselink, R. (2014). Learning apart and together: Towards an integrated competence framework for sustainable entrepreneurship in higher education. *Journal of Cleaner Production, 62*, 37–47.

Lehtonen, M. (2004). The environmental-social interface of sustainable development: Capabilities, social capital, institutions. *Ecological Economics, 49*, 199–214.

Lindner, J. (2018). Entrepreneurship education for a sustainable future. *Discourse and Communication for Sustainable Education, 9*(1), 115–127.

Lourenço, F., Jones, O., & Jayawarna, D. (2012). Promoting sustainable development: The role of entrepreneurship education. *International Small Business Journal, 31*, 841–865.

Markman, G. D., Russo, M., Lumpkin, G. T., Jennings, P. D., & Mair, J. (2016). Entrepreneurship as a platform for pursuing multiple goals: A special issue on sustainability. *Ethics, and Entrepreneurship. Journal of Management Studies, 53*.

Oeko-Tex. STANDARD 100 by OEKO-TEX. Available at: https://www.oeko-tex.com/en/our-standards/standard-100-by-oeko-tex

Parkin, S., Sommer, F., & Uren, S. (2003). Sustainable Development: Understanding the concept and practical challenge. In *Proceedings of the Institution of Civil Engineers – Engineering Sustainability* 156: 1, March 2003, 19–26.
Ploum, L., Blok, V., Lans, T., & Omta, O. (2018). Toward a validated competence framework for sustainable entrepreneurship. *Organization & Environment, 31*, 113–132.
Potluri, S., & Phani, B. V. (2020). Incentivizing green entrepreneurship: A proposed policy prescription (a study of entrepreneurial insights from an emerging economy perspective). *Journal of Cleaner Production, 259*, 120843.
QAA. (2018). *Enterprise and entrepreneurship education guidance for UK Higher Education Providers*. Quality Assurance Agency for Higher Education. www.qaa.ac.uk
Russo, M. V. (2010). *Companies on a mission. Entrepreneurial strategies for growing sustainably, responsibly, and profitably*. Stanford Business Books.
Schick, H., Marxen, S., & Freimann, J. (2002). Sustainability issues for start-up entrepreneurs. *Greener Management International, 38*, 59–70.
Schneider, G. (2018). *On file with the author*.
Statista. (2022). *Marktanteil von Bio-Lebensmitteln in Deutschland bis 2019*. Accessed March 8, 2022, from https://de.statista.com/statistik/daten/studie/360581/umfrage/marktanteil-von-biolebensmitteln-in-deutschland/
Stockholm Resilience Centre. Accessed March 25, 2022., from https://stockholmresilience.org/research/planetary-boundaries.html
Strachan, G. (2018). Can education for sustainable development change entrepreneurship education to deliver a sustainable future? *Discourse and Communication for Sustainable Education, 9*(1), 36–49.
Thelken, H. N., & de Jong, G. (2020). The impact of values and future orientation on intention formation within sustainable entrepreneurship. *Journal of Cleaner Production, 266*, 122052.
United Nations. (n.d.-a). Dept. of Social and Economic Affairs, Sustainable Development. Available at: https://sdgs.un.org/goals
United Nations. (n.d.-b). Our Common Future: The World Commission on Environment and Development. Available at: https://sustainabledevelopment.un.org/content/documents/5987our-common-future.pdf
Vuorio, A. M., Puumalainen, K., & Fellnhofer, K. (2018). Drivers of entrepreneurial intentions in sustainable entrepreneurship. *International Journal of Entrepreneurial Behavior& Research, 24*, 359–381.
Wagenknecht, S. (2016). *Reichtum ohne Gier*. Campus Verlag.
Wagner, M. (2012). Ventures for the public good and entrepreneurial intentions: An empirical analysis of sustainability orientation as a determining factor. *Journal of Small Business and Entrepreneurship, 25*, 519–531.
York, J. G., & Venkataraman, S. (2010). The entrepreneur-environment nexus: Uncertainty, innovation, and allocation. *Journal of Business Venturing, 25*(5), 449–463.

Further Reading

Daly, H. E. (1996). *Beyond growth. The economics of sustainable development*. Beacon Press.
Ivanova, E., & Rimanoczy, I. (2021). *Revolutionizing sustainability education*. Routledge.
Knoll, M. (Ed.). (1998). *Kurt Hahn: Reform mit Augenmaß. Ausgewählte Schiften eines Politikers und Pädagogen*. Klett-Cotta 1998. 389 S.
Knoll, M. (2011). *Schulreform through "Experiential Therapy": Kurt Hahn—An Efficacious Educator*. Institute of Education Sciences. U.S. Dept. of Education.
Jones, G. (2017). *Profits and sustainability: A history of green entrepreneurship*. Oxford University Press.
Russo, M. V. (2010). *Companies on a mission. Entrepreneurial strategies for growing sustainably, responsibly, and profitably*. Stanford Business Books.

Gerhard Schneider, PhD, Professor of Sustainable Development and Corporate Social Responsibility at the Business School at HES-SO University of Applied Sciences and Arts Western Switzerland at the *HEIG-VD Haute Ecole d'Ingénierie et de Gestion du Canton de Vaud* at Yverdon-les-Bains. His research focus is on sustainable management in municipalities (the integration of the SDGs into municipal management), corporate sustainability, corporate social responsibility, sustainable development, and sustainable entrepreneurship. He is responsible for the Swiss further education program in environmental law, entitled "Environmental Law for Practitioners", under the patronage of the Swiss Federal Office for the Environment and the Conference of the Cantons. From 1996 to 2016, he was a member of the Federal Team for Environmental Education of the German Mountaineering Association. He trained instructors on topics such as nature protection, ecosystems, the cultural history of the Alps, and environmentally friendly mountaineering. In 2019, he was one of the authors of the statement of Scientists for Future—the "Statement of scientists and scholars concerning the protests for more climate protection—the concerns of the young protesters are justified" and was involved in the discussion about the pricing of CO_2. With his background in natural sciences and economics, he is working at the interface between economics and science, be it life cycle analyses, the impact of the pricing of CO_2, or the link between sustainability management in municipalities and sustainability performance. After an international education at UWC of the Atlantic in the UK (South Wales), he studied Chemistry, did a PhD in Botany, and did research as a Postdoctoral Fellow at the INRA Versailles-Grignon. While working at Fribourg University, he did a postgraduate course in business.

Financial Aspect of Academic and Educational Entrepreneurship

Marius Fuchs

1 Introduction and Goals

As in many areas of life, financial aspects also play an important role in entrepreneurial activities. Financial resources are both a prerequisite and a consequence. Therefore, a serious edupreneur or academic entrepreneur needs to understand the basic rules of finance. Building a (scalable) business requires a thorough understanding of potential sources of capital, the resulting dilution effects, and other associated costs, such as limited decision-making authority.

The purpose of this chapter is to provide an introduction to both the fundamentals (Part I) and the most critical areas of seed, venture, and growth capital, including the opportunities and caveats associated with them (Part II).

Findings are summarized in the form of "impulses" and "reflections" to encourage readers to link the discussion to other aspects of the holistic conceptual framework that underlies this book.

This chapter can only cover some key elements of finance. Students and entrepreneurs are advised to consult additional literature as suggested at the end of this chapter.

2 Financial and Liquidity Planning

Finance can be reduced—in its simplest form—to the amounts of money that flow *into* and *out* of edupreneurial or academic-entrepreneurial project (Horngren et al., 2014).

M. Fuchs (✉)
Institute for Financial Services Zug (IFZ) at the Lucerne University of Applied Sciences and Art Lucerne (HSLU), Rotkreuz, Switzerland
e-mail: marius.fuchs@hslu.ch

M. Aldogan Eklund, G. Wanzenried (eds.), *Academic and Educational Entrepreneurship*, Springer Texts in Business and Economics,
https://doi.org/10.1007/978-3-031-10952-2_4

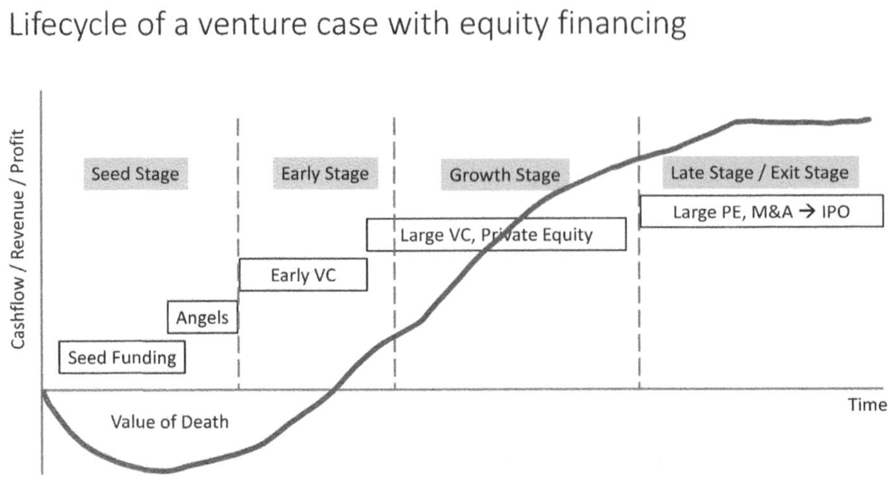

Fig. 1 An example life cycle of a risk case and its funding sources. Source: Created by the author

All entrepreneurial projects require an initial (cash) investment in order to generate a regular cash flow through operational activity. Imagine a perpetual engine that needs to be started, but afterward pretty much sustains itself.

Initially, minimal amounts of money are needed to pay for basic things such as legal advice (which may be provided for free by an institution, e.g., university), registration fees (from domain name registration to notary services or trade registry fees), rent, expenses, or salaries for helping hands (e.g., programmers and designers). As a business grows, it has specific financing needs that vary depending on the stage (Caselli & Negri, 2018).

Figure 1 shows a typical life cycle of a start-up. It starts at ground zero. In most cases, financial performance is initially dismal. The start-up consumes more money than it can raise through its operations or financing activities. However, once it survives the rough ride through the iconic "valley of death" (Al Natsheh et al., 2021), the economic outlook and funding opportunities become positive. Indeed, a large proportion of start-ups never make it past the seed stage. Many live on in a limited form, i.e., as a kind of undead zombie company that never makes it to the growth stage but always finds ways to survive for many years.

The first inflow of funds usually comes from an initial investment, known as *seed* capital. Start-up investors are usually the founders, their families or friends. Educational institutions or other private or public organizations may offer grants for start-ups. Crowdfunding has also become a popular and sometimes fruitful source of financial support for start-ups (Shelton, 2017).[1] These initial flows of money are often free. From an economic perspective, however, there is no such thing as a free

[1]Many start-ups (e.g., Initial Coin Offerings, ICO) that have successfully raised capital through crowdfunding have not necessarily fostered sustainable businesses. On the contrary, there are many cases that never managed to get beyond that early success. You can argue that they did not even

lunch. Although no legal obligations arise, there are usually expectations or moral conditions attached to such payment. It is advisable to set up simple contracts to establish clear legal and financial obligations for the initial funding. This avoids difficult discussions later on, especially in the case of the successful development of the project.

An initial seed round is usually followed by further rounds of funding as the need for cash grows with the expansion and professionalization of activities (Desai, 2019). At this stage, *angel investors* enter the scene. These are often former entrepreneurs who support start-ups. Angel investors also provide expertise and valuable access to their established network. Money that is combined with know-how and support is called "smart money."

The main difference between initial investment by friends and family and (semi) professional angel investors is that the latter usually require documentation of the planned activities, i.e., a business and financial plan. In addition, angel investors require some participation in the form of shares (see Part II). The process of finding angel investors can be arduous. Experienced entrepreneurs know that the search for money takes more time than activities related to developing or selling products and services. Common mistake founders make is being overly optimistic and underestimating the effort and time required to obtain money from an outside source (Lerner et al., 2012).

2.1 Know the Need and the State of Cash

Start-ups are—in most cases—short of cash. One may wonder why this is so. The simple answer is that no (professional) investor is willing to invest large sums upfront for something they cannot grasp. So what do investors need to take comfort in, so that they commit enough funds? The normal way is to define a possible path to sustainable positive cash flows and break it down into defined milestones. Once a milestone is reached, the next partial funding is automatically triggered. If a milestone is missed, investors and founders should review the situation before continuing their respective engagements. Both founders and investors may also conclude that there is no value in continuing. They may then walk away without further damage (Desai, 2019).

In rare cases, sponsors are very generous. However, endowing a start-up company with ample funds can spoil the young venture. Moreover, equity comes at a huge cost to founders (see Part II on dilution). Many start-ups were underfunded—in hindsight—and lost their prospects before they got started. So both underfunding and overfunding can destroy economic value and entrepreneurial careers. Knowing, or at least approximating your actual cash needs is essential for everyone involved. The liquidity plan (short-term view), budget (fiscal year), and financial plan

need to after their first successful campaign. But these are exceptions to the rule in crowdfunding campaigns.

Table 1 Example of a simple liquidity plan (fictitious example of the author)

Sales Budget & Liquidity 2022													
	January	February	March	April	May	June	July	August	September	October	November	December	EoY
Sales Budget	1,09,000	2,16,000	2,96,000	2,09,000	2,82,000	2,06,000	1,96,000	1,38,000	2,32,000	1,62,000	1,45,000	1,09,000	**23,00,000**
Cash Inflow from sales		98,000	1,80,000	2,50,000	1,95,000	2,53,000	1,85,000	1,70,000	1,38,000	2,32,000	1,62,000	1,45,000	20,08,000
Cost of Sales (cash view)	-40,000	-49,435	-95,670	-1,30,000	-95,000	-1,09,043	-74,000	-76,500	-62,100	-1,04,400	-72,900	-65,250	-9,74,298
Opex		-37,539	-37,943	-44,893	-49,893	-52,993	-38,393	-36,546	-39,143	-42,143	-40,743	-36,143	-4,56,372
Personell		-65,661	-65,661	-65,661	-65,661	-65,661	-65,661	-65,661	-65,661	-65,661	-65,661	-65,661	-7,22,271
Total	**-40,000**	**-54,635**	**-19,274**	9,446	**-15,554**	25,303	6,946	**-8,707**	**-28,904**	19,796	**-17,304**	**-22,054**	
Cash at beginning of mont	1,00,000	60,000	5,365	-13,909	-4,463	-20,017	5,286	12,232	3,525	-25,379	-5,583	-22,887	
Cash at end of month	60,000	5,365	-13,909	-4,463	-20,017	5,286	12,232	3,525	-25,379	-5,583	-22,887	-44,941	

Source: Created by the author

(medium-term view) are the most commonly used tools to determine capital or cash needs. Shelton (2017), based on decades of his own professional experience, recommends knowing the cash requirements for the next 12–15 months.

The liquidity plan shows the current and expected cash inflows and outflows. The following simple example shows a company with an initial cash balance of $100,000. Monthly sales (as per budget) and actual cash inflows (customers paying their due invoices, adjusted for bad debts), and cash outflows for expenses (for COGS, OPEX, personnel) are projected. At the end of March, the cash balance falls into negative territory. The cash balance is expected to return to a positive balance by the end of June before falling back into negative territory by the end of September (Table 1).

The company will need additional cash to survive the current fiscal year: The cash balance at the end of December is expected to be approximate -USD45 k. Simply put, if operations are to continue next year, someone will have to cover the gap. Under this plan, the company will have burned through about $145 k in cash in 2022. Either the operation becomes cash flow positive, or the financial sponsors foot the bill. They would have to cover the cash needs of the current fiscal year plus the projected cash flow gaps in the next period.

All businesses need proper liquidity planning, and there is no way around it. In most cases, a simple excel sheet is sufficient to show the gap between *planned* revenues and costs—and *actual* cash inflows and outflows. The liquidity plan is the central tool for identifying and tracking red flags (Müller-Ganz, 2019).

2.2 The Financial Plan: An Integral Part of the Business Plan

How much time and cash is needed to become a profitable company that has sustainable positive net cash flows? This is a crucial question for all investors (Lerner et al., 2012). Indeed, determining the right amount of cash needed to make a business successful is one of the most difficult tasks that founders and even professional investors face.

This leads us to the process of financial planning. Proper financial planning is closely related to business planning; it is a direct part of developing a business plan. As we shall see, planning is a multi-recursive process: ideas from the holistic conceptual framework are described in the first draft of a business plan and then further specified in the financial plan. Usually, the first versions of the financial plan do not lead to satisfactory results. This triggers a revision process of the business plan and even the conceptual framework (Shelton, 2017).

Creating a business plan is a challenging task. It forces the entrepreneur to explain and justify his idea(s). The financial plan is a distillation of the business plan. The entrepreneur is forced to cast the often vague statements of the business plan into numbers. These numbers must be structured and put into a format with standardized profit and loss statements and balance sheets (Horngren et al., 2014).

Many institutions such as banks, consultancies, or other organizations that specialize in supporting start-ups offer comprehensive, easy-to-use financial planning tools. Very often these are free of charge. These tools range from simple Excel sheets to tools that integrate different views and perspectives, such as liquidity plan, budgeted balance sheet, budgeted income statement, ratios, budgeted cash flow statement, investment plan, and budget controlling with easy-to-use variance analysis. In addition, there are numerous subscription-based or one-time payment FP&A (Financial Planning & Analysis) tools on the market.

The Fig. 2 shows a fairly detailed example of a liquidity plan monthly calculated from other input data.

In general, it is recommended to use a simple tool and focus on the content of the planning process rather than putting too much effort into evaluating and building the tool to be used (Shelton, 2017).

Several iterative steps are required to create a financial plan. First, quantities must be estimated (e.g., how many units of a particular product or service can be sold in years 1–3?). Then, the entrepreneur must set a price that (a) covers all costs plus a profit margin, (b) attempts to capture the willingness to pay of the entire target audience, and (c) is still competitive in the marketplace. Only now, with this information, is it possible to calculate revenues, costs, and expenses and derive the amount of money needed to break even.

The process of estimating revenues and costs may seem simple. However, experience teaches that very fundamental questions arise when founders are confronted with conflicting objectives and the requirement to agree on figures (e.g., prices, quantities, and costs) that are still in line with the holistic concept. The founders need to question their initial assumptions and the underlying hypothesis.

Simple validation questions include:

Is our assumption realistic that we will sell X units at the set price?
Are all costs included and reasonably calculated?
Is it a scalable business model?
Is Our company for profit or not for profit?

It is likely that the first version(s) of the financial plan are at odds with the rest of the business plan and the underlying holistic concept. The first version of the plan is always too optimistic. A rule of thumb is to estimate costs and time as accurately as

CREDIT SUISSE

Liquidity Plan

		Year		January		February		March		April		May		June		July		August		September		October		November		December	
		Total target	Total actual	Target	Actual	Target	Actual	Target	Actual	Target	Actual	Target	Actual	Target	Actual	Target	Actual	Target	Actual	Target	Actual	Target	Actual	Target	Actual	Target	Actual
	Cash sales:	0	0																								
+	Payments from accounts receivable:	0	0																								
+	Other cash receipts: a) Rent	0	0																								
+	b) Securities/interest income	0	0																								
+	c) ...	0	0																								
=	**Total receipts**	0	0	0	0	0	0	0	0	0	0	0	0	0	0	0	0	0	0	0	0	0	0	0	0	0	0
+	Purchase of goods and materials	0	0																								
+	Salaries, wages, employee benefits	0	0																								
+	Advertising	0	0																								
+	Taxes, interest on capital	0	0																								
+	Insurance	0	0																								
+	Gen. office and administrative expenses	0	0																								
+	Rent	0	0																								
+	Misc. expenditure (energy, water, etc.)	0	0																								
+	Value added tax	0	0																								
=	**Total expenditure**	0	0	0	0	0	0	0	0	0	0	0	0	0	0	0	0	0	0	0	0	0	0	0	0	0	0
=	**Gross income/outgoings**	0	0	0	0	0	0	0	0	0	0	0	0	0	0	0	0	0	0	0	0	0	0	0	0	0	0
+	Other receipts from sale of investments	0	0																								
+	Other receipts (e.g. loans granted by third parties)	0	0																								
+	Other receipts from advance payments by customers	0	0																								
+	Private deposits/capital increase	0	0																								
-	Other payments to acquire investments	0	0																								
-	Other payments (e.g. loans granted to third parties)	0	0																								
-	Other payments on account with suppliers	0	0																								
-	Private withdrawals	0	0																								
=	**Net income/outgoings**	0	0	0	0	0	0	0	0	0	0	0	0	0	0	0	0	0	0	0	0	0	0	0	0	0	0
+	Cash, post office and bank account balances	0	0	0	0	0	0	0	0	0	0	0	0	0	0	0	0	0	0	0	0	0	0	0	0	0	0
=	**Cash surplus/shortfall**	0	0	0	0	0	0	0	0	0	0	0	0	0	0	0	0	0	0	0	0	0	0	0	0	0	0
	Cash surplus used for:																										
	Cash shortfall met by:																										

Fig. 2 Example of a detailed liquidity plan (Credit Suisse, 2021)

possible—and then double both. Building a successful business takes much longer and costs much more than any bad-case scenario designed early on envisions. Experienced practitioners working with start-ups triple the initial "calculations" when evaluating the potential return on investment.

One way to deal with this is to use the first version as a best-case scenario and derive a base and a worst-case scenario from it. This triggers valuable discussions and leads to much better results—without having to start from scratch. The policy discussions can even provide the impetus to choose a different revenue or business model. The basic rule here is: Business models that consume or require as little money as possible are preferable. Such models have a lower risk profile and therefore have a higher chance of being funded by a third-party investor if the entrepreneur needs additional capital (Damodaran, 2012).

Impulse Edupreneurs and academicpreneurs should structure their business model "cash-lean," i.e., reduce capital requirements to an absolute minimum and achieve positive cash generation as quickly and directly as possible. This significantly increases the chances of obtaining financing. At the same time, undesirable dependencies on outside capital providers and the resulting dilution effects of founder shares are reduced or even avoided (cf. Part II).

Reflection Edupreneurs and Academicpreneurs working on the financial aspect—especially their financial plan—need to rethink some of their assumptions, goals, and even beliefs about some of the other aspects of their idiosyncratic holistic conceptual framework. Even though the financial aspect is only one of seven, it has a critical impact on the sustainable viability of the entire enterprise. Based on the initial calculations in the financial plan, founders are likely to be forced to discuss (fundamental) adjustments in some of the other dimensions (Fig. 3).

Founders may even review their position on whether their project is for-profit or non-profit. Financially, this decision will determine the strategy and path of seeking capital (Shelton, 2017).

In Part II, we look at possible sources of financing and their respective advantages and disadvantages. The founder's preference for some investors presupposes that the business idea is sufficiently fascinating and (financially) interesting. Once discussions with investors or other funders begin, additional feedback loops on the company's holistic concept are triggered. This is a time-consuming but, in most cases, fruitful process.

3 Sources, Dilution, and Cost of Capital

In Part I, we learned about the importance of cash flows and liquidity. Cash is the oxygen of any economic activity. The availability of oxygen must be guaranteed at all times (Müller-Ganz, 2019). In addition, we discussed that the business needs capital not only to meet its current expenses but also to pay for its planned activities

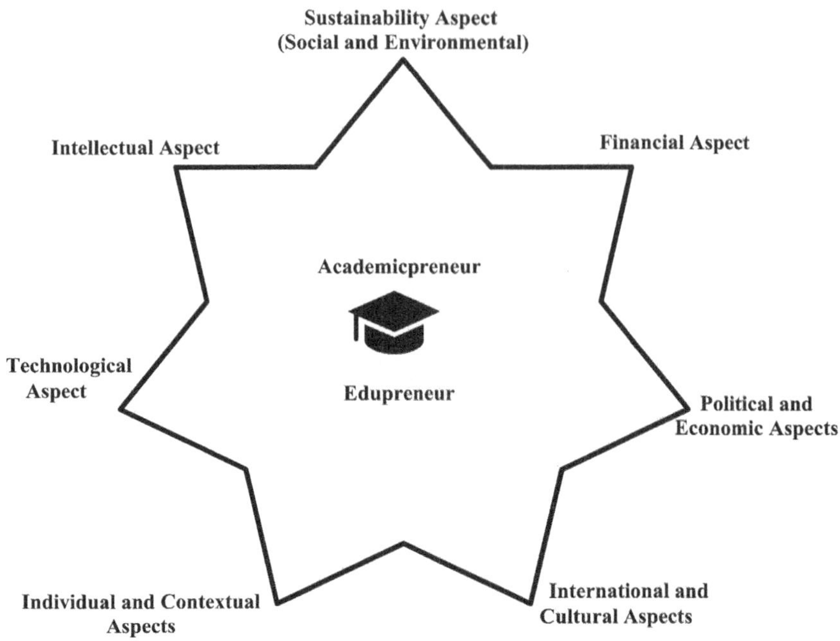

Fig. 3 The holistic conceptual framework. Source: Eklund and Wanzenried (2022)

to develop, manufacture, and distribute products and services. We learned how to calculate the future cash or capital requirements needed to achieve the goals set forth in the business plan. We also discussed that most businesses consume cash for a significant amount of time before they become cash flow positive.

When founders, family, friends, and angel investors reach their limits in funding the start-up, new outside parties must step in. There are a variety of potential partners that can be on a long list, depending on the amount of capital needed or the characteristics (Shelton, 2017). Potential partners include "the crowd," institutions that provide grants, lenders that provide loans (interest-bearing or noninterest-bearing), private investors with/without ambitious return expectations, and—at the other end of the spectrum—professional investors such as venture capital funds that only invest in very promising start-ups with high-value creation potential. Venture capitalists (VCs) are financial intermediaries that are essentially a type of specialized investment funds (Lerner et al., 2012). They receive capital contributions from institutional investors, high net worth individuals, and others across the economic spectrum and place the investments as deposits in small, private, and primarily high-technology companies with potentially high growth (Cumming & MacIntosh, 2001). Planning for exit from an investment and assessing the optimal timing for exit are of great importance (Gompers & Lerner, 1999).

For a start-up and its founders, it is very important to realize that choosing a partner is a decision that will greatly determine the future of the company and the prosperity of its current owners. It is one of the decisions in the life of a business that cannot be easily reversed. Therefore, it must be well considered. We will discuss some critical aspects and possible caveats.

3.1 A Pecking Order of Investors

Different plans require different equipment and partners. Young, loss-making businesses carry a high risk of failure. No bank is willing to provide loan financing unless there is adequate collateral or a sufficiently sustainable cash flow to pay interest and repay the loan on time. In this initial situation, equity investors are left as the remaining source of capital. Capital is provided in the form of equity or equity-like instruments (e.g., mezzanine capital, subordinated loans with conversion rights) or as grants or other "à fonds perdu" (i.e., non-repayable) structures (Desai, 2019). Here, there is an initial feedback loop to whether the enterprise should be large, medium, for-profit, or non-profit. These funding options are not completely mutually exclusive but blending them is difficult. Reputable venture capital firms, for example, will not fund a company with mid-sized market potential (Lerner et al., 2012). Investors focusing on small firms may not be professional enough to provide adequate advice and resources for a (delayed) growth phase.

For founders, a good strategy is to proceed as follows: Let us assume the start-up has had a good launch. The first products and services have received good feedback and there is further demand from satisfied customers. However, there are still many problems to solve before the products or services can be profitably deployed. The available sources of capital have been exhausted (founders, families, friends, crowd platforms), but the company desperately needs additional money to continue its operations. The founders have already identified a number of foundations (within the educational institution they are currently affiliated with and outside, e.g., through government or private entities). They have also prepared application materials. In parallel, they have begun discussions with angel investors and venture capitalists who have experience in the education sector. Many of them are offering "smart money" to sweeten their demand for a significant stake in the company in an initial round of funding. The founders see the advantage in leveraging their network and experience to grow the business. But they are also smart enough to ask for references and examples. Some investors are willing to pass on contacts without a written contract. Other investors are reluctant to be drawn in and want to sign a preliminary agreement first, which includes an advance for them and the right to include a liquidation preference clause in the investment agreement once it is drawn up. In addition, they propose that all legal costs be borne by the company.

There are two important points to consider here. Firstly, trust and gut feeling are crucial decision-making criteria. A trustworthy partner with a solid track record is invaluable, especially when things go wrong.

Second, you should be wary of investors who pretend to be professionals but are more likely to pose as consultants trying to do business and get a stake in your company on top of that. The catch is that once a shareholder has a stake in your business, you cannot get rid of them without incurring disproportionate financial and other costs. To illustrate, the aforementioned liquidation preference clause proposed by one of the potential partners means that if the company is sold, the investors will be paid first, up to the specified limits, before the founders receive any money. Depending on the terms and the transaction price, this could result in the founders not receiving a single dollar in the event of a successful sale of their company. This is certainly an extreme case, but it does happen in corporate reality, especially if the company is only a reasonably successful investment, but performs below expectation, and the investors want to get rid of it.

Other contractual reservations may arise from clauses specifying drag- or tag-along rights. These clauses may trigger a sale of the company pushed by investors despite the expressed non-consent of the founders. Again, depending on the contractual arrangements, these are potential traps that significantly shift the balance of power between shareholders without the founders noticing. The risk is extremely high when the company is desperate for a cash injection and the founders have a blind spot for anything beyond the end of the month. They are essentially giving away the future of the company and their fortune in a moment of stress.

This brings us back to the observation mentioned earlier that many financing options are mutually exclusive. However, there are some combinations that leave enough room for future moves. In general, and presumably in the field of academic and educational entrepreneurship, it makes sense to focus on grants or funds with no repayment obligations compared to third-party equity financing. There is no question that grants are hard to come by. But they are, in most cases, a "cheaper" form of start-up funding than issuing equity. Grants have one big advantage: they leave founders with the option to take on a (professional) investor at a later stage in their company's lifecycle. The later the stage, the easier and cheaper it becomes to get funding. There is another effect that occurs when a company is likely to see light at the end of its "Valley of Death": Because risks are now much lower, banks and other lenders may be willing to fund capital needs along with equity investors. As a result, the cost of capital—measured as the percentage of the total company shares that the founders must transfer—falls significantly.

Impulse Apart from the need for funding, edupreneurs and academic entrepreneurs should review the skills and capacities they have and that is needed to launch and successfully grow their start-ups. They might consider teaming up with partners who offer smart money.

Considerations When you add equity investors to your business, you have to give up shares. Edupreneurs and academic entrepreneurs should keep in mind that a small piece of a large pie (e.g., a well-positioned, profitable company of remarkable size) is still larger and more attractive in most cases than all of a small cupcake (i.e., an underperforming no-name company).

4 Summary

The financial perspective is only one aspect of the holistic conceptual framework for edupreneurs and academicpreneurs, but a very important one. Capital, cash, and regular cash flow are like oxygen that keeps the blood circulating—they are vital and need a lot of attention. Creating the financial plan as an integrated part of the business plan forces entrepreneurs to discuss and question other aspects of their conceptual framework.

This chapter has presented the main tools for controlling and forecasting liquidity and future cash needs. Start-ups have to survive their individual journey through the iconic "valley of death." This stage in a start-up's life cycle is characterized by a permanent lack of capital and resources. The risks of failure at this early stage are so great that no traditional funder (such as a bank) is willing to provide sufficient capital. Alternative sources are foundations or private investors.

Many edupreneurs and academic entrepreneurs are familiar with the system of applying for grants or interest-free (student) loans and have experience in dealing with the application and reporting process. However, there is a risk that they underestimate the difficulties and costs involved in raising equity for a share in a business. Talking to and winning over professional venture capitalists may sound exciting and is undoubtedly an accolade if achieved, but it can come at a huge cost that many founders are not aware of. Contractual clauses with rights of first refusal, ratchets and pricing mechanisms for subsequent rounds of capital may be accepted without the slightest idea of the potential (likely) impact at a later stage.

One of the goals of this chapter was to make founders aware of these risks when preparing to speak with investors. Another goal was for aspiring entrepreneurs to gain an understanding of basic documentation (i.e., business and financial plan; cash flow plan) and background checks before speaking with professional investors. Investors with a proven track record of investing smart money offer many opportunities to turn start-ups into successful, profitable businesses.

Questions

Question 1. What is the best way to get "cheap" money and avoid "expensive" capital?

Question 2. What steps are necessary to obtain external funding? (cf. Sources of funding).

Question 3. What do you think about *smart money*? What is it and where could it support a business?

Question 4. How do you feel about giving up shares in your business to gain capital and opportunities in the form of access to networks and advice?

Question 5. Is it different to invest in the education sector compared to new, fast-growing markets such as entertainment, social media, or metaverse platforms? Compare successful examples like Facebook, Twitter, Netflix, or Amazon with your ideas.

References

Al Natsheh, A., Gbadegeshin S.A., Ghafel K. , Mohammed, O., Koskela, A. , Rimpiläinen, A., Tikkanen, J., & Kuoppala, A. (2021). The causes of valley of death: a literature review. In *INTED2021 Proceedings* (pp. 9289–9298).

Caselli, S., & Negri, G. (2018). *Private equity and venture capital in Europe* (2nd ed.). Academic Press.

Credit Suisse. (2021). *Liquidity planning tool*. Accessed March 31, 2021, from https://www.credit-suisse.com/microsites/business-easy/en/firmengruendung/vorbereiten/liquiditaetsplanung.html

Cumming, D. J., & MacIntosh, J. G. (2001). The duration of venture capital investments in Canada and the United States. *Journal of Multinational Financial Management, 11*(4–5), 445–463. https://doi.org/10.1016/S1042-444X(01)00034-2

Damodaran, A. (2012). *Investment valuation – Tools and techniques for determining the value of any asset* (3rd ed.). Wiley.

Desai, M. A. (2019). *How finance works: The HBR guide to thinking smart about the numbers*. Harvard Business Review Press.

Eklund, M., & Wanzenried, G. (2022). *Academic and educational entrepreneurship: Foundations in theory and lessons from practice*. Springer.

Gompers, P. A., & Lerner, J. (1999). *The venture capital cycle*. MIT Press.

Horngren, C. T., Sundem, G. L., Elliott John, A., & Philbrick, D. (2014). *Introduction to financial accounting* (Pearson New International Edition, 11th ed.). Pearson Education Limited.

Lerner, J., Hardymon, F., & Ann, L. (2012). *Venture capital & private equity – A case book*. Wiley.

Müller-Ganz, J. (2019). *Turnaround – Restructuring and reorganization of companies*. Schulthess Management.

Shelton, H. (2017). *The secrets of creating a successful business plan*. Summit Valley Press.

Further Reading

Berk, J., & DeMarzo, P. (2020). *Corporate finance* (Global Edition, 5th ed.). Pearson.

Gompers, P. A. (1995). Optimal investment, monitoring, and the staging of venture capital. *The Journal of Finance, 50*(5), 1461–1489. https://doi.org/10.1111/j.1540-6261.1995.tb05185.x

Lerner, J. (2009). *Boulevard of broken dreams: Why public efforts to promote entrepreneurship and venture capital have failed and what to do about it*. Princeton University Press.

Marius Fuchs (Dr. oec. HSG, Swiss Certified Public Accountant) is a Senior Lecturer at the Institute for Financial Services Zug (IFZ), Lucerne University of Applied Sciences and Art Lucerne (HSLU). He is currently Head of Program for Corporate Restructuring and Turnaround Management. He held different positions in the industry and banking. He is a member of several boards of directors and advisory boards and acted previously as CEO and CFO of several VC-backed start-up companies. He can be reached at: marius.fuchs@hslu.ch

Political and Economic Aspects of Academic and Educational Entrepreneurship

Gabrielle Wanzenried

1 Introduction

The political and economic aspect is an important dimension of the holistic conceptual framework of academic and educational entrepreneurship, as outlined in Fig. 1 in the chapter "Introduction to Holistic Academic and Educational Entrepreneurship", given that a state's political-economic framework is an important determinant of its institutions, which includes universities. The importance of the political economy for academic and educational entrepreneurship has become even more important in the context of the additional role that universities have taken on over the past decades, namely, the so-called "third mission", with academic entrepreneurship participating in the socio-economic development of the local communities (see, e.g. Etzkowitz & Leydesdorff, 2000). Given this additional role, the nature of university–industry relations and knowledge transfer has become an increasingly important strategic issue for university rectors, as well as for politicians and policymakers, both as a source of revenue for universities, and as a policy tool for governments in their economic development policies (Shore & McLauchlan, 2012).

The chapter is structured as follows: Section 2 describes the changing mission of universities over the last decades, which is directly related to both necessity and the increasing intensity of policy interventions. Section 3 discusses the relationship between public policy and academic entrepreneurship, starting with the public good character of university research, how public academic entrepreneurship initiatives should be assessed, before finally discussing the risks of public policy interventions for academic entrepreneurship. Section 4 summarises the institutional factors which affect academic entrepreneurship, and Sect. 5 provides two examples

G. Wanzenried (✉)
University of Applied Sciences and Arts Western Switzerland HES-SO, Yverdon-les-Bains, Switzerland
e-mail: gabrielle.wanzenried@heig-vd.ch

M. Aldogan Eklund, G. Wanzenried (eds.), *Academic and Educational Entrepreneurship*, Springer Texts in Business and Economics,
https://doi.org/10.1007/978-3-031-10952-2_5

of major policy reforms which have had an impact on the role of universities and academic entrepreneurship. Section 7 concludes.

2 The Changing Mission of Universities

2.1 The "Third Mission" of Universities

In the past, education and research were the main missions of universities. With globalisation and the rise of the knowledge society, universities were delegated a "third mission", which is that of academic entrepreneurship and implies the participation of universities in the socio-economic development of the local communities (Etzkowitz & Leydesdorff, 1998, 2000). The role of universities has changed from being sources of academic knowledge generation and providers of well-educated human capital incorporated in their students and graduates (Audretsch & Lehmann, 2005) towards vehicles for policymakers for the promotion of growth and innovation through the higher education sector (Sandström et al., 2018). As a consequence, universities are more often seen as key actors in contributing to economic growth and fostering entrepreneurial behaviour and innovative activities, thereby being of benefit and support to private sector actors in achieving firm-level growth (Cunningham et al., 2018; Guerrero et al., 2016). Furthermore, university management increasingly highlights the "third mission" and its "societal impact" as one of the overarching goals of universities (Sandström et al., 2018).

As Rothaermel et al. (2007) outline, academic entrepreneurship includes entrepreneurial activities such as starting new businesses at universities, establishing research centres with industry, creating an appropriate way of protecting intellectual property, and licencing research results obtained at universities. Associated with these activities are the challenges that universities face. Some of these challenges are related to the policymaking level, and the structure of the higher education system and its planning, while others are related to the rules and environment, the level of resources, and the existing processes (Yadolahi & Meisam, 2014). As Lehmann et al. (2020) mention, the interactions between higher education institutions and the entrepreneurial ecosystem can be promoted in at least two dimensions: promoting and improving the internal structures and preferring of higher education institutions and taking account of the external conditions imposed by higher education policies and the business environment. Accordingly, these activities have a political-economic dimension.

2.2 The Reasons Behind the "Third Mission"

According to Compagnucci and Spigarelli (2020), the development of this "third mission" of universities is, among other factors, related to both the financial and the environmental crises, which present unprecedented challenges for society, and have contributed to the redesigning and extending of the missions of universities. In this context, the term "third mission" is used, which consists of wide-ranging and recurring concepts such as the "entrepreuneurial university", "technology transfer", and the "Triple Helix Model partnership" (Trencher et al., 2014). It also refers to an extensive array of activities performed by higher education institutions that seek to transfer knowledge not only to society in general and but also to organisations, as well as to promote entrepreneurial skills, innovation, social welfare, and the formation of human capital. Finally, it is related to the development of science and society through various forms of communication and social engagement (Rothaermel et al., 2007).

As Compagnucci and Spigarelli (2020) further outline, the transition from research universities to entrepreneurial universities originated in the USA in the late nineteenth century (e.g. Riviezzo & Napolitano, 2010). For instance, the Massachusetts Institute of Technology (MIT) and Stanford University in California represent early archetypes of such higher education institutions. They were not only the first ones to expand their traditional missions of teaching and performing research, but they were also the first movers to include more applied research with commercial relevance into their programmes. Finally, they also started to transfer knowledge to the non-academic environment as well as providing support to industry (Etzkowitz, 2003; Goethner & Wyrwich, 2020). As Blenker and Dreisler (2006) state, the entrepreneurial university is still more commonplace in the USA than in Europe. In line with this is the fact that US universities have traditionally been more based upon private funds and corporate contracts as a significant part of their overall income, and also have a more natural orientation to the market, in contrast to European universities, which are predominantly state financed. Another interesting difference between the USA and Europe is that the entrepreneurial university has emerged "bottom-up" in the USA, while, in Europe, the introduction of academic entrepreneurship is a more recent "top down" phenomenon (Etzkowitz, 2003).

In order to understand these differences better, various studies have investigated the factors determining the move towards more entrepreneurial universities (e.g. Muscio et al., 2012). Among other findings, they affirm that the limited amount of funds that universities receive from national governments has led to a funding gap, which is an important determinant. Furthermore, cutbacks in research funding systems have increased the competition between universities. Accordingly, universities increasingly consider the entrepreneurial culture as a new way of availing of the needed resources, in the form of funds, collaboration, and access both to facilities and to different sources (Mariani et al., 2018). According to Etzkowitz (2001) and Azagra-Caro et al. (2006), another driver behind this evolution is the development of techno-sciences and the growing interest of industries in university laboratories. Finally, changes in both national and international legislations on intellectual property rights have played an important role in the shift to more entrepreneurial initiatives on the part of universities (Powers, 2004). As, for example Link and Scott (2010) mention, this development has been reinforced by both national and local governments that introduced measures to promote the transformation of scientific knowledge into innovative and practical goods. A prominent example of such a measure is the Bayh-Dole Act of 1980,[1] which permitted scientists, universities, and businesses to patent and profit from discoveries made through federally funded research (Goethner & Wyrwich, 2020).

This development with its underlying drivers represents a clear change in the political economy. It has positive effects on the economic dynamics and entrepreneurial openness of universities. At the same time, this trend towards academic entrepreneurship is also criticised due to the disinvestment of the state in tertiary education (Shore & McLauchlan, 2012). Section 3.3 discusses this concern in more detail below.

3 Public Policy and Academic Entrepreneurship

3.1 University Research as a Public Good

As outlined in Sect. 2, universities have taken on a new and expanded role in recent decades. They are not only seen as providers of basic research and graduate students, but also as vehicles for regional development, and policymakers seek to promote growth and innovation through the higher education sector (Shane, 2004). According to Sandström et al. (2018), the theoretical foundation of this development lies in the public goods nature of university research: investment in research and innovation is considered to be crucial for economic growth and has a positive impact on productivity (e.g. Romer, 1990). Knowledge resulting from university research often leads to positive externalities and has thus the characteristic of a public good (Audretsch & Lehmann, 2005). The two main criteria that distinguish a public good are that it must be non-rivalrous in consumption and non-excludable. Non-rivalrous means that the good does not dwindle in supply as more people consume it; non-excludability means that the good is available to all citizens. Typically, these services are administered by governments and paid for collectively through taxation. Once acquired, knowledge can be reused infinitely, and one actor cannot prevent another from using it as well. These properties of knowledge mean that an economy can benefit greatly from investing in the development of knowledge, as this knowledge tends to spill over into the economy (Sandström et al., 2018). This particular characteristic of knowledge as a public good does, however, imply that markets are likely to under-supply it. The theoretical motivation for public investment stems from the notion that, if the benefits of new knowledge are distributed beyond those who developed it, a market economy may generate a sub-optimal amount of research and innovation (Arrow, 1962). Thus, state intervention is necessary to support academic entrepreneurship initiatives, given that private sector institutions are not likely to prioritise these activities sufficiently.

[1] Also known as the Patent and Trademark Law Amendments Act, 1980 in the USA.

3.2 Assessing Public Academic Entrepreneurship Initiatives

As outlined above, universities are no longer considered simply as providers of basic research and a skilled workforce but are increasingly seen as the engines of regional and national growth with a mission to create innovation and build up businesses (Etzkowitz, 2003). As a consequence, policymakers and academic institutions have invested extensively in initiatives for the commercialisation of academic research (Link et al., 2014). According to Sandström et al. (2018), however, it is not clear to what extent such commercialisation initiatives to support academic entrepreneurship are an effective and efficient means of promoting innovation and growth. As the authors further outline, much theoretical and empirical work has explored the conditions that best favour such commercialisation and the specific transfer mechanisms, such as university spin-offs (e.g. Perkmann et al., 2013; Djokovic & Souitaris, 2008). The underlying hypothesis of these studies is the existence of a market failure, which leads to an efficiency-enhancing perspective, i.e. companies are thought to under-invest in "good" university research with commercial potential because of appropriation problems (Martin & Scott, 2000). In response, policies are developed to "correct" this failure—often by providing incentives for universities to become actively involved in promoting entrepreneurial ventures. Another perspective is taken by Sandström et al. (2018), who focus on the question of how effective academic entrepreneurship initiatives are. As they outline, an efficient system can be viewed as one that converts input into output in a way that conserves resources. In contrast, the notion of effectiveness refers to whether or not the overall system fulfils its purpose. This is a different approach, in the sense that it allows the likeliness of the specific measures actually delivering the intended benefits and correcting market failures to be discussed. Sandström et al. (2018) provide a good example to illustrate the difference between the two approaches, which is quite important for policy interventions. Consider a policy that encourages professors to market their research results. Depending on the specific implementation, this can be very efficient in creating new businesses, but, at the same time, it can be a waste to society:

Case 1. Consider a situation in which an AE (academic entrepreneurship) initiative incentivises professors to commercialise low-value technologies. As a result, many new university spin-offs are created, but few growing companies, and, at the same time, there is a decline in university research capacity as researchers abandon their primary activities.

Case 2. Consider the alternative situation in which publicly funded AE initiatives create incentives for professors to conduct world-class research to bring their results to the market. The result is that public money crowds out private investment. Importantly, it is possible that academic entrepreneurship initiatives are efficient in transferring academic knowledge to the marketplace, but do not necessarily increase overall societal welfare. Consequently, policymakers need to be aware of these effects when evaluating alternative initiatives.

As Sandström et al. (2018) argue, the theoretical rationale for public interventions in academic entrepreneurship does not necessarily imply that policy interventions are always effective and/or efficient. As a matter of fact, public choice theory teaches us those governments and policies, just like markets, may fail under certain circumstances. In order to analyse the effectiveness and efficiency of academic entrepreneurship initiatives with the possibility of policy interventions, Sandström et al. (2018) propose using the notion of robustness, which originates in systems theory and is related to the capacity of a system to cope with stress and complexity. According to the authors, a robust system is capable of coping with uncertainties and significant variations in conditions without having its outcome adversely affected. Conversely, a system that lacks robustness experiences a sharp decline in performance when exposed to varying conditions. According to Henrekson and Rosenberg (2000), contextual factors play an important role in determining both the outcome and the success of a particular initiative. In the particular case of academic entrepreneurship initiatives, the contextual factors might be, for example national institutions, the characteristics of the regional economy, and/or the specific properties of the universities in question and would have to be taken into account. A policy system is robust if it is able to function under varying conditions. Accordingly, a properly crafted policy should be designed in a way that renders its functionality robust against/in varying conditions (Pennington, 2011).

3.3 The Risks of Public Policy Interventions for Academic Entrepreneurship

The nature of changes in the political economy with the increasing importance of the "third mission" of universities and the implied tendency towards academic entrepreneurship has its advantages but is also viewed critically by several researchers. As Compagnucci and Spigarelli (2020) argue, they warn of the impact of increased state disinvestment in tertiary education. Moreover, policymakers tend to view higher education and research as a personal, private investment, rather than as a public good (e.g. Shore & McLauchlan, 2012).

As Shore and McLauchlan (2012) further outline, the related commercialisation of academic activities is also generating new problems of an ethical and practical nature. They raise the question, for instance, of what entrepreneurship means for a public university, and how the goal of commercialisation of university knowledge may coincide with the non-profit status of public universities. With regard to possible ethical tension, they provide an example from the University of Auckland (NZ) as a good illustration: the Ethics Committee of the University of Auckland raised concerns about a new course in Bioscience Enterprise that required MA students to carry out research with a biotechnology company. Due to reasons of commercial sensitivity, almost half of the students' theses had to be placed under a ban of publication for a period of 4 or 5 years. As the authors argue, this is a potentially alarming inroad of private sector commercial interests into the principles of public education and subsidisation of private commercial research.

4 Institutional Factors Affecting Academic Entrepreneurship

As elaborated by Davis and North (1971), and outlined by Yadolahi and Meisam (2014), the environment of an institution can be seen as a set of fundamental, legal, social, and political rules, which are governed by political and economic activities. Organisations adapt their strategies and behaviour to the environmental opportunities and limitations, which represent the formal and informal institutional frameworks (Guerrero et al., 2016). The institutions determine the rules in a community, and this also has an impact on the interactions between the institutions (North, 1990, 1994). According to North (1990), there exist formal institutions, such as, e.g., political andeconomic rules or regulations, as well as informal institutions, such as, e.g., traditions and culture. Yadolahi and Meisam (2014) provide a review of the numerous studies that have investigated the effective institutional factors on academic entrepreneurship while adopting an institutional perspective. Based upon this ample literature, they develop a framework of effective factors in academic entrepreneurship by differentiating between formal and informal institutional factors. The Table 1, which is based on Fig. 1 (Yadolahi & Meisam, 2014), summarises these factors.

Based upon extensive qualitative and quantitative analyses, Yadolahi and Meisam (2014) assess the importance of these institutional factors for academic entrepreneurship and provide a ranking of their importance and derive practical recommendations for policymakers. While their analyses are made for the particular case of Iran, the following findings are relevant for other countries as well. In addition, the listing and relevance of the individual factors show the extent to which policy can influence academic entrepreneurship.

According to Yadolahi and Meisam (2014), the factor "Rules, structure and governance of the university" is considered as most important formal factor affecting academic entrepreneurship. As the authors outline, different organisational arrangements at the university level can result in different tendencies in becoming involved in the commercialisation of the results from research activities. The factor "Entrepreneurship and business education programmes" is considered as another important formal institutional factor. In line with Vohora et al. (2004), university faculty and researchers involved in identifying the commercial value of their

Table 1 Institutional formal and informal factors affecting academic entrepreneurship: based upon Yadolahi and Meisam (2014)

Formal factors	Informal factors
Rules, structures, and governance of the university Government rules and policies Academic entrepreneurship structures Intellectual property laws Entrepreneurship education programmes University–industry relationship	Academicians' attitudes towards entrepreneurship Teaching methods of entrepreneurship Role models and academic reward systems Entrepreneurial culture

Source Yadolahi and Meisam 2014

research output and involved in technology transfer activities need entrepreneurial skills in order to carry out entrepreneurial activities successfully. Yadolahi and Meisam (2014) further identify "Procedures of enforcing laws" as the most important informal institutional factor to affect academic entrepreneurship. As they outline, this factor is of great importance because it potentially affects all other formal and informal factors. Incorrect or a total lack of enforcement contributes to an unhealthy environment and to the formation of rent-seeking behaviour, leading to destructive entrepreneurial activities. With regard to this factor, the government holds special responsibilities in terms of effective policymaking, coordination, and implementation of the relevant policies. Finally, the authors identify "University-industry relationships" as another important formal institutional factor that affects academic entrepreneurship. These relationships need to be profitable for both sides.

While these factors may not have the same importance for all countries or for the stages of a country's economic development, the listed factors provide a framework to identify where and to what extent policymakers are able to impact upon academic entrepreneurship in a fruitful way.

5 Two Examples of Public Policy Reforms with Impact on Academic Entrepreneurship

5.1 The Bologna Reform in Europe as an Example of an Innovation-Driven Economy

5.1.1 The Key Characteristics of the Reform

The Bologna Process is a series of ministerial meetings and agreements between European countries to ensure comparability in the standards and quality of higher education qualifications. It was launched in 1999 by the Education Ministers of 29 European countries in an attempt to bring coherence to higher education systems across the continent, and was named after the University of Bologna, where the Bologna Declaration was signed by all 29 states. The process has created the European Higher Education Area. The Bologna Declaration followed an initiative of the Council of Europe, which adopted the Lisbon Recognition Convention on university qualifications. After 1999, it was taken up by the European Union when the Union had only 15 Member States, compared with 28 in 2011. Throughout this time, the number of states that have signed the declaration has grown, and the Bologna Process currently has 49 participating states, and it extends far beyond the current EU borders.[2]

The overarching goal of the reform was to promote mobility and strengthen the competitiveness of Europe as an education location.

[2]Information taken from https://www.goodschoolsguide.co.uk/university/europe/bologna-process-explained,https://en.wikipedia.org/wiki/Bologna_Process

The important cornerstones of the initial process are as follows[3]:

- The creation of a system of easily understandable and comparable degrees.
- The creation of a two-tier system of degrees (Bachelor/Master).
- The introduction of a credit point system (based upon the ECTS model[4]).
- The promotion of geographic mobility.
- The promotion of European co-operation in quality assurance.
- The promotion of the European dimension in higher education.
- In the follow-up conferences, the ministers agreed on the following additional measures in particular:
- The promotion of lifelong learning (2001) and the introduction of procedures for the recognition of knowledge acquired outside higher education (2005).
- The promotion of student participation (2001) and the strengthening of the social dimension (2005).
- The automatic and free issuing of Diploma Supplements (2003).
- The incorporation of the doctorate as the third stage of the new study system (2003) and the linking of the European Higher Education Area with the European Research Area (2018).
- The adoption of an overarching qualifications framework for the European Higher Education Area and the development of national qualifications frameworks compatible with it (2005).
- Closer co-operation with other regions and continents (2005) and simplified access to detailed information on the European Higher Education Area (2007).
- The strengthening of the quality assurance with the adoption of Standards and Guidelines for Quality Assurance in the European Higher Education Area ESG (2005 and revised version 2015) and the establishment of the Register of European Quality Assurance Agencies for Higher Education EQAR (2007).
- The improvement of employability (2007) and the enhancement of creative and entrepreneurial thinking (2012).
- The improvement of the quality and relevance of teaching, in particular by promoting pedagogical innovation in student-centred and research-based teaching and the use of new digital technologies (2015).
- Peer support for the implementation of the main Bologna reforms: the three-tier system, quality assurance, and recognition (2018).

5.1.2 Assessment of the Reform

As Grimaldi et al. (2012) mention, an assessment of institutional and public policies and managerial practices can yield new insights for reforming the existing policies

[3] According to https://www.sbfi.admin.ch/sbfi/de/home/hs/hochschulen/bologna-prozess.html

[4] The European Credit Transfer and Accumulation System (ECTS) is a tool of the European Higher Education Area for making studies and courses more transparent. See also under https://education.ec.europa.eu/levels/higher-education/inclusion-connectivity/european-credit-transfer-accumulation-system

and creating new mechanisms to support academic entrepreneurship. In this sense, let us look at both the intended and the unintended effects of the Bologna reform.

According to Reichert (2010), the Bologna Process has led to a new form of transnational policy development, which has triggered a multitude of national processes of decision-making. It sets soft standards and places them in a context of transnational pressure for conformity and combines top-down initiatives with bottom-up agenda setting. Furthermore, it intertwines national and European policy issues in a mutually re-enforcing way, and, through this process, it catalyses and accelerates national higher education reforms. While the intention of this process was to create a European Higher Education Area, which was fulfilled, it also has some unintended effects that exceed the intention of creating a common arena for policy exchange.

With regard to the intended effects of the Bologna reforms, most of the changes took place in areas where the reforms were clearly driven by the actors and sectors concerned. Implementation has been remarkably swift and efficient in the new two-tier curricular structures, the commonly aligned quality assurance systems and the widespread doctoral education reforms. However, progress has been slowest where hopes were highest, namely, in the planned comprehensive reforms of the teaching quality and approaches (competence and learning outcomes orientation), since these are more about changes in attitudes than mere changes in procedures and structures.

The Bologna actions also had some unintended side effects both at system and at institutional level. The consideration of the unintended effects might be even more insightful than the assessment of the intended effects. A selection of the unintended effects, according to Reichert (2010), follows here:

5.1.3 Increased Transnational Policy Osmosis

The Bologna Process has created a dense network of policymakers and institutional leaders who share best practices and strategies, so that new ideas and decisions can be transferred from one national or institutional context to another more quickly than in the past. The Bologna Process has triggered frequent transnational exchanges and political consultations between European rectors' conferences, university presidents, and the relevant authorities who face similar systemic transitions or policy dilemmas.

5.1.4 The Bologna Process' Role as a Catalyst for Other Higher Education Reforms

The Bologna rhetoric in favour of urgent qualitative improvements and international competitiveness, and the far-reaching systemic implications of the curriculum and quality goals, did not just mobilise all higher education stakeholders. Higher education also acted as a catalyst for other national reforms. Many national reform agendas went far beyond the Bologna Action Plan but were presented as inevitable components of an increasingly international higher education landscape and closely linked to the Bologna Agenda.

5.1.5 Renegotiated Institutional Profiles and "Vocational Drift"

Through the new bachelor's degrees, which focus on the employability and labour market relevance of graduates, the Bologna reforms have strengthened the vocational orientation of higher education. Consequently, they have also strengthened the position of vocationally oriented institutions such as universities, colleges, or universities of applied sciences/polytechnics, as can be seen, for example in Norway, Germany, The Netherlands, and Switzerland. Due to the growing importance attached to innovation by many countries, the non-traditional functions of universities have gained public recognition and their status has increased to such an extent that even some traditional universities are advancing the innovation and career orientation of their research and teaching programmes. This development is also related to the "third mission" of universities as discussed earlier.

5.1.6 Increasing Stakeholder Influence

In relation to the central concern of social and labour market relevance and the relevant competence profiles, the Bologna reforms have contributed to increased communication with stakeholders. Even if the dialogue in some subject areas, such as engineering, medicine, economics, business administration, and law, as well as in all career-oriented higher education institutions was already well developed, the Bologna reforms have expanded its scope and raised its profile. The influence of stakeholders has also been strengthened by the introduction of new governance structures in certain higher education institutions.

5.2 The Bayh-Dole Act of 1980 in the USA

5.2.1 The Key Characteristics of the Reform

The Bayh-Dole Act, or Patent and Trademark Law Amendments Act, is US legislation that deals with inventions arising from federal government-funded research. Sponsored by two senators, Birch Bayh of Indiana and Bob Dole of Kansas, the Act was adopted in 1980.[5] Among other effects, it gave US universities, small businesses, and non-profit intellectual property control of their inventions and other intellectual property that resulted from such funding. Perhaps the most important change of the Bayh-Dole Act is that it reversed the presumption of title. Bayh-Dole permits a university, small business, or non-profit institution to elect to pursue ownership of an invention in preference to the government.

As Markel (2013) states, the trigger for the Bayh-Dole Act was not the need to transform research, but the economic downturn of the 1970s. Oil embargoes and the resulting energy crisis, combined with the decline of the US automobile, steel, and appliance industries, led to deflation in the stock market. Experts predicted that Japan and Germany would soon dominate the world economy. Added to this were

[5] https://en.wikipedia.org/wiki/Bayh%E2%80%93Dole_Act, https://ipmall.law.unh.edu/content/bayh-dole-act-research-history-central

the consequences of the Watergate scandal which forced Richard Nixon to resign, the guardianship of Gerald Ford's presidency, and the hostage crisis in Iran during the Jimmy Carter administration.

5.2.2 Assessment of the Reform

As Grimaldi et al. (2012) state, an overall assessment of legislation like the Bayh-Dole Act is a complex task, given that it requires an integrated, multilevel approach, addressing the effects at different levels of analysis, including country-level specificities, internal organisation of public research institutions and universities, and finally individual scientists. According to Grimaldi et al. (2012), the Bayh-Dole Act has contributed to significant changes in the way universities market and disseminate technologies developed in their research laboratories and elsewhere on campuses. While there is consensus that these trends have profound implications for the management and policies of those involved in university research and commercialisation (e.g. Siegel et al., 2007), some researchers question whether the current institutional arrangements for research commercialisation are socially optimal (e.g. Kenney & Patton, 2009).

Grimaldi et al. (2012) further concluded that the increase in commercialisation associated with the Bayh-Dole Act has not led to less basic research. In addition, it may also have led to an increase in start-up activities in universities, which may have accelerated due to the increasing importance of this dimension of the commercialisation of university technologies. Finally, Grimaldi et al. (2012) raise the question of whether other countries might usefully introduce legislation along the lines of the Bayh-Dole Act. As they conclude, comparisons with the US experience could be misleading and should not be used to make predictions about the evolving characteristics of institutional property rights in Europe.

6 Recommendations for Policymakers, Governments, and Universities

As outlined above, the political and economic aspects of academic entrepreneurship are closely related to the "third mission" of universities. Compagnucci and Spigarelli (2020) propose concrete measures to enable policymakers, governments, and universities to support the strategic orientation of the "third mission" of universities. These measures reflect the political and economic dimensions of academic entrepreneurship, their socio-economic impact, and, related to this, the necessary interactions with politics, government, industry, and society.

The following selection of measures suggested by Compagnucci and Spigarelli (2020) can be attributed to four different domains:

1. The "third mission" and its interdependence with teaching and research:
   - Policy interventions should take into account all three missions of universities simultaneously, namely, teaching, performing research, and contributing to society.

- Dealing with multiple missions requires a focused strategy based upon leadership at both departmental and university levels.
- The university should analyse both the development of its internal faculty evaluation process and the perceived legitimacy of all three missions.

2. Local embeddedness of the university:
   - Universities should understand their role within the wider innovation system in order to fulfil their potential for economic development.
   - Governments, universities, companies, and communities should focus on long-term investment in all the complementary dimensions of the "third mission".
   - Universities should design structures and teaching styles, provide funds, and develop research capacities upon the basis of demand from the local context.
   - Governments should play a constructive role in creating an economic, financial, and legal environment to improve the performance of the "third mission" of universities.
   - Local governments, universities, and industry should design new forms of participative governance for research, teaching, and the "third mission", with appropriate attention being paid to students and university staff.
3. "Third mission" activities:
   - Policymakers should encourage universities to focus on "third mission" activities that have an impact on the surrounding environment, rather than simply engaging in many activities with limited impact.
   - "Third mission" activities can be improved by attracting the external expertise and financial resources of stakeholders.
   - Universities should include, among their strategic objectives, the development, co-ordination, and/or re-enforcement of those structures dedicated to providing logistical support to university staff engaged in "third mission" activities.

7 Conclusion

The political-economic dimension of academic and educational entrepreneurship is closely related to the "third mission" of universities, i.e. with academic entrepreneurship participating in the socio-economic development of communities. While this development provides valuable opportunities for the university, society, and the state, it is also associated with considerable risks. Thus, it is important that respective policy interventions take into account all three missions of universities simultaneously, education, research, and this "third mission". Moreover, politicians, state representatives, and university management should be aware of the fact that knowledge transfer between universities, industry, and society has become a topic of a strategic nature, whose importance is destined to grow in the future. Overall, there is still a lack of research into the impact of the political and economic factors on academic entrepreneurship, and more work is needed to understand better the synergies, interdependencies, risks, and opportunities of the interplay of the universities' three missions in relation to the policy interventions.

8 Summary

The political-economic aspect is an important dimension of academic and educational entrepreneurship because a state's political-economic framework is an important determinant of its institutions, which include universities. The impact of the political economy has become even more important with the changing mission of universities, the so-called "third mission", with academic entrepreneurship participating in the socio-economic development of the communities. While the involvement of higher education institutions in the socio-economic development includes real opportunities, also for the universities, public policy interventions in relation to academic entrepreneurship are also associated with risks. It is important to assess adequately the concrete initiatives and learn from the experiences of the existing policy reforms.

Questions

Question 1. Explain why the state should support academic entrepreneurship initiatives and how this is related to the nature of public goods and the possible undersupply of the good in question?

Question 2. Consider the institutional formal and informal factors affecting academic entrepreneurship. Using the example of your university and your country, find concrete examples of how policy can influence academic entrepreneurship in the long term.

Question 3. Find an example of a major policy reform like the Bayh-Dole Act of 1980 in the USA or the Bologna reform in Europe for a country in the developing world and think of possible similarities and differences in implementing such a reform in a developing country.

References

Arrow, K. J. (1962). Economics welfare and the allocation of resources for invention. In *The rate and direction on incentive activity: Economic and social factors*. National Bureau of Economic Research, Princeton University Press.

Audretsch, D. B., & Lehmann, E. E. (2005). Does the knowledge spillover theory of entrepreneurship hold for regions? *Research Policy, 34*(8), 1191–1202. https://doi.org/10.1016/j.respol.2005.03.012

Azagra-Caro, J. M., Archontakis, F., Gutiérrez-Gracia, A., & Fernández-de-Lucio, I. (2006). Faculty support for the objectives of university-industry relations versus degree of R&D cooperation: The importance of regional absorptive capacity. *Research Policy, 35*(1), 37–55. https://doi.org/10.1016/j.respol.2005.08.007

Blenker, P., & Dreisler, P. (2006). Entrepreneurship Education at University Level – Contextual Challenges. *Working Papers in Economics, 21*(149–154), 43–62.

Compagnucci, L., & Spigarelli, F. (2020). The third mission of the university: A systematic literature review on potentials and constraints. *Technological Forecasting and Social Change, 161*. https://doi.org/10.1016/j.techfore.2020.120284

Cunningham, J. A., Menter, M., & O'Kane, C. (2018). Value creation in the quadruple helix: A micro level conceptual model of principal investigators as value creators. *R&D Management, 48* (1), 136–147.

Davis, L. E., & North, D. C. (1971). *Institutional change and American economic growth*. Cambridge University Press. https://doi.org/10.1017/CBO9780511561078.

Djokovic, D., & Souitaris, V. (2008). Spinouts from academic institutions: A literature review with suggestions for further research. *Journal of Technology Transfer, 33*(3), 225–247. https://doi.org/10.1007/s10961-006-9000-4

Etzkowitz, H. (2001). The second academic revolution and the rise of entrepreneurial science. *IEEE Technology and Society Magazine, 20*(2), 18–29. https://doi.org/10.1109/44.948843

Etzkowitz, H. (2003). Research groups as quasi-firms. *Research Policy, 32*, 109–121.

Etzkowitz, H., & Leydesdorff, L. (1998). *The endless transition: A "triple helix" of university-industry-government relations (Autumn 1998)* (Vol. 36, Issue 3). https://www.jstor.org/stable/41821107

Etzkowitz, H., & Leydesdorff, L. (2000). The dynamics of innovation: From National Systems and "'Mode 2'" to a Triple Helix of university-industry-government relations. *Research Policy, 29*. www.elsevier.nlrlocatereconbase

Goethner, M., & Wyrwich, M. (2020). Cross-faculty proximity and academic entrepreneurship: The role of business schools. *Journal of Technology Transfer, 45*(4), 1016–1062. https://doi.org/10.1007/s10961-019-09725-0

Grimaldi, R., Kenney, M., Siegel, D. S., & Wright, M. (2012). 30 years after Bayh-Dole: Reassessing Academic entrepreneurship. *SSRN Electronic Journal*. https://doi.org/10.2139/ssrn.1821239

Guerrero, M., Urbano, D., Fayolle, A., Klofsten, M., & Mian, S. (2016). Entrepreneurial universities: Emerging models in the new social and economic landscape. *Small Business Economics, 47*(3), 551–563. https://doi.org/10.1007/s11187-016-9755-4

Henrekson, M., & Rosenberg, N. (2000). Designing efficient institutions for science-based entrepreneurship: Lesson from the US and Sweden. *Journal of Technology Transfer*.

Kenney, M., & Patton, D. (2009). Reconsidering the Bayh-Dole Act and the current university invention ownership model. *Research Policy, 38*(9), 1407–1422.

Lehmann, E. E., Meoli, M., Paleari, S., & Stockinger, S. A. E. (2020). The role of higher education for the development of entrepreneurial ecosystems. *European Journal of Higher Education, 10*(1), 1–9. https://doi.org/10.1080/21568235.2020.1718924

Link, A. N., & Scott, J. T. (2010). Government as entrepreneur: Evaluating the commercialization success of SBIR projects. *Research Policy, 39*(5), 589–601.

Link, A. N., Ruhm, C. J., & Siegel, D. S. (2014). Private equity and the innovation strategies of entrepreneurial firms: Empirical evidence from the small business innovation research program. *Managerial and Decision Economics*. https://doi.org/10.1002/mde.2648

Mariani, G., Carlesi, A., & Scarfò, A. A. (2018). Academic spinoffs as a value driver for intellectual capital: The case of the University of Pisa. *Journal of Intellectual Capital, 19*(1), 202–226. https://doi.org/10.1108/JIC-03-2017-0050

Markel, H. (2013). Patents, profits, and the American people — The Bayh–Dole Act of 1980. *The New England Journal of Medicine, 369*, 794–796.

Martin, S., & Scott, J. T. (2000). The nature of innovation market failure and the design of public support for private innovation. *Research Policy, 29*. www.elsevier.nlrlocatereconbase

Muscio, A., Quaglione, D., & Scarpinato, M. (2012). The effects of universities' proximity to industrial districts on university-industry collaboration. *China Economic Review, 23*(3), 639–650. https://doi.org/10.1016/j.chieco.2011.07.001

North, D. C. (1990). A transaction cost theory of politics. *Journal of Theoretical Politics, 2*(4), 355–367. https://doi.org/10.1177/0951692890002004001

North, D. C. (1994). Economic performance through time. *The American Economic Review, 84*(3), 359–68, http://www.jstor.org/stable/2118057

Pennington, M. (2011). 27-4-11-mark-pennington.

Perkmann, M., Tartari, V., McKelvey, M., Autio, E., Broström, A., D'Este, P., Fini, R., Geuna, A., Grimaldi, R., Hughes, A., Krabel, S., Kitson, M., Llerena, P., Lissoni, F., Salter, A., & Sobrero, M. (2013). Academic engagement and commercialisation: A review of the literature on university-industry relations. *Research Policy, 42*(2), 423–442. https://doi.org/10.1016/j.respol.2012.09.007

Powers, J. B. (2004). R&D funding sources and university technology transfer: What is stimulating universities to be more entrepreneurial? *Research in Higher Education, 45*(1), 1–23. https://doi.org/10.1023/B:RIHE.0000010044.41663.a0

Reichert, S. (2010). The intended and unintended effects of the Bologna reforms by. 22(1).

Riviezzo, A., & Napolitano, M. R. (2010). *Italian universities and the Third mission A longitudinal analysis of organizational and educational evolution towards the "entrepreneurial university"*.

Romer, P. M. (1990). *Endogenous technological change*.

Rothaermel, F. T., Agung, S. D., & Jiang, L. (2007). University entrepreneurship: A taxonomy of the literature. *Industrial and Corporate Change, 16*(4), 691–791. https://doi.org/10.1093/icc/dtm023

Sandström, C., Wennberg, K., Wallin, M. W., & Zherlygina, Y. (2018). Public policy for academic entrepreneurship initiatives: A review and critical discussion. *Journal of Technology Transfer, 43*(5), 1232–1256. https://doi.org/10.1007/s10961-016-9536-x

Siegel, D. S., Veugelers, R., & Wright, M. (2007). Technology transfer offices and commercialization of university intellectual property: Performance and policy implications. *Oxford Review of Economic Policy, 23*(4), 640–660. https://doi.org/10.1093/oxrep/grm036

Shane, S. (2004). *Academic entrepreneurship: University spinoffs and wealth creation*. Edward Elgar.

Shore, C., & McLauchlan, L. (2012). "Third mission" activities, commercialisation and academic entrepreneurs. *Social Anthropology, 20*(3), 267–286. https://doi.org/10.1111/j.1469-8676.2012.00207.x

Trencher, G., Yarime, M., McCormick, K. B., Doll, C. N. H., & Kraines, S. B. (2014). Beyond the third mission: Exploring the emerging university function of co-creation for sustainability. *Science and Public Policy, 41*(2), 151–179. https://doi.org/10.1093/scipol/sct044

Vohora, A., Wright, M., & Lockett, A. (2004). Critical junctures in the development of university high-tech spinout companies. *Research Policy, 33*(1), 147–175. https://doi.org/10.1016/S0048-7333(03)00107-0

Yadolahi, F. J., & Meisam, M. (2014). *Institutional Factors Affecting Academic Entrepreneurship: The Case of University of Tehran* (Vol. 47, Issue 55).

Further Reading

Cai, Y., & Amaral, M. (2021). The triple helix model and the future of innovation: A reflection on the triple helix research agenda. *Triple Helix, 8*(2), 217–229. https://doi.org/10.1163/21971927-12340004

Gabrielle Wanzenried, Dr. rer. pol., MSc Econ LSE is a professor of finance and real estate at the School of Management and Engineering (HEIG-VD), Yverdon of the University of Applied Sciences and Arts Western Switzerland HES-SO since Sept 2019, where she is the lead of the research group Finance, Governance and Sustainability at the Interdisciplinary Institute of Business development (IIDE). She studied at the University of Bern, the London School of Economics, and UC Berkeley. Before joining the HEIG-VD, she was a professor of corporate finance at the Institute of Financial Services Institute of the Lucerne University of Applied Sciences and Art. Her research and teaching topics are Corporate Finance, Real Estate, Entrepreneurship, and the Ageing Economy. Over the years, she has led several research projects, provided consulting services to practice partners, and written numerous publications on these topics. In addition to her academic work, Gabrielle Wanzenried is co-founder and co-chair of a housing cooperative specialising in retirement homes (www.zuhauseambielersee.ch) and president of the board of the Thiébaud-Frey Foundation (www.laprairiebellmund.ch), a cultural institution that promotes talented young musicians in the field of classical music and organises concerts for this purpose in its own cultural centre in Bellmund near Biel, Switzerland.

International and Cultural Aspects of Academic and Educational Entrepreneurship

Vincent Grèzes and Line Pillet

It is through education that culture is transmitted. [. . .] the authentic transmission of Value is from soul to soul, from one mind to another mind.
Edouard Sans, foreword to The Glass Bead Game, Hermann Hesse

1 Introduction

Academic entrepreneurship activities are defined by Klofsten (1998) as large-scale science projects, contracted research, consulting, patenting, and licensing, spin-off firms, external teaching, sales, and testing. Indeed, entrepreneurship in higher educational institutions can take several forms (Rasmussen, 2004); moreover, the types of agents and types of entrepreneurial projects must be taken into consideration. On the one hand, educational entrepreneurship refers to education businesses that lead to a massive improvement in education (Smith, 2006), where education entrepreneur is the "change agent" who combines business acumen with education expertise (Hess, 2006). On the other hand, academic entrepreneurship involves a university faculty that establishes a new company or institution project (Hayter, 2017).

According to Eklund and Wanzenried (2020) Holistic Conceptual Framework of the seven aspects of academic and educational entrepreneurship, there are seven

V. Grèzes (✉) · L. Pillet
University of Applied Sciences and Arts Western Switzerland, Sierre, Switzerland
e-mail: vincent.grezes@hevs.ch; line.pillet@hevs.ch

M. Aldogan Eklund, G. Wanzenried (eds.), *Academic and Educational Entrepreneurship*, Springer Texts in Business and Economics,
https://doi.org/10.1007/978-3-031-10952-2_6

aspects that are required to lead an edupreneur to success: (1) financial, (2) political and economic, (3) social and environmental, (4) international and cultural, (5) individual and contextual, (6) intellectual, and (7) technological.

The specificity of international aspects of entrepreneurship has been identified as new and innovative activities that create value and growth in organizations beyond national frontiers. (Oviatt, 2005) Therefore, internationalization in academic entrepreneurship contexts can be related to several actions of opportunity seeking. As identified in the open innovation processes (Gassmann & Enkel, 2004), internationalization aspects of academic entrepreneurship can be included in an *outside-in process of innovation*, enriching a project through the capture of international aspects, an *inside-out process of innovation*, by transferring ideas to the outside environment, or a *coupled process of innovation*, by creating alliances of knowledge and developing new projects with international aspects.

The purpose of this chapter is to analyze the international and cultural aspects that academic entrepreneurs must take into consideration and propose a conceptual framework for analyzing higher educational institutions (HEI) regarding their international settings to support or hinder academic entrepreneurship.

In the remainder of this paper, we will firstly present the international and cultural factors that any entrepreneur must take into consideration in an international business development context. Secondly, we will present several settings and management conditions that can support or hinder international and cultural sensitivity in academic contexts.

2 Internationalization and Cultural Aspects

2.1 The Notions of Distances

According to Ghemawat (2001) notion of firms, which can be extended to entrepreneurs, one ought not to focus only on geographical dimensions of internationalization. Indeed, the author proposes several dimensions of distance that matter in international business activities.

Cultural distance is increased by different languages, different ethnicities, different religions, different social norms, and the lack of connective ethnic or social networks. These elements affect particularly industries with high linguistic content (e.g., TV), activities related to national identity (e.g., food), or containing country-specific quality associations (e.g., wines).

Administrative and political distance is increased by the absence of shared monetary or political association, presence of political hostilities, and weak legal and financial institutions. These elements affect particularly industries that foreign governments view as staples (e.g., electricity), as building national reputations (e.g., aerospace), or as vital to national security (e.g., telecommunications).

Geographic distance is increased by the lack of common borders, waterway access, adequate transportation, or communication links, physical remoteness and by different climates. These elements affect particularly industries with low value-toweight ratio (e.g., cement), industries that are fragile or perishable (e.g., glass, fruit), and industries in which communications are vital (e.g., financial services).

Economic distance is increased by different consumer incomes, different costs and quality of natural, financial, and human resources, and different information or knowledge. These elements affect particularly industries for which demand varies by income (e.g., cars) or industries in which labor and other cost differences matter (e.g., garments).

The author recommends analyzing those aspects in relation to the pertinent industries and observes that industries are not equally sensitive to the different distances. These several types of distance are elements of knowledge regarding international projects that must be taken into consideration by any academic entrepreneur as key informational success factors.

2.2 The Notions of Culture

The definitions of culture are various in academic literature, and in fact, there is no common definition. In this section, we will focus on two specific approaches to culture that can enlighten academic entrepreneurs regarding the diversity and the dimensions of the concept.

2.2.1 Culture as an Invisible Distance

According to Hall (1959), "Culture is communication, and communication is culture" (Hall, 1959, p. 186). The author developed the theory of proxemics that explains the types of personal distances maintained by people depending on social settings and cultural backgrounds (Hall, 1966). According to Hall, the main differences between cultures are related to three dimensions that we summarize in the remainder of this section.

The relation to *context* conditions fundamentally the meaning of the words used and the understanding of the message. The more people exchange words, the stronger their context will be, and the easier the interpretation of the message will be. In a low-context situation, the message will require the most explicit information. In a cultural context where people are used to a lot of detailed information, people can feel like not being sufficiently informed by a person used to communicating with more help from contextual knowledge.

The relation to *time* allows Hall to propose two kinds of cultures: monochronic ones w people here, tend to do one thing at a time, and polychronic ones, where people are used to dividing time to manage several activities at a time.

The relation to *space* is based on the principle that everybody disposes of a *situational personality*. This consideration leads to four notions of distance, such as *intimate distance* or interpersonal distance with contact, *personal distance* or interpersonal distance without contact, *social distance* which is the "limit of power on other," and *public distance*, outside of the circle of individual concern.

Hall (1966) discusses the impact of cultural differences based on proxemics and warns against risks of population inflow to cities all around the world, creating a

Melting Pot with unexpected risks based on ignorance of the cultural atoms that compose it.

2.2.2 Culture as a Programming of the Mind

According to Hofstede (2001), culture is "the collective programming of the mind that distinguishes the members of one group or category of people from another, where the mind stands for thinking, feeling and acting, with consequences for beliefs, attitudes and skills" (Hofstede, 2001, p. 5). Hofstede defines culture as a programming of the mind based on five main cultural dimensions. The main aspects of these five dimensions are presented below.

Power distance is related to personal acceptance of unequal distribution of power within a group. High-power distant people will be reluctant to express disagreement. Low power distant people will easily contradict their superiors.

Uncertainty avoidance is related to the way people cope with uncertainty and risk. High uncertainty avoidant people tend to avoid ambiguous situations and prefer structured and predictable environments. Low uncertainty avoidant people are more curious about differences.

Masculinity vs. femininity is relative to gender roles. Masculinity is more oriented toward competition, recognition, and challenge. Femininity is more focused on home, children, and people.

Individualism vs. collectivism is relative to the relationships between individuals and the group. Individualists are more concerned about themselves and their immediate families. Collectivists are integrated within strong and cohesive groups that protect them in exchange for loyalty.

Time orientation is the cultural aspect related to people's concern with the past, present, and future. Hofstede distinguishes between short-term people, concerned with the past and the present, and long-term people, oriented and concerned more with the future.

These five dimensions are dichotomies that can be used to distinguish between different cultures. At a management level, *internationalization success depends on several notions of distance, including cultural distance*. These notions of distance are important in the entrepreneurial journey in terms of opportunity and risk management. At a personal level, common points through the different dimensions of culture come out of the comparison, such as *different cultures relying on different values* and *culture not being innate but acquired* by subjects.

In the next sections, we will consider the conditions and vectors of internationalization and cultural aspects in the context of academic entrepreneurship.

3 Attitude Toward International and Cultural Aspects

To analyze factors that support or hinder academic entrepreneurship, the following section focuses on the attitudes of both subjects of our study: the entrepreneur and the higher educational institution. We will present the conditions of absorptive capacity of the subjects such as the ability to value, assimilate, and apply new knowledge to improve organizational learning (Cohen, 1990). Hence, the following sections present conditions of entrepreneurs and personal attitudes toward internationalization and cultural aspects (A), before analyzing the organizational side and its absorptive capacity toward internationalization and cultural aspects (B).

3.1 Personal Attitudes Toward Internationalization

To be able to take advantage of the potential for internationalization and cultural aspects of internationalization, entrepreneurs, and higher educational institutions must be aware of several degrees of knowledge transfer. To give some direction to measuring this degree of knowledge, the next section is dedicated to intercultural sensitivity (1) and cultural awareness (2).

3.1.1 Intercultural Sensitivity

Landis and Bhagat (1996) argue that intercultural sensitivity is crucial to enabling people to live and work with others from different cultural backgrounds. This consideration is particularly important in the context of coupled processes of innovation.

According to Bennett (1993), the development of intercultural sensitivity follows several steps from ethnocentric stages of resistance to ethnorelative stages of openness.

The ethnocentric stages of resistance are (1) *denial*, the lowest degree of openness to cultural differences; (2) *defense*, with development of sensitivity relative to the denial stage, with a sentiment of threat emerging in the perception of cultural differences; (3) *minimalization* which is the last stage of resistance with the attempt to preserve the centrality of one's own world view.

With a new way of seeing cultural difference, the ethnorelative stages of openness begin: the *acceptation* stage is important because it characterizes the subjectivization of cultural aspects, allowing relativization of differences and the capacity to imagine other frames of reference than our own; *adaptation* is the stage when by accepting differences, we can change our behaviors and our way of thinking; finally, *integration* is the last stage of openness when a person is capable of adapting to several cultures after a long time living in various locations.

3.1.2 Cultural Awareness

Numerous studies have measured international sensibility through the concept of cultural awareness (Howell, 1982). Indeed, Howell (1982) applied these learning steps to cultural consciousness. *Cultural awareness* is defined as "learning to work with people from diverse cultural backgrounds, using interpersonal communication, relationship skills, and behavioral flexibility" (Rew, 2003, p. 250). This awareness includes four stages:

- *Unconsciousness of incompetence.* When the individual does not understand the deficit of knowledge from which he suffers, and therefore is not aware of misinterpreting a foreign behavior.
- *Awareness of incompetence.* When the individual understands that he lacks the competence to complete a task, and therefore is aware of misinterpreting a foreign behavior but knows nothing about it.
- *Competence awareness.* When the individual understands and knows how to complete a task and can perform it in a strongly conscious way; he reflects on his behavior and consciously tries to modify it to increase efficiency.
- *Unconsciousness of competence.* When an individual can perform a task easily without being aware of it, like second nature, he/she has practiced and integrated effective communication behaviors.

To take advantage of international and cultural aspects, entrepreneurs must develop cultural sensitivity and cultural awareness at least at the levels of ethnorelativism with competence awareness. Personal absorptive capacities of international and cultural aspects, such as cultural sensitivity and cultural awareness, must be supported by higher educational institutions. The next section will discuss the characteristics of the conditions of absorptive capacity of academic organizations.

3.2 Organizational Attitudes Toward Internationalization

Organizational learning theory (Cangelosi, 1965) purports that to be competitive in a changing environment, companies must adapt their actions to achieve their goals and optimize the degree of alignment between expected and achieved results. For learning to occur, companies must *make a conscious decision to change* in response to circumstances, to consciously *link the action to the result*, and to *remember the result*.

According to Cangelosi (1965), initial learning takes place at the individual level. However, it becomes organizational learning once the information is shared, formalized, and stored in the organization to be transmitted and used.

According to Dill (1999), *organizational learning* refers to an organization that maximizes learning opportunities toward organizational changes, and the *learning organization* is based on the process of learning in the organizational context.

In the academic context, Dill (1999) describes the way universities become "learning organizations" to improve their skills of knowledge creation to enhance teaching and learning, and to modify their behavior to reflect this new knowledge. The author analyzed the framework proposed by Garvin (1993) regarding learning organizations in academic contexts and proposes *five elements of architecture of the academic learning organization*.

The *culture of evidence* is a core element in the problem-solving process of improving teaching and learning. Dill (1999) proposes to publicly define and defend measures of student learning upon which academic units can base their teaching processes.

The *improved coordination of teaching units* is based on the observation that successful problem solving also requires improved coordination, communication, and accountability structures among faculty members, e.g., curriculum coordinators and faculty committees dedicated to the coordination of teaching and learning within academic units.

Learning from others is the action of seeking out knowledge from others, e.g., organizing study tours as a means of identifying curricular innovations or benchmarking professional curricula against international standards.

University-wide coordination of "learnings" proposes the development of a pan-university level of coordination and support structures, responsible for the allocation of funds supporting experiments and innovation in teaching and learning.

Transfer of knowledge was the least conspicuous element among the case studies and refers to processes and structures encouraging internal transfer of knowledge to improve core processes.

According to Dill (1999), those architectural elements allow universities to better adapt their capacities to new environments.

As exposed in this section, the quality of the internationalization process, which is the basis of knowledge improvement, relies on the attitudes of agents. On the one hand, academic entrepreneurs, such as students and staff, should adopt an ethnorelative attitude, with at least the third level of cultural awareness—a share of knowledge of cultural differences. On the other hand, higher educational institutions must adopt architectural elements to develop absorptive capacities to enrich their organizational learning process and then to provide entrepreneurs an ever-enhanceding and suitable environment to encourage academic entrepreneurship.

4 Conclusion

In this chapter, we firstly presented the international and cultural factors that any entrepreneur must take into consideration in an international business development context. At a management level, we saw that *internationalization success depends on several notions of distance, including cultural distance*. At a personal level, we saw that *different cultures rely on different values* and *that culture is not innate but acquired* by the subjects.

In the second section, we discussed settings and conditions that support or hinder the international and cultural sensitivity of entrepreneurs in academic contexts. We saw that the quality of the internationalization process depends on the attitudes of agents. Academic entrepreneurs, such as students and staffs, should adopt an ethnorelative attitude, with at least the third level of cultural awareness. Higher educational institutions must adopt architectural elements to develop absorptive capacities and provide entrepreneurs a continuously improving and suitable environment to promote academic entrepreneurship.

Finally, Edupreneurship's success toward international and cultural aspects depends on the personal attitudes of entrepreneurs and on the devices that HEIs set up to promote intercultural sensitivity among students and staffs.

5 Summary

The purpose of this chapter was to analyze international and cultural aspects that academic entrepreneurs must take into consideration to support or hinder academic entrepreneurship. We elaborated on international and cultural aspects to be taken into consideration to successfully undertake an academic entrepreneurship journey, such as cultural, administrative, geographical, and economic distance. We deepened our understanding of cultural distance by summarizing the most used sociological approaches. Finally, we discussed the personal and institutional factors that can support or hinder entrepreneurship success, such as cultural sensitivity, cultural awareness, and the concept of academic learning organizations.

Questions

Question 1. Why are international and cultural aspects important for academic entrepreneurship?

Question 2. What are the settings of cultural sensitivity that an academic institution can manage?

Question 3. What are the characteristics of an academic learning organization?

References

Bennett, M. J. (1993). Towards Ethnorelativism: A development model of intercultural sensitivity. In R. M. Paige (Ed.), *Education for the intercultural experience*. Intercultural Press.

Cangelosi, V. E. (1965). Organizational learning: Observations toward a theory. *Administrative Science Quarterly, 10*(2), 175–203.

Cohen, W. M. (1990). Absorptive capacity: A new perspective on learning and innovation. *Administrative Science Quarterly, 35*(1), 128–152.

Dill, D. (1999). Academic accountability and university adaptation: The architecture of an academic learning organization. *Higher Education., 38*, 127–154.

Eklund, M., & Wanzenried, G. (2020). *Academic and educational entrepreneurship: Foundation in theory and lessons from practice*. Springer.

Garvin, D. A. (1993). Building a learning organization. *Harvard Business Review, 71*(4), 78–84.

Gassmann, O., & Enkel, E. (2004). Towards a theory of open innovation: Three core process archetypes. In *Proceedings of the R&D Management Conference*. Lisbon.

Ghemawat, P. (2001). *Distance still matters, the hard reality of global expansion*. Harvard Business Review.

Hall, E. T. (1959). *The silent language*. Doubleday and Co.

Hall, E. T. (1966). *The hidden dimension*. Doubleday.

Hayter, C. L. (2017). Who is the academic entrepreneur? The role of graduate students in the development of university spinoffs. *The Journal of Technology Transfer, 42*, 1237–1254.

Hess, F. M. (2006). Entrepreneurship, risks and reinvention. In F. M. Hess (Ed.), *Educational entrepreneurship: Realities, challenges, possibilities* (pp. 1–21). Harvard Education Press.

Hofstede, G. (2001). *Culture's consequences* (2nd ed.). Sage Publications.

Howell, W. S. (1982). *The empathic communicator*. Wadsworth.
Klofsten, M. J.-E. (1998). Academic entrepreneurship in the European context: A comparative study. *Babson entrepreneurship research conference*. Babson.
Landis, D., & Bhagat, R. S. (1996). *Handbook of intercultural training* (2nd ed.). Sage.
Oviatt, B. M. (2005). Defining international entrepreneurship and modeling the speed of internationalization. *Entrepreneurship Theory and Practice, 29*(5), 537–554.
Rasmussen, R. (2004). The university spin-off process. *NCSB 2004 Conference 13th Nordic Conference on Small Business Research.*
Rew, L. B. (2003). Measuring cultural awareness in nursing students. *The Journal of Nursing Education, 42*, 249–257.
Smith, K. P. (2006). What is educational entrepreneurship? In F. M. Hess (Ed.), *Educational entrepreneurship: Realities, challenges, possibilities.* Harvard Education Press.

Further Reading

Voda, A. I., & Florea, N. (2019). Impact of personality traits and entrepreneurship education on entrepreneurial intentions of business and engineering students. *Sustainability, 11*, 1192.
Van Auken, H., Fry, F., & Stephens, P. (2006). The influence of role models on entrepreneurial intentions. *Journal of Developmental Entrepreneurship, 11*, 157–167.

Further Readings About Internationalization Factors at the Industry Level

Ghemawat, P., & Mallick, R. (2003). *The industry-level structure of international trade networks: A gravity-based approach*. Harvard Business School working paper.

Further Readings About the Analysis of Effects of Internationalization Settings on Cultural Sensitivity

Anderson, P. H., Lawton, L., Rexeisen, R. J., & Hubbard, A. C. (2006). Short-term study abroad and intercultural sensitivity: A pilot study. *International Journal of Intercultural Relations, 30*, 457–469.
Soria, K. M., & Troisi, J. N. (2014). Internationalization at-home alternatives to study abroad: Implications for students' development of global, international, and intercultural competencies. *Journal of Studies in International Education, 18*, 260–279.

Vincent Grèzes, PhD, is an Associate Professor of Management, specialized in Strategic Management, International Management, and Open Innovation, at the University of Applied Science and Arts Western Switzerland (HES-SO) in Sierre, Valais. He holds a PhD in Competitive and Strategic Intelligence and leads the Competitive Intelligence module of the HES-SO Innokick Master in Lausanne, Switzerland. His research interests are focused on Business and Open Innovation, Competitive Intelligence, aimed at private and public decision makers, the Creation of Shared Values, and Pedagogical Innovation.

Line Pillet is a Professor in systems thinking and sustainable team leadership at the University of Applied Sciences and Arts Western Switzerland (HES-SO) and leads the Institute of Entrepreneurship and Management (IEM) at HES-SO Valais-Wallis. She holds a Master of Arts degree from the University of Geneva with a specialization in Philosophy of Management (CAS) from the University of Fribourg and Agile Governance (CAS) from HEIG-VD. She is active in economic networks as a founding member of the Swiss Cercle of Women Administrators, president of the Association of Women SME leaders in Western Switzerland, and member of several advisory boards and juries. Her research focuses on governance and Complex Systems Dynamics.

Individual and Contextual Aspects of Academic and Educational Entrepreneurship

Mehtap Aldogan Eklund

The purpose of this chapter is to discuss the individual and contextual aspects of the holistic academic and educational entrepreneurship framework (academic and edu e-ship framework), which has already been introduced by the editors in the introduction chapter. Specifically, this chapter elaborates on how individual and contextual aspects, such as personality traits, age, education, skills, e.g., impact the success of academic and educational entrepreneurs.

Entrepreneurship is a complex and multidimensional concept. Similar to corporate entrepreneurship, both educational entrepreneurship (edu-preneurship) and academic entrepreneurship (acapreneurship/academicpreneurship) involve four interacting factors for new venture creation (Kuratko et al., 2014). These four factors are grouped as follows: individual factors, environmental factors, organizational factors, and venture process. According to Kuratho and Hodgetts (2007), the individual factors that are one of the important factors include the following variables: the need for achievement, locus of control, risk-taking propensity, job satisfaction, previous work experience, entrepreneurial parents, age, and education. Brockhaus (1982) has also used these individual factors to differentiate the types of entrepreneurs. David McClelland's theory posits that an entrepreneur's psychological characteristic as a need for achievement represents a general driver of entrepreneurship (McClelland, 1961). As Gartner (1985) stated, the differences in the background, the personality of an entrepreneur, the capacity for innovation, and risk-taking propensity are the foremost important factors to differentiate an entrepreneur from a non-entrepreneur.

Personality traits play an important role to predict entrepreneurial behavior and to differentiate corporate entrepreneurs from academic and educational entrepreneurs. Personality traits can be measured broadly. Entrepreneurship literature provides us

M. Aldogan Eklund (✉)
University of Wisconsin-La Crosse, La Crosse, WI, USA
e-mail: meklund@uwlax.edu

M. Aldogan Eklund, G. Wanzenried (eds.), *Academic and Educational Entrepreneurship*, Springer Texts in Business and Economics,
https://doi.org/10.1007/978-3-031-10952-2_7

with a breadth of knowledge about entrepreneurial traits, such as being a good leader and learner, optimistic, risk-tolerant, disciplined, dedicated, creative, proactive, confident, passionate, persistent, curious, self-motivated, goal-oriented, team player, and self-aware (Gartner, 1989). Prior scholars also investigated whether entrepreneurs have any distinguishing characteristics or not. Beugelsdijk and Noorderhaven (2005) reported that entrepreneurs distinguish themselves from the rest of the population in a number of ways. For example, they are individually oriented, which means that they have a higher level of individual responsibility, effort, and ethics of working hard, compared to the rest of the population.

In contrast to a wide range of entrepreneurial traits, scholars are agreed upon the big five personality traits that directly impact the success or failure of all types of entrepreneurs, which is called the "Big Five Model" or "five-factor model of personality." This model is made up of the following personality traits—extraversion, emotional (in)stability (neuroticism), conscientiousness, agreeableness, and openness to experience (Costa & McCrae, 2008). Sahin et al. (2019) conducted a survey study and they concluded that the Big Five model is a successful tool for understanding multiple configurations of personal characteristics that lead to a high level of entrepreneurial intention. Shimoli et al. (2020) have also named the Big Five traits as an "entrepreneurship success traits" since those are the significant predictors of the likelihood of entrepreneurial intention, creation, and success. Furthermore, Zhao and Seibert (2006) performed a meta-analysis review on the previous studies about the big five personality dimensions to examine the relationship between personality and entrepreneurial status. The results of their analysis revealed that entrepreneurs scored higher on conscientiousness, openness to experience, and emotional stability, and scored lower on agreeableness. However, no significant difference was noted in extraversion. Liang et al. (2015) examined the relationship between entrepreneurs' Big Five personality traits and their perceived enterprise performance as an indicator of success. They have found that extraversion, conscientiousness, agreeableness, and openness to experience are positively related to the social enterprise (SE) performance, but there is a curvilinear relationship (U-shaped) between neuroticism (emotional instability) and SE performance. The study of Postigo et al. (2021) has taken a step forward by discussing the "Big Eight Model" of entrepreneurial behavior. They were inspired by the specific traits of enterprising personality when this model was developed. It includes the following eight traits: self-efficacy, autonomy, innovativeness, internal locus of control, achievement motivation, optimism, stress tolerance, and risk-taking (Postigo et al., 2021).

Bergner (2020) illustrated the connection among Big Five traits, cognitive ability, and vocational interest. Vocational or occupational interest means meaningful individual differences in work-related behaviors and environments. Bergner (2020) found that both Big Five traits and vocational interests boost the entrepreneurs' cognitive ability, which has a direct impact on their emergence and success. Similarly, Salgado et al. (2003) stated that intellectually challenging occupations require higher cognitive ability, so it may result in entrepreneurial intention for the person having conscientiousness and emotional stability. According to social cognitive theory and institutional theory, there is a direct nexus between the higher cognitive ability of entrepreneurs, entrepreneurs' self-efficacy, and alertness to new opportunities, which promote opportunity entrepreneurship (Boudreaux et al., 2019; Omar et al., 2019). The study of Kolb and Wagner (2014) stated that Big Five traits, higher cognitive ability, and motivation for both tangible and intangible value creations are key success factors for the entrepreneurs, but especially for academic entrepreneurs (acapreneurs). Vega-Gómez et al. (2020) have also emphasized the importance of Big Five traits for both academic and educational entrepreneurs because Big Five are the antecedents of entrepreneurial skills.

For the contextual model of entrepreneurship, the interplay between personal characteristics and contextual influences shaping the entrepreneurial activities, such as gender, age, education, socioeconomic resources, occupation, competencies, and social skills is discussed. For instance, Leick et al. (2022) stated that the likelihood of individuals engaging in entrepreneurial activities is highest at the age of 25–34 years, and after the age of 34 years, it decreases continuously. Occupation, education, and sex are the other relevant determinants of entrepreneurial behavior. Schoon and Duckworth (2012) defined entrepreneurship as the employment status of being self-employed and owning a business. They realized that sex is the significant contextual determinant of entrepreneurship because they found that men were significantly more likely to be self-employed than women and one in every five entrepreneurs was a female (Schoon & Duckworth, 2012). They also noted that social skills are positively related to entrepreneurial intention. The association among age, social skills, and academic attainment is strongly linked to entrepreneurial intention at age of 34 years, which is similar to the finding in the study of Leick et al. (2022). Furthermore, family background factors are also a predictor of later entrepreneurial activities. Moreover, Bernardino et al. (2018) investigate the differences between men and female social entrepreneurs from the perspective of Big Five traits. It is noted that women and men social entrepreneurs only differ in agreeableness (women scored more highly); however, there are no significant differences in the other four personality traits. For education, Sandhu et al. (2011) and Roman and Maxim (2017) have reported that not the education itself, but the entrepreneurial education has a positive and significant effect on entrepreneurial inclination.

For academic entrepreneurship, it is defined as entrepreneurial activity that is beyond the traditional academic roles of teaching and research. Academic entrepreneurial activity is grouped under three categories: formal commercial activities (including licensing and spinouts), informal commercial activities (including consultancy business and contract research), and noncommercial activities (including informal advice and public lectures (Abreu & Grinevich, 2013)). It is noted that prior scholars have generally investigated academic entrepreneurial activities, but only a few studies have focused on the motivation of the individual academics and the individual and contextual characteristics of acapreneurs resulting in emergence and success, which is the gap in the entrepreneurship research. Abreu and Grinevich (2013) are the few scholars who studied the individual and contextual aspects of acapreneurs. They have noted that age and gender are the predictors of academic entrepreneurial activities and acapreneurs do care more about the social and intangible value creation instead of tangible and commercial value. It is also found that senior academics are more likely to engage in informal and noncommercial activities, such as consultancy, contract research, informal advice, and public lectures, compared to younger scholars. On the other hand, younger academics prefer being involved in formal commercial activities, e.g., licensing and spinouts, which create economic value. For the gender, female academics have shown to have more difficulties in formal and informal commercial activities due to the challenge of making business and industry contacts, so they prefer noncommercial activities that create social and intangible values. Klofsten and Jones-Evans (2000) and Samo and Huda (2019) have similar results from the perspective of age and gender. They have grouped informal commercial activities and noncommercial activities as "soft academic entrepreneurship activities" and formal commercial activities as "hard academic entrepreneurship activities." Similarly, they revealed that senior and female academics are more likely to engage in soft activities, on the other hand, male and young academics prefer hard activities. Bin et al. (2018) have examined the family-related contextual factors of acapreneurs and they have concluded that there is a direct association between acapreneurs coming from families with a good financial situation and hard academic entrepreneurship activities. Sandhu et al. (2011) agree that family influence is one of the significant variables for the entrepreneurial inclination, right after the personal characteristics. Bin et al. (2018) also highlighted that academic entrepreneurs differ from nonacademic entrepreneurs in the creation of an organization as a result of academic education, and gender is a significant factor in academic entrepreneurial activities. For instance, male scholars are more likely to become acapreneurs than female scholars because male researchers are more risk tolerant. For educational entrepreneurship, similar to academic entrepreneurship, the prior research has overlooked investigating how the motivation, individual, and contextual characteristics of educational entrepreneurs (edupreneurs) differ from those of corporate entrepreneurs. It is recommended that future studies in the entrepreneurship discipline focus more on academic and educational entrepreneurship because it is still waiting to be explored, especially the individual and contextual aspects of edupreneurs and acapreneurs. Mooradian et al. (2016) elucidated that the three main individual characteristics of educational entrepreneurs are perseverance, passion, and social responsibility. Edupreneurs tend to pursue long-term challenging goals with perseverance and passion for social value creation.

To sum up, this chapter has elaborated on the individual and contextual aspects of entrepreneurship by providing examples from prior research. It is noted that the Big Five traits are important for all entrepreneurs. Moreover, for academic and educational entrepreneurs, three other traits (perseverance, passion, and social mindset) bring success and emergence (Smith et al., 2014; Mooradian et al., 2016). In addition to the personality traits, age, gender, social skills, cognitive ability, and family-related contextual factors are the significant determinants of academic and educational entrepreneurial intentions.

1 Summary

This chapter is about the individual and contextual aspects of the holistic academic and educational entrepreneurship framework (academic and edu e-ship framework), and it elaborates on how individual and contextual aspects, such as personality traits, age, academic attainment, social skills, competencies, family background, e.g., impact the success of entrepreneurs and academic and educational entrepreneurs.

Questions

1. What are the big five personality traits that lead to a high level of entrepreneurial intention? Explain.
2. Which contextual factors could be the significant determinants of an entrepreneurial intention? Discuss
3. At which age there is a strong nexus among social skills, academic attainment, and entrepreneurial intention? What could be the reason behind this? Elaborate.
4. For academic entrepreneurs, is there any difference between the female and male entrepreneurs in their academic entrepreneurial intentions? Explain.

References

Abreu, M., & Grinevich, V. (2013). The nature of academic entrepreneurship in the UK: Widening the focus on entrepreneurial activities. *Research Policy, 42*(2), 408–422. https://doi.org/10.1016/j.respol.2012.10.005

Bergner, S. (2020). Being smart is not enough: Personality traits and vocational interests incrementally predict intention, status and success of leaders and entrepreneurs beyond cognitive ability. *Frontiers in Psychology, 11*, 204–204. https://doi.org/10.3389/fpsyg.2020.00204

Bernardino, S., Freitas Santos, J., & Cadima Ribeiro, J. (2018). Social entrepreneur and gender: What's personality got to do with it? *International Journal of Gender and Entrepreneurship, 10*(1), 61–82. https://doi.org/10.1108/IJGE-07-2017-0040

Beugelsdijk, S., & Noorderhaven, N. G. (2005). Personality characteristics of self-employed; an empirical study. *Small Business Economics, 24*(2), 159–167. https://doi.org/10.1007/s11187-003-3806-3

Bin, A., de Oliveira Gavira, M., Botelho Figueira, J., & Mariano Bezerra de Carvalho, T., Monteiro Salles-Filho, S. L., & Basile Colugnati, F. A. (2018). Profile of academic entrepreneurship in Brazil. *Innovation & Management Review, 15*(4), 394–415. https://doi.org/10.1108/INMR-07-2018-0054

Boudreaux, C. J., Nikolaev, B. N., & Klein, P. (2019). Socio-cognitive traits and entrepreneurship: The moderating role of economic institutions. *Journal of Business Venturing, 34*(1), 178–196. https://doi.org/10.1016/j.jbusvent.2018.08.003

Brockhaus, R. H. (1982). The psychology of the entrepreneur. In C. A. Kent, D. L. Sexton, & K. H. Vesper (Eds.), *Encyclopedia of entrepreneurship* (pp. 39–56). Prentice-Hall.

Costa, P. T., & McCrae, R. R. (2008). The revised neo personality inventory (neo-pi-r). In G. J. Boyle, G. Matthews, & D. H. Saklofske (Eds.), *The SAGE handbook of personality theory and assessment* (Vol. 2, pp. 179–198). Sage.

Gartner, W. B. (1985). A conceptual framework for describing the phenomenon of new venture creation. *The Academy of Management Review, 10*(4), 696–706. https://doi.org/10.2307/258039

Gartner, W. B. (1989). Some suggestions for research on entrepreneurial traits and characteristics. *Entrepreneurship Theory and Practice, 14*(1), 27–38.

Klofsten, M., & Jones-Evans, D. (2000). Comparing academic entrepreneurship in Europe: The case of Sweden and Ireland. *Small Business Economics, 14*(4), 299–309. https://doi.org/10.1023/A:1008184601282

Kolb, C., & Wagner, M. (2014). Crowding in or crowding out: The link between academic entrepreneurship and entrepreneurial traits. *The Journal of Technology Transfer, 40*(3), 387–408. https://doi.org/10.1007/s10961-014-9346-y

Kuratho, D. F., & Hodgetts, R. M. (2007). *Entrepreneurship: Theory, process, and practice* (7th ed.).

Kuratko, D. F., Hoskinson, S., Kuratko, D. F., & Antal, N. (2014). *Innovative pathways for university entrepreneurship in the 21st century* (1st ed., Vol. 24). Emerald.

Leick, B., Falk, M. T., Eklund, M. A., & Vinogradov, E. (2022). Individual-contextual determinants of entrepreneurial service provision in the platform-based collaborative economy. *International Journal of Entrepreneurial Behavior and Research* (ahead of print). https://doi.org/10.1108/IJEBR-09-2020-0585

Liang, C.-T., Peng, L.-P., Yao, S.-N., & Liang, C. (2015). Developing a social enterprise performance scale and examining the relationship between entrepreneurs' personality traits and their perceived enterprise performance. *Journal of Entrepreneurship, Management and Innovation, 11*(3), 89–116. https://doi.org/10.7341/20151135

McClelland, D. (1961). *The achieving society*. Van Nostrand Reinhold.

Mooradian, T., Matzler, K., Uzelac, B., & Bauer, F. (2016). Perspiration and inspiration: Grit and innovativeness as antecedents of entrepreneurial success. *Journal of Economic Psychology, 56*, 232–243. https://doi.org/10.1016/j.joep.2016.08.001

Omar, N. A., Ullah Shah, N., Abu Hasan, N., & Ali, M. H. (2019). The influence of self-efficacy, motivation, and independence on students' entrepreneurial intentions. *Journal of Nusantara Studies (JONUS), 4*(2), 1–28. https://doi.org/10.24200/jonus.vol4iss2pp1-28

Postigo, Á., Cuesta, M., García-Cueto, E., Prieto-Díez, F., & Muñiz, J. (2021). General versus specific personality traits for predicting entrepreneurship. *Personality and Individual Differences, 182*, 111094. https://doi.org/10.1016/j.paid.2021.111094

Roman, T., & Maxim, A. (2017). National culture and higher education as pre-determining factors of student entrepreneurship. *Studies in Higher Education (Dorchester-on-Thames), 42*(6), 993–1014. https://doi.org/10.1080/03075079.2015.1074671

Sahin, F., Karadag, H., & Tuncer, B. (2019). Big five personality traits, entrepreneurial self-efficacy and entrepreneurial intention: A configurational approach. *International Journal of Entrepreneurial Behaviour & Research, 25*(6), 1188–1211. https://doi.org/10.1108/IJEBR-07-2018-0466

Salgado, J. F., Anderson, N., Moscoso, S., Bertua, C., de Fruyt, F., & Rolland, J. P. (2003). A meta-analytic study of general mental ability validity for different occupations in the European Community. *Journal of Applied Psychology*, 1068–1081. https://doi.org/10.1037/0021-9010.88.6.1068

Samo, A. H., & Huda, N. U. (2019). Triple helix and academic entrepreneurial intention: Understanding motivating factors for academic spin-off among young researchers. *Journal of Global Entrepreneurship Research, 9*(1), 1–15. https://doi.org/10.1186/s40497-018-0121-7

Sandhu, M. S., Sidique, S. F., & Riaz, S. (2011). Entrepreneurship barriers and entrepreneurial inclination among Malaysian postgraduate students. *International journal of entrepreneurial behaviour & research, 17*(3), 428–449. https://doi.org/10.1108/13552551111139656

Schoon, I., & Duckworth, K. (2012). Who becomes an entrepreneur? Early life experiences as predictors of entrepreneurship. *Developmental Psychology, 48*(6), 1719–1726. https://doi.org/10.1037/a0029168

Shimoli, S. M., Cai, W., Abbas Naqvi, M. H., & Lang, Q. (2020). Entrepreneurship success traits. Do Kenyans possess the desired entrepreneur personality traits for enhanced E-entrepreneurship? Case study of Kenyan students in the People's Republic of China. *Cogent Business & Management, 7*(1), 1847863. https://doi.org/10.1080/23311975.2020.1847863

Smith, R., Bell, R., & Watts, H. (2014). Personality trait differences between traditional and social entrepreneurs. *Social Enterprise Journal, 10*(3), 200–221. https://doi.org/10.1108/SEJ-08-2013-0033

Vega-Gómez, F. I., Miranda González, F. J., Chamorro Mera, A., & Pérez-Mayo, J. (2020). Antecedents of entrepreneurial skills and their influence on the entrepreneurial intention of academics. *SAGE Open, 10*(2), 215824402092741. https://doi.org/10.1177/2158244020927411

Zhao, H., & Seibert, S. E. (2006). The big five personality dimensions and entrepreneurial status: A meta-analytical review. *Journal of Applied Psychology, 91*(2), 259–271. https://doi.org/10.1037/0021-9010.91.2.259

Mehtap Aldogan Eklund received a PhD at the University of St. Gallen, Switzerland. She is an Assistant Professor in Accounting at the University of Wisconsin-La Crosse, USA. She is currently on the editorial board of the SN Business and Economics journal and is a regional governance partner at Board Foundation (BF). Previously, she worked as an Associate Professor in Norway. Before her PhD, she worked for 7 years as an auditor in two of the Big 4 auditing firms in Europe, the USA, and the Caribbean. She has published articles and a book on corporate governance and accounting.

Technological Aspect of Academic and Educational Entrepreneurship

Ergün Akgün and İpek Altinbasak Farina

1 Introduction: Role of Edupreneurs in the New Era

Entrepreneurship is the process of creating, developing, and transforming a product, service, or system through demonstrating enterprise behavior and conducting utility and value creation activities (Galloway & Brown, 2002). According to another definition, entrepreneurship is the journey of creating economic value and employment by developing a product or service with the inherent creative power of humanity (Audretsch, 2012; Drucker, 1986). Innovations throughout humanity have subsumed the factors that direct the individual; the entrepreneur who leads the enterprise in this journey (Bygrave & Hofer, 1992). For example, while the primary capital of the industrial society encompasses muscle power and natural resources, the capital of the information society is depicted by the knowledge and the knowledge production capacity of people (Castells, 2004; Drucker, 1986). Therefore, the process of change from an industrial to an information society is an important milestone for entrepreneurship. In this context, educational entrepreneurship (edupreneur) and academic entrepreneurship (academicpreneur) concepts, two terminologies widely used in the literature, attract considerable attention. While an academic entrepreneur is defined as a university lecturer who establishes a new company or institution based on technologies derived from university research or commercializes a research project with high-income expectations (Lacetera, 2009), educational entrepreneur is also defined as the change agent (Hess, 2007) who presents innovative methods with his knowledge and experience in order to create permanent change. Actually, edupreneurs are expected to be the leaders in establishing a new education mindset in line with the needs of the twenty-first century.

E. Akgün (✉) · İ. A. Farina
Bahçeşehir University, Istanbul, Turkey
e-mail: ergun.akgun@de.bau.edu.tr; ipek.altinbasak@eas.bau.edu.tr

M. Aldogan Eklund, G. Wanzenried (eds.), *Academic and Educational Entrepreneurship*, Springer Texts in Business and Economics,
https://doi.org/10.1007/978-3-031-10952-2_8

According to Eklund and Wanzenried (2020)'s Holistic Conceptual Framework on Edu-Academic E-ship, there are seven aspects which are required to lead an edupreneur to success: financial, political and economic, international and cultural, individual and contextual, intellectual and technological. Although all of them are closely interlinked, the rapid technological advances in the twenty-first century create a sudden need for new approaches, especially in education. The characteristics of the new generations, the effects of globalization, and the recent experiences brought by the COVID-19 pandemic put forward the importance of technology for a successful edupreneur. Therefore, edupreneur is the right person to present innovative ideas to improve the education system via technology.

In this chapter, the changing landscape of education is introduced first by putting an emphasis on the characteristics of new generations. Afterward, the technological tools that can be used by edupreneurs to improve the education system are presented. The impact of COVID-19 on education and how different countries responded to it are also summarized in the following section. The chapter concludes with recommendations to edupreneurs in order to cope with the changing educational requirements of the new Era through the use of technology.

2 Changing Landscape of Education and the Needs of the New Generations

The education system has always been designed to meet the requirements of the age it serves. In this context, the skills which are necessary to create the best workforce, to improve the intellectual development of the society's members and consequently create a better World are expected to be the main goals of the system. However, it is a fact that the educational system of today has been created within the framework of the needs of the industrial society. Therefore, the current system has limitations in meeting the basic needs of the information society where individuals can access information in a fast and accurate way. Furthermore, the current education system has been criticized for not being able to prepare the labor force needed by the business world. That is why individuals need to have new skills or take on new roles in order to succeed in the changing work environment. Within the scope of all these facts presented, making education more efficient and effective is a necessity as well as making quality education more accessible for everyone (World Economic Forum, 2020).

With the spread of technology and its availability, the learning experience has become available anywhere, anytime (Ally, 2007; Sharples, 2013). Mobile learning, distance education technologies can be cited as examples for overcoming the time and space limitations in education. The use of those new technologies spread faster with the improvement of the technological infrastructure and new devices in the World.

Recent studies show that today, at least one in ten adults in the World has a computer or smartphone (Pew Research, 2019). Therefore, it can be claimed that technology is more accessible and available today. Individuals have the opportunity to communicate with each other and access content from anywhere at any time. The quick spread and adaptation of technological tools have caused changes in the behavior of people. Especially, young people are used to fulfill their basic needs such as daily shopping, socialization, and communication through technology (Prensky, 2001). One of the concrete examples of this situation is social media user statistics. Social media users, whose number may be expressed in billions, spend most of the day on these platforms (Everson et al., 2013). Along with the time spent on social media, a significant change is observed in individuals' consumption habits and preferences (Ruths & Pfeffer, 2014; Schivinski & Dabrowski, 2016). On the other hand, this change has been reflected in the learning experience as the shortening of the attention span of the students (Holt et al., 2013). As a result, short and high-quality learning contents should be prepared in line with the shortened attention span of the students. In other words, content that is high in image quality and can be completed in a short time should be prepared for the students of today. Furthermore, it is becoming more and more important to increase student involvement in the course, encouraging them to take active roles in contrast to the content in which students remain a passive audience.

While considering the changes in the education environment, it has to be noted that students from different generational cohorts learn in different ways as well. The concept of generation is described by Egri and Ralston (2004) as a type of national subculture that reflects the value priorities. The research proves that the members of a generational subculture have similar beliefs, values, and logical processes, which shape their way of thinking, acting, reasoning, processing information, working, organizing, and leading (Balda & Mora, 2011). There are five generational cohorts classified in the literature: The Silent Generation (or Veterans; born between 1933 and 1945); Baby Boomers (born between 1946 and 1964); Generation X (born between 1965 and 1976); Generation Y/Millennials (born between 1977 and 1994), and Generation Z (born between 1995 and 2010). Although there is no consensus among scholars on the exact year intervals, it is observed that there are significant generational differences in terms of values, behavior, perception of life and expectations (Altinbasak-Farina et al., 2014). Today, Gen Y'ers constitute 33% of the world's population, and they will comprise 50% of the USA workforce by 2020 and 75% of the global workforce by 2030 (Miester, 2012). In previous research among studying Gen Y'ers, it is observed that they like dynamic environments and get bored easily. They use social media and technology effectively (Altinbasak-Farina et al., 2014). The Generation cohort which is on the ladders of the education system is Generation Z, or Gen Z for short, and is the cohort succeeding the Millennials (or Gen Y). Many scholars attempted to understand the learning styles, motivations, and perspectives of Gen Z to work better with them. In their book "Generation Z Goes to College," Seemiller and Grace (2016) highlighted the characteristics making this generation unique. Besides their open-mindedness, creativity, and desire to create an impact on the World, Gen Z members, being born and raised in the Internet age, are also called "Digital Natives" or "the Net Generation." They are very good at using technology, can find any information very quickly, and are connected to others through social networks (Seemiller & Grace, 2016).

This generation presents serious challenges to HR professionals, educators, and all others in the workforce (Tulgan, 2013). Therefore, an edupreneur should understand the different skills of those youngsters and should be able to introduce the best educational tools which will prepare them to the business world.

3 The New Technologies to Support Edupreneur

In this section, the distance education technologies will be described, current technological tools will be explained, personalized education, and how technology may help the students to develop multiple new skills will be discussed. Furthermore, technological pedagogical content knowledge and digital learning tools will be elucidated to highlight how the technology may help to improve the education quality.

3.1 Distance Education Technologies

Considering the current state of technology, it is clear that the learning experience cannot be confined to school walls solely. For this reason, there is a need to prepare and present content that students can access from anywhere, anytime. In particular, technology will stand out in providing an individualized and collaborative learning environment while providing a competency-based experience that supports the motivation of the individual (Microsoft, 2020). For instance, the literature reveals that technology stands out with examples of how a collaborative learning experience is more practicable by offering individuals the opportunity to work together independent of time and place (Engstrom & Jewett, 2005; Resta & Laferrière, 2007).

At this point, learning management systems (LMS) are one of the preferred tools (Alias & Zainuddin, 2005). An LMS is a system that enables individualization of the learning experience through the management of learning contents and monitoring students and teachers (Horvat et al., 2015). Actually, the LMS is not only used to deliver learning content to the students, but also it provides comprehensive statistics to instructors such as how much of the content is completed and how much of the specified learning objective is achieved. Those detailed statistics called learning analytics enable the evaluation of the student 360 degrees and also help to individualize the learning experience. Learning analytics enable data-based decisions to be made in planning the learning experience. Besides, a comprehensive report on the quality of the evaluation process can also be obtained through the LMS as well as the provision of a statement by the teacher about the suitability of the educational content for administrative purposes.

Educational institutions use LMS to reduce costs, eliminate geographic constraints, be more accessible and increase the quality of education. However, LMS is preferred not only for educational institutions such as K-12 or universities, but also for staff training and orientation processes of institutions. Especially nowadays, when students stay away from the physical environment of the school due to the COVID-19 epidemic faced by the whole world, LMS stands out in terms of providing students with learning content and following their academic development closely. Therefore, it is possible to say that LMS has become a basic need for all institutions where learning experience exists, especially educational institutions.

Via learning management systems, shared files with cloud Technologies (Mousannif et al., 2013), special videos prepared in accordance with the course content (Geri, 2012) and interactive materials (Dobrzański et al., 2006) are presented to students in a time-independent manner to complete the requirements of the learning experience. It is quite common today to create lessons with content that allows people to study regardless of time and place. Nevertheless, it is also possible to enrich the learning experience with created materials such as books, videos, or presentations. Video conferencing tools, which are frequently used today, can be used to meet with students synchronously. Today, due to the physical limitations of social distance in the classroom, educational activities from the K-12 level to the university level are carried out with video conferencing tools in many countries of the World. This experience shows that it is possible for people living in different parts of the world to learn together regardless of geographical distances. Also, it has become much more possible for those who want to continue their professional development and to receive an education regardless of time and place. Web 2.0 tools are also frequently used in both video conferencing tools and traditional classroom settings to deliver instant feedback, convey learning content to students, and make learning content more engaging (Chou & Chen, 2008). Web 2.0 tools save teachers' time in providing quick feedback to students and preparing content. When evaluated from the students' point of view, meeting with Web 2.0 tools in the learning experience creates an important opportunity for them to gain digital competencies.

3.2 Current Technologies in Education

Today's students have difficulties in transferring the knowledge they have accumulated in school to real-life situations. Considering the international exam results of the countries, it can be stated that there is clear evidence of this problem. In this context, it is recommended to prepare learning activities based on real-life problems (Hung et al., 2008). However, it is not always possible to bring real-life examples to the learning environment due to security, time, and cost reasons. At this point, augmented reality (AR) and virtual reality (VR) applications are recommended. Studies show that bringing real-life examples to the learning environment supports conceptual learning by enriching the learning experience (Ho et al., 2017; Kurilovas, 2016). In addition, AR and VR applications allow the students to take an active role in the learning experience. Therefore, it offers alternative ways to transform the learning experience with AR and VR.

Bloom (1984), in his study titled *2-Sigma Problem*, revealed that students' success can be increased by 80–85% with applications for eliminating learning deficiencies with after-school activities, small group activities, and follow-up tests.

However, the above-mentioned studies (Guskey, 2007; Senemoğlu, 1987; Slavin, 1987) such as after-school activities, control tests, feedback correction, and small group work, which were suggested to support student success, are not applicable because they create overtime and extra workload for teachers. Today, with artificial intelligence, student development is followed step by step, determining the deficiencies of the student and saving time and cost in presenting solutions (Microsoft, 2020). In the studies, it was concluded that providing instant and systematic feedback, as well as learning content for the needs of artificial intelligence-based students, supports academic success and performance development (Dekker et al., 2020; Luckin & Cukurova, 2019).

3.3 How to Develop Multiple New Skills Through Technology?

With the developments in technology, the skills needed to succeed have changed over time. In the third decade of the twenty-first century, the individuals are required to know how to have access to accurate and up-to-date information quickly. Furthermore, they have to be curious, collaborative, and think creatively and analytically (Short & Keller-Bell, 2021). In addition to all these skills, it is expected that the individual be aware of and sensitive to both local and global problems (Whorton et al., 2017).

Considering the current needs of the World, it would not be wrong to describe Massive Open Online Courses (MOOCs) as the future of education. With MOOCs, it has become possible to access the lectures of many reputable universities and experts in their fields from all over the World. In other words, MOOCs are platforms that enable individuals who wish to improve their knowledge and competencies by taking courses from leading academicians/professionals and also by creating a network of people with similar interests. With MOOCs, students are basically entitled to follow the asynchronous content presented to them, execute their assignments and receive a certificate as a result. Furthermore, these processes enable the students to realize projects together with people from a completely different cultures and geographies.

With the acceleration of the revolutionary processes of technology, the production, sharing, and dissemination of information have gained momentum today. Hence, information has become omnipresent and accessible. However, the production of qualified information is still very difficult and time consuming. At this point, collaborative studies are needed to produce qualified information and to make this information accessible. Open Educational Resources (OER), which has a very similar structure to MOOCs, is in the foreground at this point. With OER, where information is produced and shared together at the same time and place, it is possible to overcome obstacles such as cost, as well as time and geographical barriers related to education. That is why, OER is described as an up-to-date and modern way to access qualified information (Darwish, 2019). Especially as stated in the Sustainable Development Goals of the United Nations (2015), the dissemination of quality education is critical for the future of the world. Therefore, the crucial role of

MOOC, OER, and m-learning (mobile learning) in educational sciences is to make it possible to realize a sustainable transformation in general by increasing the opportunity to access qualified education for all segments of the society and all stakeholders (Casserly, 2007; Darwish, 2019; Geith & Vignare, 2008; Koseoglu & Bozkurt, 2018; Zawacki-Richter et al., 2020).

3.4 How to Reinforce the Personalized Education?

Today, technology allows almost everything to be personalized. The clothes, the food, the recommended list of books, TV series, and the music may be tailored according to each individual's preferences. In marketing, even the services are co-created with the customers in order to meet the individual expectations. Therefore, education should also be individualized, and the learning experience should be personalized according to the pre-learning, habits, and personality traits of the individual so that better learning outcomes can be attained (Aslan & Reigeluth, 2015).

In the traditional education system, a certain number of students are congregated in a classroom and are inculcated with the same content, ignoring their individual characteristics. However, personalized education presents a more flexible structure where each student is offered a content according to his/her interests and at his/her own learning pace. Therefore, the educational institutions and practitioners have to build an individual-centered structure and reconstruct the system according to different levels of expertise for each field, prepare infrastructures that will support the learning of students by following their development step by step. Therefore, for personalized education, it is necessary to plan in four different ways: (1) individual learning and career plan, (2) support system in line with the interests and needs of the individual, (3) planning for the habits and goals of the individual, and (4) coaching (Reigeluth, 2012).

However, an education system based on variables such as the individual's needs, interests, and learning pace has also been criticized in terms of its design, management, and sustainability (An & Reigeluth, 2011). It is argued that it is costly and time consuming, cannot be applicable in real life due to the workload it will create for teachers (Watson & Reigeluth, 2008). It is a fact that, besides the actual teaching, teachers' weekly working hours may reach 50 h due to preparation of teaching activities, providing feedback to students, material development, professional development activities, and managerial activities (Bryant et al., 2020). However, it has to be acknowledged that in this era, technology is making a student-centered system more applicable, less costly, and less time consuming (Watson & Reigeluth, 2008). Watson et al. (2015) state that it is possible to personalize teaching and provide a lifelong education through technology which will render the content preparation, measurement and evaluation, and tracking of student development much easier. McKinsey Global Institute (2020) offers predictions that with the widespread use of artificial intelligence, much of the workload of instructors, especially pre- and post-teaching activities, will be automated by 2030.

Artificial intelligence is used in many different processes in education. Frequently artificial intelligence stands out today:

- In personalizing the learning experience by making suggestions in line with parameters such as learning styles, abilities, and learning performance of each student in the classroom.
- In providing instant and systematic feedback to students by automating measurement and evaluation processes.
- In supporting the academic success of students with instant student tracking.
- In making the existing learning permanent.
- In creating a collaborative work environment (Andriessen & Sandberg, 1999; Guilherme, 2019; Karsenti, 2019).

Certain scholars have stated the concern that artificial intelligence-based applications may eliminate the need for teachers in the learning process (Nabiyev & Erümit, 2020). However, artificial intelligence is expected to support the development of students by easing the workload of teachers (McArthur et al., 2005). Studies show that artificial intelligence applications create new opportunities for teachers' pre-teaching preparation and teaching experience for enrichment and development (Popenici & Kerr, 2017). In other words, artificial intelligence is expected to eliminate inequality of opportunity in education and provide qualified education for everyone (Timms, 2016).

Artificial intelligence is beneficial not only in learning-teaching processes but also in educational management. For example, education managers benefit from using artificial intelligence in various managerial processes such as budgeting, student applications and registration, course management, purchasing activities, expenditure management, and facilities. In this way, a more sustainable management approach can be established. Therefore, it can be claimed that artificial intelligence will stand out in the improvement of all sub-processes related to the education system.

3.5 How Can Technology Help to Improve the Education Quality?

When evaluated in terms of education, technology is considered to be an important tool that accelerates the diffusion process of change and increases its impact area and certainly is the catalyst of the change process. Therefore, for edupreneur, it is an opportunity and an imperative to benefit from technology for all innovations related to the improvement of education quality. However, this point is a must to follow current practices closely in order to develop effective solutions for the learning problem or need. As shown in Fig. 1, according to the 2020 Horizon Report (Brown et al., 2020), in the education system of tomorrow, individuals will be able to use artificial intelligence to adapt to their own learning speed, HyFlex approach, a more flexible learning experience, open educational resources and microcredit applications for more accessible education. By gaining the required

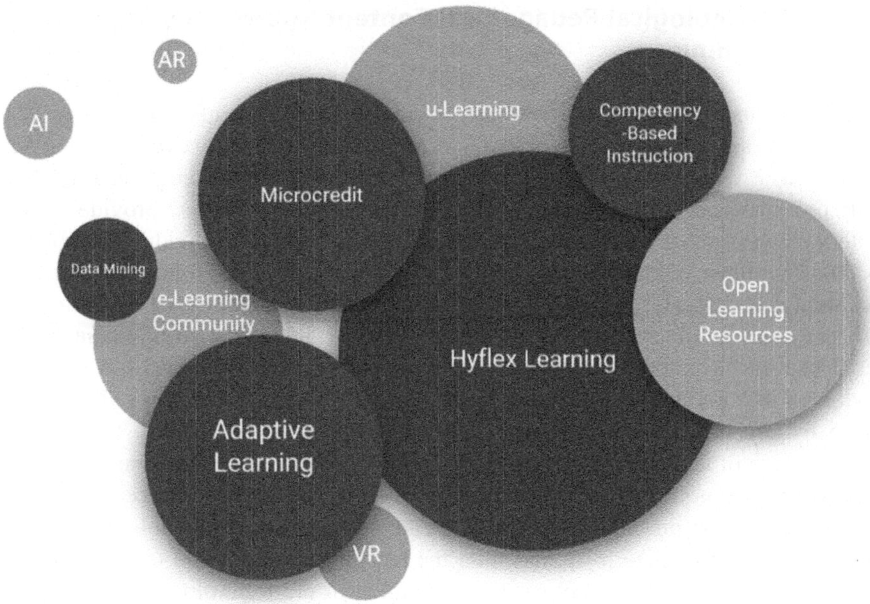

Fig. 1 Current issues in educational technologies-the Horizon Report (Brown et al., 2020)

competencies with these, it will be possible to offer experiences enriched with applications such as digital learning environments, AR and VR to continue learning outside the walls of the school. Therefore, it is possible to say that learning will be a lifelong process, while tomorrow's education becomes a structure that offers a more flexible experience to the individual compared to today. Considering this situation, there will be a need for new applications that will solve learning problems with new technologies in the near future.

In addition, it is not possible for an innovation, introduced to any system, to receive the same reaction from all stakeholders. To clarify, Rogers (2002) underlines that a society's acceptance of innovation takes time and correct communication strategies need to be developed for this process. In that sense, it is also important to produce solutions for the stakeholders to adopt the innovation brought to the system. For instance, explaining this innovation to people from many different sources speeds up the spread and adoption of innovation.

Change in education becomes a problem that spreads over time and is sometimes difficult to solve. About this issue, Reigeluth and Duffy (2019) argue that the process of making a change in education is equivalent to solving a complicated problem. The most important factor that makes the process difficult is that education, as an open system, is in constant interaction with the social system and there are many different aspects to be controlled (Squire & Reigeluth, 2000). Therefore, in order to overcome the difficulties of making a change in an unstable structure, a multidirectional and systematic perspective should be taken (Reigeluth, 2012).

3.6 Technological Pedagogical Content Knowledge, Digital Learning

The importance of the digital learning environment in students' motivation, academic success, and knowledge transfer cannot be ignored. However, for qualified education, it would not be the right approach to consider technology as a tool that only provides access to learning content. Quality education aims to provide society with the workforce it needs and to raise happy and competent individuals (UNICEF, 2000). Therefore, in order to achieve this goal, it is necessary to follow the scientific developments closely, organize all stakeholders and move forward by taking the process from a systematic perspective (Banathy, 1995). This requirement brings along the need for stakeholders who can utilize technology effectively. An investigation of the literature reveals that people who do not use technology show resistance to any new technology offered to them (King & He, 2006). In addition, effective use of technology is required to improve the learning experience. In other words, it is not enough to put the technology into the learning environment or to have it purchased. For this reason, in addition to mastering this technology, teachers should be able to utilize it by matching the teaching methods and techniques with their learning goals. This competence is detailed in the technological pedagogical content knowledge (TPACK) model for teachers in Fig. 2 (Koehler & Mishra, 2009).

Within the scope of technological pedagogical content knowledge, the following items are considered: (1) recognizing any tool or equipment used in a technological knowledge course; (2) pedagogical knowledge teaching-learning methods and strategies; (3) mastery of field knowledge of the course content; (4) technological pedagogical knowledge to be able to determine the appropriate method for a technological tool; (5) determining a method in accordance with the pedagogical content knowledge course subject; and (6) choosing the appropriate technology for the technological content knowledge course content. Finally, the last item of technological pedagogical content knowledge in the model includes (7) planning and presenting by choosing the method and technology appropriate to the course content. Sickel (2019) points to technological pedagogical content knowledge as the only way technology can improve the learning experience. In cases where the teaching process is not built on the TPACK framework, technology will remain as the tool that conveys the learning content to the student or the stimulus that reveals the behavior. Therefore, in order for teachers to gain competence within the scope of technological pedagogical content knowledge, it is necessary to support their development from the pre-service period (Suharwoto & Niess, 2001). In this context, the use of MOOCs and video conferencing tools stand out (Hanson-Smith, 2016; Israel et al., 2009; Tømte, 2019). However, the use of developing technologies for this need is important in terms of the quality of education.

TPACK is a roadmap for teachers to bring technology, pedagogy, and content to integrate with technology in education. However, the questions about how and for what purpose the technology will be used in the learning environment have not been answered in TPACK. At this point, the SAMR model, which responds to how technology should be positioned in the learning environment from a hierarchical

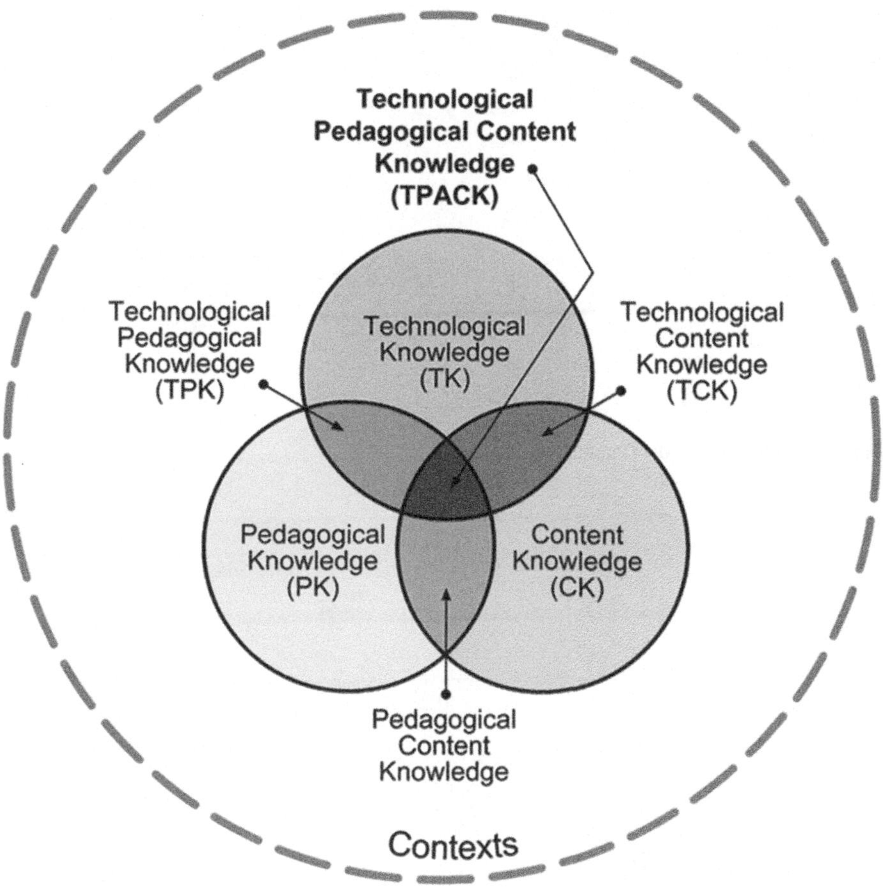

Fig. 2 Technological pedagogical content knowledge (Koehler & Mishra, 2009)

perspective, stands out (Hilton, 2016). The SAMR model is a general framework for how the teacher chooses, uses, and evaluates technology. The SAMR model consists of four steps: Substitution, Augmentation, Modification, and Redefinition.

In the substitution step, technology does not make a functional contribution to the learning and teaching process compared to the current situation. A typical example of substitution is for the teacher to reflect on a presentation he/she prepared before the lesson with a projector instead of writing on the blackboard. In the augmentation step, technology is used in the learning process in a way that will provide functional development and improvement. An example of a technology integration belonging to the augmentation step is to receive homework with online file sharing instead of printed material to give instant and fast feedback to students. In the modification step, technology is expected to create a statistically significant and important functional change in the teaching process. In other words, in the modification step, it is aimed to redesign the task of using technology and to approach the task from

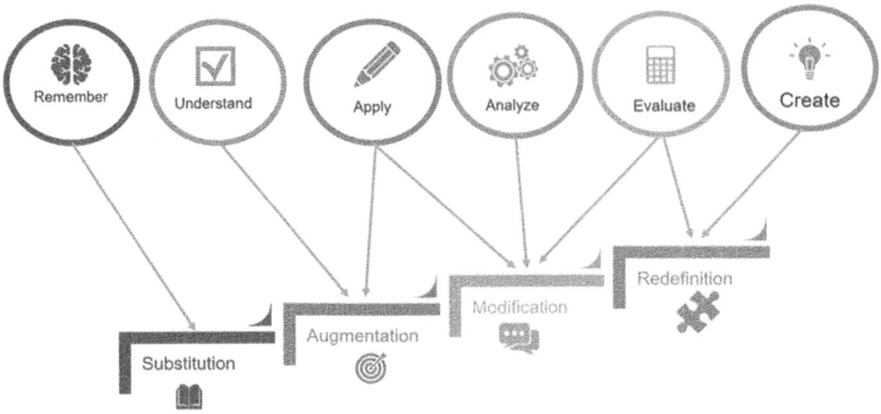

Fig. 3 The SAMR model (Puentedura, 2013)

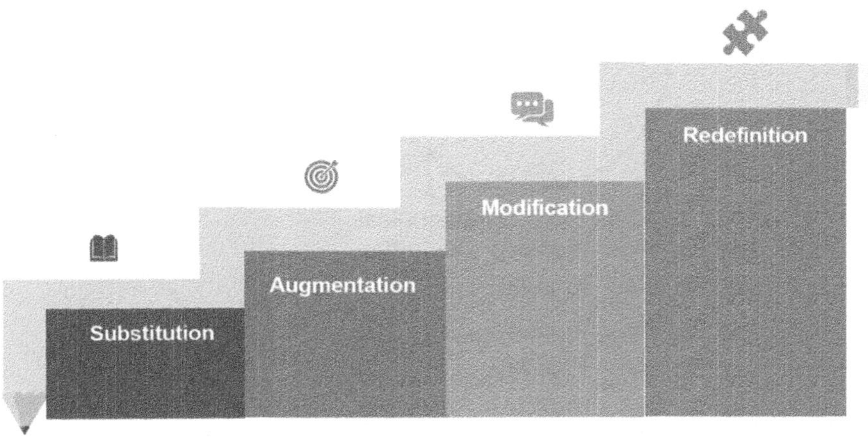

Fig. 4 Bloom's taxonomy and SAMR (Bloom et al., 1956)

different perspectives. In the final stage, redefinition, technology is intended to deepen the learning experience. The steps for the model are presented in Fig. 3.

The SAMR Model is associated with Bloom's taxonomy in enriching students' academic success and conceptual learning experience in the learning process. Accordingly, it is sufficient to replace the technology with newer technology in the learning objectives at the remembering and understanding level. However, the functional contribution of technology should also be included in the process of learning at the application, analysis, and evaluation level. At the creativity step, technology is expected to be an element that enriches and deepens the learning experience for a learning objective. The relationship between SAMR and Bloom's taxonomy is presented in Fig. 4.

4 How to Transfer the Information Acquired at School to 4. Distance Education?

4.1 How Different Countries and Education Institutions Responded to the Pandemic?

Distance education is an interdisciplinary field that develops over time and serves well in responding to learning needs and guiding open education practices (Bozkurt, 2019; Zawacki-Richter et al., 2020). Moore (1989) defines distance education as an approach in which the students participate in the learning activities that the instructor (s) planned, regardless of the time and place, and the learning content is presented in the printed or electronic (digital) form. According to another definition, distance education is carrying out the communication and interaction between the instructor and the student for learning purposes in a planned manner via technologies such as books, letters, videos, video conferences, and audio recordings (Alkan, 1987). Considering both definitions, the emphasis is placed on interactions between different parties and via different channels to ensure greater involvement of students in the learning process in distance education (Moore, 1989). For this reason, both synchronous and asynchronous contents are used in well-planned and qualified distance education applications. In other words, while meeting students simultaneously with video conference calls, providing students with a rich learning experience with quizzes and interactive videos in the process is a must for distance education.

With the advances made in information and communication technologies, it is seen that distance education technologies are frequently used in different levels of higher education, especially in professional development. However, for distance education, March 2020 has been an important turning point. Coronavirus (COVID-19), which emerged in China in December 2019, first affected the entire Asian continent and then Europe and the Americas. Following these developments, the World Health Organization (WHO) classified COVID-19 as a global epidemic in March 2020 (WHO, 2020). In order to prevent the transmission of this virus and prevent the spread of the epidemic, the whole world has made serious restrictions on social life with strict rules. Within the scope of these restrictions, steps have been taken to realize learning-teaching activities with distance education technologies at all educational levels, including pre-school to higher education. Thus, more than 1.5 billion students of all ages from around the world have been affected by school and university closures due to COVID-19 (UNESCO, 2020; UNICEF, 2020).

With the interruption of face-to-face teaching activities, countries have determined their road maps in line with their infrastructure and facilities. UNESCO (2020) states that, in this process, countries mostly benefit from video conferencing tools as well as mass broadcast media such as television and radio. However, during this process, most of the students who had access to the contents found the learning activities inefficient (UNICEF, 2020). In addition, with the interruption of face-to-face education, inequality of opportunity in education has increased, while vulnerable children and youth are disproportionately harmed (UNESCO, 2020). In response to this situation, UNESCO (2020) has taken measures and offered solutions for students to continue their education, considering that education is a fundamental human right. However, it is clear that all of these have very limited effects on the process. In particular, the course of the epidemic and the rapid digital transformation experienced show that distance education technologies will always be a part of the learning process (Bozkurt & Sharma, 2020). Therefore, countries need to invest in the infrastructure and qualified workforce required for educational technologies, especially distance education.

5 Last Remarks and Conclusion

It has been argued that meaningful learning cannot be achieved due to the fact that today's education system decreases the attention of students, directs them to memorization, and assumes that all students learn in the same way. Therefore, there are also some loudly expressed opinions that the traditional understanding of "school" is coming to an end. In the face of these criticisms and opinions, the education system should be enriched with opportunities for students to apply the knowledge they have learned. Therefore, problem-based learning is one of the prominent approaches. Problem-based learning is an approach based on understanding and problem solving, which puts the student in the center, helps to improve the field knowledge in which the student performs effective learning and uses problem-solving skills (Mayo et al., 1993). It contributes to the educational essence of the students who take responsibility and act independently and become independent learners in lifelong learning.

Another approach that stands out in the reorganization of learning environments is project-based learning. Project-based learning is an approach that enables students to build a bridge between real life and learning experience by working in teams and improving their planning, decision-making, and time management skills (Railsback, 2002). With this approach, it is ensured that students experience the processes of research, reconstruction, and solution generation by taking responsibility for their own learning. For this reason, the project-based learning approach offers the students the opportunity to apply the abstract knowledge they have acquired.

Creating both project- and problem-based learning activities are very costly, time-consuming, and often creates security problems. Studies show that technology solves the cost, time, and security problems that arise in learning environment design (Clark, 2001). For example, simulations and digital games are important solution partners.

In addition to all these, today there is a need for a specialized workforce rather than adults who are knowledgeable about everything. At this point, certificate programs and lifelong learning activities become prominent so that people can excel in a field. In addition, universities also have an important mission in this context. Universities should provide students with the opportunity to receive the highest quality education from the most competent person in the field they want to specialize in. For instance, certificate programs can be created with agreements between universities and student mobility can be a preferred part of them. Similarly, it is very important to increase cooperation between sectors and universities. The necessary infrastructure should be established for the preparation of content that combines the experience in the sector and the knowledge of universities. For example, students' internship or work experience can be accredited as course credits. Similarly, arrangements can be made for people experienced in a sector to successfully complete certificate programs and to be accepted as course credits. Practices made within this scope have recently taken place in the literature with microcredit applications.

More than two decades of the twenty-first century are over. Today, the World is facing a global pandemic that has not been witnessed for more than a Century. The years 2020 and 2021 are expected to be the years of discerning the main problems of the World and of creating a deep learning which will help to the progress of the World in terms of using the resources with more care, more sharing and with a global partnership spirit. Education for sure is the main leverage to achieve "a Better World" objective.

In this period, technology has permitted people from all around the World to access to information, to services, to products and also to education. Edupreneur's main goal is to bring a new philosophy supported by new tools, technologies, approaches to educational field in order to improve the quality of education. Therefore, he/she has to be the person observing all the changes in the environmental forces, taking into consideration the economic, legal, natural, demographic, cultural, and technological developments. The needs of the era may change the generations in education or in the workforce may change but the technology will continue to expand rapidly. Therefore, technology is expected to be indispensable in the school education and as well as in lifelong learning processes. Edupreneur should pioneer the best methods which will fit to the education field and improve their applications, and usage through leadership. The examples of different technological tools presented for the use of edupreneur in this chapter will for sure deepen and extend in the near future, but the desire and the spirit of improving the education quality should be sustained.

6 Summary

The fast and disruptive transformations stemming from advances in technology are reshaping many systems in the World. Parallel to these, it is apparent that the education system also should be reorganized to meet the requirements of the era. Mixing the two important disciplines, namely education and entrepreneurship in a single pot, edupreneur should be the catalyzer and creator of this new education landscape. Understanding that new generations have different abilities and expectations and acknowledging the necessities of success in business life, edupreneur either inside or outside the classroom, should follow the developments in order to improve the quality of education. Today, technology is providing immense tools to achieve this goal. This section aims to present a general framework on different technological tools that edupreneurs may benefit from in their learning-teaching processes.

Questions

Question 1. Can X generation continue its dominant role in the new era? Which generation presents stronger skills as new edupreneurs? Why?

Question 2. What are the considerations when designing a learning experience for the generation Z? Why is that?

Question 3. What are the opportunities and challenges that technology presents to edupreneurs?

Question 4. What is the effect of students being from different generations on learning design?

References

Alias, N. A., & Zainuddin, A. M. (2005). Innovation for better teaching and learning: Adopting the learning management system. *Malaysian Online Journal of Instructional Technology, 2*(2), 27–40. https://citeseerx.ist.psu.edu/viewdoc/summary?doi=10.1.1.119.9362

Alkan, C. (1987). *Eğitim teknolojileri*. Ankara.

Ally, M. (2007). Guest editorial: Mobile learning. *The International Review of Research in Open and Distance Learning,* 8(2). http://www.irrodl.org/index.php/irrodl/article/view/451/918

Altinbasak-Farina, I., Arda-Ayaz, O., & Bicer, B. (2014). Targeting millennials in an emerging market: A qualitative study on the value systems of generation Y in Turkey. *European Journal of Research on Social Sciences, 1*(2), 12–18.

An, Y. J., & Reigeluth, C. (2011). Creating technology-enhanced, learner-centered classrooms: K–12 teachers' beliefs, perceptions, barriers, and support needs. *Journal of Digital Learning in Teacher Education, 28*(2), 54–62.

Andriessen, J., & Sandberg, J. (1999). Where is education heading and how about AI. *International Journal of Artificial Intelligence in Education, 10*(2), 130–150.

Aslan, S., & Reigeluth, C. M. (2015). Examining the challenges of learner-centered education. *Phi Delta Kappan, 97*(4), 63–68.

Audretsch, D. (2012). Entrepreneurship research. *Management Decision, 50*(5), 755–764.

Balda, J. B., & Mora, F. (2011). Adapting leadership theory and practice for the networked, millennial generation. *Journal of Leadership Studies, 5*(3), 13–24. https://doi.org/10.1002/jls.20229

Banathy, B. H. (1995). Developing a systems view of education. *Educational Technology, 35*(3), 53–57.

Bygrave, W. D., & Hofer, C. W. (1992). Theorizing about entrepreneurship. *Entrepreneurship Theory and Practice, 16*(2), 13–22. https://doi.org/10.1177/104225879201600203

Bloom, B. S. (1984). The 2 sigma problem: The search for methods of group instruction as effective as one-to-one tutoring. *Educational Researcher, 13*(6), 4–16. https://doi.org/10.2307/1175554

Bloom, B., Englehart, M. Furst, E., Hill, W., & Krathwohl, D. (1956). *Taxonomy of educational objectives: The classification of educational goals. Handbook I: Cognitive domain*. Longmans, Green.

Brown, M., McCormack, M., Reeves, J., Brook, D. C., Grajek, S., Alexander, B., Weber, N., et al. (2020). 2020 educause horizon report teaching and learning edition (pp. 2–58). EDUCAUSE.

Bozkurt, A. (2019). Intellectual roots of distance education: A progressive knowledge domain analysis. *Distance Education, 40*(4), 497–514. https://doi.org/10.1080/01587919.2019.1681894

Bozkurt, A., & Sharma, R. C. (2020). Emergency remote teaching in a time of global crisis due to CoronaVirus pandemic. *Asian Journal of Distance Education, 15*(1), i–vi.

Bryant, J., Heitz, C., Sanghvi, S., & Wagle, D. (2020). *How artificial intelligence will impact K-12 teachers*. Retried February 10, 2021, from https://www.mckinsey.com/industries/public-and-social-sector/our-insights/how-artificial-intelligence-will-impact-k-12-teachers

Casserly, C. (2007). The economics of open educational resources. *Educational Technology, 47*(6), 14–19.

Castells, M. (2004). *The network society: A cross-cultural perspective*. Edward Elgar.

Chou, P. N., & Chen, H. H. (2008). Engagement in online collaborative learning: A case study using a web 2.0 tool. *Journal of Online Learning and Teaching, 4*(4), 574–582.

Clark, R. E. (Ed.). (2001). *Learning from media: Arguments, analysis, and evidence*. IAP.

Darwish, H. (2019). Open educational resources (OER) Edupreneurship business models for different stakeholders. *Education and Information Technologies, 24*(6), 3855–3886. https://doi.org/10.1007/s10639-019-09962-8

Dekker, I., De Jong, E. M., Schippers, M. C., Bruijn-Smolders, D., Alexiou, A., & Giesbers, B. (2020). Optimizing students' mental health and academic performance: Ai-enhanced life crafting. *Frontiers in Psychology, 11*, 10–63. https://doi.org/10.3389/fpsyg.2020.01063

Dobrzański, L. A., Honysz, R., & Brytan, Z. (2006). Application of interactive course management system in distance learning of material science. *Journal of Achievements in Materials and Manufacturing Engineering, 17*(1–2), 429–432.

Drucker, P. (1986). *Innovation and entrepreneurship*. Harper.

Egri, C. P., & Ralston, D. A. (2004). Generation cohorts and personal values: A comparison of China and the United States. *Organization Science, 15*(2), 210–220.

Eklund, M., & Wanzenried, G. (2020). *Academic and educational entrepreneurship: Foundation in theory and lessons from practice*. Springer.

Engstrom, M. E., & Jewett, D. (2005). Collaborative learning the wiki way. *TechTrends, 49*(6), 12–15. https://doi.org/10.1007/BF0276372

Everson, M., Gundlach, E., & Miller, J. (2013). Social media and the introductory statistics course. *Computers in Human Behavior, 29*(5), 69–81. https://doi.org/10.1016/j.chb.2012.12.033

Galloway, L., & Brown, W. (2002). Entrepreneurship education at university: A driver in the creation of high growth firms? *Education+ Training, 44*(8/9), 398–405.

Geith, C., & Vignare, K. (2008). Access to education with online learning and open educational resources: Can they close the gap? *Journal of Asynchronous Learning Networks, 12*(1), 105–126.

Geri, N. (2012). The resonance factor: Probing the impact of video on student retention in distance learning. *Interdisciplinary Journal of E-Learning and Learning Objects, 8*(1), 1–13.

Guilherme, A. (2019). AI and education: The importance of teacher and student relations. *AI & SOCIETY, 34*(1), 47–54. https://doi.org/10.1007/s00146-017-0693-8

Guskey, T. R. (2007). Closing achievement gaps: Revisiting Benjamin S. Bloom's learning for mastery. *Journal of Advanced Academics, 19*(1), 8–31. https://doi.org/10.4219/jaa-2007-704

Hanson-Smith, E. (2016). Teacher education and technology. *The Routledge Handbook of Language Learning and Technology*, 210–222.

Hess, F. M. (2007). The case for educational entrepreneurship: Hard truths about risk, reform, and reinvention. *Phi Delta Kappan, 89*(1), 21–30.

Hilton, J. T. (2016). A case study of the application of SAMR and TPACK for reflection on technology integration into two social studies classrooms. *Social Studies, 107*(2), 68–73.

Ho, S. C., Hsieh, S. W., Sun, P. C., & Chen, C. M. (2017). To activate English learning: Listen and speak in real life context with an AR featured u-learning system. *Journal of Educational Technology & Society, 20*(2), 176–187.

Holt, K., Shehata, A., Strömbäck, J., & Ljungberg, E. (2013). Age and the effects of news media attention and social media use on political interest and participation: Do social media function as leveller? *European Journal of Communication, 28*(1), 19–34.

Horvat, A., Dobrota, M., Krsmanovic, M., & Cudanov, M. (2015). Student perception of Moodle learning management system: A satisfaction and significance analysis. *Interactive Learning Environments, 23*(4), 515–527.

Hung, W., Jonassen, D. H., & Liu, R. (2008). Problem-based learning. *Handbook of research on Educational Communications and Technology, 3*(1), 485–506.

Israel, M., Knowlton, E., Griswold, D., & Rowland, A. (2009). Applications of video-conferencing technology in special education teacher preparation. *Journal of Special Education Technology, 24*(1), 15–25.

Karsenti, T. (2019). Artificial intelligence in education: The urgent need to prepare teachers for Tomorrow's schools. *Formation et profession, Chronıque Technologies en Education, 27*(1), 112–116. https://doi.org/10.18162/fp.2019.a166

King, W. R., & He, J. (2006). A meta-analysis of the technology acceptance model. *Information & Management, 43*(6), 740–755.

Koehler, M., & Mishra, P. (2009). What is technological pedagogical content knowledge (TPACK)? *Contemporary Issues in Technology and Teacher Education, 9*(1), 60–70.

Koseoglu, S., & Bozkurt, A. (2018). An exploratory literature review on open educational practices. *Distance Education, 39*(4), 441–461. https://doi.org/10.1080/01587919.2018.1520042

Kurilovas, E. (2016). Evaluation of quality and personalisation of VR/AR/MR learning systems. *Behaviour & Information Technology, 35*(11), 998–1007.

Lacetera, N. (2009). Academic entrepreneurship. *Managerial and Decision Economics, 30*(7), 443–464. https://doi.org/10.1002/mde.1461

Luckin, R., & Cukurova, M. (2019). Designing educational technologies in the age of AI: A learning sciences-driven approach. *British Journal of Educational Technology, 50*(6), 2824–2838. https://doi.org/10.1111/bjet.12861

Mayo, P., Donnelly, M. B., Nash, P. P., & Schwartz, R. W. (1993). Student perceptions of tutor effectiveness in a problem-based surgery clerkship. *Teaching and Learning in Medicine: An International Journal, 5*(4), 227–233. https://doi.org/10.1080/10401339309539628

McArthur, D., Lewis, M., & Bishary, M. (2005). The roles of artificial intelligence in education: Current progress and future prospects. *Journal of Educational Technology, 1*(4), 42–80.

McKinsey Global Institute. (2020). *Future of work Turkey's talent transformation in the digital era.* Retrieved February 10, 2021, from https://www.mckinsey.com/~/media/mckinsey/featured%20insights/future%20of%20organizations/the%20future%20of%20work%20in%20turkey/future-of-work-turkey-report.pdf

Miester, J. (2012). *Three reasons you need to adopt a millennial mindset regardles of your age.* Retrieved February 10, 2021 from https://www.forbes.com/sites/jeannemeister/2012/10/05/millennialmindse/?sh=6f9a4e9b4ee4

Microsoft. (2020). *The class of 2030 and life-ready learning: The technology imperative A summary report.* Retrieved February 10, 2021, from https://education.minecraft.net/wpcontent/uploads/13679_EDU_Thought_Leadership_Summary_revisions_5.10.18.pdf

Moore, M. G. (1989). Editorial: Three types of interaction. *American Journal of Distance Education, 3*(2), 1–7.

Mousannif, H., Khalil, I., & Kotsis, G. (2013). Collaborative learning in the clouds. *Information Systems Frontiers, 15*(2), 159–165. https://doi.org/10.1007/s10796-012-9364-y

Nabiyev, V., & Erümit, A. K. (2020). Yapay zekanın temelleri, öğrenmesi, problemleri ve eğitimde yapay zeka. In V. Nabiyev & Erümit (Eds.), *Eğitimde Yapay Zeka Kuramdan Uygulamaya* (pp. 2–34). Pegem.

Pew Research Center. (2019). *Mobile fact sheet.* Retrieved February 10, 2021, from https://www.pewresearch.org/internet/fact-sheet/mobile/

Prensky, M. (2001). Digital natives, digital immigrants part 2: Do they really think differently? *On the Horizon, 9*(6), 1–6.

Popenici, S. A., & Kerr, S. (2017). Exploring the impact of artificial intelligence on teaching and learning in higher education. *Research and Practice in Technology Enhanced Learning, 12*(1), 1–13.

Puentedura, R. R. (2013). *SAMR: Moving from enhancement to transformation.* Retrieved from http://www.hippasus.com/rrpweblog/archives/000095.html

Railsback, J. (2002). Project-based instruction: Creating excitement for learning. By Request Series.
Reigeluth, C. M. (2012). Instructional theory and technology for the new paradigm of education. *Revista de Educación a Distancia, 2012*(32), 1–18.
Reigeluth, C. M., & Duffy, F. M. (2019). The school system transformation process: Guidance for paradigm change in school districts.
Resta, P., & Laferrière, T. (2007). Technology in support of collaborative learning. *Educational Psychology Review, 19*(1), 65–83.
Rogers, E. M. (2002). Diffusion of preventive innovations. *Addictive Behaviors, 27*(6), 989–993.
Ruths, D., & Pfeffer, J. (2014). Social media for large studies of behavior. *Science, 346*(6213), 1063–1064.
Schivinski, B., & Dabrowski, D. (2016). The effect of social media communication on consumer perceptions of brands. *Journal of Marketing Communications, 22*(2), 189–214. https://doi.org/10.1080/13527266.2013.871323
Seemiller, C., & Grace, M. (2016). Generation Z *goes to college*. Wiley.
Senemoğlu, N. (1987). Tam öğrenme modeli-yararları ve sınırlılıkları. *Eğitim ve Bilim, 66*(12), 28–34.
Sickel, J. L. (2019). The great media debate and TPACK: A multidisciplinary examination of the role of technology in teaching and learning. *Journal of Research on Technology in Education, 51*(2), 152–165. https://doi.org/10.1080/15391523.2018.1564895
Sharples, M. (2013). Mobile learning: Research, practice and challenges. *Distance Education in China, 3*(5), 5–11.
Short, M. N., & Keller-Bell, Y. (2021). Essential skills for the 21st century workforce. In *Research anthology on developing critical thinking skills in students* (pp. 97–110). IGI Global.
Slavin, R. E. (1987). Mastery learning reconsidered. *Review of Educational Research, 57*(2), 175–213.
Squire, K. D., & Reigeluth, C. M. (2000). The many faces of systemic change. *Educational Horizons, 78*(3), 143–152.
Suharwoto, G., & Niess, M. (2001). *How do subject specific teacher preparation program that integrate technology throughout the courses support the development of mathematics pre-service teachers' TPCK*. Retrieved February 10, 2021, from http://eusesconsortium.org/docs/Site_With_Gogot.pdf
Tømte, C. E. (2019). MOOCs in teacher education: Institutional and pedagogical change? *European Journal of Teacher Education, 42*(1), 65–81.
Timms, M. J. (2016). Letting artificial intelligence in education out of the box: Educational cobots and smart classrooms. *International Journal of Artificial Intelligence in Education, 26*(2), 701–712. https://doi.org/10.1007/s4059
Tulgan, B. (2013). Meet generation Z: The second generation within the millenial cohort. *Rainmaker Thinking Inc*, 1–13.
UN. (2015). *The goals*. Retrieved from March, 5, 2021, from https://sdgs.un.org/goals
UNESCO. (2020). *COVID-19 education response*. Retrieved February 10, 2021, from https://en.unesco.org/covid19/educationresponse/globalcoalition
UNICEF (2020). *UNICEF and Microsoft launch global learning platform to help address COVID-19 education crisis*. Retrieved February 10, 2021, from https://www.unicef.org/press-releases/unicef-and-microsoft-launch-global-learning-platform-help-addresscovid-19-education
UNICEF. (2000). *Defining quality in education*. Retrieved February 10, 2021, from https://pdf4pro.com/view/defining-quality-in-education-home-page-unicef-aefce.html
Watson, W. R., Watson, S. L., & Reigeluth, C. M. (2015). Education 3.0: Breaking the mold with technology. *Interactive Learning Environments, 23*(3), 332–343. https://doi.org/10.1080/10494820.2013.764322
Watson, S. L., & Reigeluth, C. M. (2008). The learner-centered paradigm of education. *Educational Technology*, 42–48.

WHO Director-General's Opening Remarks at the Media Briefing on COVID19. (2020, March). https://www.who.int/director-general/speeches/detail/who-director-general-s-opening-remarks-at-the-media-briefing-on-covid-19%2D%2D-22-june-2020

Whorton, R., Casillas, A., Oswald, F. L., & Shaw, A. (2017). Critical skills for the 21st century workforce. *Building Better Students: Preparation for the Workforce*, 47–72. https://doi.org/10.1093/acprof:oso/9780199373222.001.0001

World Economic Forum. (2020). *Resetting the future of work agenda: disruption and renewal in a post-covıd world.* Retrieved February 10, 2021, from http://www3.weforum.org/docs/WEF_NES_Resetting_FOW_Agenda_2020.pdf

Zawacki-Richter, O., Conrad, D., Bozkurt, A., Aydin, C. H., Bedenlier, S., Jung, I., Kerres, M., et al. (2020). Elements of open education: An invitation to future research. *The International Review of Research in Open and Distance Learning, 21*(3), 319–334. https://doi.org/10.19173/irrodl.v21i3.4659

Ergün Akgün is an assistant professor at the Faculty of Educational Sciences, Bahçeşehir University. He also works as a director at Distance Education Application and Research Center, Bahçeşehir University. With more than 10 years of experience, he provides expertise and consultancy in the fields of distance education, data mining in education, and artificial intelligence in education. Contributing to the literature by making various studies in these fields, Ergün Akgün also takes part in conferences and workshops. After completing his undergraduate education at the Department of Basic Education, Muğla Sıtkı Koçman University, he continued his master's degree in Computer and Instructional Technologies at Hacettepe University. In this master thesis, he focused on the subject of students' participation and engagement in situation-based computer-enhanced collaborative learning. He completed his doctorate education at the Department of Basic Education, Dumlupınar University in 2017. In his doctorate thesis, he worked on modeling the success of primary school teacher candidates in science and technology teaching with artificial neural networks.

İpek Altınbaşak Farina received her MBA degree from West Georgia State University in 1991 after graduating from the Department of Business Administration, Boğaziçi University. İpek Altınbaşak Farina, who worked at the management levels at Unilever Komili Holding, completed her doctorate at Boğaziçi University in 2004 and has been working as a lecturer at Bahçeşehir University since 2004. She has worked at various management levels within the university and still works as the Strategic Marketing and Brand Management Graduate Program Coordinator.

Intellectual Aspect of Academic and Educational Entrepreneurship

Gabrielle Wanzenried

1 Introduction

More than 15 years ago, Cherwitz (2005) highlighted a problem that has since become even worse: public research universities face enormous challenges in the twenty-first century, namely, waning fiscal support, a loss of public confidence, and a persistent lack of diversity. In addition, they must serve society, which is—maybe—the most compelling challenge. While these statements were made in the North American context, they are probably also valid for Europe and other regions of the world as well. The time is ripe for increased university engagement, socially relevant research and learning, and cross-disciplinary forms of inquiry that require complex social issues. The problems of our time increase the urgency of this demand.

Intellectual entrepreneurship provides one of several existing solutions to this challenge, and it is also a powerful mechanism to reposition universities as a vital and responsive part of our society. Intellectual entrepreneurship is a philosophy and vision of education, which views academics as innovators and agents of change. As is noted on the website of the University of Texas [1], the focus lies in creating cross-disciplinary and multi-institutional collaborations designed to produce intellectual advancements with a capacity to provide real solutions to the problems of our world, and the needs of our society.[1]

This chapter explains the foundations and meaning of intellectual entrepreneurship. Based upon a concept first developed by Johannisson et al. (1999),

[1] http://www.ut-ie.com/about-ie.html visited on March 30th 2022

G. Wanzenried (✉)
University of Applied Sciences and Arts Western Switzerland HES-SO, Yverdon-les-Bains, Switzerland
e-mail: gabrielle.wanzenried@heig-vd.ch

M. Aldogan Eklund, G. Wanzenried (eds.), *Academic and Educational Entrepreneurship*, Springer Texts in Business and Economics,
https://doi.org/10.1007/978-3-031-10952-2_9

R.A. Cherwitz initiated the intellectual entrepreneurship programme at the University of Texas, and this was the start of an extremely fruitful and rich experience implemented in many other institutions since.

The intellectual aspect of entrepreneurship is an important part of the holistic conceptual framework as outlined in the Introduction of this book as outlined in Fig. 1 below. The essence of intellectual entrepreneurship provides an almost ideal foundation for the work of "edupreneurs" and "academicpreneurs". With the academic world as a starting point, they confront the real problems of our world and develop concrete solutions.

The chapter is structured as follows: Section 2 lays the foundations while discussing definitions of entrepreneurship and intellectual entrepreneurship, explaining the constituents and purposes of intellectual entrepreneurship and defining the intellectual entrepreneur. Section 3 describes the intellectual entrepreneurship initiative at the University of Texas, where the concept was first employed and very successfully implemented. Section 4 discusses challenges and solutions for implementing intellectual entrepreneurship, and why successful "edupreneurs" and "academicpreneurs" are at the same time intellectual entrepreneurs, and Sect. 5 concludes.

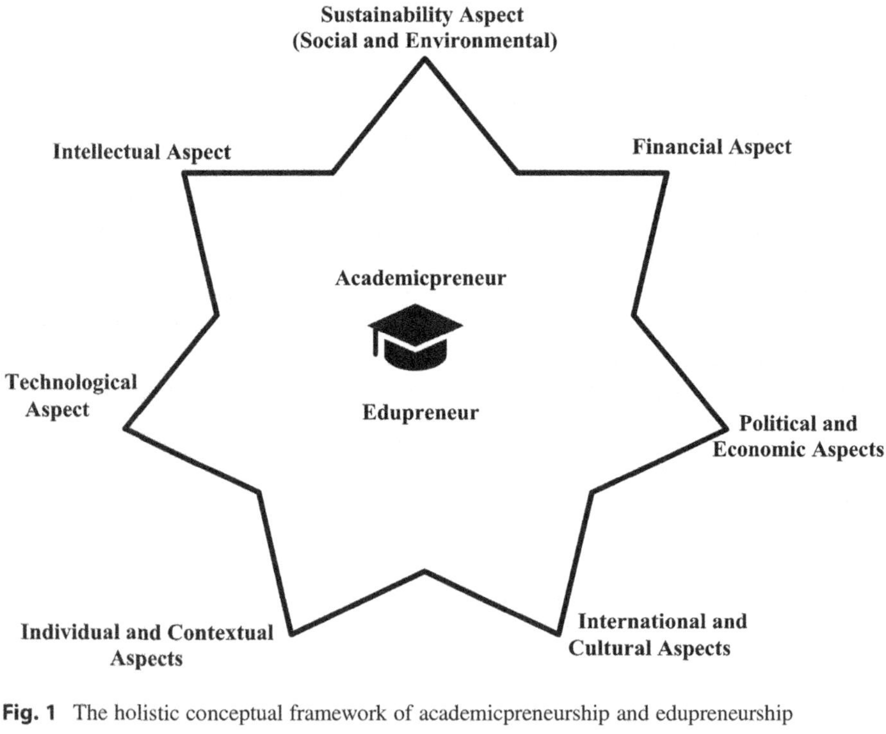

Fig. 1 The holistic conceptual framework of academicpreneurship and edupreneurship

2 Definitions, Constituents, and Purposes of Intellectual Entrepreneurship

2.1 Definitions of Entrepreneurship

Let us start with what is understood by entrepreneurship before explaining what is meant by intellectual entrepreneurship. Many definitions exist but let us focus on a few of them:

- In the spirit of Gartner et al. (1992) and Johannisson et al. (1999) perceive entrepreneurship as the emergence of (new) business activity, and they associate entrepreneurship with organising endeavours in different contexts.
- Kuratko (2006) describes the entrepreneurship outcome as strategic change management, which includes setting vision, mission, and core values, as well as implementation mechanisms. In effect, the entrepreneur pursues novel processes and methods to capitalise on opportunities by creating value (Brown & Ulijn, 2004).
- As mentioned by Abosede and Onakoya (2013), the entrepreneurial process is seen as a key aspect of the dynamism of economic crisis (renewal), during which less efficient firms fail and are replaced by more efficient ones, in a continuous process of creative destruction (Schumpeter, 1942). Entrepreneurship as a process gives people more jobs, creates new inventions and ideas, increases and/or stimulates national income, and thus can impact economic development.

2.2 The Three Constituents of Intellectual Entrepreneurship

Johannisson et al. (1999) define intellectualism, academia, and entrepreneurship as the three constituents of intellectual entrepreneurship. Figure 2, which is taken from Abosede and Onakoya (2013), who adapted the original representation, outlines how the three constituents of intellectual entrepreneurship relate to each other.

According to Stankiewicz (1994), academic entrepreneurship flourished in the 1980s as a strategy for commercialising scientific knowledge. Also, academics, science parks, and entrepreneurship are three closely related phenomena that have been frequently addressed in research (Roberts, 1991). However, according to Massey et al. (1992), the potential of academic respectively high-tech entrepreneurship is often overstated. Even though intellectualism and high formal (academic) education typically overlap, many intellectuals are mavericks.

Intellectualism involves learning, scholarship, and informed and critical thinking. The intellectual is a specific variant of the intelligent practitioner who, unlike the general trait, is strictly associated with reason and thought (Sowell, 1980). Etzioni (1968) identifies the three dimensions of an intellectual as (1) the possession of a broad and diversified knowledge base, (2) a critical mindset that considers thoroughly before acting, and (3) independence of thought. The term "intellectual entrepreneurship" represents the application of rationality and intuition within the

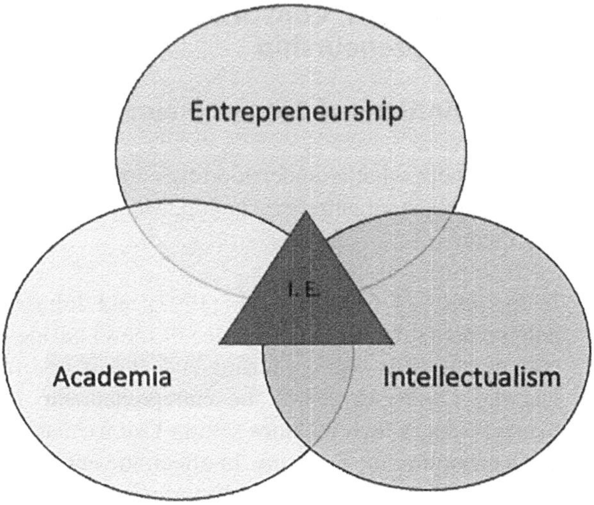

Fig. 2 The constituents of intellectual entrepreneurship. Source: Abosede and Onakoya (2013)

learning cycle and in a different context. While entrepreneurial skills represent risky experimentation and decisive action, intellectual skills involve reflection and conceptualisation in expanding the frontiers of knowledge. Intellectual entrepreneurship requires, on the one hand, collaboration with people to generate ideas and, on the other, the engagement of people with other required skills and resources in order to realise a project (Abosede & Onakoya, 2013).

The intellectual and the entrepreneur share several characteristics in their organising function. Both act independently, but work with others only in mutually beneficial relationships or enforced collaboration. Thus, the intellectual approaches challenges with analytical skills, while the entrepreneur faces challenges with agency. For both intellectuals and entrepreneurs, the constant change appears to be the normal state, as they both embody the concept of creativity (Chia, 1995).

According to Abosede and Onakoya (2013), intellectual entrepreneurship involves a willingness to seek opportunities, to accept the responsibilities that come with them, and to embrace the uncertainty that comes with initiating true innovation. Intellectual entrepreneurship is based upon the belief that intellect is not limited to science, and that entrepreneurship is not limited to, or synonymous with, business.

As Johannisson et al. (1999) outline, entrepreneurship and intellectuality are usually juxtaposed. However, in an increasingly complex context for entrepreneurial activity, there is an opportunity to mobilise the skills of intellectuals in commercial processes. They associate intellectual entrepreneurship with a particular way of pursuing an entrepreneurial career.

Intellectual entrepreneurship leverages the knowledge resources available within a university and empowers both the faculty and the students to be agents of change, both internally and externally (Cherwitz & Hartelius, 2007).

2.3 Purposes of Intellectual Entrepreneurship

Abosede and Onakoya (2013) consider the following key drivers as purposes of intellectual entrepreneurship:

1. *Sustaining entrepreneurial education*: Intellectual entrepreneurship offers an authentic philosophical foundation for sustaining cross-campus entrepreneurship education. This stands in line with Cherwitz and Darwin (2005), who consider the purpose of intellectual entrepreneurship as nurturing and educating "citizen-scholars" throughout the citadel of learning.
2. *Harnessing resources*: Intellectual entrepreneurship is based upon the body of knowledge contained within the walls of the university. As a consequence, the faculty and the students may become change agents both within and outside the university (Cherwitz & Hartelius, 2007). Recognising the rich humanistic traditions upon which the university is based, intellectual entrepreneurship harnesses the core philosophy of Western education, and transforms the paradigm of master-apprentice-entitlement into a new paradigm of invention, ownership, responsibility, collaboration, and implementation (Cherwitz & Hartelius, 2007).
3. *Shaping the business world*: Intellectual entrepreneurship influences and shapes today's world through its research findings and innovative ideas. For higher education institutions to be relevant to the world, intellectual entrepreneurship is needed in order to connect the academic mission with society.

2.4 The Intellectual Entrepreneur

It is important to realise that intellectual entrepreneurship does not exist without intellectual entrepreneurs, and the latter have specific characteristics. According to Cherwitz and Sullivan (2002), successful and resilient academic professionals are intellectual entrepreneurs. Intellectual entrepreneurs appreciate the important value of their scientific expertise and are able to create bold, but achievable, visions for its use. Intellect is not limited to academia, and entrepreneurship is not limited to business. As Cherwitz and Sullivan (2002) further outline, intellectual entrepreneurs, both inside and outside the university, are willing to take risks, seize opportunities, and mobilise all available resources in order to realise their visions; they understand the importance of collaboration and teamwork, and have the passion and skills to apply and sustain their expertise across careers in various settings.

As Abosede and Onakoya (2013) argue, intellectual entrepreneurship—as a concept—suggests the application of rationality and intuition within the learning cycle, and contextually "outside the box", that is to say, in new imaginative ways which are non-traditional. While entrepreneurial skills represent risky experimentation and decisive action, intellectual skills involve reflection and conceptualisation in expanding the boundaries of knowledge. Intellectual entrepreneurship requires, on the one hand, collaboration with people in order to generate ideas and, on the other, the engagement of people with other required skills and resources in order to realise a project. The intellectual and the entrepreneur share several characteristics in their organising functions. Not only do they act independently, but they also work with others only in mutually beneficial relationships or enforced collaboration situations. Thus, the intellectual approach challenges with analytical skills, while the entrepreneur does so with agency. For both intellectuals and entrepreneurs, constant change appears to be the normal state, as they both embody the concept of creativity (Chia, 1995).

3 The Intellectual Entrepreneurship Initiative at the University of Texas as Pioneer Concept

The intellectual entrepreneurship initiative at the University of Texas as a pioneering institution goes back to Professor Emeritus Richard Cherwitz as founder and director of the Intellectual Entrepreneurship Consortium. The Intellectual Entrepreneurship Consortium (IE) began at the University of Texas' Graduate School in 1996. In 2006, IE became part of the newly created Division of Diversity & Engagement, a vice-presidential portfolio dedicated to integrate diversity into the core mission of the university and community engagement into teaching, research, and service.[2]

As the university describes itself, the IE is an interdisciplinary initiative whose mission is to educate "citizen-scholars"—individuals who creatively use their intellectual capital as a lever for social good. Since its inception, IE programmes have enrolled approximately 10,000 undergraduate and graduate students, having the added effect of increasing diversity in higher education. Over time, the programme has been endorsed by dozens of university chancellors, presidents, and leaders in higher education.[3]

The vision behind the initiative, as summarised by Beckman and Cherwitz (2009), is as follows:

> Imagine if students could discover their lives' true passions and commitments and from the very beginning function as intellectual entrepreneurs—designing their education to pursue those paths. The Intellectual Entrepreneurship Consortium at the University of Texas at Austin has this as its objective. Sponsored by and part of the portfolio of the vice president for diversity and community engagement, the IE brings together 12 colleges and schools at the university. The mission of the consortium is to educate citizen-scholars—individuals who creatively use their intellectual capital as a lever for social good.

As the authors further outline, the IE is neither a programme nor a compartmentalised academic unit or institute. It is an intellectual platform and student-centred educational philosophy for instigating learning across disciplinary boundaries, promoting diversity in higher education, and generating collaboration

---

[2] https://diversity.utexas.edu/2016/05/16/intellectual-entrepreneurship-consortium-celebrates-20th-anniversary/

[3] http://www.ut-ie.com/articles/cherwitz-retires.pdf

between academia and society. Consortium initiatives pertain to the undergraduate experience, graduate studies, faculty research, and connections between the university and the community.

According to Beckman and Cherwitz (2009), the success of IE lies in its groundbreaking approach: (1) connecting with society, (2) putting research to work, and (3) demonstrating that education can become more responsive and accountable. They see IE as a blueprint for the intellectual entrepreneur as a new type of academic: these citizen-scholars are part of a growing body of intellectuals, whose research simultaneously contributes to academic disciplines and to society.

As McDowell (2013) outlines, in the IE process, student participants negotiate a type of contract that exposes them to graduate work using graduate student mentors, allows them to work outside their chosen area of study, or involves them in external internships, as some of the options available. Also, IE students use their knowledge and expertise to solve real problems facing the community. As an example, IE students solved the problem of overcrowded emergency rooms in hospitals by using the scholarly methodology of oral history to implement programmes for increasing diversity and promoting culturally sensitive communication in local schools.

Even though intellectual entrepreneurship was first implemented at the University of Texas, the basis of the concept was laid in 1995 by Thomas Dandridge, Bengt Johannisson, and Stefan Kwiatkowki, who developed an empirical framework for IE (Johannisson et al., 1999). While the University of Texas is clearly the pioneering institution, IE has been endorsed by other scholars of other prestigious universities, such as the Ohio State University, Stanford University (CA), the University of California, the University of Syracuse (NY), and the University of North Carolina (Cherwitz, 2012).

As Cherwitz and Sullivan (2002) outline, the success of IE derives from its four core values: (1) vision and discovery, (2) ownership and accountability, (3) integrative thinking and action, and, finally, (4) collaboration and teamwork.

First, intellectual entrepreneurs develop visions for their academic and professional work by imagining the realm of possibilities. Second, after discovering more about themselves and their expertise, intellectual entrepreneurs take responsibility for acquiring the knowledge and tools required to bring their vision to fruition. Third, intellectual entrepreneurs know the limitations of partial knowledge and working in a vacuum. For intellectual entrepreneurs, synergy is more than a buzzword; something greater than the sum of the parts is produced when people engage in integrative thinking.

Finally, people in collaborative relationships make integrative thinking and synergy possible. Intellectual entrepreneurs understand that new ideas are generated when people and networks are viewed as the primary resource.

4 Challenges and Solutions for Intellectual Entrepreneurship

According to Cherwitz and Sullivan (2002), intellectual entrepreneurship asks individuals to "think about who they are", to take ownership of their education, and to apply their visions to systems of culture and society by using new discoveries to meet individual and community needs.

As Beckman and Cherwitz (2009) argue, intellectual entrepreneurship challenges learning communities to be accountable for their discoveries. Both faculty and students earn degrees, which is a privilege often taken for granted. The motive for earning a degree is undoubtedly individual, but when the impact of education beyond the individual is considered, the core purpose of education in a social context is encountered. Intellectual entrepreneurship challenges graduates to find new applications for an advanced degree that goes beyond tenure. Students and faculty identify opportunities by exploring an environment conducive to positive change that will be beneficial because of their degree, not in spite of it. This sense of empowerment helps to create the change agents who recognise the potential of their degree, and the value and the rewards of personal accountability. As the authors further outline, while a university may be able to design a cross-campus entrepreneurship programme today, without an overarching philosophy to guide the implementation, curriculum design, and sustainability of such a programme, stagnation may occur sooner than expected. These initiatives must be able to respond to changes in leadership at all levels, uncertain funding streams, changes in popular culture, varying levels of student preparation in secondary schools, and a host of other possibilities.

Given these considerations, several hurdles must be overcome for a successful implementation of intellectual entrepreneurship. Abosede and Onakoya (2013) summarise the most important challenges and the possible solution approaches as follows:

Personality Trait Challenges There is no clear-cut profile for a successful intellectual entrepreneur. Intellectual entrepreneurs come from different genders, races, age groups, and income levels. They also differ in terms of education and experience. However, research shows that most successful entrepreneurs share certain personal characteristics, including commitment, creativity, determination, leadership, flexibility, self-confidence, passion, and intelligence (Acs, 2006). Conversely, most academics lack some of these traits. Each entrepreneur possesses these traits in varying degrees. If the entrepreneur has deficits in certain areas, someone with the necessary traits can be hired to perform the tasks. The most important strategy is to be aware of one's strengths and build on them.

Conventions Academics are guided by principles and conventions about how to teach, publish, conduct research, and behave at professional conferences. In addition, each academic field has its own set of principles and rules. The specific variants indicate what is considered valid knowledge in that field and what roles and status are assigned to its/the members. All of this can have a negative impact on facilitating intellectual entrepreneurial collaboration with other academic and entrepreneurial researchers (Clemens & Cook, 1999). Urban and rural should be able to intersect without violating academic conventions.

Change Management Institutional change requires more than good ideas and innovative programmes, but efforts made over many years. However, efforts to transform academia through entrepreneurship have met with stiff resistance. As Abosede and Onakoya (2013) outline, the humanistic ideals forming the foundation of higher education have proven difficult on the altar of economic expediency. As they further argue, this is perceived by many as detrimental to the liberal arts, even though the academic and entrepreneurial traditions share certain commonalities: namely, faculty support, visionary leadership, and the development of innovative curricula. However, many universities have also found that defining intellectual entrepreneurship in a way that fits their goals and institutional culture is critical to the successful operation and long-term promotion of entrepreneurship (Clemens & Cook, 1999).

Legal Protection of Intellectual Property Rights As Abosede and Onakoya (2013) further argue, the respect for individual property rights is very important, and the institutional legal system has to protect those rights. Without property rights, there are no incentives to create and invest. The law must protect intellectual property for intellectual entrepreneurship to flourish. Similarly, innovations have to be legally protected through copyrights, trademarks, and patents in order to encourage entrepreneurs to take the risks necessary to invest in new products and methods (The World Bank, 2006).

Creating a Business Culture Abosede and Onakoya (2013) mention further that governments should encourage the promotion of intellectual entrepreneurship, which can be achieved by making it easier for intellectuals (individuals and organisations) to learn entrepreneurial skills, and by rewarding outstanding entrepreneurial achievements.

Funding R&D and Innovations In order to fund R&D or to start a new business, intellectual entrepreneurs often face difficulty raising the necessary capital. As Abosede and Onakoya (2013) outline, there exist several funding options and sources for entrepreneurs to explore, such as venture capitalists (capitalists), microfinance, government grants, as well as foundations, in addition to financial institutions.

Strategic Collaborations According to Abosede and Onakoya (2013) many in academia are responsible for their own intellectual isolation because they do not leave their academic world and do not engage with society. Similarly, journal articles, books, and other academic materials are produced for the minority only. It would be necessary to have a broad intellectual and philosophical platform in order to have a change through entrepreneurship with strategic collaborations between academia and the business world.

Given the key characteristics of intellectual entrepreneurship, its purposes, opportunities, but also its challenges, as described above, it has become clear why the intellectual aspect is a very important, even a constituent, element for edupreneurship and academicpreneurship, respectively. As mentioned earlier, entrepreneurship and intellectuality are closely related, and mobilising the resources of intellectuals in the commercial processes represents an immense opportunity for entrepreneurs (Johannisson et al., 1999). At the same time, entrepreneurial thinking and entrepreneurial activities empower both faculty and students and allow them to become agents of change who address the real problems of the world (Cherwitz & Hartelius, 2007).

5 Conclusion

As Cherwitz and Sullivan (2002) mention, intellectual entrepreneurship is a way of thinking that goes back to our earliest Western intellectual traditions, to a time when theory and practice were united. Bringing together the demands for action and the equally unrelenting demands for reflection that characterize the new electronic and global marketplace, the term "intellectual entrepreneur" describes a new form of connection between academia and the world, and between the academy and its own deepest traditions.

Intellectual entrepreneurship is more than a specific programme or professional development tool; it is a philosophy of graduate education. It is also a philosophy for how universities should collaborate more with their communities in solving complex problems.

The University of Texas was the pioneering institution to develop the intellectual entrepreneurship initiative since 1996. The success of these efforts does not lie in any single aspect of design or in simply adopting the principles of intellectual entrepreneurship. Rather, it is the recognition that these initiatives are authentic to the mission of higher education because of their grounding in the philosophy of intellectual entrepreneurship. This return to the purpose of higher education is embraced by the participants, as they find unique applications of their education for bettering society. This realisation—coupled with considerable intellectual effort and the freedom to find new potential in the object of study—empowers students and faculty alike.

According to Beckman and Cherwitz (2009), intellectual entrepreneurship is an academic engagement with the goal of changing lives. It also expands the mission of higher education from "advancing the frontiers of knowledge" and "preparing tomorrow's leaders" to "serving as an engine of economic and social development".

Especially nowadays, in our globalised world, with the interdependence and high complexity of our current societal problems, which also require appropriate solutions, IE represents a great opportunity to address the challenges of our social, economic, and ecologic systems. It would be desirable for the IE initiative to be taken up and implemented by as many other universities around the world as possible, thus contributing to solving the problems of our time, be they small or large.

6 Summary

Intellectual entrepreneurship was created against the background that public research universities were facing the challenges of waning fiscal support, a loss of public confidence and a persistent lack of diversity, and the request from the public for them to serve society. As a consequence, there was a clear demand for an increased university engagement, socially relevant research and learning, and cross-disciplinary forms of inquiry into complex social issues. Intellectual entrepreneurship is a philosophy and a vision of education, which views academics as "innovators" and "agents of change". The focus lies in creating cross-disciplinary and multi-institutional collaboration designed to produce intellectual advancements with a capacity to provide real solutions to the problems of our world and the needs of our society. The University of Texas was the pioneering institution to develop the intellectual entrepreneurship initiative since 1996 and to employ the core values of intellectual entrepreneurship, enabling students to have greater agency in and ownership of their education. Since then, many universities all over the world have adopted this approach to learning, teaching, thinking, and interacting with the society.

Questions

Question 1. Explain the core values of intellectual entrepreneurship according to Cherwitz and Sullivan (2002) and illustrate with four concrete examples how the values, which are at the same time principles, can be implemented in a concrete way.

Question 2. Explain what is meant by "citizen-scholar" and what lies behind the emergence of this concept.

Question 3. Find specific examples of how students enrolled in intellectual emergency programmes have found meaningful solutions to real-world problems.

References

Abosede, A. J., & Onakoya, A. B. (2013). Intellectual entrepreneurship: Theories, purpose and challenges. *International Journal of Business Administration, 4*(5). https://doi.org/10.5430/ijba.v4n5p30

Acs, Z. J. (2006). How is entrepreneurship good for economic growth? *Innovations, MIT Press Journal (Winter)*, 97–107. Retrieved from http://www.mitpressjournals.org/doi/pdf/10.1162/itgg.2006.1.1.97

Beckman, G. D., & Cherwitz, R. A. (2009, July–September). Intellectual entrepreneurship: An authentic foundation for higher education reform. *Planning for Higher Education.*

Brown, T. E., & Ulijn, J. (2004). *Innovation, entrepreneurship and culture: The interaction between technology, progress and economic growth*. Edward Elgar. isbn:1-84376-346-X, 248 pp.

Cherwitz, R. A. (2005, November/December). A new social compact demands real change—Connecting the University to the Community. *Change*.

Cherwitz, R. A. (2012). Toward entrepreneurial universities for the 21st century. *Stanford Social Innovation Review*. https://doi.org/10.48558/HGMC-9M64

Cherwitz, R. A., & Darwin, T. (2005). Crisis as opportunity: An entrepreneurial approach to productivity in higher education. In J. Miller & J. Groccia (Eds.), (pp. 58–68). Anker. Retrieved from https://webspace.utexas.edu/cherwitz/www/articles/prod_univ.pdf

Cherwitz, A., & Hartelius, E. J. (2007). Making a great 'engaged' university requires rhetoric. In J. Burke (Ed.), *Fixing the fragmented public university: Decentralization with direction* (pp. 265–288). Anker.

Cherwitz, R. A., & Sullivan, C. A. (2002). Intellectual entrepreneurship A vision for graduate education. *Change: The Magazine of Higher Learning, 34*(6), 22–27. https://doi.org/10.1080/00091380209605565

Chia, R. (1995). From modern to postmodern organizational analysis. *Organization Studies, 16*(4), 579–604.

Clemens, E. S., & Cook, J. M. (1999). Politics and institutionalism: Explaining durability and change. *Annual Review of Sociology, 25*, 244–266. Available at:. https://doi.org/10.1146/annurev.soc.25.1.441

Etzioni, A. (1968). Toward a theory of guided societal change. *Social Casework, 49*(6), 335–338.

Gartner, W. B., Bird, B. J., & Starr, J. A. (1992). *Acting 'as if': Differentiating entrepreneurial from organizational behavior* (Entrepreneurship theory and practice) (pp. 13–31).

Johannisson, B., Kwiatkowski, S., & Dandridge, T. (1999). Intellectual entrepreneurship: Emerging identity in a learning perspective. In S. Kwiatkowski & L. Edvinsson (Eds.), *Knowledge Café for intellectual entrepreneurship* (pp. 29–46). Leon Kozminski Academy of Entrepreneurship and Management.

Kuratko, D. F. (2006). A tribute to 50 years of excellence in entrepreneurship and small business. *Journal of Small Business Management, 44*, 483–492.

Massey, D., Quintas, P., & Wield, D. (1992). *High-tech fantasies; Science parks in society, science and space*. Routledge. xiv + 272 pp.

McDowell, J. J. (2013). On the theoretical and empirical status of the matching law and matching theory. *Psychological Bulletin, 139*, 1000–1028.

Roberts, N. C. (1991). Towards a synergistic model of power. In J. M. Bryson & R. C. Einsweiler (Eds.), *Shared power* (pp. 103–121). University Press of America.

Schumpeter, J. A. (1942). *Capitalism, socialism, and democracy*. Harper and Brothers. pp. x, 381.

Sowell, T. (1980). *Knowledge and decisions* (422 pp). Basic Books.

Stankiewicz, R. (1994). Spin-off companies from universities. *Science and Public Policy, 21*(2), 99–107.

The World Bank. (2006). *Doing business 2007: How to reform*. A Co-publication of the World Bank and the International Finance Corporation. Retrieved from www.worldbank.org. Higlight

Further Reading

Cherwitz, R. (2005, July/August). Creating a culture of intellectual entrepreneurship. *Academe*, 5(91).

Cherwitz, R. A., Van, C. A., & Stewart, T. (2002). Intellectual entrepreneurship and outreach: Uniting expertise and passion. *Journal of Higher Education Outreach and Engagement, 7*(3), 123.

Cutcliffe, J. R. (2003). Reconsidering reflexivity: Introducing the case for intellectual entrepreneurship. *Qualitative Health Research, 13*(1), 136–148. https://doi.org/10.1177/1049732302239416

Devine, K. (2001). Developing intellectual entrepreneurship: For graduate students, communication is a basis for success. *The Scientist, 15*(5), 32.

Faulkner, L. (2005, February 13). *The changing relationship between higher education and the states*. Robert H. Atwell distinguished lecture, 87th annual meeting of the American Council on education, Washington, DC.

Griffith, V. (2003, June). *Emergency room remedies: Intellectual entrepreneurship program enables grad students to apply academic expertise to complex community problems*. University of Texas Web Feature Story.

Grund, L. (2001). UT intellectual entrepreneurship program promotes social change via 'synergy groups': Program educates students to be citizen-scholars through collaborative partnerships. *On Campus, 28*(8), 12–13.

Gabrielle Wanzenried, Dr. rer. pol., MSc Econ LSE is a professor of finance and real estate at the School of Management and Engineering (HEIG-VD) in Yverdon of the University of Applied Sciences and Arts Western Switzerland HES-SO since Sept 2019, where she is the lead of the research group Finance, Governance, and Sustainability at the Interdisciplinary Institute of Business development (IIDE). She studied at the University of Bern, the London School of Economics, and UC Berkeley. Before joining the HEIG-VD, she was a professor of corporate finance at the Institute of Financial Services Institute of the Lucerne University of Applied Sciences and Art. Her research and teaching topics are Corporate Finance, Real Estate, Entrepreneurship, and the Ageing Economy. Over the years, she has led several research projects, provided consulting services to practice partners, and written numerous publications on these topics. In addition to her academic work, Gabrielle Wanzenried is co-founder and co-chair of a housing cooperative specializing in retirement homes (www.zuhauseambielersee.ch) and president of the board of the Thiébaud-Frey Foundation (www.laprairiebellmund.ch), a cultural institution that promotes talented young musicians in the field of classical music and organizes concerts for this purpose in its own cultural centre in Bellmund near Biel, Switzerland.

Part II

Practical Insight and Cases on Academic Entrepreneurship

The Case of USN School of Business Campus Bø: A "Small" Rural Player in Applied Academic and Educational Entrepreneurship in Norway

Runar Gundersen and Birgit Leick

1 The Concept of the Study Program and the Lecturers' Commitment

Already in the first study year when the students start the program "Bachelor in Innovation and Entrepreneurship" (Innovasjon og entreprenørskap, in Norwegian) at Campus Bø, they get acquainted with a specific mode of teaching and learning. Central to the Bø model is that the students are encouraged to learn about themselves and other individuals, while studying the concepts and models in entrepreneurship and innovation management. The entire study program motivates the students to continuously self-reflect on their entrepreneurial aspirations, attitudes, and capabilities. While a major part of these entrepreneurship students will start a career in an established company or organization after having finished the program, part of the students trained in the Bø entrepreneurship education will turn into entrepreneurs. These prospective entrepreneurs will benefit from the Bø model as they will start developing their ideas and business plans early in the study program. To this aim, the curriculum of the program is structured so that the students can work with their own entrepreneurial ideas in every single course, and, in the courses, through the specific topics addressed and the way they are taught.

As an example, when the students learn about entrepreneurship in the first semester course "Entrepreneurship and Society" (Entreprenør og samfunn, in Norwegian), they understand why the knowledge about the historical background of the theories, the main interpretations of the theories in research and teaching, and their applications to real-life cases cannot be looked at in isolation. Already at this stage, the students are encouraged to share their ideas and translate them into languages that fellow students, lecturers, and external stakeholders might understand. Such key

R. Gundersen (✉) · B. Leick
USN School of Business, University of South-Eastern Norway, Bø, Norway
e-mail: Runar.Gundersen@usn.no; Birgit.Leick@usn.no

M. Aldogan Eklund, G. Wanzenried (eds.), *Academic and Educational Entrepreneurship*, Springer Texts in Business and Economics,
https://doi.org/10.1007/978-3-031-10952-2_10

learning outcomes are implemented in every single course of the program. Another example is the course "Student Enterprises" in the final (third) year of the study program: in this course, the main task for the students is to establish their own company and present it with a business plan; the students taking this assignment will work in groups and demonstrate their ability to understand the entire curriculum during the 3-year bachelor education. More importantly, the students will give proof that the learning outcomes in the curriculum can be practically used for their own start-up enterprises and that they have the ability to become an entrepreneur.

Within the study program, the university lecturers highlight the theories and research aspects because the students need to know about the 'why' and 'how' concerning the theoretical frameworks and practical tools needed. An example is *marketing knowledge and skills* which are addressed across various courses: in the traditional marketing courses, students learn about how to sell an existing product or service to customers. Within the Bø model of entrepreneurship education, by contrast, the students learn how to use the marketing theories in a different way—we like to call it "*reverse engineering*": Depending on the type of project, the students must decide in a first step which information is needed for the project, for instance, when they need to develop supplier and customer relationships for the market entry. The marketing methods and concepts will be subsequently chosen according to these needs, which are ultimately guided by the entrepreneurial idea in the background.

At the same time, the Bø model of entrepreneurship education is characterized by a strong commitment to incubate the student enterprises, which represent start-ups in the countryside and span across various industries and sectors and accompany them in their subsequent years of operation in the market. The *lecturers* act as *incubator* and, simultaneously, turn into an important *internal-external consultants to the student enterprises* over time. The start-up companies incubated that originate from the student enterprises during the study program are sustainable in the sense that the students as entrepreneurs can develop their own ideas toward gaps in the real-world markets and recognize opportunities based on these gaps that meet a demand and survive in the market with the potential for subsequent firm growth and internationalization. Numerous examples of regional companies that were originally born, incubated, and accompanied by means of a tight student–lecturer interaction in Bø demonstrate the success of the model.

2 The Individual and Contextual Aspects

Taken from the aims and goals of the study program, the students are confronted at an early stage with entrepreneurship as a potential occupational field. Even though the goal of the bachelor program is not necessarily to create entrepreneurs that start their own companies, the development of entrepreneurial skills and implementation of entrepreneurial thinking to the students are integral parts of the program, which they might use both in their own start-up companies and a work profession with established companies and public organizations.

This set-up leads to a self-selection bias. Students attending the program are a mix of "young and hopeful" idealists who want to become entrepreneurs and "young grown-up" people that have previously been working as either self-employed entrepreneurs or employees in companies and organizations. The young and hopeful students have mainly finished their high school degree in Norway and choose entrepreneurship education as their first study program. The latter students have often been working in dynamic work environments, for example, in the oil sector, health and welfare provision, and technical professions. Common to these sectors is that employees must understand the needs of fast changes regarding markets, policies, technology, and society. Within the program, the lecturers challenge the students to understand why leaders in companies from such sectors make decisions as they do. These students are moreover a mix of immigrants and national Norwegian students, which both have their specific backgrounds and preferences to choose the study program. One common ground is that they are committed to the idea that they all contribute to making changes to the economy, the policy arena, or society with their own business ideas. Taken together, many of the students taking the study program in "Innovation and Entrepreneurship" start with their own entrepreneurial ideas and work with these ideas throughout the entire program. Theories and concepts, as it seems, matter less for them than the development of their entrepreneurial ideas and skills. This is the core of the individual and contextual aspects, resulting from a positive self-selection bias.

2.1 The Technological Aspect

Students attending the program have various entrepreneurial ideas. When they attend the first courses at the beginning of their entrepreneurship studies, these ideas are simplistic—ranging from developing their own, healthy recipes for cooking to how to save the world from climatic changes. Throughout the bachelor's program, from the early start with their idea to commercialization, the students are challenged on the technological aspects that affect a startup's ability to succeed. For instance, one student had the idea to set up a new platform to highlight specific types of products from the hardware industry. While working on this topic, the student discovered major technological challenges and concluded that setting up a platform is not enough. The student also experienced a lack of appropriate marketing channels for the products he wanted to sell through the platform, which is dog food. This example illustrates how broad the range of ideas can be that students bring to the study program and how the original ideas can change during their work within the different courses and across the topics and tasks.

Therefore, the lecturers in the study program encourage the students to continuously discuss and develop the technological aspects of the ideas they are working with. Technology can either act as a barrier—for instance, digital platforms are dependent on a high number of users and need to rapidly grow in terms of traffic—or an enabler—in this case, the student would not have developed the concept of marketing for dog food without the existence of the digital platform technology.

2.2 The Intellectual Aspect

As a matter of fact, the intellectual aspect is paramount for all entrepreneurs and companies. The only valuable asset an entrepreneur possesses is the brain as the repository of all relevant knowledge. Within the program, a specific course is dedicated to the management of intellectual property by entrepreneurs. This course is connected to topics addressed in other courses, such as business development, marketing, project management, and ethics.

The intellectual aspect of the Bø model of entrepreneurship education is about encouraging innovation and creating relationships of trust between entrepreneurs and stakeholders, fostering fair play in the marketplace, and benefitting users and consumers as well as society. By supporting the creation of knowledge and the development of innovative, new, and improved products, the students are empowered to improve the quality of people's lives and provide more value to users and consumers.

The intellectual aspect is vital to the students' learning process because everything still depends on the human brain that secures frontier development with a new generation of entrepreneurs, such as those incubated in Bø. "Reverse engineering" is used as a key and overarching pedagogical approach to achieve this goal. Most importantly, the management of intellectual property rights is taught in an independent course that takes up the knowledge the students have gained from the other, more traditional, courses in entrepreneurship education programs. Because the IP theme is highlighted by including vital elements from all the other courses, the Bø model creates greater awareness among potential entrepreneurs about the importance of intellectual property rights and their management.

This is, indeed, a distinctive approach that sets the Bø model apart from other educational programs for entrepreneurs in the Nordic countries, because the course does not only shed light on legal issues in connection with intellectual property rights management but also illuminates the business-related aspects: for instance, how to use and protect intellectual property rights in connection with the business plan or during negotiations with various stakeholders. The clue here is that the course builds on tacit knowledge provided by part of the lecturers, who are entrepreneurs themselves. The students will thereby learn about cutting-edge trends and gain expert knowledge that is commonly not provided through the academic system. The experiences of established entrepreneurs are transferred to the new generation of potential entrepreneurs.

2.3 Sustainability, Social, and Environmental Aspects

All the specific courses in the study program address one or several of the United Nation's Sustainable Development Goals (SDGs). One of the goals is SDG No. 17, Partnerships for the Goals. This goal is considered in the program as a fundamental building block as it encourages cross-cultural and interdisciplinary collaborative relationships. For an entrepreneur, it is vital to know and understand other people's needs and goals to succeed. All ideas that the students bring to the study program are in one way or another founded in some basic needs, either arising from the students themselves or others. Having this in mind, the lecturers also strive to teach the students that any new ideas need to provide value for themselves and others to enable the scalability of their business idea and contribute to business, societal, and policy development.

As an example, a key global challenge is a low water quality and water contamination, which result in a lack of access to clean water for many people in the world. The World Health Organization (WHO) stated that they expect 50% of the global population to live in water-stressed areas by 2025. Surprisingly, this global problem is an issue that some of the Bø entrepreneurship students are well aware about. Within the course "Student Enterprises," a student group wanted to develop a portable water purification system. This idea challenged the students in every single aspect of their knowledge. First, as business students, they were not enrolled in technical and engineering study programs. Second, no one in their group had a technical background that could be used to develop a prototype. Having this in mind, their lack of knowledge also stressed the fact that they could not produce a sufficient requirement specification for a prototype. As a consequence, collaboration was a must for them. To produce this requirement specification, they needed to know more about how people in water-stressed areas live, and they had to learn about the major technical solutions for water purification and how to introduce this technical product to the markets.

This example demonstrates how societal and environmental needs belong to the spectrum of ideas that students develop on their own and that are taken up and developed during the entire study program.

2.4 The Financial Aspect

In the Bø model of entrepreneurship education, financial aspects are addressed repeatedly because they represent another important issue when it comes to the transformation of a rough business idea into a real-life start-up–and even a grown-up company. Entrepreneurs need to approach various financial sources and learn from other companies about how they get funded, how they have presented themselves to get successfully funded and how they managed to apply this knowledge for a successful pitch of their ideas and subsequent business growth. In the study program, the students learn how they themselves can apply knowledge from "best cases" to secure the financial side of their own start-up business.

In the academic lectures, there are traditional economic-financial courses that prepare the students for this challenge. In addition, specific topics related to funding agencies, angel investors (business angels, venture capitalists), and traditional investors are addressed in the program. Moreover, financial aspects are continuously taken up by the lecturers throughout the entire curriculum. Each course highlights specific financial-economic questions to the potential future entrepreneur to ensure that the students understand the link between financial issues and other topics that matter for entrepreneurship practice. In the end, the financial aspects are the decisive part of a start-up enterprise when entrepreneurs must dedicate most of their time convincing others that everything they are going to do concerning their idea is developed based on risk reducing facts.

2.5 The Political and Economic Aspect

The political and economic aspect refers to the formal and informal rules, norms, and laws as well as regulatory-juridical issues that future entrepreneurs will meet at the local-regional, national, and international levels. As the topics and business ideas that the students bring to their classes vary in terms of industry-specific and regulatory questions, the content of the courses is customized to fit the specific sectors that the entrepreneurship students are dealing with. For example, in the "Student Enterprises" course, students have been working with mental health issues that addressed their fellow students' challenges. In this case, both the political and economic aspects, such as regulation, are strict when it comes to the handling of personal information and confidentiality. It involves a high degree of complexity. By contrast, other students in the same course may want to start their own concept restaurant where they need to consider the local-regional and national legislation.

Within this spectrum, the economic aspect is also important because, for instance, the students opening their concept restaurant will have to apply for trainings about legislation for offering alcoholic beverages and they need to get a license to sell. In the course, the lecturers, together with the students, specify such legal-economic-political issues as much as possible to aid the students with this task. As for the financial, political, and economic aspects within the study program, the overarching goals of the lecturers are to support the students in increasing their communication skills and getting first-hand information on the planning and methods about how to address regulations and laws.

2.6 The International and Cultural Aspect

Within the course "Business Development" in the study program, cross-cultural communication, and international business policy are important aspects addressed by the lecturers. Depending on the students' own ideas, the specific topics vary greatly. This, again, links the international-cultural aspects—that is, for instance, understanding and meeting the cultural differences between European and Asian business understandings and behavior—to the intellectual and property rights aspects. These topics are closely intertwined with the technological aspects and the students' understanding of technology for their venture.

In addition, the technological side also depends on the political and economic situation. Several student enterprises have been working with solutions for the financial sector. One of the student enterprises was developing a new type of screen to prevent the insight when people entered their pin code with ATM bank machines.

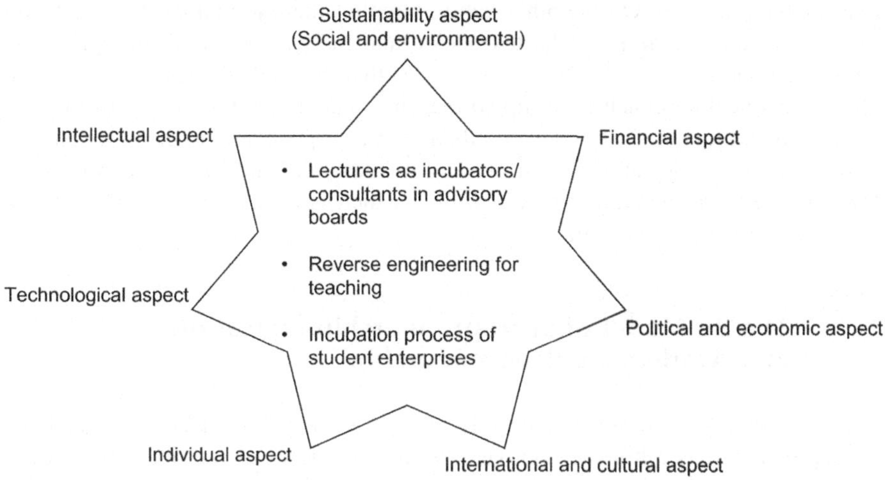

Fig. 1 Key aspects of the Bø model of entrepreneurship education. Source: Created by authors

This problem represented a threat to security within the banking sector as the existing access barriers for insight were designed with a high risk of increased card fraud due to lack of effective insight barriers with a universal design. Moreover, the solutions used was not adapted in such a way that visually impaired people could use ATMs in a way that gave them good insight and at the same time prevented access from unauthorized persons.

Since Norway is a high-cost country for product development, the students had to find a supplier delivering the prototypes from a low-cost country such as the People's Republic of China. To secure that the knowledge was not spread out, the students had to split up the production of the prototype by using three different suppliers and assembling the finished product (prototype) upon arrival in Norway. In this way, they managed to secure their own intellectual property rights during the product development phase.

Another example of a student enterprise was 360 Innovator SE (now the company Zwipe AS) that also was working on the issue of card fraud through identification challenges and solutions within the financial sector, notably with credit and debit cards. In this project, the students were depending on the knowledge of persons outside of Norway and Europe. To establish international networks that could provide such knowledge, the relevant cultural background of the countries where these persons were located and their ethics related to their cultural background were investigated in the courses. Moreover, the political-institutional system including religious-ethical norms were a relevant factor studied to bring this student enterprise to life.

Altogether, referring to the holistic framework (Fig. 1), these examples demonstrate how all courses with their content in the entire bachelor's program in Innovation and Entrepreneurship on Campus Bø are interconnected. The curriculum in the program builds on research input, on the one hand, by challenging established concepts and theories. On the other hand, it applies them to real-world cases: even though the same learning goals, textbooks, and theories are used throughout the years, the courses are customized to the cases that the students want to work with. The pedagogical approach is set up so that the students do not only learn to apply theories to textbook cases but develop their own enterprise around them. Because of this specific pedagogical approach, we call this teaching and learning approach the "*Bø model of entrepreneurship education*," which is closely intertwined with *the holistic conceptual framework*.

3 The Bø Model of Entrepreneurship Education and Academic Entrepreneurship

The Bø model of entrepreneurship education is closely associated with academic entrepreneurship as a holistic approach because it addresses the needs of students that want to start their own company during the study program, and it is also linked to the needs of society. More specifically, academic entrepreneurship according to the Bø model of entrepreneurship education is tailored to the needs of regional, national, or international businesses and ensures that both the students and the lecturers recognize the importance of firm growth beyond the start-up stage. This means that the lecturers in Bø establish *"advisory boards" for the companies born in the study program* and accompany these new companies during their first years on the market to make sure that they can develop and grow.

Through these boards, important elements and topics associated with a new company—product/service development, marketing and sales, strategy and firm growth, corporate governance, intellectual property rights and risk analysis, and business model change and development—are continuously discussed with the (former) students from an applied perspective. A specific focus is that they are supported in finding the right networks to stay viable and remain in the market. These topics are those taught in entrepreneurship education in Bø.

It is important to emphasize that the student enterprises and the start-ups evolving from them are not affiliated with a traditional, institutionalized *business incubator* run by the university lecturers, but they are rather an *incubation process* in the initial start-up period to support the students on their way to establish a viable company that survives in a market.

According to Sherman and Chappell (1998, p. 313), a business incubator is an "*economic development tool primarily designed to help create and new businesses in a community.*" Sherman and Chappell (1998, p. 313) also note that business incubators "*help emerging businesses by providing various support services, such as assistance in developing business and marketing plans, building management teams, obtaining capital, and access to a range of other more specialized professional services. They also provide flexible space, shared equipment, and administrative services.*"

Bearing this common understanding of business incubators in mind, the specific academic entrepreneurship approach applied in Bø represents a *floating, dynamic, and adaptive incubation process* rather than a fixed model. It is more *open and flexible* compared to the traditional tech-incubation organizations and institutionalized programs that exist all over Europe, including Norway. These incubator programs and organizations in Norway are typically equipped with governmental funding. However, the Bø model appeals to various small businesses across industries and sectors, for example, small handcraft and service start-ups. All newly founded student enterprises are followed up intensively and supported to be embedded in an optimal incubation environment, including important networks, after the start-up stage. By this token, the *lecturers* engaged in the entrepreneurship education become themselves *part of the incubation environment* (for instance, as investors) and accompany the businesses in their *advisory boards* formally or informally, which renders them *academic entrepreneurs* in this specific understanding.

A key characteristic of the lecturers is that they are committed to provide the newly established student enterprises with an incubation environment that matches both the needs of the companies and the regional or national economy. Therefore, the Bø model of academic entrepreneurship is not stuck in the existing models in entrepreneurship education and business development but stays *flexible* and *driven by emerging trends and formal norms* for start-ups and young companies.

Within entrepreneurial education, it is vital that the students experience firsthand that what they learn about economics or intellectual property rights is just as important as, for example, what they learn about project management, marketing, ethics, and organizational theory. Because of this, when a student enterprise is planned—as any other start-up business—the team of lecturers and students in Bø starts a process where they jointly seek to answer questions such as the following ones:

- How does the organization need to be built?
- How can prototypes be developed?
- How does the company get funds and how can it reach out to customers and markets in the best possible way with its products and services?

To answer these questions, the lecturers and students need to understand that there are strong links between all subjects taught within the field of entrepreneurship education and any other formal/informal competences the people behind the idea may possess.

Throughout the educational process, students also need to learn that *all processes must have a beginning and an end*. The first step of a process, the beginning, also applies to entrepreneurship and entrepreneurial actions. The latter step, an end, is less clear with entrepreneurship and entrepreneurial actions. As a matter of fact, if a business is to survive in a demanding and competitive market, it can never stop evolving. However, at some point, it must be possible for a start-up enterprise, such as a student enterprise, to state that the company framing is done, and the entrepreneurs then need to recognize that the business has *transitioned into the intrapreneurship phase*. When this happens is not important because entrepreneurship and intrapreneurship are largely about the same thing.

3.1 The Zwipe Case

The former student enterprise that is portrayed in this section is an example of how such incubation processes through academic entrepreneurship in the Bø model of entrepreneurship education can take place. Zwipe started as 360 Innovator SE, and it is now Zwipe AS, listed on Euronext Growth Market in Norway and Nasdaq First North Growth Market in Sweden. Kim Kristian Humborstad, the co-founder of Zwipe AS and its CEO during the first 10 years, started his bachelor studies in Innovation and Entrepreneurship in 2006 at USN School of Business in Bø (formerly called Telemark University College).

Also in the case of Zwipe: from the very beginning, the lecturers guided the incubation processes and represented an important part of the incubation environment for the student enterprise. In the following case description, the questions (*in italics*) represent the overarching guidance provided by the academic lecturers to the incubated student entrepreneurs. This guidance was in the first stage a more informal process along with the courses that the students took in the study program; during later stages of the firm growth, the guidance was coordinated by means of advisory boards in which the lecturers were active.

4 How the Initial Idea Evolved During the Study Program?

During the first semester, all students in Bø participate in the course "Entrepreneur and Society" and learn about entrepreneurship theories and practice, including a history of theories and concepts throughout the nineteenth and twentieth centuries. At the same time, the students will also have their first encounters with real-life start-up companies and their founders when they will seek to understand their challenges and compare the finding from interviews with start-up founders with academic articles and theories taught in the course.

After having attended this course, in the spring of 2007, Kim ended up in a group with Mads and Joakim in the consecutive course "Product Development." Their assignment in the course was to identify and uncover a problem or a need with an important impact on the society. Being young students, the trio agreed that there was a huge problem within restaurants and clubs with people illegally entering events at a lower age than the 18-year adult age limit. In the course, the students developed the research question: *How to prevent a 17-year-old from entering a disco with an 18-year age limit?*

The trio worked on this issue in this course and in later courses, and they developed a concept of an electronic identification card that restaurants and clubs could check against a database. The response from the businesses was positive. However, as the project was developed further, it turned out that the implementation of the idea was not easy to achieve. One question they had to answer was: *How to build and maintain such a database, and for whom should it be available?* Another tricky question raised was: *What type of technology should they use to achieve secure identification and how to integrate such technology in,* e.g., *an ID card?*

5 The Early-Stage Incubation Process as a Journey to the Final Business Idea

During their research on these questions, Kim and his fellow students received numerous indications that they were on the right track of developing "something big" with their idea. They also uncovered major issues to the privacy and data management for this type of ID handling. As the investigation and analysis of the possibilities for their idea progressed, it became clear that the most obvious needs and opportunities for a system that could provide secure identification was found in another sector than the original one.

In 2007, the estimated card fraud in Europe was totaling 200 million euros, and the prognoses for the next years indicated a significant increase. These factors and the challenges the students experienced with privacy policies and legislations for handling critical personal information within an ID card led them to shift their focus to the obvious lack of security in credit and debit cards.

The question they addressed was then: *Could it be possible to integrate a biometrical identification system directly into the payment cards where the only solution to activate a transaction was a unique fingerprint from a living person?*

With this revised business idea and concept, another question emerged: *has all the effort they had made with the ID card been wasted?* No, was the answer. Every single detail revealed in their work with the original idea was vital, as they found out. The critical elements for data handling and privacy policies helped the team to narrow down the number of possibilities about how to build a prototype. All fingerprints are unique, and they do not display any critical personal information, such as date of birth, or social security number. Another subsequent question they had to address was what type of fingerprint technology was available on the market? And *what would it take to achieve this?*

During their research, they did not find any similar solutions to their new idea for secure identification. *Could it be that no one had ever done something like this before?*

As Innovation and Entrepreneurship students with various backgrounds—Kim as a racecar driver in Europe and the USA, Mats as a supervisor at an ICA supermarket, and Joakim with 1 year as manager in a clothing store—nobody from their group had any technical background. *How could an idea like this be realized, and would the big Fintech providers have faith in three young students without any in-depth knowledge about the technology and product development?* One thing was obvious; this was the start of a long journey on bumpy roads and through wild hurricanes.

In the phase of transforming their idea to fit a new concept, the first step was to rewrite the original business idea (or business plan) and establish some new criteria that could provide them with a unique selling point. This new idea was first named Biowave.

Biowave was described as an innovative combination of wireless non-contact communication, fingerprint technology, and database management. The concept of this new type of payment card was in a draft stage, and the concept was adaptable to the planned alterations in the infrastructure of payment. The keywords for their new product idea were:

- Wireless communication—to replace the magnetic stripe or a chip.
- Fingerprint scanner—to replace the need for PIN code.
- Energy harvesting—no battery needed.
- Database management—locally storage of matching data within the card.

Based on this new set up, the trio received the following assignment from their supervisor: "Try to divide the tasks and write a first requirement specification for each of them." The question was now *what they needed to know in addition to what they have learned so far about how to manage and draft their first requirements specifications?*

6 Building the First Prototype: In a Garage

What the trio already knew at that time was that RFID (radio frequency identification) has already been in use during the 1940s in World War II to identify "friend or foe" aircraft. RFID was also a standard within contemporary wireless communication. Moreover, the team learned that it was possible to harvest energy through magnetic fields. In addition, they knew that there were several suppliers of microchips, such as Texas Instruments, that could be suitable for data handling. Furthermore, potential suppliers of fingerprint sensors were located "just around the corner." All these products were needed to create a functional model, which was built for other purposes. Because of this, it was unlikely that they would fit into a product with the size of a credit card.

Based on this challenge, their next critical question in the start-up process was: *how could a first prototype be built?* At this stage, the start-up team had arrived at a point where they realized that they had to specify what they aimed to develop—including the type of competences they needed to fill their own knowledge gap.

This was the start of an intensive network-building process, both nationally and internationally, in which the goal was to establish contacts with the best engineers in wireless communication, programmers, and data security. The question was now: *how could the trio, as inexperienced students, appear interesting and attractive to knowledgeable people who were most probably well-established actors in their respective markets and professions?*

The answer to this question was threefold. First, they had to get to know the respective industries and learn to speak their "languages" as skilled people were needed. To this aim, the trio attended fairs and conferences throughout Europe.

Second, they had to make convincing presentations without revealing possible patentable solutions. The students felt well prepared for this task based on the courses about intellectual property rights they had attended during their study program in Bø. Therefore, they used all their acquired knowledge about communication techniques. Third, they had to visualize their idea. This was solved in a way that we know from all entrepreneurs: they built a first functional dummy of a prototype—in their lectures garage.

7 Network Building and Competitions

Spending the next semester with network building and attending student enterprise competitions at regional, national, and international levels, the start-up team ended up winning the prize for Europe's most innovative product. With their first "professional" advisory board, consisting of their lecturer and professionals from their networks within the program established, it was time for the final step out in the real world. All their work during the study program they had attended in Bø had prepared the team for the next big challenge, which was about convincing financial investors, including private investors and governmental actors, such as Innovation Norway, that their business idea was future-oriented and important enough to be financially supported.

The "race" was on, now everything needed to go seamless, and it was the right time to transfer all knowledge from the study program to practice. This was all about planning, convincing, and implementation. A "golden rule" was established by the lecturers: *promise to deliver a maximum of 75% of what was achievable if half of the people involved ended up being sick—and deliver 15% more than promised.*

From this time on, Kim spent most of his time travelling around the world organizing the different teams who worked on various parts for the first product as he kept building a strong interdisciplinary network. The core activity was to cover the functions of competence building, marketing, support, product development, and innovation. Living the days like being swung in a vortex of challenges and impressions from partners, competitors, and other stakeholders, it was crucial to establish a strong intellectual property rights strategy for the whole organization to secure all possible trade secrets and build an intellectual property rights portfolio for the enterprise. Moreover, it was crucial to demonstrate that the technology worked and that it was easier to use and safer than the other solutions available on the market.

At this time, there was no big player that offered anything similar—the beginning of Zwipe happened 2 years before Apple launched their I Phone 5 with a fingerprint sensor! Therefore, the need to prove the functionality was urgent, the gap in the market was evident, and they had to seize this window of opportunity before a big international player closed this gap. The team knew that a formal cooperation with MasterCard or Visa was the safest way to a market and a proof that their product was unique and superior to other well-known solutions.

8 The Proof of Concept

The solution to demonstrate the functionality for such a "proof of concept" was in the security sector. By introducing *Biowave access card*, which enabled an individual to authenticate oneself not through something you know, but through something you are, your biological fingerprint, there was a fair chance to demonstrate that the concept worked. It provided simultaneously the highest level of security and was easy to use for both corporate customers and end users. The card itself was based on the same contactless card platform as the payment card that was under development: without PIN codes, magnetic stripes, or an external database containing sensitive personal information.

Kim then had to find out about: *who will attend this pilot and be our demanding customer with high credibility?* The answer was found where it all started, at the former university college in Bø where he took his bachelor studies. The *Biowave Access pilot* went on for about 8 months and demonstrated what had to be improved to fit the payment solution. Overall, the pilot was a success, and it was time for the next big step before a more formal cooperation with the big card suppliers could become a reality. The team was getting ready for a new trail, this time for contactless payment with identification through fingerprint.

Again, there was an open question about *which actors could serve as demanding customers and where could the new enterprise find 50–100 people that would act as end users—spending their own money using an unknown new payment solution?* Moreover, *where could the team find the banks, individuals, and shops that were willing to participate in such a demanding pilot test?*

As for the *Biowave Access pilot*, the answer was, again, found in Bø. In cooperation with a local bank, *Sparebanken Din*, the university, its student canteen, and local shops, the first contactless transaction verified by a fingerprint was introduced in 2013.

9 Cooperation with MasterCard

Three days before Apple initially launched Apple Pay, on October 17th, 2014, after successful tests with some very encouraging results, Zwipe and MasterCard launched their cooperation to bring a new payment card with NFC (Near Field Communication) and a biometric fingerprint sensor to the market. A new era for the Norwegian start-up and former student enterprise from Bø began, and the focus on further development, patents and partners continued—all that was once considered "a wild dream." After having funded the enterprise mostly by self-financing and minor private placements, the company was now ready to bring in larger investors. The first of those "big investors" was on board in October 2015, the Chinese technology giant Kuang-Chi Group which invested $5 million to a 20% stake.

The development of the technology grew tremendously, and in 2019, the former student enterprise was listed on the Euronext Growth Market on the Oslo stock exchange and further on the Nasdaq First North Growth Market, Sweden, in 2020.

10 Once an Entrepreneur, Always an Entrepreneur

After successfully having developed and established an international lead company within the biosecurity sector, Kim is still aiming at new goals. After years of intensive work, from a student start-up enterprise that turned into a listed international company, he found that the time was right to head for new adventures. As he kept investigating new opportunities and ideas that demand complex interdisciplinary knowledge, he recently revitalized the contact with his former university lecturers on Campus Bø to explore if his new ideas could be of common interest, that is, academically and commercially.

Maybe all the entrepreneurial processes will start all over again, together with new and young entrepreneurs and supported by their lecturers and supervisors from the study program? The answer lies, as always, in the future.

11 Key Facts

In 2009, two of the students from TUC that established the former Student Enterprise, 360 Innovator SE, Kim Kristian Humborstad and Joakim Egseth Solberg, founded the company, now named Zwipe AS. Their goal and focus were to develop frontier biometric authentication solutions by combining the security of biometrics with the convenience of contactless payment.

By a strong commitment to innovate across borders, Zwipe became a global workplace after a few years. As of today, May 31, 2022, Zwipe owns four subsidiaries: Zwipe America Inc., Zwipe Germany GmbH, Zwipe Singapore Ltd., and Zwipe UK Ltd.

Zwipe's listed market value on the stock exchange, Nasdaq First North Growth Market in Stockholm, on this date is 644,536,648.00 SEK (equal to US$66.4 million).

12 Summary

Entrepreneurship education is an important lever to incubate nascent student enterprises. Academic lecturers and mentors can become important elements of an incubation environment and steer the process of starting and growing a student enterprise. The Bø model of entrepreneurship education highlights that even a small player, such as a rural campus of a former university college, can represent a flexible and open incubation environment. The Zwipe case demonstrates why flexibility and openness, but also the continuous guidance through advisory boards of student enterprises are important tools for successful entrepreneurship, built from both academic and educational entrepreneurship blocks.

Questions

Question 1. In the Zwipe case, which parts of the story can be linked to the different areas within the Holistic Academic and Educational Entrepreneurship Framework?

Question 2. After reading the examples on how the students have been working related to the seven aspects in the Holistic Conceptual Framework, what (if any) common challenges do these examples have?

Question 3. Zwipe is a textbook case of a fast-growing, successful student enterprise in a high-tech sector. Which key lessons can nascent student entrepreneurs and their academic mentors and academic incubators, respectively, learn about how to grow a start-up into a successful business?

References

Sherman, H., & Chappell, D. S. (1998). Methodological challenges in evaluating business incubator outcomes. *Economic Development Quarterly, 12*(4), 313–321.

Further Reading

Beyhan, B., & Findik, D. (2018). Student and graduate entrepreneurship: Ambidextrous universities create more nascent entrepreneurs. *Journal of Technology Transfer, 43*(5), 1346–1374.

Culkin, N. (2013). Beyond being a student: An exploration of student and graduate start-ups (SGSUs) operating from university incubators. *Journal of Small Business and Enterprise Development, 20*(3), 634–649.

Morris, M. H., Shirokova, G., & Tsukanova, T. (2017). Student entrepreneurship and the university ecosystem: A multi-country empirical exploration. *European Journal of International Management, 11*(1), 65–85.

Runar Gundersen is the Program Coordinator for the bachelor's program in Innovation and Entrepreneurship at the University of South-Eastern Norway. He is specialized in and teaches Intellectual Property Rights, Business development, Entrepreneurial Project Management, and Student Enterprise. He is the founder and co-founder of more than 15 Norwegian start-ups. Runar has attended various company boards, and he is currently engaged in five start-up advisory boards. In 2015, he was awarded the prize "Entrepreneurship teacher of the year" in Norway.

Birgit Leick is a Professor in Innovation and Entrepreneurship and teaches in the bachelor's program in Innovation and Entrepreneurship at the University of South-Eastern Norway. She is specialized in, and teaches the foundational course "Entrepreneurship and Society" and "SME Structures and Dynamics." She is also an active researcher in entrepreneurship, SME and business economics, and regional development. Personal webpage: https://sites.google.com/site/birgitleick/home

Academic Entrepreneurship at the Lucerne University of Applied Sciences and Arts, Switzerland

Christian Hohmann and Patrick Link

1 Introduction

This chapter presents a case study of how Academic Entrepreneurship is implemented at the Lucerne University of Applied Sciences and Arts (LUASA). The case study examines which aspects of the framework for academic and educational entrepreneurship are most important to entrepreneurs during each stage of the start-up development process used at LUASA. It mainly analyzes and describes which needs the start-ups have in which phase of the process, to which of the seven aspects they can be assigned, and what conclusions can be drawn from this.

As a basis, this chapter introduces LUASA and its entrepreneurship program Smart-up. Second, the process underlying the program is presented, which the ten ventures considered in the case study have gone through. In the analysis of the ten qualitative interviews with one founder of each venture, the experiences of the entrepreneurs in the individual aspects of the framework are discussed in more detail. Finally, key factors for the successful coaching and support of a start-up in an academic environment will be derived based on the findings.

LUASA offers a variety of Bachelor's and Master's programs. Figure 1 shows the structure of the university and its main academic offering. As a part of its fourfold mandate, LUASA also offers applied research and services for third parties.

LUASA supports start-ups of university members in the cross-university program Smart-up. The program itself is not tied to any specific institute or school, and all organizational units of the university support it. Smart-up was established to foster entrepreneurial thinking and behavior among all university members (especially students) and within the university. The aim is to offer what is necessary to successfully find the right idea and to implement it. By linking Smart-up to all

C. Hohmann (✉) · P. Link
Lucerne University of Applied Sciences and Arts (HSLU), Lucerne, Switzerland
e-mail: christian.hohmann@hslu.ch; patrick.link@hslu.ch

M. Aldogan Eklund, G. Wanzenried (eds.), *Academic and Educational Entrepreneurship*, Springer Texts in Business and Economics,
https://doi.org/10.1007/978-3-031-10952-2_11

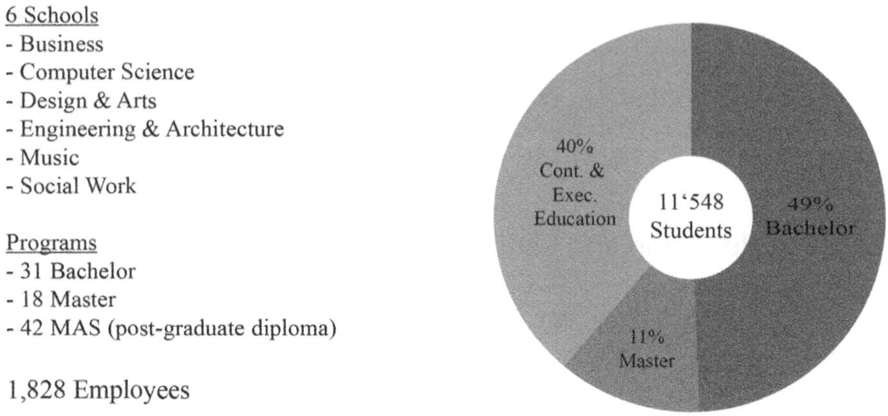

Fig. 1 Facts and Figures 2019, Lucerne University of Applied Sciences and Arts (Hochschule Luzern, 2020)

faculties of the university, the program follows a holistic approach, in which all seven aspects of the framework for academic and educational entrepreneurship can be considered if necessary. Smart-up is using the university as a network of experts. Most of the coaches who support the start-ups with their knowledge are lecturers at LUASA and are not directly involved in the start-up itself.

Smart-up is aimed at all university members, who learn about the program through various information channels. About 10% of all those interested take the first steps and follow up on their ideas. Three percent manage to successfully start a business while studying or working at the university. Over the last few years, more than 200 start-ups have been founded by students, alumni, or employees, and most have been supported by Smart-up.

2 The Four-Step Process in the Development of Start-Ups

Smart-up follows a four-step process (Fig. 2) in the development and coaching of the supported start-ups by combining Design Thinking and Lean Start-up (Link et al., 2019). The start-ups go through the four phases, whereby the questions and needs of the start-ups change.

Ideally, these phases are passed through linearly. This ideal path is shown in Fig. 2. The dotted line shows the most probable scenario: Start-ups spend a certain time in one phase iterating their idea, prototype, or solution until they reach the next goal represented by bullets one to four. For example, a researcher with an idea for a new solution enters the first phase and stays there until there is a clear picture about a potential customer and their problems. However, a step back to an earlier phase is also possible. In this case, an entrepreneur would drop back from the second phase into the first phase due to new findings about the customers and their problems. The individual phases of the process are introduced in more detail below.

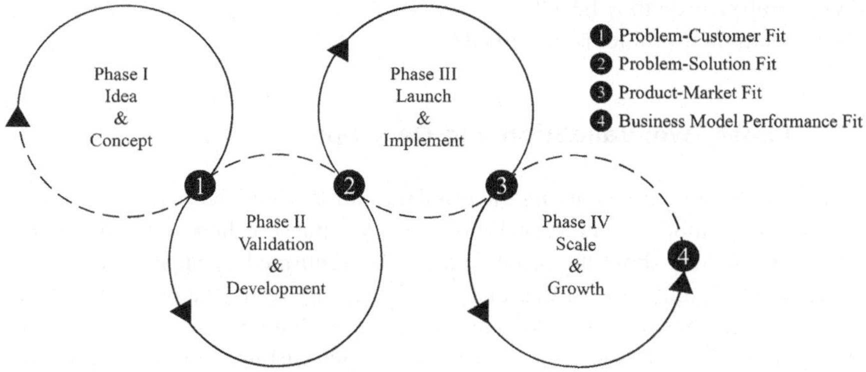

Fig. 2 The four-step process in the development of start-ups (Grossmann & Link, 2018)

2.1 Phase One: Idea and Concept

The first phase is about identifying a problem worth solving or an idea that solves a real problem. The goal of the first phase is to achieve the so-called problem-customer fit. In this phase Design Thinking is used. Design Thinking is a methodology and at the same time a way of thinking that enables the solving of complex problems and promotes the development of new ideas, focusing on the user. A first prototype simulates the solution for the customer, allowing the entrepreneur to test the user's needs extensively and to really understand the problem (Lewrick et al., 2018).

As mentioned, the key is to find a problem that is worth solving. There are basically two ways to find suitable business ideas: the hunter method and the gatherer method. With the gatherer method, people carry a small notebook for several weeks, writing down all ideas, problems, and suggestions for a business idea. From time to time, these notes are looked at, the ideas are clustered and they are combined with each other. In the hunter method, one tries to find specific search fields based on one's experiences, interests, and abilities (Link, 2016).

An important point, especially in Academic Entrepreneurship, is to ask if a university member is really an entrepreneur and ready for this journey. Starting and building up a business requires great willpower and perseverance. It is worthwhile seeking advice from experts and learning what it takes to be successful as an entrepreneur. An important point to clarify is how much one is willing to invest and lose (affordable loss), i.e., first and foremost how much time and how much financial resources (Sarasvathy, 2008).

Often, students get stuck with their first idea. Coaches then need to motivate them to find other ideas for solutions and think in variations. In this way, ideas can be found that create greater added value.

The main questions to be answered in this phase are:

- Are you an entrepreneur?
- Who are the customers?

- What problems do they have?
- How could their problems be solved?

2.2 Phase Two: Validation and Development

The second phase is about solving the problem for the client and finding an optimal solution. The goal of the second phase is to validate the so-called problem-solution-fit. The assumptions about the problem are to be confirmed by appropriate testing. Step by step the solution is further elaborated and improved. The problem-solution fit is a statement about the extent to which an offer that has been developed, or that is to be developed ("solution"), is seen by the target customer or target user as a solution to a problem that is relevant to the target group.

The development of the solution is done by designing, presenting, and testing prototypes. At first, the prototypes are very simple and have low resolution. The goal is to understand the critical elements and find the best solution for the problem. The best solution is the one that meets the customer's needs in a simple and minimal way, so that it can be sold to customers. Different tools and types of prototypes can be used, depending on the learning objectives (Lewrick et al., 2020).

The main approach in this phase is Lean Start-up. Through continuous customer feedback and hypothesis testing, conclusions are drawn as early as possible in product development. This keeps the process lean and reduces the probability of failure. Lean Startup explains or describes this process as a "build-measure-learn cycle" (Ries, 2017). Eric Ries, one of the founders of the Lean Startup methodology, formulates the approach toward problem-solution-fit as follows (Ries, 2017):

- Does the customer's problem really exist?
- Does the planned solution solve the problem better than existing alternatives?
- Does the solution deliver real change?

The problem-solution-fit test is not (yet) about testing a concrete product—it is too early for that. Initially, it only aims to find out whether the type of solution seems attractive to the target group or not. The early low-resolution prototypes used in this stage can also be called pretotypes. The term pretotyping is made up of the words "pretend" and "prototyping." It is a method of testing new product ideas quickly and cheaply (Savoia, 2011). Pretotyping starts before prototyping. The later prototyping is much more time-consuming and cost intensive. When the prototypes become more functional, they are eventually called "minimal viable products" (MVP) in Lean Start-up language.

In order to determine the problem-solution-fit and describe the business model the Lean Canvas is used. The Lean Canvas is an iterative process that is used to evaluate the assumptions behind the value proposition and business model (Maurya, 2012).

The main questions to be answered in this phase are:

- What added value is offered to the customers?
- How will this solution earn money?
- Who is in the team?
- How to build the solution?

2.3 Phase Three: Launch and Implement

The third phase is about implementing the project and introducing the product/service to the market. The result of this phase is the product-market fit. The product-market fit is the central milestone in the life of a start-up. It marks the end of the learning phase in which the founders strive to understand their future customers and develop the first marketable version of their product. It means that the product is developed to such an extent that the market finds it attractive and the venture prepares for the next phase of scaling.

To achieve this, the start-up must continue to work on the product, customer, and business levels. At the product level, the product (or service) must be developed, either by converting the MVP into a marketable product or by developing the product from scratch with clear requirements derived from the MVP. Developing an MVP can be done in a linear way, e.g., the waterfall model based on a requirements specification, or in an iterative and agile way, e.g., with Scrum, based on a product backlog.

On the business side, the company must be completely set up. The build-up of long-term resources, especially headcount, should be done carefully. "Make, buy or partner" decisions and eventual partnerships should be well examined.

Building up the business level includes:

- Building the team and defining roles and competences.
- Building up a partner network, e.g., in the area of supply chain or sales and distribution.
- Protecting intellectual property (IP).
- Establishing a risk compass to keep track of the risks (including those that endanger liquidity).
- Defining the most important internal processes to ensure quality.
- Selecting the most appropriate business model.

Selecting the most appropriate business model includes defining the architecture of the value creation. Business analogies can help. According to Gassmann, 90% of new business models are a recombination of existing business models (Gassmann et al., 2014).

On the customer side, the customers need to be ready to accept the new product or service, the market entry needs to be planned, and the sales funnel needs to be built. Co-creation is an important part of the implementation phase. The third phase shows whether customers really buy into the offer. Consequently, success at this stage means that the products and services create added value for the customer and gain a foothold in the market. Through the acquisition of new customers and responding to their feedback, it becomes clear how well the marketing concept works and where the solution may still need to be improved.

The main questions to be answered in this phase are:

- How to promote the product/service?
- How to get the first paying customers?
- What legal form to choose?
- What type of business to choose?

2.4 Phase Four: Scale and Growth

The fourth phase shows whether the business model works and whether the financial goals (sales, growth, and profit) can be achieved. The business model and the value proposition are constantly optimized and adapted to the different needs of the (new) target groups in order to successfully continue growth.

The result of this phase is the business model-performance-fit. It proves that the business is performing as expected. In case of any deviations between the previously assumed performance and the real results, counter actions are implemented, and/or the growth engine and scaling are enabled.

In this phase, the growth strategy is developed. Ideally, the growth loop also promotes the hook model (NoGood, 2019). New customers are found in the growth loop. They engage with the output and decide to try the product. Then users complete the desired actions which trigger the hook model and the output. The output is the external creation that is seen outside the ecosystem of the current user base. This fosters new users. The action in the hook model fosters the reward of satisfied user needs. The interest of the user encourages product engagement. This allows the investment and anticipation of future rewards and triggers internal and external cues that prompt the user to take action. The hook model acts as a complement to the steps of the core engagement loop (Lewrick, 2021).

Continuously scaling and growing the business requires more financial resources than the first three phases. Depending on the degree of innovation of the idea and the stage of the company, there are various ways to raise capital. In addition to the classic financing options such as "family, friends, and fools" or through a partnership with a "business angel," there are also numerous funding awards, foundations, and venture capital (VC) companies, which provide start-ups with the necessary financial resources at an early stage.

The main questions to be answered in this phase are:

- How to raise capital?
- What contracts and patents are needed?
- How to grow the company?

3 Cases from the Lucerne University of Applied Sciences and Arts

For this case study, ten cases have been analyzed from more than 200 cases supported by the Smart-up program at the Lucerne University of Applied Sciences and Arts. The selected start-ups are all related to one or more of LUASA's Schools of Business, Computer Science, Engineering, and Architecture. Table 1 shows a list of the companies analyzed for the case study.

At the time of setting up their companies, half of the founders were students, and the other half were academic staff. Most of the companies are product-based businesses, only one of the ventures is exclusively active in service business. The offerings of four companies are focused toward the B2C market, while the other six operate almost exclusively in the B2B market. The start-ups operate in six different business sectors. The company size varies from 3 to 40 employees at the time of the survey. The companies are all in the two final phases of the four-step process described above. Consequently, all the company founders were able to give an insight into their work during the four different phases, according to the seven aspects of the framework.

As part of the analysis, the founders, or co-founders of the ten start-ups were asked about the seven different aspects of the framework, their motivation and intentions, the biggest obstacles, and the most important success factors on their journey so far. Qualitative interviews with a semi-structured questionnaire were conducted to analyze the companies. Figure 3 shows a graphical representation summarizing the results for each aspect. The four sub-circle segments correspond to the four phases of the process. The color of each segment represents the importance of the aspect in the respective phase. A respective graphical summary closes each individual section in the following chapter.

Table 1 List of the analyzed companies (created by authors)

Company name	Phases reviewed	Business sector
Awaptec GmbH	1,2,3,4	Building technology
Chipeno GmbH	1,2,3,4	Food
ConceptIris GmbH	1,2,3	Home furniture and houseware
Cowa Thermal Solutions AG	1,2,3	Building technology
Flimatec AG	1,2,3,4	Energy
SCALORIC GmbH	1,2,3,4	Home furniture and houseware
Anonymous	1,2,3	Digital Health
Swisens AG	1,2,3	Precision mechanics and optics
Thingdust AG	1,2,3,4	Building technology
Yamo AG	1,2,3,4	Food

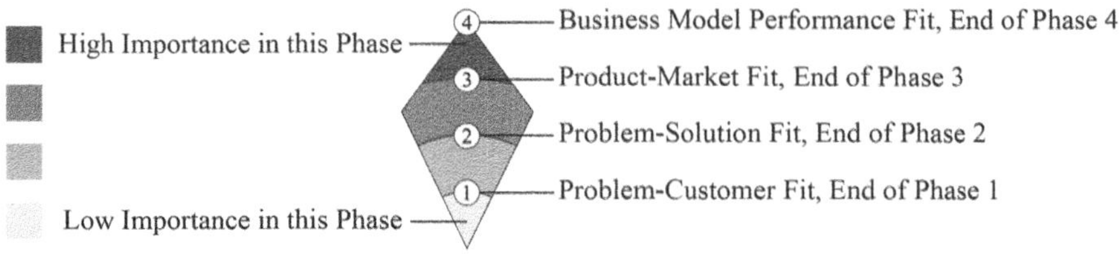

Fig. 3 Graphical representation of the results for each aspect (created by authors)

Fig. 4 Summary individual aspect (created by authors)

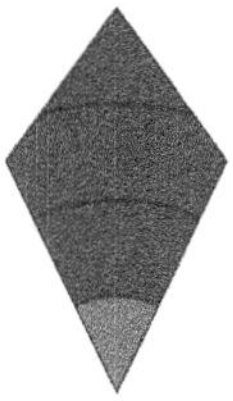

3.1 Individual and Contextual Aspects

Individuals have been shown to take greater responsibility for decisions and their outcomes when they gain control over their own destiny (Cherwitz & Sullivan, 2002). The founders participating in the case study strive for self-employment in order to pursue their own interests as well as live and work in a self-determined manner. They follow a vision that they develop by noticing problems in their environment and the opportunities that are apparent to them. To this extent, they prioritize the achievement of their vision over short-term financial success, which is easier to achieve in the context of employment. Some of the founders also indicated that they were inspired to pursue their own business idea early in their life by family role models.

Smart-up is an entrepreneurship program that, like similar programs at other universities, aims to positively influence the entrepreneurial motivations and attitudes of students and academic staff. This positive influence in general has already been confirmed by research. It appears that students gain a more realistic perspective on the lifestyle and skills they need for a successful career as an entrepreneur through such programs (Hayter et al., 2017). Some of the founders, who have already established their start-ups as students, said that they intentionally chose a study program in which the relevant entrepreneurial skills are taught, and in which it is possible to integrate their own first experiences with their venture into their lessons.

Individual aspects play a central role in most of these start-ups from the very first steps of the process (Fig. 4). As soon as the founders realize that the idea they have found has relevance for potential customers, they see their vision confirmed and pursue it.

3.2 Financial Aspect

Whichever stage of development their business is at, the most tangible resource for any entrepreneur is money. Going further, the capital market open to for-profit organizations differs significantly from the one for nonprofit organizations (Smith & Peterson, 2006). Among the founders supported by Smart-up, two different groups can be identified in terms of their financing strategy. One group focuses on deliberate slow organic growth, while the other relies on external financing for various reasons. Those companies that are prepared and willing to integrate external investors into their projects gain greater and faster access to the market.

Depending on the technological complexity of its solution, a start-up may need to acquire substantial financial resources at a very early stage to prove the technological feasibility of its project in the first place. The university itself can greatly reduce the financial needs of the companies in the first two phases by providing non-financial resources (such as laboratory facilities, premises, etc.). In this case, the entrepreneurs mainly contribute their time, which is necessary to implement their ideas.

LUASA cannot support the start-ups financially. However, if the founders are academic employees of the university, they can remain employed at the university with a reduced workload through flexible employment conditions. This gives the entrepreneurs financial security in the early stages of their ventures. By cooperating with the university at an early stage, it is also possible for the start-ups to attract additional funding from private and public funding institutions. This funding supports the start-ups in determining feasibility up to the development of a first functioning prototype or MVP.

In phases three and four of the process, the need for financial resources increases very sharply (Fig. 5), especially for product-based business models. Figure 5 will look different for ventures whose focus is on the development or exploitation of a new technology. In this case, financial aspects will have a significantly higher importance.

3.3 Technological Aspect

Promoting the exchange of knowledge, skills, and technology with business and society is part of LUASA's mission (Konkordatsrat der Fachhochschule Zentralschweiz, 2011). The importance of technology transfer activities in publicly funded universities has increased more and more in recent years (Wood, 2011).

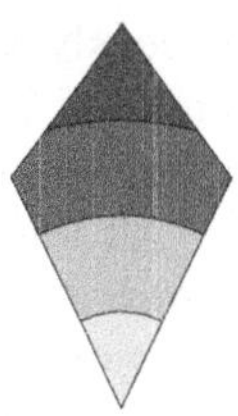

Fig. 5 Summary financial aspect (created by authors)

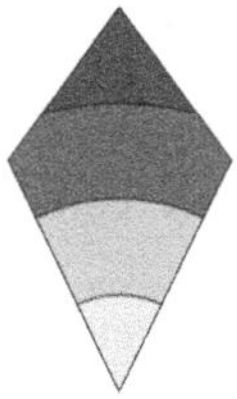

Fig. 6 Summary technological aspect (created by authors)

One form of technology transfer out of universities leads to the establishment of new ventures. Those founders who work as scientific employees in a research center at the time they establish their start-ups make partial use of the knowledge about the technologies under development. This is not the direct exploitation of new technologies, but rather the adaptation of the new knowledge into a related technological field. The scientific employees interviewed use the LUASA network and the exchange among all scientific staff to find like-minded people for their projects. At the same time, the technological expert knowledge of all employees at the university is available to the founding teams, so that gaps in technological know-how can be filled quickly.

Technology itself plays a very different role in the development of the start-ups surveyed. Half of the companies analyzed use the current possibilities of digitization for their value proposition, by solving problems they have observed in their personal and professional environment with the help of state-of-the-art technologies such as artificial intelligence and the Internet of Things. The motivation for these founders comes exclusively from a longer personal experience with the problem. This experience is a success factor for these companies.

For the interviewed entrepreneurs, on average the latest technologies only play a role in the later phases from market entry or in later growth, as Fig. 6 shows. For those companies whose business model is based on the exploitation of current technologies, continuous monitoring, or further development of the technologies relevant to them from the first phase of the four-step process is of central importance. In this case Fig. 6 would show higher importance in the first two phases. They strive for a technological leadership role in their business field. Mastering the technology at an early stage is a success factor here.

3.4 Sustainability Aspect

All the founders in the case study take environmental and social sustainability very seriously. However, these aspects only play a central role for those companies whose business model is particularly affected by them. These companies show in their entire communication how important these values are to them.

All founders strive to achieve sustainable financial success with their ventures, which assures them financial independence. In this respect, the sustainable development of the company takes precedence over personal financial success.

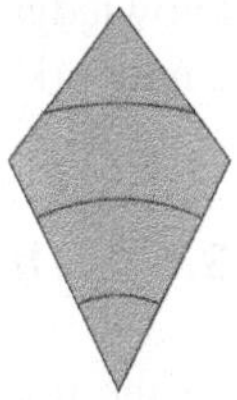

Fig. 7 Summary sustainability aspect (created by authors)

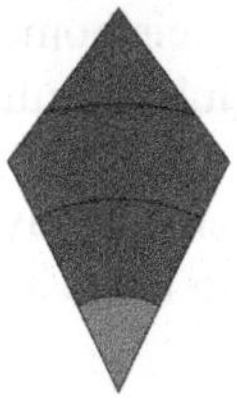

Fig. 8 Summary intellectual aspect (created by authors)

It can be seen that sustainability is important to all of the entrepreneurs from the beginning of the first phase (Fig. 7), even if some of them are only able to implement these aspects in their business model in later phases of their development.

3.5 Intellectual Aspect

One of the claims of Intellectual Entrepreneurship is to train individuals who are responsible for their own education and use their intellectual assets to contribute to disciplinary knowledge (Cherwitz, 2005). All entrepreneurs interviewed take this responsibility for themselves and their businesses. Therefore, intellectual aspects play a central and important role in all the companies analyzed, albeit at different phases in the four-step development process.

The entrepreneurs who started their venture during their studies emphasize how well they were able to connect and consolidate the content and skills taught during their studies with the experience gained during the start-up phase of their company. They benefit from exchanges with the lecturers, who also provide them with customized support on specific issues during the development of their business idea.

All interviewees see a great intellectual enrichment in their business. Through their entrepreneurial activity, they are inevitably forced to deal with new areas of knowledge again and again. The relevant areas of knowledge change with the development phases of the four-stage process. Particularly in the case of technology-driven business models, the focus in the first phases is on ensuring technological feasibility and minimizing technological risks. Business knowledge around team building and organizational development plays a stronger role in the last two phases (Fig. 8).

The decisive success factors for the intellectual development of entrepreneurs are straightforward access to the relevant knowledge carriers and the associated knowledge transfer to the entrepreneur. It is crucial that entrepreneurs have access to a network of experts.

3.6 International and Cultural Aspects

At the time of the survey, international and cultural aspects played a rather minor role among the participating founders. Most of the start-ups market their products in their home market or in the German-speaking region of Europe, which has only minor cultural differences. Only one company exhibits real cultural differences within the team structure. The differences resulting from the different perspectives are perceived as enriching. All companies surveyed assign the international aspects to the last two of the four phases (Fig. 9).

3.7 Political and Economic Aspects

The political and economic aspects are assessed very differently by the companies in the case study. About half of the companies base parts of their business model and thus their existence on political and economic efforts and trends. For these companies, these aspects are relevant within the first phases of the four-stage process. For the other companies, political and economic factors only play a role at a much later stage (Fig. 10). One of the biggest obstacles in this context is seen in the current rules for exporting goods from Switzerland to the European Union.

All the interviewed founders are aware of the potential public support programs. However, these are not perceived in the same way by all. Here too, a different strategic orientation of the companies can be identified.

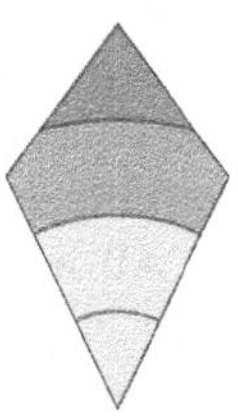

Fig. 9 Summary international and cultural aspect (created by authors)

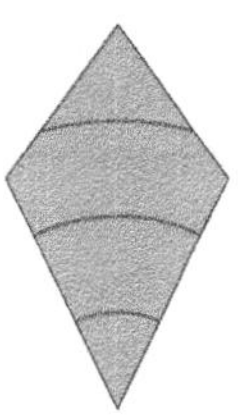

Fig. 10 Summary political and economic aspect (created by authors)

4 Conclusion

From the interviews with the founders, it is evident that the seven aspects of the framework must be weighted differently for the companies depending on their business model. The same applies to the importance of the aspects in the phases of the four-step process, which depends strongly on the start-up's intended value proposition. Figure 11 shows the importance of the various aspects of the framework in each phase of development for the start-ups analyzed here. The phases are shown in the diagram from the inside to the outside. For ventures whose focus is on the development or exploitation of a new technology, the importance of technological and financial aspects is significantly greater in the first two phases.

Figure 11 also shows that the importance of the individual aspects changes significantly throughout the phases. In the beginning, individual, intellectual, sustainable, and political aspects dominate. In the end, technological and financial aspects play a greater role, while the importance of sustainable and political aspects decreases in proportion.

Recommendations for the coaching of the individual start-ups can be derived from the examination of the ten ventures by comparing the statements on the seven aspects of the framework with the four-step process.

In phase one "Idea & Concept," the coaching should focus on individual aspects, such as the readiness for entrepreneurship, and intellectual aspects, such as the know-how required to solve the problem. Depending on the business model, the consideration of sustainable, political, and economic aspects plays an important role in this phase as well.

In phase two "Validation & Development," the same aspects play a central role. However, the challenges change. It must be clarified which intellectual property rights already exist, what the competition in the target market looks like and how a sustainable business model can be created. The knowledge and awareness required for these topics must be built up among the entrepreneurs.

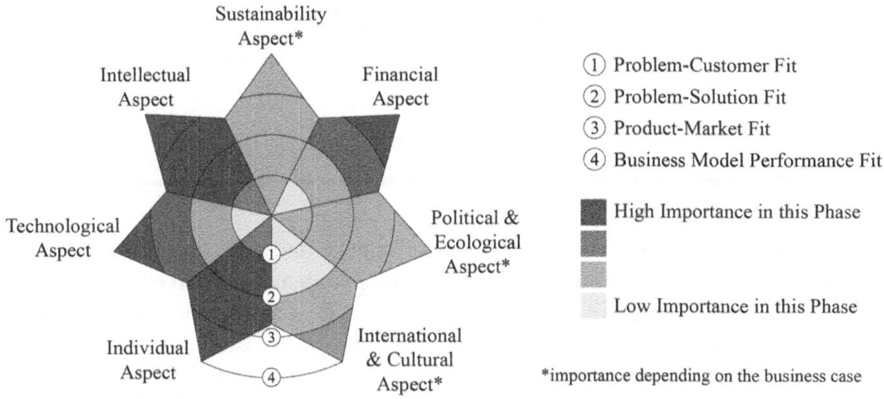

Fig. 11 Importance of the different aspects over the four phases (created by authors)

In phase three "Launch & Implement," technological and financial aspects are crucial in all business models. Market entry means a high technological challenge with a change in its focus: the attention is now on manufacturability and no longer just on feasibility. This requires initial financing, which must be secured. These aspects must be considered in successful coaching.

For coaching in phase four "Scale & Growth," all seven aspects of the framework are relevant, depending on the business model. The growth of this phase results in questions in subject areas that arise from the establishment and continuous improvement of business processes.

Overall, the importance of financial aspects increases from phase to phase. In ventures where the feasibility of a complex technical system must be clarified first, financial aspects are already highly relevant in the first two phases. The success factor in this area is knowing which financing options are available to start-ups in which phase, and how these can be tapped for the company.

Similar patterns can be observed for the technological aspects. In start-ups whose focus is on establishing a new technology in the market, technological aspects play a central role from the very first phase. For all other start-ups, the technological aspects increase from phase to phase and play a central role from the time of market entry in phase three. The success factor is mastery of the technologies required for creation. If the start-up does not have its own know-how in this area, it is crucial to gain access to the relevant knowledge as quickly as possible.

Individual and intellectual aspects play a central role from the first phase. One success factor is the individual involvement and identification of the founding team with the problem to be solved. The ambition to solve a self-experienced problem is often the central motivator for the founders. The founders' intellectual gain depends strongly on access to the relevant knowledge. All founders can acquire knowledge independently. This process is supported when they are connected to the relevant knowledge holders.

The results of the survey show that the key success factor for any start-up is easy access to a network of experts, customers, suppliers, and financing partners who can help them quickly clarify the current issues at each stage of development. The Smart-up program of the Lucerne University of Applied Sciences and Arts makes the knowledge of all university members available to the founders as a network of experts.

5 Summary

In 2012, the Lucerne University of Applied Science and Arts (LUASA or HSLU) started a project to foster entrepreneurship among students and university members. Today, the Smart-up project has been transformed into a university-wide program to inspire all university members to set up their own businesses, and to support the entrepreneurs and ventures along their journey. Smart-up has developed an iterative four-step coaching and support process for the development of start-ups. The case study presented in this chapter has analyzed ten different cases supported by the program. The analysis focuses on the specific needs of the different start-ups according to the seven aspects of the framework for academic and educational entrepreneurship in each phase of the process.

The case study shows that the individual and intellectual aspects are most important for the entrepreneurs in the first phases of the process. Financial and technological aspects are relevant at the beginning only for those ventures whose goal is to establish new technologies in the market. In general, the importance of these two aspects increases in the later phases and they dominate all other aspects in the end. The other three aspects of the framework, i.e., sustainability, international, and cultural aspects, as well as political and economic aspects, vary in importance for the analyzed companies and depend very much on the company's specific business model. Sustainable as well as political and economic aspects are equally relevant throughout the four phases, while international and cultural aspects gain in importance in the later phases.

Smart-up's coaching and support for entrepreneurs is tailored based on these findings. For example, topics such as access to the necessary technical knowledge and commitment to entrepreneurship must be clearly addressed at the beginning and discussed with anyone considering creating a business.

Questions

Question 1. What are the key phases in the development of a start-up? What are the deliverables of each of those phases?

Question 2. The financial aspect gets more and more important. Explain the changing focus over the four phases.

Question 3. Individual and intellectual aspects play a central role from the first phase. Explain why.

References

Cherwitz, R. A. (2005). Diversifying graduate education: The promise of intellectual entrepreneurship. *Journal of Hispanic Higher Education, 4*(1), 19–33. https://doi.org/10.1177/1538192704270901

Cherwitz, R. A., & Sullivan, C. A. (2002). Intellectual entrepreneurship a vision for graduate education. *Change: The Magazine of Higher Learning, 34*(6), 22–27. https://doi.org/10.1080/00091380209605565

Gassmann, O., Frankenberger, K., Choudury, M., & Haefner, N. (2014). *The business model navigator: 55 models that will revolutionise your business*. Pearson.

Grossmann, L., & Link, P. (2018). *Zentralschweizer start-up map*. Retrieved February 24, 2021, from https://www.startup-map.com/

Hayter, C. S., Lubynsky, R., & Maroulis, S. (2017). Who is the academic entrepreneur? The role of graduate students in the development of university spinoffs. *The Journal of Technology Transfer, 42*(6), 1237–1254. https://doi.org/10.1007/s10961-016-9470-y

Hochschule Luzern. (2020). In Hochschule Luzern (Ed.), *Hochschule Luzern, facts and figures 2019*. Hochschule Luzern. https://www.hslu.ch/en/lucerne-university-of-applied-sciences-and-arts/about-us/portrait/facts-and-figures-2019/

Konkordatsrat der Fachhochschule Zentralschweiz. (2011). Zentralschweizer Fachhochschul-Vereinbarung. In Konkordatsrat der Fachhochschule Zentralschweiz (Ed.), *520* (Vol. 5). Rechtssammlung Kanton Luzern: Kanton Luzern.

Lewrick, M. (2021). *Business Ökosystem design*. Franz Vahlen Verlag AG.

Lewrick, M., Leifer, L., & Link, P. (2020). *The design thinking toolbox: A guide to mastering the most popular and valuable innovation methods*. Wiley.

Lewrick, M., Link, P., & Leifer, L. J. (2018). *The design thinking playbook: Mindful digital transformation of teams, products, services, businesses and ecosystems*. Wiley.

Link, P. (2016). How to become a lean entrepreneur by applying lean start-up and lean canvas? In *Innovation and entrepreneurship in education* (Advances in digital education and lifelong learning) (Vol. 2, pp. 57–71). Emerald Group.

Link, P., Fontana, V., & Zeier, R. (2019). Smart-up: How to foster entrepreneurial thinking and acting at a university. In D. Remenyi (Ed.), *5th teaching innovation and entrepreneurship excellence awards 2019 at ECIE19*. ACPIL.

Maurya, A. (2012). *Running lean: Iterate from plan A to a plan that works* (The lean series) (2nd ed.). O'Reilly.

NoGood. (2019). *Acquisition loops: How the world's best brands build & sustain growth*. Retrieved March 3, 2021, from https://nogood.io/2019/10/01/growth-acquisition-loops-funnel/

Ries, E. (2017). *The lean startup: How today's entrepreneurs use continuous innovation to create radically successful businesses* (Currency International ed., First International edition ed.). Currency.

Sarasvathy, S. D. (2008). *Effectuation: Elements of entrepreneurial expertise*. Edward Elgar Publishing.

Savoia, A. (2011). *Pretotype it*. Retrieved October 12, 2017, from http://www.pretotyping.org/uploads/1/4/0/9/14099067/pretotype_it_2nd_pretotype_edition-2.pdf

Smith, K., & Peterson, J. L. (2006). What is educational entrepreneurship? In F. M. Hess (Ed.), *Educational entrepreneurship: Realities, challenges, possibilities*. Harvard Education Press.

Wood, M. S. (2011). A process model of academic entrepreneurship. *Business Horizons, 54*(2), 153–161. https://doi.org/10.1016/j.bushor.2010.11.004

Christian Hohmann is the co-head of the Smart-up program and lecturer for product innovation and design thinking at Lucerne University Applied Sciences and Arts where he also heads four continuous education programs at the nexus of engineering and business. He is co-author of the book "The Design Thinking Toolbox." At LUASA, he built up an International Study week on Design Thinking in cooperation with Larry Leifer, Stanford University, and the continuous education programs "CAS Innovation & Technology Management" and "CAS Industrial Transformation & Project Management." He has a background in precision engineering and business administration and worked in and for different enterprises in various industry sectors.

Patrick Link is a professor of product innovation at the Lucerne University of Applied Sciences and Arts School of Engineering and Architecture. He studied Mechanical Engineering and got his doctorate in the field of innovation management at ETH Zurich. After that, he worked for Siemens in various positions. He is co-editor of the books "The Design Thinking Playbook" and the "The Design Thinking Toolbox." At the LUASA, he built up the start-up support initiative "Smart-up" and the advanced education program "CAS Design Thinking" and designed the "CAS Agile Product Engineering." His research and teaching interest are in the field of agile product management, Design Thinking and entrepreneurship/Lean Start-up, and the combination of these approaches.

In Praise of Acapreneurship: Aspiring for the Best of Both Worlds by Spanning the Boundaries of Academia and Entrepreneurship

Michael Hilb

1 Introduction

The opportunity to reflect on your own activities, behaviors, and motivations does not occur often. An entrepreneur strives to understand the needs of customers. An academic focuses on observing the behavior of research subjects and linking it to theory. The task for this article is different: I am asked to reflect on my behavior as a person who, among other things, considers himself both an academic and an entrepreneur.

As with any role that someone takes on, it is important to distinguish between thinking and acting. While the former is shaped by a mindset, the latter forms a community of like-minded people, i.e., a sphere. What does this mean for the roles of academic and the entrepreneur?

2 Being an Academic and an Entrepreneur

2.1 Thinking and Acting Like an Academic

The guiding principle of an academic is the search for truth, even though everyone knows that the truth does not exist. As such, academics are open to debate and have the ability and interest to engage in discourse on any matter, weighing all arguments for and against a thesis. In the absence of a scientific method, academics apply the same dialectical approach to define how they arrive at a conclusion. Overall, the mindset is tailored to answering the question "Why?".

M. Hilb (✉)
University of Fribourg, Fribourg, Switzerland
e-mail: michael.hilb@unifr.ch

M. Aldogan Eklund, G. Wanzenried (eds.), *Academic and Educational Entrepreneurship*, Springer Texts in Business and Economics,
https://doi.org/10.1007/978-3-031-10952-2_12

The institutionalized framework of academics is academia, the world of universities and other research institutions dedicated to advancing knowledge through discovery and teaching. As with entrepreneurial ecosystems, the academic ecosystem consists of those who provide funding, whether government or private institutions, and those who use the money. While some of the knowledge consumers are also driven by markets, such as students or the public seeking advice from experts, the other part of consumption is purely non-market. The institutional environment is designed to avoid any market acceptance, such as the peer review system for evaluating studies, or the tenure system that grants academics lifetime tenure without market scrutiny in the interest of academic freedom. While there is competition within the system, i.e., who gets published and who gets tenure, the ecosystem is insulated from outside influences and is often self-governing to exclude outside forces such as market competition.

2.2 Thinking and Acting Like an Entrepreneur

The entrepreneur is a well-researched species. Hundreds of studies have been conducted to conceptualize *homo entrepreneurius*. From all these studies, certain characteristics crystallize. In addition to curiosity and drive, entrepreneurs should master the art and science of identifying and seizing opportunities without being opportunistic. To achieve this, entrepreneurs challenge conventions and anticipate trends that others do not yet see and are guided by the question "Why not?".

The entrepreneurial sphere, i.e., the institutionalized community in which entrepreneurs operate, can be described as an ecosystem in which new institutions are created, whether in the form of a business, a social movement, or a political party. In all cases, entrepreneurs succeed in gaining a following and creating either wealth, an ideology, or power. To achieve this, entrepreneurs are embedded in an ecosystem consisting of the providers of capital, talent, and services, alliance partners, and those who consume the outcome of entrepreneurial activities. The ecosystem partners are often well-developed institutions, such as venture capital or fundraising organizations, which stand on their own. As a result, competition is fierce in this ecosystem, promoting those that add value and crushing the others that do not.

3 Combining the Worlds of Academia and Entrepreneurship

How can we best leverage insights from the entrepreneurial and academic worlds? We will explore different approaches to connecting the two worlds by considering the academic who applies an entrepreneurial mindset, the entrepreneur who thinks like an academic, and finally defining the boundary-spanning acapreneur who bridges the boundaries of entrepreneurial and academic thought and action. In this way, we will offer a simple taxonomy of acapreneurship by defining in which domain the discovery and dissemination of knowledge take place.

3.1 The Entrepreneurial Academic

An academic is not an academic: Academics find various ways to apply the entrepreneurial mindset to excel in their field:

- *Capture a market niche*: Identifying a scientific area and, within it, a research gap is the core of any scientific investigation and positioning. As in any market, there is supply and demand in scientific inquiry. While there are many incentives for researchers to focus on hot topics, whether for funding, career advancement, or attention, these topics tend to attract many peers, making it highly competitive to get noticed and published. Consequently, scientists who anticipate trending topics and understand the market for scientific knowledge are well prepared to identify scientific opportunities earlier and thus take advantage of them.
- *Understand the target audience*: Another trait of an entrepreneur is customer centricity. This is not just an intellectual conviction, but a matter of survival for an entrepreneur. If the customer is not willing to pay for a product or service, the business will not survive. An entrepreneurial academic understands these mechanisms and strives to understand the different audiences he or she must address to be successful: the scientific community, school administrators, students, funders, or the public. Because the expectations of the various audiences are different, an entrepreneurial scientist recognizes and responds to these differences by exceeding their respective expectations.
- *Succeed with scarce resources*: There are few academics who do not complain about a lack of funding or at least have many ideas on how to invest additional funds in their research. In this sense, an academic shares the fate of an early-stage entrepreneur: having limited financial resources, he or she must be creative to make the best use of the restricted finances available. Constrained resources often lead to a competitive advantage, as entrepreneurs must take a lean and agile approach for the sake of survival. Scientists who see resource scarcity as an opportunity for agility and speed can achieve the same advantage over large, well-funded research consortia, which often lack speed and agility and are not infrequently shaped by political machinations and struggles for power and money.

3.2 The Academic Entrepreneur

Since academics can learn from entrepreneurs, entrepreneurs are advised to draw inspiration from the academic mindset to become even more effective and successful as entrepreneurs:

- *Think in terms of hypotheses*: A core competency of any scientist, whether in the natural or social sciences, is to generate meaningful hypotheses that can be empirically tested with rigor. Hypotheses are at the heart of the deductive approach to research, a key concept for ensuring progress in the creation and validation of knowledge. Given scarce resources and lack of prior experience, the

ability to derive meaningful hypotheses about products and markets is critical to the success or failure of entrepreneurs. Entrepreneurs as academics simply cannot afford to derive all knowledge in a purely inductive approach.
- *Apply evidence-based reasoning*: Equally important as thinking in hypotheses is testing them. Here, successful entrepreneurs often borrow from the book of a thorough researcher, relying entirely on data rather than gut instinct to reach their conclusions. Empirical evidence is at the heart of scientific thinking, as it should be when testing in a business context where the results of such tests can lead to significant changes in strategic direction, i.e., realignment.
- *Understand complex systems*: Finally, the ability of scientists to deal with complex systems and multidimensional explanatory patterns is another transferable skill that can prove valuable to an entrepreneur. He or she is typically dealing with several complex systems simultaneously, e.g., the market, the investment opportunity, regulation, etc., and must find ways to mentally simplify the complexity without lapsing into of simplistic reasoning. This ability also enables entrepreneurs to construct meaningful theories about the various systems that allow them to anticipate dynamics that might directly affect their venture.

3.3 The Boundary-Spanning Acapreneur

While the patterns described above can be effective, the real power of combining the two approaches lies in new business models. Five models are described below that are the result of overcoming the boundary between entrepreneurial and academic mindsets and spheres:

- *The intellectual property realtor*: Treating the result of scientific investigation, the scientific discovery, as the product of a venture can be seen as a first type of acapreneurship. In this model, the scientific discovery is considered intellectual property (IP) that can be traded, i.e., sold, licensed, or given away for free. The IP entrepreneur must identify and exploit opportunities where their product can add more value than competing IP products. In this model, the product comes from academia, while its application is clearly rooted in entrepreneurship, requiring both an academic and an entrepreneurial mindset. As a result, this acapreneur seeks to break through the entrepreneurial sphere by offering better science-based technology.
- *The education venture builder*: Educational entrepreneur model is related to the intellectual property model in that the product of an entrepreneurial venture is scientific in nature. Unlike the IP model, acapreneur does not primarily market codified knowledge, but rather a process that enables others to become more effective. Moreover, educational entrepreneur competes in the core area. As a result, this acapreneur seeks to disrupt the academic sphere by offering an alternative model of education.
- *The venture-driven inventor*: The venture-driven inventor approach aims to drive scientific discoveries through entrepreneurship. In this model, a company is

created specifically to enable scientific discoveries that would not be possible in a traditional scientific setting. Well-known examples include the space ventures of some of the wealthiest entrepreneurs. While their ventures aim to advance science, their goal is to convert the discovery into a new business. As a result, this acapreneur seeks to disrupt the entrepreneurial sphere.

- *The data-venture empiricist*: Partially related to the former model, but still distinct, is the data-venture model. In this approach, a company is created with the objective of collecting empirical data that can be used by researchers to expand their knowledge. Such an enterprise is necessary because there are no other organizations that have, or are willing to share, the relevant data. This is another case where an acapreneur is attempting to disrupt the academic sphere.
- *The thought leader*: Finally, there is a model that seeks to intervene neither directly in the entrepreneurial nor in the academic sphere, but rather in the court of public opinion. The thought leader model aims to combine the perceived need for knowledge from the entrepreneurial sphere with the knowledge generated in the academic sphere. In this sense, it translates the "E" into the "U" of knowledge, to use the music metaphor.[1] As a result, the entrepreneur seeks to disrupt the public sphere, which indirectly affects both the entrepreneurial and academic spheres.

4 Conclusion

Acapreneurship, as outlined above, can take many forms and shades, depending on how academic and entrepreneurial spheres are influenced, but also depending on the mindset applied. In summary, we have outlined seven types of acapreneurship, providing a simple taxonomy of acapreneurship (see Fig. 1).

These different types of acapreneurship share an underlying logic; that combining the best of both worlds leads to value-added results, whether it is simply a complementary mindset or a true boundary crossing. In many cases, the results are not just added creativity and innovation, but real progress and contributions in the respective fields.

The benefits of such behavior are often acknowledged, but so are the obstacles faced by true acapreneurs. Some of those deeply rooted in one of the spheres and lacking experience and exposure to other contexts may see the value in combining different perspectives or fear the disruptive power of such combinations. Although such a taxonomy may prove persuasive to some of them, the real power of acapreneurship can only be experienced when acapreneurship becomes a personal endeavor and not just a theoretical construct.

[1] The division of music into serious music (E for "ernst") and light music (U for "unterhaltend") is a classification scheme for evaluating music in Germany. The classification plays an important role not only in remuneration in a public redistribution system, but also in public discourse about culture.

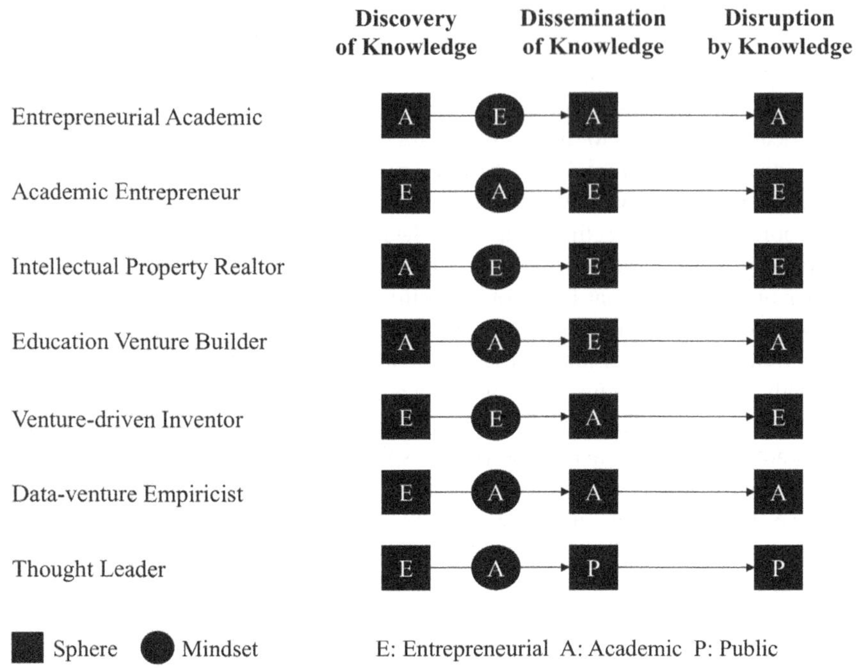

Fig. 1 Exhibit: A taxonomy of acapreneurship

5 Summary

This chapter intends to show how the entrepreneurial and academic worlds can benefit from a greater diversity of integration. It addresses the specifics and commonalities of both worlds and makes recommendations for how synergies can be more effectively harnessed. A taxonomy of acapreneurship is proposed through seven hybrid forms of entrepreneurship and academia. The article concludes with a call for action to acknowledge and appreciate the contributions of acapreneurs.

Questions

Question 1. How to successfully apply entrepreneurial thinking to academia?
Question 2. How to successfully apply academic thinking to entrepreneurship?
Question 3. What are the different approaches to transcending the boundaries between academia and entrepreneurship?

Michael Hilb is a titular professor at the University of Fribourg, Switzerland, and teaches strategy, entrepreneurship, and corporate governance at universities in Asia and Europe. He is the founder of DBP Group and serves on various corporate and foundation boards. Michael holds a PhD from the University of St. Gallen, Switzerland, and was a visiting fellow at INSEAD and Harvard University.

Academic Entrepreneurship: Pay, Peace, and Passion

Hermann J. Stern

1 Introduction

I want to take you on a journey. It's my journey as an academic and an entrepreneur. It's a story of a passionate business ethics doctorate selling a more reliable way to pay executives. It outlines my struggles as an entrepreneur driven by passion who's learned about what motivates people, the importance of "pain," and how the most unexpected circumstances can sometimes be the best for one's business.

What others are still learning is that you can't pay someone else to be motivated or passionate. And yet, year after year, executives are paid large sums with the hope that they will be motivated to do well. I studied this topic, and through trial and error as an entrepreneur developed a framework to help organizations better compensate their executives.

I share my story with you here so you can gain your own insights, find your own passions and motivations, and learn what I mean by pay, peace, and passion. This is an exert from an autobiography about my entrepreneurial adventure story that I share on Medium and in a planned book.

2 Finding a Customer Benefit

At my business school, the University of St. Gallen in Switzerland, we learned that you need potential benefits, a value proposition, to have a business. If your customers have benefits, you have a business. My initial business was helping Swiss companies with executive compensation—a nicer word if you don't want to

H. J. Stern (✉)
Obermatt, Zürich, Switzerland
e-mail: hjs@obermatt.swiss

M. Aldogan Eklund, G. Wanzenried (eds.), *Academic and Educational Entrepreneurship*, Springer Texts in Business and Economics,
https://doi.org/10.1007/978-3-031-10952-2_13

bluntly say "pay," "compensation," or the excessively long British version "remuneration."

I thought we had the answer to the reason why executives weren't correctly motivated. The solution was economic value add (EVA), a funny term in German, because in that language it also means "Eve." Nothing is virgin about EVA, the German "Eve" of financial metrics, as I would learn soon. In the beginning, we were convinced that executive compensation should be based on EVA. EVA is a form of profit metric in corporate financial reporting. So basically, we thought that executive compensation needed to be based on a smarter way of calculating profits.

What we didn't realize at the time is that compensation doesn't build motivation or passion in a person. Compensation *compensates* people for the pain they gain from having to work. It provides *peace*, as the word "pay" comes from that the Latin *pācāre*, which means to make peaceful. So, employees stay peaceful if they are paid for their work. It's as true for executives as it is for employees. We wrongly thought that if we had a better way of calculating profits, that if we could measure better, executives would be more motivated.

Selling consulting is a good way to start a business for an academic because it doesn't require much capital. For me this meant that I would be my own boss with no investors to report to, so I could take action when I saw the need for it. The necessities of starting a business occupy new entrepreneurs quite a bit, but at the end of the day you only need to incorporate and find an office. My first office was the window bench at my father's law firm, which, obviously, took care of the incorporation. So we were up and running 3 days after our founding lunch on the terrace of the restaurant Gasthaus Obermatt on Lake Lucerne on August 24, 2001. We named the company after the restaurant, Obermatt, and Rämistrasse 5, close to the picturesque Bellevue Square in Zürich, became the first "headquarters" of us proud startup entrepreneurs.

Sitting at the small window desk behind the secretary of my dad's precious wood and leader coated office, I started to research the topic of executive compensation to learn how to best sell it. When my father's friend, Marc, visited from New York City, I was eager to tell them about my new venture and hear what he would have to say. Marc had run several businesses successfully. His company was the first to provide paid information services over the telephone in New York. He had his ups and downs. When the lid on premium phone charges was lifted in the 1980s, they could charge larger fees for more expensive information. Teenagers' large phone bills led to a backlash that almost killed his company, as he had to return the money for services he himself had to pay for.

Father and Marc took me to the historical Kronenhalle restaurant across the Rämistrasse where they had most of their meals together when Marc was in town. The crisp white tablecloths and original Chagall paintings on the walls made a perfect setting for pitching my compensation consulting business idea. Marc was dismissive: "You want to know what a good compensation plan is?" he asked with his nasal New York accent. "I tell you a good compensation plan. Load up the CEO with as much debt as you can and have him purchase shares in your company. That's a good compensation plan. He will work his ass off to make sure the company is successful." I had nothing to counter this. I felt like the red Robespierre beef on my plate—mostly rare and cut to pieces. Not even Kronenhalle's infamous Chocolate mousse dessert with crème de Gruyere could lift my spirits that day.

I decided to walk along the lake to think this new startup killer argument through. The fresh air helped, and I conceived of an idea—this type of activity has helped me many times during my career as an entrepreneur. I decided to give Marc's bonus plan a try and analyze it on real companies.

3 Getting the First Customers

When you start a company, it is very similar to finding a job. You have to put yourself in the right light and start talking to people about you and your product. Our first customer was the local TV station, Star TV. The owner, Paul Grau, knew my father and needed a company valuation to attract a new investor. I could never completely rule out the possibility of closing this deal because Paul wanted to maintain good relations with my dad who was an intellectual property lawyer distributing licensing revenues to TV stations. Using your network feels a little bit like cheating at the beginning, but that's not true. Our entire life is based on our relationships. If you start a business, you have to use them like you use them to get a partner to play tennis or go sailing.

Luckily, calling friends also helped me find my second customer. Marcel Chiappori worked for Swisscom and introduced me to their strategy department that needed education on EVA. I learned that the friends who understand your situation are more likely to help. I also turned into successful friends. But for some reason, these people help you less. It's difficult to say why. Maybe it's because they have more to lose and work hard to maintain their own success. I once received work from a bank director who knew me from university. He asked me to run some calculations over Christmas. Because it was urgent and Christmas didn't really leave time to get the papers right, I did all the research during the holiday season without a written contract. When I showed him the result in early January, he was very happy. When I sent him the invoice for my work at the end of the month, he sent an email saying that there wasn't a contract. What do you do in these situations? I decided to let it go. You don't want a fight with your customers. It is much better to just move on.

Despite all my good contacts with prospects through friends and business relations, most companies seemed not to care about increasing their productivity through better bonus plans. How was that possible? How can one be indifferent to a proven benefit? I suspected that they just didn't understand it. With our EVA compensation plan, they would not link bonuses to share prices; they would link them to an annual improvement of EVA. I felt that my problem was communication. We had to find a better way to spread the word.

4 Publishing Is the Marketing of Academic Entrepreneurs

Corporate compensation systems were wrapped in secrecy in the early years of the new millennium. There were no corporate remuneration reports and the government stayed clear of all interventions. The world was still in order and running smoothly a dozen years after the Berlin Wall fell. There was no need for regulations, no transparency of pay in Switzerland. But we needed something to sell. Rather than asking for government regulations to make this field more professional, I teamed up with the aspiring young professor Simon Peck from the University of St. Gallen to do the first large-scale survey of Swiss compensation practices and publish a booklet (Stern & Peck, 2003). I hired students to help me get questionnaires out and answered. We called many in person to make sure that they responded. The result was a report that secured us the admiration of the big four accounting firm PwC partner Robert Kuipers. He came to our survey launch and congratulated from his seat in the audience. This was very encouraging. Suddenly, we were someone, respected by renowned peers with data that was interesting for everybody, including our leading competitors. We even got recognition by prestigious newspaper *NZZ am Sonntag* that received the study prior to publication (Tip: always give the press exclusivity). Journalist Katharina Fehr structured the story around the fact that there is too little performance orientation in Swiss compensation systems (Fehr, 2003).

Now that we were published in the largest and most respected Sunday paper in Switzerland, I expected the phone to ring non-stop from Monday. It didn't. Instead of waiting any longer for people to read our press and booklets, I started to send my articles directly to my prospects. This became my preferred marketing method. With an empirical study on an interesting topic, you may get into the press. This allows you to print the coverage and send it to prospects. You benefit double: first, you get co-branding with a well-established media company that acts like a quality stamp. Second, you get your message to your prospects.

Sending our publications to our prospects individually and making sure they arrived was labor intensive and not uplifting, but it got us customers that paid the bills. Because of these successes, we set out to write an entire book, which turned out to be a lot of work. When it was finally published in 2004, we received even less recognition than we received for our executive compensation pamphlet a year before. I guess it was because the book is theoretical, and the study was empirical. Theory is hard to sell, especially to businesspeople. Don't do it to attract customers. The book didn't help in any way to bring our business forward. Because it consumed our full attention, the year became our financially most difficult one in our entire history. This is one of the reasons I now focus on online publishing on our website and selected trade journals. This allows me to better package my messages and to keep them accessible for a long time. Books are bad at both.

The final punch for my self-employed compensation consulting phase came from the wine and beer bottling company Vetropack on the outskirts of Zürich. Quite early in a project, the CFO plainly told me that EVA doesn't work for bottlers. Their lengthy investment cycle made the flaws of EVA apparent. I developed this into a teaching example that I bring whenever a smart student proposes EVA bonus plans.

The reason is simple: Bottling companies have excessively long investment cycles. They need huge tubs for heating glass until it melts. Because of the high temperatures, these tubs get used up over time. They get thinner and thinner. After 20 years they need to be replaced. The year they are replaced are extra-difficult years. The company needs to replace the tub and deliver bottles at the same time. More effort is required by management and employees. Despite that additional effort, an EVA plan would punish them dearly for this new investment, not only because of the additional costs in that year but also because of the flaws in the EVA calculation: Because capital costs have been going lower and lower every year when the tubs get depreciated because of the lower value of the tubs, EVA went higher and higher. At the time of replacement, the capital costs explode because the tubs are new and valuable. I realized right then that our EVA bonus plans wouldn't work for them, but they wouldn't work for any other company with capital expenditures either. This was when I decided to move to financial research and abandon executive compensation consulting.

5 Useful Products Don't Sell in a Crisis

During the time that I felt less and less confident about EVA bonus plans, I started to work with the new financial databases that became ever larger, thanks to the expansion of Internet use by corporations.

There is a crucial difference between consulting and research. Consulting is personal. You want to know the consultant well that consults you. Research isn't personal. You want the research done well and don't care much about who does it. For me that meant moving from being "self-employed" to being an "entrepreneur" with a scalable business model. Consultants can't really scale their business because it depends on their personalities. In effect, they are self-employed freelancers. Research firms are companies; they are scalable. Their owners are entrepreneurs. Becoming an entrepreneur for me was much more attractive than staying a self-employed consultant.

So I started again. I hired a career coach. It was the first time I spent money on consulting and many more consultants would follow. Spending money on external help speeds things up. Entrepreneurs don't become entrepreneurs because they want to make money, they become entrepreneurs because of a passion. Bill Gates didn't program because he wanted to be one of the richest people. He programmed because he found it so fascinating. For him, his wealth must be a welcome side-effect. In those days on my own I lived from the hand to mouth, thankful that my wife had a reliable job.

Helmut Elben, the head of strategy at esteemed Swiss manufacturer Georg Fischer, was my first customer for financial research. He was my light at the end of the tunnel. The ticket to more meaningful and more exciting work. As his company was among my shortlist of desirable customers, I called him 1 day and he invited me to their headquarters at Schaffhausen, just above the Rhine fall. When I told Helmut about the financial databases, I had access to, he was convinced that he could be onto something. We didn't really know what to do with all that data. So we worked on finding uses together.

We felt that the problem was to turn bewildering database information into something that tells a story. Most people hate statistics, which means that most customers dislike our data mining of financial databases. I had to find a way to hide the statistics and get people excited about what was hiding in the numbers. My choice was to use graphs instead of numbers.

A painful old weakness of mine suddenly became a strength. Early in my life I realized that I would mix up words and numbers without being able to explain why. When I looked at what I had written a little later, it would contain very obvious mistakes. Words would be missing, numbers copied erroneously. I couldn't explain why. It was so obviously wrong that the only thing I derived from these experiences was fear. Fear of making a dumb mistake. The result was that I slowly stopped looking at numbers directly. Whenever possible I tried to plot them in a graph. Graphs turned out to be much safer than the numbers themselves. Because of this regular exercise of turning numbers into graphs, I became good at interpreting them. This also made me understand what is needed for a good graph to tell a story.

My "second Helmut" was Paul Hälg, the CEO of a publicly quoted company! I had certainly moved one level up. Paul wanted to show professionalism to his investors. He wanted to manage his three divisions like a portfolio of companies, a little bit like a private equity firm. For this, he needed analysis that his CFO couldn't do. That's why he came from Altorf, the village in the middle of the Alps just below the majestic Gotthard pass to Zürich, the city of finance. Right there in the lobby of the new Hyatt, Paul became my largest customer, double the size of Georg Fischer, who was the second largest and three to five times the size of my typical customers. The papers were signed in the following days.

This was very encouraging. I had an enthusiastic head of strategy who helped me develop the tools and I had the CEO of an industrial conglomerate with three divisions who uses the research in their investor conferences. This was it. I cut ties with my compensation consulting past, and I invested even more into growing this new and exciting business. I decided to write a book with all the new tools and the rationale for why you should be using them. This would allow me to forget about the first book, which was about compensation and EVA, both of which I found completely silly by that time. The second book was written quickly. I wasn't dragged down by endless discussions, as I was the only author this time. In less than a year, my new book was published, this time about market-oriented management (Stern, 2007). We launched in the former stables of the Zürich cavalry, now a trendy place for eating, drinking, and dancing.

The book itself didn't sell that well, but I expected already this from my earlier publishing experiences. I needed the book mainly for proving to people how serious we were about our new field. It looked good on the panel of a public podium or on the meeting table of a prospective client.

Because not many people read books and I needed new marketing stories, I decided to go public with our research. This was the time the idea of the Obermatt rankings was born. We used our performance measurement method to calculate Operating Ranks for the largest 100 Swiss companies.

The months following the first ranking were reaffirming. I was regularly on the phone finding new clients. We added customers from such diverse fields as measurement instruments, beer breweries, automotive suppliers, and IT consulting companies. The business was growing fast. In 2008 it exploded by a factor of five. I continued investing. By now, there was no question I would ever go back to compensation consulting. My new financial research business was so much more interesting than consulting. It was an enterprise with a product.

However, by fall of that fateful year, Lehman Brothers had collapsed, and stock prices crashed. Nobody had money for indexing company performance. It isn't sufficient to provide a useful product; it isn't enough to have a benefit. If the rain comes in, customers disappear from the streets. Worst of all, this is quite unpredictable.

6 Pain Creates Business

It was eerily quiet in the first quarter of 2009. What looked like explosive growth the year before was about to evaporate into nothing. A decade later our income from measuring corporate performance for management purposes would be less than 10% of our revenues. By spring it was clear we had a problem. If I didn't find a solution quickly, I would need to let half of my staff go. I didn't sleep well anymore. Certainly, my employees were young and would find other jobs, but it also meant that I would lose all their knowledge and need to train new staff later. I needed to keep my people on board longer. I had already passed on my salary a couple of months earlier, and money was running out quickly. Fortunately, the summer before, I gave a speech at a board seminar and decided to watch the speaker before my presentation. It was Professor Rolf Dubs, an economic scholar I admired since high school. He was retired, but he kept teaching seminars for board of director members. Rolf taught the importance of cash flow that day. It took him an hour to walk through the three simple steps of cash flow from operating activities, cash flow from investing activities, and cash flow from financing activities. He concluded by saying that a cash flow forecast is now the single most important piece of information he requests from his management teams. The reason was very simple: no company ever went bankrupt for any other reason than running out of cash.

I started maintaining my own cash flow forecast right there in summer of 2008. By spring 2009, it became my holy grail. I checked it almost every day. It would tell me how long our cash would last. I still do this on a monthly basis. The cash flow projection for the next 18 months became the single most important financial tool to manage my company. The profit and loss statements are needed for optimizing the business, the cash flow projection is needed for its survival. There is nothing more important for an entrepreneur than making sure the cash doesn't run out. It was a humbling experience at that time and still is. All the beautiful research we do with indexing performance is interesting, but when it comes to making sure the company survives, it turns into an irrelevant luxury.

In April 2009, I stood before the decision to fire half my staff because there wasn't enough money in June to pay the salaries. When I shared the difficult news with my team, my senior analyst Doris asked why I didn't request payroll protection from social insurance. After all, we had paid our dues for 10 years by then. I didn't know about that at all, but it took me less than an hour to fill out the online form, and 3 days later the Swiss payroll protection program confirmed that they would pay 80% of my payroll. My employees still got almost what they made before, but I didn't have to pay for it. Of course, they were free to seek new employment and I had a lot less capacity, but the most important thing was that I didn't have to fire them. This was a crucial ingredient for the success that would follow later.

What was I about to do? The business I had built up over the last 5 years was about to come to a complete stop. I needed to find other sources of income. The obvious choice was to find a job. Indeed, I did apply to a University of Applied Sciences in an alpine village and did supply a job application to a client who needed a CFO. There wasn't much hope of changing my career at the age of 45 years after having been self-employed for over a decade. I had zero corporate management experience. So, I needed to focus on what I could sell with my company Obermatt. With a heavy heart, I revisited executive compensation, this time using our Operating Index for performance measurement. The idea was indexed executive compensation. Performance relative to peers decides the level of variable pay. I combined the compensation experience from the beginning and the later acquired financial research experience.

The credit crisis was my wake-up call. I needed a new product and I developed it with rigor. This time, I didn't just call up potential customers, this time, I documented my product with its benefit in an article and a book contribution, a new website, and a product brochure. It wasn't consulting anymore. I wasn't saying, "This is my hourly rate and I just charge whatever you need." This time, I was able to say, "This is what you get, this is the price we charge, and these are your benefits." My sales trainer called it the price sandwich: first you tell them what your product includes, then you say the price, and immediately you list the benefits from the perspective of the customer. It became my only way to talk about prices, and still is today. Listing the delivery items builds up understanding for the price, and listing the benefits afterward relates the price to what the customer actually needs.

Düsseldorf is where I received the most important insight into my entrepreneurial life. Invited by the visionary and enthusiastic Martin Handschuh and his employer A.T. Kearney to a roundtable, we wanted to learn from nature by the biologist Jörg Kretzschmar who spoke about "wisdom of the crowd" and "swarm intelligence," which had just become fashionable with the newly emerging network technologies. Kretzschmar started with the simple statement, "I don't know if there is much we can learn from nature. The only law in nature that is of any significance is very basic: If it doesn't hurt, keep doing it. If it hurts, find another way to avoid the pain."

"Avoid the pain" is the most important behavioral law in nature. And it's true for humans, too. I suddenly realized that the indifference that I found when telling people about the cool new features of my Index products was simple due to an absence of pain. Those that bought, had pain. Paul Hälg of Dätwyler needed to prove that he manages his conglomerate like a professional asset manager. He used our Strategy Index research to prove it to his shareholders. Dr. Michael Bischoff of Daimler wanted to justify a bonus payment despite below-target performance because he felt it was deserved. He used our Bonus Index research to prove that some pay is warranted. Ernst Bärtschi of Sika, another early client, wanted a bonus for an outstanding company despite excessively high internal targets. He got it with our Bonus Index.

7 Giving Up

Then the "recession—no bonus" pain disappeared for my clients. For a decade, the market would only know one direction: UP. Nobody wanted to be compared with a booming market, certainly not if it meant linking compensation to it. The result was that our Bonus Index services stayed flat for several years. I published a magazine where we tried to finance our CEO rankings with advertising revenue. I learned to program and created a stock investing web site based on the Obermatt indexing method where we hoped for subscription revenue. I started a video blog to make it popular. I volunteered to teach. For 7 years, I spent more than half a million dollars on purchasing development services and 80% of my time working on new services that even today only provide a couple of hundred dollars in monthly revenue. By 2018, the verdict was unavoidable: I needed a new job and I needed to say farewell to Obermatt. I started to take long walks for inspiration, the most memorable one being an August fasting march of 3 days around the lake of Zurich. Fasting had the effect that I had lots of time to think. While I learned that food isn't that important and that energy can pop up suddenly even after 3 days of hunger, I didn't learn anything more for my future.

It was my wife, Candace, who found a course on social entrepreneurship at INSEAD, which I immediately liked. As a student, I always wanted to study in Paris, and INSEAD had always been my first choice. So the dream of INSEAD was still alive when her recommendation came. Social entrepreneurship sounded interesting, especially after earning a living from excessive executive compensation. It would also mean a partial revival of my dissertation on philosophy and economics. I didn't hesitate and signed up for the surprisingly affordable week at the famous post-war first pan-European business school in a picturesque park just 1 h south of the city of love.

I got so committed to a new beginning that I even decided to sell Obermatt. I figured that a performance measurement business for executive compensation purposes could better grow within a full-service human resources consultancy. I did what most people advise against in such a situation: I asked my team. They would be the most affected. I told them my plan of selling and staying in a larger company where they would find more secure jobs. They weren't convinced. I could tell that there was fear of being sucked up and spit out from a vast organizational beast. It wasn't entirely wrong. I had similar fears. So I told them that we should go step by step and that I would only do it if I had their full support. We started writing the business plan and were up for a surprise. The previous year had actually been better than expected. The plan showed year-on-year growth of 21% in 2018 and a projection of 18% for 2019. This would be the third year of double-digit growth. Even better, we had a profit margin of 30%. That's high by any standard. I needed to verify this and looked at the large performance rating companies. Thomson Reuters had a margin of 20%, Fitch a margin of 35%, and Moody's a margin of 40%. The economics of my miniscule operation were the same as those of the big guys, and they were good. "This should be easy to sell," I thought, "Especially if we can show the growth that we have." If we grow the business to $3 million, we have $1 million in profit, and a valuation that easily exceeds $10 million with our growth rate. I became optimistic about being able to offload the headache and go someplace else.

This was a surprising turn of events. I was running a performance rating company and had not been aware of its own performance. How was that possible? I think I wasn't aware of this positive development because I focused fully on the stock research product that had become my new baby. The performance rating services, the lifeblood of our business, were only there to finance it. I started to look for a broker to help me sell the company. Interestingly enough, I suddenly got cold feet. I wanted to sell a company that was still small and may get acquired cheaply while it would be worth a lot more in 3–5 years when revenues were higher. I had a team that could execute it. The only thing I needed to do was to invest in more marketing and sales, something that I largely avoided when working on the stock research product. I decided to wait to start the sale until my social entrepreneurship course was completed at INSEAD.

The Social Entrepreneurship Program (ISEP) class at INSEAD required hardly any preparation for someone like me who studied new research for developing new products all the time. The program included a "town hall" meeting where students could pitch their social entrepreneurship ideas on the first night. I basically had two options: I could speak about making stock research accessible to the masses, my new baby. This business even had a category in social entrepreneurship called financial literacy, albeit hardly used by any social entrepreneur as finance is not really their main passion. I could also talk about making executive pay more socially acceptable. On the train to Paris, looking out the window at the prairies flying by at 300 km an hour, I weighed in on the pros and cons of each business. I stayed undecided on that train ride all the way to the Paris suburb Fontainebleau where INSEAD is located.

When I prepared for my INSEAD pitch of "plural incentives" as I called it originally, I realized that non-economic factors—today more popularly known as economic, social, and governance (ESG) performance—could actually solve the profit conundrum. ESG reporting provides the opportunity to compensate for the shortcomings of today's profit reporting. ESG reporting sees employee development not as a cost but as a benefit. The same goes for employee satisfaction, safety, and other inclusion achievements. ESG reporting doesn't deduct customer service as a cost, it adds customer satisfaction as a benefit. ESG rewards managers for being responsible to the environment today, not only 10–20 years into the future when the costs of external effects from the company's activity come back, hunting it, and lowering profit at a time when nobody is left who can be held accountable. With ESG incentives, executives get rewarded for lowering those risks and improving corporate governance.

When I pitched my theory to my fellow INSEAD students, I felt energized. I was surprised that I developed the pitch in less than an hour before the town hall. This is when I started to look into executive compensation for sustainability. Today, we call it the Triple Bottom Line Index. I returned to the offices, never looked at the business plan again and started to develop an ESG executive compensation product.

Getting clients for ESG executive compensation was much easier than anything I had experienced before. I asked three of my existing clients and received three invitations for a sales presentation. It was March 2020, and the pandemic was on its overseas flight West. The three sales calls became Zoom sessions and they turned into a whopping two first clients. I never had such a success with my previous products. It was a rewarding experience. We talked about how to make the world a better place, and everybody wanted to be part of it. With enthusiasm I prepared for the first workshops. And as I had done many times before, I started to write.

This time I was actively looking for pains. Where does ESG hurt the most? And more importantly, where does ESG performance hurt the company and the management team the most? My buyers are the companies. If it doesn't hurt them, I can't sell, no matter how beneficial the product is. I decided the pain area as climate change. It has been a long time since I heard the last climate change denier. Indeed, all of my clients were worried about inevitable and unpredictable climate change by spring 2020. So, I wrote about the "E" for the environment in ESG. This time, I wanted to address the emotional side of my readers. I didn't want to say, "Please add climate metrics to your executive compensation." I felt that this is a plea that leads to nowhere. It had to be stronger: "Manager bonuses against climate protection?" was the title of the first article.

This time, I wanted to be part of a movement. So I searched for coauthors. With such an enticing topic, you can get the best. All my coauthors were professors. I even managed my first single-authored article in the United States on "Better Bonus Plans for ESG" in WorldatWork, the gold standard in executive compensation. A couple of weeks later I learned that one of the world's top legal scholars, Professor Lucian A. Bebchuk at Harvard Law School included my contribution in one of his regular newsletters.

The Triple Bottom Line Index is beautiful. It is intuitive. Everybody understands the numbers 0–100. It is universal. Any metric can be turned into the 0–100 indexing range. It doesn't require putting difficult moral values on people's lives. Two accidents are better than three, irrespective of what cost you put on people's well-being. And it's easy. Everyone understands it immediately.

8 Taking Off

The pain for our service to thrive arrived from a place I could have never envisioned. It's the smallest creature in the world that keeps us all busy these days. The Coronavirus not only made business much more unpredictable, it also made it much more volatile. 2020 would become the year when I acquired the largest number of new index clients, and for reasons I still do not completely comprehend, the pandemic also made sustainable investing practices a priority. You would think that a crisis makes people turn to what they know best. It makes them want to be safe and focus on their self-interest. But this is not what happened in the year of Coronavirus. ESG investing went through the roof. Maybe people have acquired a new humbleness. Maybe they understand now that we have to look for more than just last year's profit. It is difficult to say what caused it, but here it is: an invigorated quest for more sustainable management. Suddenly, most corporations are looking for good ESG ratings.

With a clear pain to relieve and the welcome momentum from the pandemic to take better care of each other and our environment, we were on a roll. We outperformed our own revenue expectations by three times and before a year past after my ISEP class, we already had the first recurring customer for our newly baptized Climate Index. A lot had to come together: The interest in ESG, the pandemic to make it a pain, our passion for performance measurement and data mining, our experience with indexing, and our reference client list in providing executive compensation "rating/performance evaluation" services to public companies for over a decade.

Obermatt—and above all me—are on a roll. Financially, my dissertation in business ethics "paid off." I'm almost a little ashamed to say this because "ethics paying off" is actually an oxymoron. Three things came together: my passion for economics, my 20 years of deep practical knowledge of executive compensation, and my enthusiasm for philosophy. It couldn't have been planned. Steve Jobs couldn't have planned to create the world's most beautiful technical interface when he studied calligraphy.

I myself couldn't have planned *anything* that I accomplished as an entrepreneur. I followed my passion, made sure I was paid enough to survive, and the world showed me where my niche is. Of course, no niche opens itself up without hard work. It needs both: The passion and effort that you put into the business and the opportunity in society to welcome your efforts. I don't think other entrepreneurs are different in this aspect. It certainly is the only way to create an enterprise.

9 Holistic Academic Entrepreneurship Framework

9.1 Individual and Contextual Aspects

I learned the hard way that the better, more rational solution isn't the one that drives you or your business forward. It has been a passion that has kept me and my business going in the face of adversity. My drive has never been to get rich or famous; what has driven me is my interest in being an entrepreneur who seeks out new and better ways of doing things. I have also been driven by personal relationships that have educated and inspired me.

9.2 Financial Aspect

It's not money that drives entrepreneurs, it's always a passion. Yes, entrepreneurs want to make money, but this is not what makes them take substantial risks. If money is the main driver, many jobs offer a more secure path to riches than heading out on your own. Financing my company was through consulting assignments. This is a good way to avoid having to beg for money someplace else.

9.3 Political and Economic Aspects

When we started the company in 2001, executive compensation was entirely unregulated. In 2013, Switzerland passed a law to require more compensation transparency and made some of the practices illegal. This propelled a drive for better executive compensation and with it better performance measurement, the core competency of our operation.

9.4 Sustainability Aspect

With the pandemic, the quest for sustainability, also referred to as ESG for environment, social, and governance, became the new mantra in executive compensation. This allowed us to transfer our knowledge from financial performance measurement into the area of sustainability performance measurement, a new and much larger market for our services.

9.5 Intellectual Aspect

When I tell people, I'm specialized in financial analysis, most of them refer to the area as "rather dry." However, our type of financial analysis was completely developed in-house, requiring a huge intellectual effort that included many publications, videos, speeches, and even a couple of books. Being an entrepreneur in my area would not be possible without significant intellectual capabilities.

9.6 Technological Aspect

Technology helped us apply our methods to 10,000 stocks worldwide, enabling us to provide stock research almost for free by using algorithms. It would have been impossible to publish our CEO rankings without a huge database and algorithms that took hours to complete a ranking. Finally, we invested heavily in proprietary technology that helped us distribute our financial research in a more meaningful way.

9.7 International and Cultural Aspects

At Obermatt, we entertain a very unique and inclusive culture. While we were diverse from day one, we go even further, making all financial information transparent to all employees and allow employees to propose and decide upon their compensation themselves. Everything is first discussed in the team, even such delicate matters as the trade-sale of the company.

10 Summary

This academic entrepreneurial case is driven by the life story of Hermann J. Stern. Dr. Stern started up Obermatt based on his academic experience on executive compensation at the University of St. Gallen in Switzerland. It is an interesting and didactic case for nascent academic entrepreneurs.

Questions

Question 1. What is a customer benefit that generates a business, and how do you find it?

Question 2. What are some of the strategies an entrepreneur can use to find customers?

Question 3. What role do publication and education (both formal and self-education) play in an entrepreneur's journey?

Question 4. Is it more important to get things right the first time, or to fail and try again?

References

Fehr, K. (2003, March 23). Der Leistungslohn ist nicht immer an Leistung gekoppelt. *NZZ am Sonntag*, p. 49.

Stern, H. J. (2007). *Marktorientiertes Value Management*. Wiley-VCH.

Stern, H. J., & Peck, S. (2003). *Executive compensation Switzerland: Trends in vergütungsstrukturen für führungskräfte*. Obermatt.

Further Reading

Eklund, M. A., & Stern, H. J. (2021). How COVID-19 reshapes businesses and executive pay for sustainability. *Corporate Governance and Sustainability Review, 5*(1), 107–119.

Hostettler, S., & Stern, H. J. (2007). *Das Value Cockpit*. Wiley-VCH.

Stern, H. J. (2016). *Hermann Stern speech on executive compensation fairytales for cfa institute*. https://www.youtube.com/watch?v=BlJui5NB6Z0.

Stern, H. J., & Watter, R. (2020). Manager-Boni contra Klimaschutz? In *Gesellschafts- und Kapitalmarktrecht* (pp. 78–88).

Welte, P., & Stern, H. J. (2020, September). *Zur Einbeziehung der relativen CO2-Leistung in die Vorstandsvergütung nach dem ARUG II*. IRZ – Zeitschrift für Internationale Rechnungslegung.

Hermann J. Stern Dr. oec HSG, is the managing owner of the financial research company Obermatt since August 2001. He has developed the indexed performance measurement and triple bottom line ESG compensation methodologies and published them at universities, in the media, and research. Before Obermatt, he worked at Compaq (HP), Swisscom and UPAQ. His video blog at obermatt.com helps private investors manage their own retirement savings. Dr. Stern earned his doctorate in philosophy and economics under Prof. Peter Ulrich at the Institute for Business Ethics at the University of St. Gallen.

Academic Entrepreneurship: The Case of Coursera

Ayla Esen, Yasin Kütük, and Ümmügülsüm Zor

1 Introduction

Coursera is a platform that offers courses, certificates, specialization, and online degree programs provided by institutional partners (universities and companies). It was launched as a for-profit company in April 2012 by two Stanford Computer Science professors, Daphne Koller and Andrew Ng. Coursera started initially hosting courses from six universities. As of 2021, there are more than 200 institutional partners of Coursera and the platform has reached 77 million learners from around the world in the last year. The organization's vision is "a world where anyone, anywhere has the power to transform their life through learning" (Coursera, 2021).

The initiative is a timely response to the ongoing technological and economic disruption the world has been going through. On the one hand, increasing income inequality and poverty has led to an opportunity gap in education. Higher education is hardly affordable for many. On the other hand, digitalization is changing the workplace and there is an increasing demand for upskilling and reskilling of the workforce to adapt to the future of work. Moreover, the COVID-19 pandemic has accelerated the transformation of learning and education processes to the online

A. Esen (✉)
Bahçeşehir University, Istanbul, Turkey
e-mail: ayla.esen@eas.bau.edu.tr

Y. Kütük
Altinbas University, Istanbul, Turkey
e-mail: yasin.kutuk@itu.edu.tr

Ü. Zor
Sakarya University, Sakarya, Turkey
e-mail: ummugulsumzor@sakarya.edu.tr

M. Aldogan Eklund, G. Wanzenried (eds.), *Academic and Educational Entrepreneurship*, Springer Texts in Business and Economics,
https://doi.org/10.1007/978-3-031-10952-2_14

mode. One cannot overemphasize the importance of Coursera's mission in this era of the "new normal."

Coursera serves as an exemplary case of academic entrepreneurship for several reasons. First, the co-founders of the company are from a university context that fosters entrepreneurship. Second, Coursera is one of the most popular massive online open course (MOOC) providers in the education technology market. And third, the founders of the company strongly emphasize the "social" purpose of Coursera accompanying its mission.

The aim of this chapter is to present the case of Coursera by examining the context where the initial idea was generated, looking into the main motivations of the co-founders of Coursera, and generating insights on academic entrepreneurship accordingly. In exploring the Coursera case, our chapter will adopt "the holistic conceptual framework on academic and educational entrepreneurship" developed by the editors of this book.

2 The Story

The origins of distance education go back to the eighteenth century. Back then, correspondence education emerged as the first mode of distance education where the instructor and the students were not in the same place as opposed to traditional face-to-face education (Harting & Erthal, 2005). Over time, postal services as a tool for distance education was replaced by online tools and channels in line with technological developments.

Courses using distance education were initially designed to train audiences who could not enroll in in-class higher education programs for a variety of reasons, such as economic condition or geographic distance. The initial success of distance education led this mode of training to evolve in terms of context as well as the mode of information transfer in accordance with technological advancements, especially the increased use of computers (Moe, 2015). Web-based education was basically viewed as a new mode of content delivery and was not considered a "massive learning" tool yet. In the meantime, however, the idea of using computers in education was not new to Stanford University. The first experimental design of computer-based teaching went back to the mid-1960s.

Using online platforms as a vehicle to deliver education for a mass level of participation has become possible thanks to technological advancements (Jacot et al., 2014). All these advancements might constitute the roots of today's modern MOOC systems, including Coursera. The first professional MOOC platform was Connectivism and Connected Knowledge (CCK08) which was designed by George Siemens and Stephen Downes in 2008 both for students who paid tuition for the program at the University of Manitoba and for the "outside participants" who enrolled for free but did not earn any credits (Mabuan, 2019). In the following years, there were several initiatives at Stanford University. Stanford University offered trial versions of three mass online courses in 2011: *Databases, Machine Learning,* and *Introduction to Artificial Intelligence* (Ng & Widom, 2014). The main purpose of this initiative was to provide high-quality training for everyone. The program was able to fulfil its goals as more than 100,000 learners signed up for each course. Even though it is still not clear who used the term MOOC the first time, the origins of today's modern MOOC might be attributed to these three courses offered by Andre Ng, Peter Norvig, Sebastian Thrun, and Jennifer Widom (Ng & Widom, 2014). In the meantime, Daphne Koller was trying to improve the in-class experience for her students through a novel set of education design principles that is known today as *the flipped class*. Koller later referred to her initiation as an effort intended to ensure "free class time for more meaningful interaction." The apparent success of these two initiatives in terms of high demand from learners paved the way for MOOC systems, including Coursera and other similar platforms such as Udacity and edX (Severance, 2012). Even though Coursera is not the first MOOC platform established, its launch is considered as a facilitator for the boost of MOOCs (Loya et al., 2015).

Koller and Ng have emphasized their awareness of the world's grand challenges and their motivation to contribute to the solution of social problems in various platforms so far. In one of her talks, Daphne Koller stated (The Qualcomm Institute, 2013):

> We are very fortunate as are many other countries in the developed world in having education available to us; that's not true for many countries in the world where there just isn't the capacity there to accommodate the people who want and deserve an education.

Similarly, Andrew Ng summarized his motivation in an interview as (FranceinSF, 2013):

> I want to live in a world where students no longer have to choose between paying for tuition and for groceries. I want to live in a world where a poor kid born in Africa has nearly the same opportunity as a kid born in the wealthy suburb of DC.

As two academic entrepreneurs aspire to provide an opportunity for "education to anyone, anywhere," Koller and Ng launched Coursera as a "social edu-preneurship company" in April 2012 (Ng & Widom, 2014). The two co-founders set out to fill the opportunity gap in the higher education system stemming from the fact that higher education is not affordable for many individuals throughout the world, and that "there is not much intellectual supply in the world for everyone," as Koller puts it (Ng & Widom, 2014; Severance, 2012).

3 What Numbers Tell: The Impact of Coursera

Coursera reached more than 70 million learners around the world in 2020. Prospective students have access to detailed information on courses offered through well-designed and customized web pages for each course on Coursera.

Data obtained from the introductory pages of 4515 individual courses on Coursera's web site reveal that Coursera has reached at least 289 billion views and

Table 1 Descriptive information on courses offered via Coursera

	Min	Mean	Max	Sum
Enrollments	2	32,345.6	3,779,672	146,040,216
Review score (over 5)	3	4.6	5	
Score	58	95.6	100	
Views	146	63,942.0	14,208,655	288,698,277

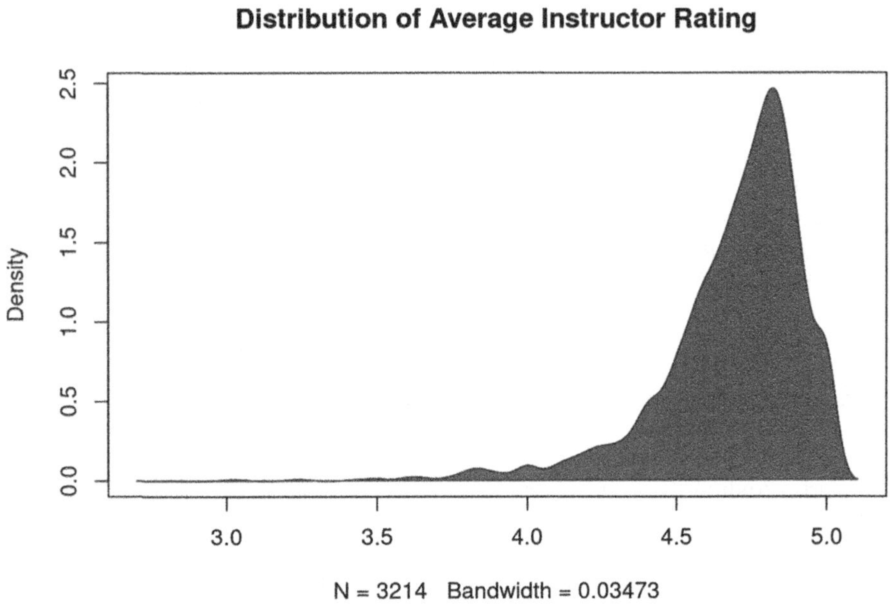

Fig. 1 Distribution of average instructor rating, Source: created by authors

146 billion enrollments through these 4515 courses[1] (Table 1). This indicates a conversion rate of nearly 50%, highlighting the positioning of Coursera as a lovemark in the education sector. As seen in Table 1, average number of views of courses is almost 64,000, while the most viewed course has reached almost 15 million views.

There are several success factors behind the popularity of the platform. We have delved into some numbers that provide insight on a set of competences that distinguish Coursera from its peers.

User Satisfaction with Instructors Instructors of courses offered by Coursera receive significantly high ratings from users, as seen in Fig. 1. The average instructor

[1]Data presented in this section has been compiled from the introductory web pages of 4515 individual courses in December 2020 from www.coursera.org

Table 2 Highest course page views in Coursera (top 10)

Course name	# of views	Review score
COVID-19 contact tracing	14,208,655	4.9
Machine learning	7,277,982	4.9
Technical support fundamentals	4,703,790	4.8
Programming for everybody (getting started with python)	3,919,725	4.8
The science of well-being	3,483,309	4.9
Excel skills for business: essentials	3,353,559	4.9
The bits and bytes of computer networking	3,125,402	4.7
Financial markets	2,291,155	4.8
Crash course on python	2,112,891	4.8
Neural networks and deep learning	2,053,761	4.9

Source: Created by Authors

Table 3 Highest course enrollments on Coursera (top 10)

Course name	# of enrollments	Course review score
Machine learning	3,779,672	4.9
The science of well-being	3,150,679	4.9
Learning how to learn: powerful mental tools to help you master tough subjects	2,657,154	4.8
Programming for everybody (getting started with python)	1,998,459	4.8
English for career development	1,143,923	4.8
COVID-19 contact tracing	1,073,026	4.9
Successful negotiation: essential strategies and skills	949,673	4.8
Chinese for beginners	877,773	4.8
Neural networks and deep learning	877,483	4.9
Financial markets	788,551	4.8

Source: Created by Authors

rating is around 4.75 (out of 5). (Number of votes per instructor vary from minimum five votes to a maximum of 37.5 K votes per instructor.)

Content Relevance and Usefulness The popularity of Coursera also stems from the content of courses that meet the needs of learners. The period in which this study was conducted coincided with the period in which the COVID-19 pandemic was most severe in the world. Therefore, as seen in Table 2, the most viewed course page belongs to the "COVID-19 Contact Tracing" course, with approximately 14 million views. It is followed by the "Machine Learning" course taught by Andrew Ng, with approximately seven million views.

Regarding enrollment frequencies, the "Machine Learning" course also appears to be the most enrolled course (Table 3). Moreover, it has managed to convert more than half of the seven million views into enrollments. "The Science of Well-Being"

Fig. 2 Wordcloud of course subtitles at Coursera, Source: Created by Authors

course taught by Laurie Santos is the second most enrolled course (Prof. Santos has also earned the title of Top Instructor in her field).

It is no coincidence that the most popular courses in Coursera (in terms of the total number of views and enrollments) are closely related to the current upskilling and reskilling needs of the workforce. The harsh adverse effects of COVID-19 are reflected in increasing unemployment levels that boost the demand for MOOCs (Ariker, 2021). According to World Economic Forum's *Future of Jobs Report*, the top three job roles increasing in demand across industries are (1) data analysts and scientists, (2) AI and machine learning, and (3) big data specialists, whereas the top three skills for 2025 are listed as: (1) analytical thinking and innovation, (2) active learning and learning strategies, and (3) complex problem-solving (World Economic Forum, 2020). The most popular courses in Coursera reflect the upskilling and reskilling efforts towards the future of work as well as the increasing demand for personal development and well-being in the COVID-19 pandemic environment.

Serving a Diverse Community In line with its vision of "a world where anyone, anywhere has the power to transform their life through learning," Coursera has adopted an international expansion strategy in terms of both the partnerships established and learners reached. To ensure that the educational content is accessible by anyone, anywhere, courses on the Coursera platform often include subtitles in at least one language.

As depicted in Fig. 2, most courses offer English subtitles. English, as the most frequently utilized subtitle language, is followed by Russian, Spanish, Chinese, Portuguese, and Arabic languages, respectively. Students also have access to courses in multiple languages, including Spanish, Chinese, French, and Italian, as the number of Coursera's international partners increase.

4 Seven Aspects of Academic Entrepreneurship for Coursera

In this section, we will focus on the entrepreneurial characteristics of Coursera's co-founders through utilization of the holistic conceptual framework on academic and educational entrepreneurship developed by the editors of this book. Academic entrepreneurship is defined as "an umbrella term which refers to the efforts and activities that universities and their industry partners undertake in hopes of commercializing the outcomes of faculty research" (Wood, 2011, p. 153). In their seminal work on university entrepreneurship, Rothaermel et al. (2007) list entrepreneurial activities of universities as encompassing a broad set of initiatives, including "patenting and licensing, creating incubators, science parks, university spin-outs, and investing equity in start-ups (p. 691)." Coursera, a for-profit organization founded by two university professors, serves as an interesting case for academic entrepreneurship. Academicpreneurs of Coursera and their achievements can be analyzed in multiple aspects:

Sustainability Aspect The primary motivation behind the formation of Coursera was a strong drive for creating social impact through providing access to world-class learning to all. In that sense, co-founders Koller and Ng seem to possess the characteristics of social entrepreneurs. Nicholls (2008) defines social entrepreneurship as "a set of innovative and effective activities that focus strategically on resolving social market failures and creating new opportunities to add social value systemically using a range of resources and organizational formats to maximize social impact and bring about change" (p. 23). Social entrepreneurs make deliberate efforts to solve social problems, aspiring for large-scale systemic change (Light, 2009). The concept of sustainable entrepreneurship also resonates with the characteristics of Coursera's main mission and strategies. Sustainable entrepreneurs contribute to creating solutions to social and environmental problems through income-generating activities.

Koller and Ng have mentioned on numerous occasions that the social impact Coursera creates is more important than maximizing profits. According to the Coursera 2020 Impact Report, the organization is creating value in multiple ways by "achieving human progress through learning" (Coursera, 2020):

- Providing free content to learners for developing future-ready skills
- Building partnerships with quality educators from around the world
- Coronavirus response initiatives
- Social impact programs for refugees

Coursera is a public benefit corporation (a new form of organization that combines aspirations of for-profit and non-profit organizations) and has recently received a B Corp™ certification. B Corp is "an organization that has taken the B impact assessment and scored sufficient points on its environmental and social impacts as scored by the B Lab organization to become a Certified B Corporation" (Shields & Shelleman, 2017, p. 12). The certification requires companies to have goals over and to be assessed under five categories, namely environment, workers, customers, community, and governance. These initiatives towards contributing to a more sustainable world are extensions of Koller and Ng's initial mission, as Coursera CEO, Jeff Maggioncalda, puts it (Maggioncalda, 2021):

> Daphne Koller and Andrew Ng founded Coursera with a mission to provide universal access to world-class learning. While our purpose, strategy, and practices have always been consistent with B Corp requirements, the demand Coursera has experienced during the COVID-19 pandemic calls for us to play an even greater role in empowering communities and institutions. This is one of the reasons we are now committing to a higher standard of purpose and impact through third-party validation, public transparency, and legal accountability.

Intellectual and Technological Aspects Intellectual and technological aspects of entrepreneurship by Koller and Ng are significantly shaped by their educational and social backgrounds. Both co-founders pursued academic degrees in top universities. Ng received his bachelor's degree from Carnegie Mellon, his master's degree from MIT, and his PhD from UC Berkeley. Koller received her bachelor's and master's degrees from Hebrew University of Jerusalem, and her PhD from Stanford University. In one of her well-known talks, Koller (2012) introduced herself as follows:

> Like many of you, I'm one of the lucky people. I was born to a family where education was pervasive. I'm a third-generation PhD, a daughter of two academics. In my childhood, I played around in my father's university lab. So it was taken for granted that I attend some of the best universities, which in turn opened the door to a world of opportunity.

Similarly, Ng positioned himself as privileged because of the opportunities he was provided by his family. In an interview, he said (Pitney, 2017):

> I think when I was about six, my father bought a computer and helped me learn to program. A lot of computer scientists learned to program from an early age, so it's probably not that unique, but I think I was one of the ones that was fortunate to have had a computer and could learn to start to program from a very young age.

Koller and Ng studied computer science in top universities and taught computer science for many years. Both co-founders were innovators in their fields of expertise: Ng's initial attempt for online machine learning classes and Koller's introduction of flipped learning in her classes can be listed as examples among the many pioneering initiatives they have pursued. A solid educational background and technological as well as academic expertise fostered the creative and innovative skills of the two academic entrepreneurs. Koller (2020) highlighted the importance of the technological expertise of the founder in research and development focused companies in one of her talks:

> In companies that are very strongly R&D-focused, having a technical co-founder is absolutely essential because it's fine to have an understanding of whatever the user needs and so on. [. . .] So I think it's really important to have a strong technical foundation in these companies.

Individual and Contextual Aspects There is a considerable amount of research in entrepreneurship literature focusing on the relationship between an individual's personal characteristics and entrepreneurial capabilities (Stewart et al., 1999; Gartner, 2001; Beugelsdijk & Noorderhaven, 2005). Characteristics such as need for achievement, risk-taking propensity, innovativeness, internal locus of control (being self-motivated), hard work, and self-confidence are widely addressed by entrepreneurship scholars as drivers of entrepreneurial orientation. It would not be wrong to say that Coursera's co-founders reflect these individual characteristics along with a strong sense of social awareness and mission. Both co-founders continue exploiting new opportunities through starting new companies, making new strategic partnerships and taking additional roles in a variety of organizations.

International and Cultural Aspects Both Ng and Koller lived and worked in diverse cultural settings (whether it be national or organizational cultures) in different periods of their lives. The multicultural and interdisciplinary nature of Coursera co-founders' personal and professional experiences shaped their attitudes towards diversity and inclusion. In an interview, Andrew Ng talked about the value of these experiences for him (Pitney, 2017):

> I was also fortunate to have gotten to live and work in many different places. I was born in the U.K., raised in Hong Kong and Singapore, and came to the U.S. for college. Then for my own studies, I have degrees from Carnegie Mellon, MIT, and Berkeley, and then I was at Stanford. I was very fortunate to have moved to all these places and gotten to meet some of the top people. I interned at AT&T Bell Labs when it existed, one of the top labs, and then at Microsoft Research. I got to see a huge diversity of points of view.

Koller (2020) also highlighted the importance of a diverse and interdisciplinary culture from a similar standpoint as Ng:

> I think in order to address some of the critical problems that we're facing, one needs to really build a culture of people who work together from different disciplines, each bringing their own insights and their own ideas into the mix.

Co-founders' attitudes are reflected in how Coursera is designed and managed: a learning platform serving a diverse community, shaped by the interdisciplinary experience of a diverse team, providing courses from a wide variety of disciplines.

Political and Economic Aspects Coursera is one of the many enterprises incorporated by members of Stanford University. The university's entrepreneurial culture acted as one of the main drivers behind the initiation of Coursera. This culture is continuously supported by the economic and political dynamics surrounding Stanford University, as it stands at the center of the entrepreneurial ecosystem of Silicon Valley. Adams (2020) refers to Stanford University as an academic anchor facilitating entrepreneurial action. Stanford's entrepreneurs generate trillions of dollars every year and generate millions of jobs in Silicon Valley. This economic contribution leads to increased government support to the university as well. Entrepreneurship education and research are also the strong sides of the university.

Coursera, along with all other MOOC providers, might be considered as an actor in a shared economy where people transfer services online for a fee or for free by promoting sharing rather than owning (Cornejo-Velazquez et al., 2020). This unique form of economic environment might connect stakeholders around the world to be able to add value by employing excess or sharable resources (Hamari et al., 2016). The sharable resource in the MOOC case is the transfer of education where service providers—in this case, professors—teach millions of students online, instead of teaching smaller groups in a physical classroom environment. It seems that this new form of educational service has potential for the future as the market size for e-learning platforms is expected to reach USD375 billion by the end of 2026 (Wadhani & Gankar, 2020).

Financial Aspect Koller and Ng started Coursera to democratize higher education; therefore, the company is mainly known for its free courses. This might be seen as kind of a naïve dream. To ensure sustainable long-term success, Koller and Ng focused on a solid business model as well. Coursera is funded by venture capital together with a business model that has been evolving since its foundation.

The surprising fact is that Coursera seems to have no revenue plan initially (Adam, 2012) even though it was established as a profit-seeking organization. Unique and immature market structure made it more difficult to predict the supply and demand for the future. Initially, the business model included the sale of verified course certificates. Later with the initiation of "Coursera for Business," the company added revenues from the corporate e-learning market to its business model. This new product was followed by the launch of a monthly subscription model for specializations. "Coursera for Governments and Nonprofits" was later added to the product portfolio. Additionally, Coursera is now offering degree programs working with partner universities to offer bachelor's and master's degrees.

Currently, Coursera generates revenue through tuition fees, verified certification, degrees, specialization, recruiting programs, employee training, and sponsorship, and they focus on financial sustainability, continuous improvement, partner acquisition, and expanding the scope of services for value proposition (Cornejo-Velazquez et al., 2020). The more partnership agreements are formed with universities and institutions, the more recognition Coursera certification receives around the world. This cycle therefore creates unique value and improvement. Prestigious universities offer free courses, modules, or programs. This provides further recognition in the higher education ecosystem, so the certification becomes valuable. Certification creates revenue to improve the services even further. This cycle represented the initial revenue generation method until Coursera started to generate revenue from other services such as the Amazon partnership program (Fischer et al., 2014).

It might be said that Coursera has created its own sustainable financial structure where revenue is generated through course enrollments, providing a platform for others and taking advantage of economies of scale to provide free education for interested learners. Rather than being an NGO that generates funds through donations to provide free education, Coursera creates its own ecosystem where different parties are involved in revenue creation.

5 The Story Goes on: Coursera IPO

Coursera has recently capitalized on remote education becoming increasingly essential every day, as the company has been listed on New York Stock Exchange (NYSE) as of March 2021 (McKenzei, 2021). CEO Maggioncalda addressed email subscribers on March 31, 2021, highlighting Coursera's vision once again (Pierce Onos, 2021):

> Today, Coursera is taking a step forward by becoming a publicly-traded company on the NYSE. As a public B Corp, we are committed to using our resources to further our vision of creating a world where anyone, anywhere has the power to transform their life through learnings. Today and always, every member of Coursera, along with our partner community of more than 200 university and industry educators, aspires to continue reducing barriers to world-class education so we can all collaborate, learn and advance together. Thank you for being a part of this community of problem-solvers, leaders, and change-markers—and for showing the world how to learn without limits.

Being an ed-tech company, Coursera continued to grow despite (or, on the contrary, thanks to) the pandemic. The online platform realized a market cap around USD5.1 million on the day it went public.

6 Conclusion

As one of the key players in the MOOC industry, Coursera continues to stand out from its competitors. The main drivers of Coursera's competitive advantage are grouped under three pillars as depicted in Fig. 3.

Trends in the macro environment played an important role in Coursera's success. Ng and Koller's recognition of the window of opportunity was timely. There was an unfulfilled need for accessible and quality education, and education technologies were ready to support MOOC platforms. In addition, concerns about the future of jobs and the future of the workplace had increased awareness of and demand for reskilling and upskilling initiatives. As discussed previously in this chapter, the entrepreneurial culture at Stanford University also acted as a catalyst within the Silicon Valley context.

Coursera would not be in its current position if it weren't for the motivation and capabilities of academic entrepreneurs, Koller and Ng. Individual characteristics, educational and professional backgrounds as well as their strong sense of mission can be listed among the main drivers of Coursera's success.

Coursera's establishment at the right time by the right people fueled the competitiveness of the company in its initial years. As the company grew, it was seen that this was not a one-time achievement. Rather, the competitive advantage was

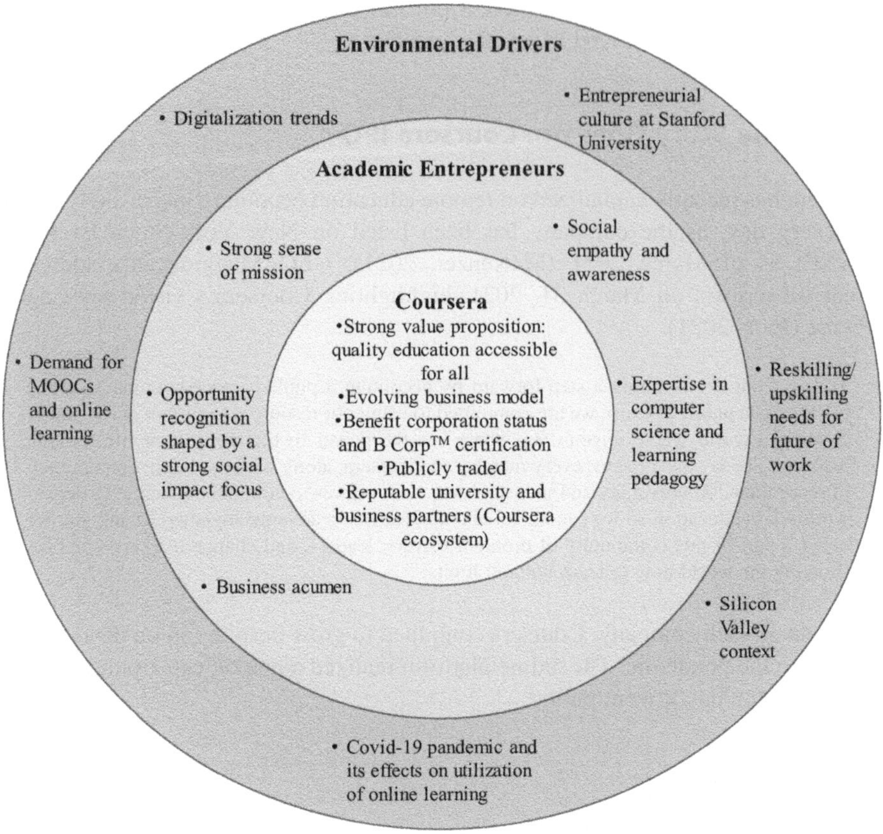

Fig. 3 Drivers of Coursera's competitive advantage, Source: Created by Authors

sustainable. The main reason behind a sustainable competitive advantage is the company's strategic approach over the years. A strong value proposition, an evolving and innovative business model, strategic partnerships, and governance capacity are the building blocks behind an outperforming business strategy.

Technological and economic disruptions accompanied by disruptions in labor markets will be shaping the agenda of the next decade. Demand for developing new skills due to the fast pace of technology-driven job creation will continue to grow. As a platform that has set out to address these challenges, Coursera will have to continuously evolve in order to sustain its competitive advantage in the online learning market.

7 Summary

This chapter focused on the story of Coursera, one of the world's leading MOOC platforms. Coursera was launched as a for-profit company in April 2012 by two Stanford Computer Science professors, Daphne Koller and Andrew Ng. The company is an exemplary case for academic entrepreneurship due to the supportive entrepreneurial culture at Stanford University and to academic entrepreneurs who successfully integrated their sense of mission with their expertise and skills towards "a world where anyone, anywhere has the power to transform their life through learning." "The holistic conceptual framework on academic and educational entrepreneurship" developed by the editors of this book was utilized to explore the Coursera case. It is concluded that Coursera's sustainable competitive advantage is based on the co-founders' sense of mission, ability to recognize the window of opportunity for online learning platforms, and a sound and dynamic business strategy supported by the Coursera ecosystem.

Questions

Question 1. What role can universities play in supporting the entrepreneurship ecosystem?

Question 2. What are the critical success factors for MOOCs in higher education?

Question 3. What are the underlying motivations of Daphne Koller and Andrew Ng for establishing Coursera?

Question 4. How has Coursera differentiated itself from similar online learning platforms?

References

Adam, S. (2012). *Is Coursera the beginning of the end for traditional higher education?* Retrieved April 2, 2021, from https://www.forbes.com/sites/susanadams/2012/07/17/is-coursera-the-beginning-of-the-end-for-traditional-higher-education/?sh=7243be12ae42

Adams, S. B. (2020). From orchards to chips: Silicon Valley's evolving entrepreneurial ecosystem. *Entrepreneurship and Regional Development*, 1–21. https://doi.org/10.1080/08985626.2020.1734259

Ariker, C. (2021). Massive open online course (MOOC) platforms as rising social entrepreneurs: Creating social value through reskilling and upskilling the unemployed for after COVID-19 conditions. In M. Afacan Findikli & D. Acar Erdur (Eds.), *Creating social value through social entrepreneurship* (pp. 284–306). IGI Global.

Beugelsdijk, S., & Noorderhaven, N. (2005). Personality characteristics of self-employed; An empirical study. *Small Business Economics, 24*(2), 159–167.

Cornejo-Velazquez, E., Clavel-Maqueda, M., Perez-Lopez-Portillo, H., & Lyubimova, E. (2020). Business model of learning platforms in sharing economy. *Electronic Journal of e-Learning, 18*(1), 102–113.

Coursera. (2020). *2020 impact report*. Retrieved February 4, 2021, from https://about.coursera.org/press/wp-content/uploads/2020/09/Coursera-Impact-Report-2020.pdf

Coursera. (2021). *About Coursera*. Retrieved February 4, 2021, from https://about.coursera.org/

Fischer, H., Dreisiebner, S., Franken, O., Ebner, M., Kopp, M., & Koehler, T. (2014). Revenue vs. costs of MOOC platforms: Discussion of business models for xMOOC providers, based on empirical findings and experiences during implementation of the project iMooX. In *7th International Conference of Education, Research and Innovation (ICERI2014). Conference Proceedings* (pp. 2991–3000).

FranceinSF. (2013). *Interview with Andrew Ng, co-founder of Coursera* [video]. Retrieved January 15, 2021, from https://www.youtube.com/watch?v=sUO3Pk0nOCM

Gartner, W. B. (2001). Is there an elephant in entrepreneurship? Blind assumptions in theory development. *Entrepreneurship Theory and Practice, 25*(4), 27–39.

Hamari, J., Sjöklint, M., & Ukkonen, A. (2016). The sharing economy: Why people participate in collaborative consumption. *Journal of the Association for Information Science and Technology, 67*(9), 2047–2059.

Harting, K., & Erthal, M. J. (2005). History of distance learning. *Information Technology, Learning, and Performance Journal, 23*(1), 35–44.

Jacot, M. T., Noren, J., & Berge, Z. L. (2014). The flipped classroom in training and development: Fad or the future? *Performance Improvement, 53*(9), 23–28.

Koller, D. (2012). *What we're learning from online education, TED talk* [video]. Retrieved January 15, 2021, from https://www.youtube.com/watch?v=U6FvJ6jMGHU&t=21s

Koller, D. (2020). *Stanford women in data science (WiDS) conference 2020* [video]. Retrieved January 15, 2021, from https://www.youtube.com/watch?v=7TlZ7l0J76o

Light, P. C. (2009). Social entrepreneurship revisited: Not just anyone,anywhere, in any organization can make breakthrough change. *Stanford Social Innovation Review, Summer*, 21–22.

Loya, A., Gopal, A., Shukla, I., Jermann, P., & Tormey, R. (2015). Conscientious behaviour, flexibility and learning in massive open on-line courses. *Procedia-Social and Behavioral Sciences, 191*, 519–525.

Mabuan, R. (2019). *A MOOC camp-based flipped classroom: Integrating MOOCs into university curriculum*. DLSU Research Congress 2019.

Maggioncalda, J. (2021). *Coursera receives B Corp™ certification. Coursera Blog*. Retrieved February 14, 2021, from https://blog.coursera.org/coursera-receives-b-corp-certification/

McKenzei, L. (2021). *MOOCs failed, short courses won*. Retrieved March 20, 2021, from https://www.insidehighered.com/news/2021/03/09/coursera-ipo-filing-reveals-company-successfully-monetizing-moocs

Moe, R. (2015). The brief & expansive history (and future) of the MOOC: Why two divergent models share the same name. *Current Issues in Emerging Elearning, 2*(1), 2.

Ng, A., & Widom, J. (2014). *Origins of the modern MOOC (xMOOC)*. Retrieved March 30, 2021, from http://robotics.stanford.edu/~ang/papers/mooc14-OriginsOfModernMOOC.pdf

Nicholls, A. (2008). *Social entrepreneurship: New models of sustainable social change*. Oxford University Press.

Pierce Onos, J. (2021). *What to know about Coursera's 2021 IPO*. Retrieved August 15, 2021, from https://public.com/learn/what-to-know-about-courseras-2021-ipo

Pitney, N. (2017). *Inside the mind that built Google brain: On life, creativity, and failure*. Retrieved March 30, 2021, from https://www.huffpost.com/entry/andrew-ng_n_7267682

Rothaermel, F. T., Agung, S. D., & Jiang, L. (2007). University entrepreneurship: A taxonomy of the literature. *Industrial and Corporate Change, 16*(4), 691–791.

Severance, C. (2012). Teaching the world: Daphne Koller and Coursera. *Computer, 45*(8), 8–9. https://doi.org/10.1109/mc.2012.278

Shields, J. F., & Shelleman, J. M. (2017). A method to launch sustainability reporting in SMEs: The B Corp impact assessment framework. *Journal of Strategic Innovation and Sustainability, 12*(2), 10–19.

Stewart, W. H., Jr., Watson, W. E., Carland, J. C., & Carland, J. W. (1999). A proclivity for entrepreneurship: A comparison of entrepreneurs, small business owners, and corporate managers. *Journal of Business Venturing, 14*(2), 189–214.

Wadhani, P., & Gankar, S. (2020). *eLearning Market size worth over $375bn by 2026*. Retrieved April 2, 2021, from https://www.gminsights.com/pressrelease/elearning-market

Wood, M. S. (2011). A process model of academic entrepreneurship. *Business Horizons, 54*(2), 153–161.

World Economic Forum. (2020). *The future of jobs report 2020*. Retrieved March 30, 2021, from http://www3.weforum.org/docs/WEF_Future_of_Jobs_2020.pdf

The Qualcomm Institute. (2013). *The online revolution: Education for everyone—Daphne Koller, Coursera, Inc* [video]. Retrieved February 14, 2021, from https://www.youtube.com/watch?v=09tvsd3TGlk&t=353s

Further Reading

Daniel, J., Cano, E. V., & Cervera, M. G. (2015). The future of MOOCs: Adaptive learning or business model? *International Journal of Educational Technology in Higher Education, 12*(1), 64–73.

Sandler, M. R. (2010). *Social entrepreneurship in education: Private ventures for the public good*. R&L Education.

Shane, S. A. (2004). *Academic entrepreneurship: University spinoffs and wealth creation*. Edward Elgar.

Wright, M. (2007). *Academic entrepreneurship in Europe*. Edward Elgar.

Ayla Esen is an Assistant Professor of Management and Organization at Bahcesehir University, Istanbul. Her professional experience includes 10 years as an expert and consultant in strategic management, organizational development, and participatory approaches such as the search conference. She holds MBA and Ph.D. degrees in management and organization, along with an undergraduate degree in industrial engineering. Dr. Esen's research interests mainly focus on the relationship between business and society; she has several publications and conference papers on corporate social innovation. Dr. Esen has also studied topics related to strategic management such as cooperative strategies, scenario planning, and participative management processes.

Yasin Kütük is an Assistant Professor of Economics at Altinbas University. He holds BA in Economics and Philosophy, MA in Economics with an award-winning thesis. He earned his Ph.D. in Economics from Istanbul Technical University with a dissertation entitled "Essays on Estimation Methods: Three Comparative Essays on Econometrics and Machine Learning." He is mainly specialized in computational social science (CSS) covering deep learning, natural language processing, and applied/theoretical econometrics. He teaches these for 4 years at Altinbas University in the Department of Economics and also publishes in CSS.

Ummugulsum Zor is an Associate Professor of Accounting. She holds a BA in Business Administration, Master of Professional Accountancy, and Ph.D. in Accounting and Auditing. Her professional experience includes management and consultant positions mainly in managerial accounting. Her research interests relate to SME management, resource efficiency, and sustainable accounting. She manages several social projects with local governments in rural areas for improving the equal distribution of academic resources for disadvantaged groups. She works as a visiting professor at Sakarya University.

The Case of Academic Entrepreneurship at the HES-SO Valais-Wallis: Business eXperience

Line Pillet, Vincent Grèzes, Sherine Seppey, and Blaise Crettol

1 Introduction

Founded in 1998, the HES-SO University of Applied Sciences (UAS) and Arts of Western Switzerland is a network of 28 higher education institutions located in the 7 cantons of French-speaking Switzerland. With more than 21,000 students (27% international students), the HES-SO is the largest UAS in Switzerland. Bachelor's and master's degrees are delivered in six faculties: Arts & Design, Business, Management & Services, Engineering & Architecture, Music & Performing Arts, Health Sciences, and Social Work. The HES-SO also offers a wide range of continuing education programs (MAS, EMBA, DAS, and CAS). Applied research and development are integral to the HES-SO's mission. Each school has close ties with institutes, laboratories, or research units that carry out innovative projects with a variety of partners at regional, national, and international levels. The results of this research are channeled back into the study programs and provide cutting-edge learning to students enhancing graduates' continued employability and consequently social and economic sustainability. Professors and lecturers come directly from the field, bringing along comprehensive scientific qualifications together with know-how from real-life implementation and references to concrete cases from actual practice. The study programs build upon the pre-existing practical competencies of their students. They offer scientific reflection and further development by connecting theoretical content with the concrete practical work experience students have already gained.

At the international level, the HES-SO is one of 14 universities included in U-Multirank for Switzerland (umultirank.org). In 2020, its overall performance

L. Pillet (✉) · V. Grèzes · S. Seppey · B. Crettol
Institute of Entrepreneurship and Management, University of Applied Sciences and Arts Western Switzerland, HES-SO Valais-Wallis, Sierre, Switzerland
e-mail: line.pillet@hevs.ch; vincent.grezes@hevs.ch

M. Aldogan Eklund, G. Wanzenried (eds.), *Academic and Educational Entrepreneurship*, Springer Texts in Business and Economics,
https://doi.org/10.1007/978-3-031-10952-2_15

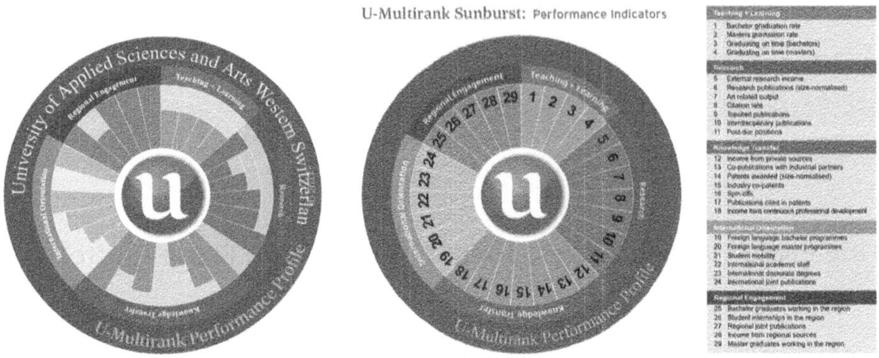

Fig. 1 HES-SO U-Multirank performance profile (source: www.hes-so.ch)

profile across the 5 U-Multirank dimensions showed top performance across various indicators, with 9 "A" (very good) scores:

- Knowledge Transfer (indicators 13: Co-publication with industrial partners; 17: Publications cited in patents; 18: Income from continuous professional development)
- International Orientation (22: International academic staff; 24: International joint publications)
- Regional Engagement (25: Bachelor graduates working in the region; 27: Regional joint publications; 28: Income from regional sources; 29: Master graduates working in the region) (Fig. 1).

2 Academic Entrepreneurship at the HES-SO and the Business eXperience

Entrepreneurship plays an important role at the HES-SO. It is not limited to entrepreneurship courses and programs but is considered as a central to achieving the HES-SO's overall economic and social goals. Indeed, as evidenced by experts, academic entrepreneurship is a well-recognized driver of regional and national economic development (Hayter et al., 2017). Research shows that individual university faculty often act as the primary entrepreneurial agent for the dissemination and commercialization of new knowledge generated in universities (Hayter, 2013, 2015). However, recent studies suggest that students also play a critical role in the establishment and early development of university spinoff companies (Boh et al., 2016; Hayter, 2016; Lubynsky, 2012) and that university culture and entrepreneurship can positively impact the entrepreneurial motivations and attitudes of students (Boh et al., 2016; Pittaway & Cope, 2007). How students are initially exposed to entrepreneurship matters: while most education programs focus on teaching entrepreneurship in a classroom setting, learning-by-doing and building relevant social networks are far more effective in spurring entrepreneurial behavior (Rasmussen & Sorheim, 2006; Shah & Pahnke, 2014). Entrepreneurship is the recognition, evaluation, and pursuit of opportunity in diverse contexts (Christensen et al., 1989). It is expressed in observable behavior such as founding an organization (profit or non-profit) or leading a project within an organization to meet market needs, interests, or wants through creative combination of resources to deliver superior value (Schumpeter, 1934; Casson, 1982). Although the entrepreneurial setting differs from corporate and bureaucratic contexts, entrepreneurial behavior may occur in small or large organizations (intrapreneurship). Entrepreneurship is situational and varies among nations and regions over time and among individuals (Reynolds et al., 2001; Thurik & Dejardin, 2011). It is therefore this entrepreneurial behavior and mindset that should be first and foremost stimulated and developed.

This is precisely the perspective of the Business eXperience (BeX) program launched in 2003 at the HES-SO Valais-Wallis, one of the 28 Higher Education institutions affiliated with the HES-SO. The program was designed to support academic entrepreneurship and to promote an entrepreneurial mindset, interdisciplinary approach, and ability to work in teams among undergraduate students from different disciplines (business administration, tourism management, computer science, life technologies, and systems engineering) over one whole academic year (September–June) while establishing their own ventures. Since BeX's launch in 2003, more than 500 students have attended this program and some 100 entrepreneurial initiatives have flowered, some of which have successfully broken into markets. Shining examples are KeyLemon (20 employees) a 3D face recognition software company founded in 2008 in Martigny, the innovative tourism player Travelise (10 employees) which has been offering surprise trips to Switzerland and Europe since 2016 with the aim of promoting a low-impact way of traveling to meet local populations while adopting eco-responsible behavior, or the company Nivitec which was the recipient of the SwissLife Select Business eXperience 2018 Award for its innovative and personalized solutions in the field of safety and rescue through drone technology. This overview would be incomplete if we did not also mention the former BeX academicpreneurs who started their own business years later after identifying a specific need in their industry. An emblematic example is the entrepreneur Sébastien Bruchez who, after BeX, entered the world of mass distribution. He quickly identified a need in the villages of the lateral valleys in the Valais Alps and launched his retail grocery business Edelweiss Market in the French-speaking part of the Valais-Wallis Canton. In October 2019, he sold his brand to 13*PAM Valais Market, a major employer in the region with 56 retail outlets, 300 employees, and 9800 products from 150 local producers.

Recognizing the strategic importance of these developments, the Head of the Entrepreneurship and Management Institute (IEM) of the HES-SO Valais-Wallis decided to hold half-day session offsite with her team to undertake a global assessment of BeX. The offsite session took place in July 2020. This opportunity allowed the head of the BeX program to report on the main achievements of the program to-date while outlining the major issues and latest developments. The presentation was supplemented by the 6 BeX coaches' insights given the active role they play in the follow-up process. Overall, the results were qualified as very encouraging. However, the BeX executive team agreed on the fact that more could be done to better bring together and coordinate activities and strengthen overall team dynamics among BeX academicpreneurs. Therefore, it was decided to use the Holistic Conceptual Framework of the seven aspects of academic and educational entrepreneurship (Academic & Edu E-Ship) developed by Eklund and Wanzenried to carry out a comprehensive review of the program in order to gain some new insights into academic entrepreneurship and identify both areas of strength and areas for improvement for future development.

3 Exploring the Seven Aspects of the Holistic Framework

As explained in the theoretical section of this book, the holistic framework is based on seven interdependent and mutually reinforcing pillars: (1) sustainability (societal and environmental), (2) financial, (3) political and economic, (4) international and cultural, (5) individual and contextual, (6) technological, and (7) intellectual. In this section, we showcase how the framework was applied to BeX for closer analysis and critical reflection in constant striving for improvement.

3.1 Sustainability (Societal and Environmental)

Sustainability has become a critical area of focus for the HES-SO over the years, which resulted in the decision of the HES-SO Rectorate to adopt an overall sustainability strategy in 2018. A monitoring system has been introduced to assess the HES-SO's contributions to sustainable development in the fields of research, teaching, and operations (Plateforme de durabilité|HES-SO Haute école spécialisée de Suisse occidentale (hes-so.ch). An initial sustainability report was published in 2020 which will be repeated every 2 years.

All BeX activities fall in line with the HES-SO sustainability strategy. This is evidenced by an eco-friendly culture (waste management, energy savings, and promotion of low-impact mobility), awareness-raising initiatives (conferences, workshops, etc.), the introduction of the Laval University Sustainable Business Model Canvas in 2020 to encourage students to embrace sustainability (economic, environmental, and sociocultural aspects) as a core for their business model, as well as experts' interventions and practical guidance on significant ethical and legal issues to be considered when starting a new venture. Special emphasis is given to productive entrepreneurship, which creates economic wealth through innovation and filling gaps in the market, unlike non-productive entrepreneurship where entrepreneurial talent is dissipated seeking subsidies from government agencies, for example privileged monopoly positions or individual tax and regulatory exemptions, or destructive entrepreneurship. The key idea in defining unproductive and destructive entrepreneurship is that not everything that is entrepreneurial is necessarily desirable. There is no obvious connection between entrepreneurship and genuine productivity. Productivity, defined from a purely politico-economic perspective, reflects society's ability to meet real needs, create capabilities (Stanford Encyclopedia of Philosophy, n.d.), and to promote human flourishing. Some entrepreneurs contribute to it, but others do not. Both short-term and long-term effects should therefore be considered as some "negative" activities may have a positive but short-term impact on either the performance of a company or its contribution to the growth of the economy, while in the long term, the same activity might lead to harmful output with consequent effects on society, the economy, and the environment.

Other significant actions on sustainability include students' participation in national initiatives such as a Sustainability Week as well as participation in calls for proposals such as the funding program "U Change—Student Projects for Sustainable Development 2021–24" run by the Network for Transdisciplinary Research (td-net) of the Swiss Academies of Arts and Sciences and supported by the HES-SO with matching funds.

The findings of this analysis show that the sustainability aspect of academic & Edu framework is well covered in BeX, and that these efforts need to be continued and intensified.

3.2 Financial Aspect

With respect to the financial dimension of academic & edu e-ship framework, it is important to underline that the BeX program has been designed to ensure that students benefit from sufficient opportunities to test the viability of their entrepreneurial projects on the market. Financial viability is therefore a key component of the strategy. Special emphasis is placed on the business plan. Creating this plan provides students with deep understanding of the business (customers' needs and location, competition, marketing strategy, etc.) and provides tangible help by aligning everyone with the vision and strategy going forward. This formal strategic planning process plays an important role in improving overall satisfaction with strategy development. BeX students also benefit from the professional support of a financial coach as well as ongoing training on entrepreneurial finance, such as the sources of entrepreneurial financing and entrepreneurial financial planning. They are also trained for an optimal use of the powerful suite of integrated software iManagement developed and made available in open access by a professor of the HES-SO Valais-Wallis.

Since students come from different disciplines and not only from business administration, but it is also essential that they understand accounting including the main financial statements (balance sheet, income statement, and statement of cash flow), the jargon on the field, and the meaning of key financial ratios. Each BeX venture is also allocated a seed funding of some 5000 CHF to support the business until it can generate cash of its own and is put into contact with business angels and private individuals willing to invest time and money in small, newly founded companies with innovative projects. They are also regularly encouraged to take part in startup competitions such as venture.ch and the "Prix Créateurs BCVs" awarded by the Cantonal Bank of Valais or to apply for admission to startup accelerator programs such as Venture Kick or CimArk.

These elements suggest that the financial aspect of academic & edu e-ship framework is well covered in BeX, and that students are well supervised and properly trained.

3.3 Political and Economic Aspect

At the political and economic level, BeX students are kept alert on how political and economic systems of countries shape institutional setup and offer an opportunity or put up barriers to entrepreneurs. The nature of the relationships among entrepreneurship, economy, and politics are discussed by providing examples from factor-driven, efficiency-driven, and innovation-driven economies. The favorable and unfavorable circumstances of economic and political systems are exemplified from the perspective of academic entrepreneurship through BeX alumni's stories and entrepreneurs' testimonies, and regular interactions with government representatives as well as community and business leaders allow for immediate immersion in the regional entrepreneurial ecosystem. It should also be noted that a special half-day event is organized at the end of the program so that students can make valuable contacts for the future and get to know existing support mechanisms that will enable their business to get off the ground.

This analysis suggests that the political and economic aspect of the holistic framework would certainly deserve to be further explored in the future.

3.4 International and Cultural Aspect

The holistic framework also highlights the importance of international and cultural settings as critical factors that either support or hinder entrepreneurship. This finding is confirmed by the Global Entrepreneurship Monitor (GEM) that shows with relevant facts and figures that entrepreneurial activity and success are highly dependent on the contexts within which they occur (Bosma et al., 2020). Any decision to start and run a new venture is taken in a specific context, encompassing a wide range of local and national conditions that may facilitate or hinder the new venture. For instance, a country or region may encourage entrepreneurial activity by providing quality education in schools and colleges, including entrepreneurship training, or may discourage that same activity by having exorbitant business registration fees or burdensome local regulation and bureaucracy. Each national context is different, and while entrepreneurial activity can persist in the most difficult circumstances, it can also fail to flourish even in the most favorable conditions.

In the Valais-Wallis Canton, authorities believe that developing entrepreneurial thinking is an important part of preparing young people for the future. Youth entrepreneurship education is seen as instrumental in developing important soft skills such as communication and collaboration, creativity, problem solving, and critical thinking. BeX coaches take an active leadership role in this effort by offering their expertise in programs such as "Apprendre à Entreprendre (learning to be entrepreneur" targeting young adults in secondary schools or the equivalent.

According to GEM, Switzerland is the top-ranked country in terms of offering highly supportive environments for entrepreneurial activity, followed closely by the Netherlands and Qatar. Driving factors are financing, market dynamics, access to professional services, and a high level of diversity in terms of culture, languages, and disciplines. BeX students benefit directly from this conducive environment. Although international business opportunities are not excluded from consideration, the vast majority of BeX ventures focus on serving the domestic market. Students are aware that the era of globalization and standardization is over. Consumer communities are becoming increasingly diverse—in terms of ethnicity, wealth, lifestyle, and values, and the demand for local products and services is growing. In response, companies are starting to customize their offers to local markets, rolling out different types of products and alternative approaches to pricing, marketing, staffing, and customer service. They are moving away from standardization and towards localization. Customization encourages local experimentation and is difficult for competitors to track, let alone replicate. BeX companies take advantage of these trends and are trained to co-design approaches to actively involve all stakeholders (e.g., partners, customers, citizens, end users) in the design process to help ensure that results meet their needs and are usable.

These considerations demonstrate that the international and cultural aspect of the holistic framework are adequately addressed in the program.

3.5 Individual (the Academicpreneur)

The individual aspect of the holistic framework outlines the specific challenges of academicpreneurs and the rare blend of skills they must possess. They must have the attributes of academics, including inner drive, rigor, and technical skills, and also possess the attributes of entrepreneurs, such as the ability to recognize business opportunities and create value for the customer, and the willingness to take risks, combined with essential soft skills like leadership, interpersonal skills, and the ability to work in teams and make effective decisions. Doing it successfully requires taking a holistic approach to entrepreneurship taking into consideration the distinctive human characteristics, personality traits, and entrepreneurial, social, networking, managerial, and technical skills of academicpreneurs.

BeX takes pride in meeting those needs. Business coaches closely follow the teams throughout the academic year through weekly situation reports, and a professional coach specializing in human behavior offers her assistance in personal and organizational development, conflict management, and team development. She is accredited to use the research-based psychometric tool Leonardo 3.4.5 that helps identify the potentials and the talents of the individuals inside their entrepreneurial environment. Personal attributes of individuals are categorized within four psychological dimensions: interpersonal relationships (rather introverted or extroverted), information processing (rather practical or conceptual), decision-making (rather analytical or emotional), and work management (rather structured or open). The tool also measures fundamental attitudes in relation to five strategic polarities of the company: time, organization, the axis of values (consensus or focus), the axis of process or product orientation, and the axis of piloting (stability or instability). The answers are used to determine the main function for which students have the most affinities, as well as one or two secondary functions and a hierarchy of preferences. This helps improve students' effectiveness as well as their personal and organizational development.

The network of BeX alumni also plays an important part in students' entrepreneurial life acting as role models and serving as a helpful source of guidance and inspiration. Alumni are particularly involved in four key moments that punctuate the BeX academic year: (1) at the beginning of the year, at the 2-day offsite "BeX Camp," alumni challenge the students on their entrepreneurial projects; (2) at mid-year, at the BeX general assembly, critical feedback on project performance is provided to help students fine tune their approach and make adjustments if circumstances so required; (3) a few months later during the practice defense of the business plans, alumni challenge the students on the content and form of their work, and (4) finally, at the end of the academic year, a large public event is organized where alumni provide open and constructive feedback on the project as a whole. This analysis leads us to conclude that the individual aspect of the holistic framework is given proper consideration.

3.6 Technological

With reference to the technological aspect of the framework, there is no doubt that advances in technology have led to major changes in the way businesses have operated over the years. The way technology has recently impacted entrepreneurship and small businesses is a prime example of this. BeX academicpreneurs take advantage of the opportunities provided by technology to target their specific audiences and reach out to potential customers in greater numbers. They benefit from the professional support of tech experts and have practical, hands-on training (e.g., digital marketing and social media, cloud computing) in order to get the skills they need to use digital technologies in an effective way.

Recent events related to the Covid-19 pandemic have created new challenges for BeX startups, making it harder to keep up with what matters the most to their business—their customers and their teams. This has made it necessary to develop new approaches to teamwork to get the work done. The HES-SO takes all necessary measures to provide a favorable environment that is conducive to learning, including excellent facilities and a supportive community of professionals and experts. Interdisciplinary collaboration is encouraged, for instance with the School of Engineering and the Institute of Information Systems, enabling students to quickly obtain the detailed and reliable information and support they need to develop their activities. With respect to technology, which is ever increasing importance, it is imperative that this aspect of the holistic framework be further developed and strengthened in the years ahead.

3.7 Intellectual

Lastly, as shown in the framework, academicpreneurs should also be intellectual entrepreneurs who own and are accountable for their education and who utilize their intellectual assets to add to disciplinary knowledge and as a lever for social good. They are innovators and agents of change (Cutcliffe, 2003; Cherwitz & Sullivan, 2002). Innovation requires entrepreneurs, and they in turn need a supportive environment: an innovation ecosystem of business and finance people, educators, and regulators who together create a climate within which new and established businesses can innovate and thrive.

This is precisely the kind of environment that BeX has created over the years bringing together government representatives, academics as well as community and business leaders. This broad network of experts is also instrumental in the development of the BeX program which is steadily improving to adapt to ever-evolving society and business requirements.

4 Lessons Drawn from the Exploration of the Seven Aspects of the Holistic Framework

This exploration of the seven aspects of the holistic framework reveals that most dimensions are currently well addressed by BeX, but that more could be done to foster innovation and to use the whole potential of academic entrepreneurship to engage further with external communities to promote business for good and create more value for all stakeholders. The holistic framework represents an excellent starting point for such analysis. However, from our perspective the framework tends to focus on the individual academic entrepreneur with little emphasis on the collaborative dimension of academic entrepreneurship, which is, from our experience gained in BeX, a key driver for success. In order to maximize learning from this case, complementary research was therefore undertaken to provide an assessment of the collaborative dimension of BeX entrepreneurial teams in order to provide useful input and make a contribution to the implementation of the holistic framework. To that end, the Belbin Team Role methodology was applied.

5 Teamwork: The Cornerstone of Academic Entrepreneurship

An extensive body of literature indicates the importance of teamwork to the success of innovative projects (Hoegl & Gemuenden, 2001). But what makes a team effective? This is a question that the BeX executive team asked itself and thought about multiple times given the fact that BeX entrepreneurial ventures are always collaborative endeavors. A common approach to this question takes the perspective that the team is the sum of its parts. Meaning, the sum of the individuals that are on the team, their traits, strengths, weaknesses, and preferences and the way those interact with one another. This then leads to utilizing individual assessment as a tool for capturing a simplified representation of the individuals on the team, understanding them in isolation and then looking at the team aggregate to understand their interplay and the areas where the team as a whole is particularly strong or likely to have blind spots.

Experience has taught us that to really understand teams we also need to look at them holistically as teams. If we think of teams as complex systems (which they are like any human system), some attributes of the system will only manifest themselves at a certain level of the system and not in others, because the attributes are a result of interactions between the parts and not of the parts themselves. In other words, simply bringing together academicpreneurs, even when very talented and motivated, and expecting them to work as a team is not enough. The fact is, if individuals lack effective interaction, the team might face significant setbacks such as potentially destructive "us and them" attitudes (a high risk in interdisciplinary teams), delayed projects and product launches diminishing competitive edge in a rapidly changing marketplace, an inability to work around cultural and geographical barriers in an increasingly global economy, ineffective use of time sorting out interpersonal issues instead of ensuring deliverable quality and timely project completion.

5.1 Methodology

Our research started with abductive reasoning and data collection in the field. Semi-directed interviews were conducted with the 6 BeX coaches (4 women and 2 men with an average experience of 8 years in BeX) to learn about their experience in BeX and collect their feedback and observations. Three major elements emerged from the discussion: *the relatively homogenous composition of entrepreneurial teams*, usually composed according to students' personal affinities (natural relationships) or their interest in a specific project proposed by a student, a dominance of *solo leadership* taken by the project owner or the most influential person in the team, and *gradual disengagement* of some team members halfway through the project. These observations led us to the following finding: teams can become imbalanced if their members have too similar profiles (background, experiences, cultures, etc.) and styles of behavior (often the case in affinity teams) with negative impact on their performance. Generally, if team members have similar weaknesses, the team as a whole may tend to have those weaknesses too. Likewise, if team members have similar strengths, they may tend to compete (rather than co-operate) on the team tasks and responsibilities that best suit their natural style. BeX would therefore benefit from having more diverse teams. This finding was confirmed by recent research (Rock & Grant, 2016; Hunt et al., 2018) showing that working with people from diverse backgrounds may challenge the brain to overcome its stale ways of thinking and sharpen its performance which leads to improved and more accurate group thinking and decision-making. The Belbin Team Role methodology (www.belbin.com) was then identified as the best available option to achieve this goal, given its scientific validity and successful implementation in tens of thousands of organizations throughout the world to enhance individual and team performance.

Dr. Meredith Belbin developed the Belbin Team Roles Theory in the 1970s, based on how individuals perform in a team environment. He observed that people in teams tend to assume different team roles, which is done rather autonomously and without conscious decision-making. As a result, Belbin defined a team role as "a tendency to behave, contribute and interrelate with others in a particular way." Belbin team roles were then born, which highlighted nine different functions that a team must undertake in order to be truly effective and successful. Team roles are broken down into three categories according to their primary focus: thought oriented, people/social oriented, and action oriented. Each team role has its strengths and allowable weaknesses (areas to be aware of and potentially improve), and important contributions to make to a team.

The nine team roles are:

- Thought oriented roles: Plants (PL) who are the creative innovators who come up with new ideas and approaches, Monitor Evaluators (ME) who are best at analyzing and evaluating ideas that other people (often Plants) come up with, and Specialists (SP) who have specialized knowledge that is needed to get the job done.
- People/social oriented roles: Coordinators (CO) who guide the team to what they perceive are the objectives and are able to recognize the value each team member brings to the table, Team Workers (TM) who provide support and make sure that people within the team are working together effectively, and Resource Investigators (RI) who explore available options, develop contacts, and negotiate for resources on behalf of the team.
- Action oriented roles: Shapers (SH), who challenge the team to improve, Implementers (IMP) who put ideas into action and get things done, and Completer Finishers (CF) who ensure thorough, timely completion.

Belbin suggests that, by understanding their roles within a particular team, individuals can develop their strengths and manage their weaknesses as a team member, and so improve how they contribute to the team. However, it should be borne in mind that behaviors and interpersonal styles within a team are to some extent dependent on the situation: this relates not only to the own natural working style, but also to the interrelationships with others, and the work being done. A person may behave and interact quite differently in different teams or when the membership or work of the team changes.

The Belbin methodology starts with an online Self-Perception Inventory (SPI) completed by at least four Observer Assessments (OA), meaning short surveys for managers and coworkers to complete, based on the behaviors they witness every day. These inform and enrich an individual's own view with a practical, democratic, evidence-based measurement on observable behaviors and their impact upon a team. It results in a team overview identifying who plays which team roles in a team.

The Belbin approach was introduced to the 6 BeX coaches who completed their individual Belbin team roles profile (SPI, OA) before the beginning of the academic year under the guidance and supervision of a Belbin Professional Practitioner. This resulted in improved understanding of Belbin, enhanced ownership of and appropriate application of the method and tool with respect to teamwork.

At the beginning of the academic year, then, Belbin was introduced to the 42 undergraduate students of the 2020–2021 BeX intake and each student was invited to complete their individual Belbin team roles profile (SPI, OA). A detailed explanation of each Belbin profile was provided with specific emphasis on behavioral strengths and potential contributions to a team. BeX teams were then composed according to students' Belbin profiles striking a balance between thought, people/social and action roles, and other important criteria such as the diversity of skills/academic fields work experience, geographical origins, and gender (Fig. 2).

Once teams had been set up (6 teams of 5, and 2 teams of 6), a session was organized where team members were invited to share preferred team roles within the team and highlight potential strengths and weaknesses. This resulted in a clearer insight into both individual and collective contributions, leading to more productive working on entrepreneurial project discussion and selection.

Feedback from students and coaches on the session was very positive as expressed here: "Students enjoyed completing their Belbin team role profile and sharing their strengths as individuals and teams," "The team composition is much more neutral and objective," "As students don't know each other, they are focused on the project, what binds them are BeX and their project," "Students are more focused and open to other team members."

After 6 months of project activity, an evaluation was carried out through a survey of the 6 BeX coaches and a selection of 24 BeX students in order to measure the impact of Belbin on the teams' performance and dynamics. Although no significant effect was noted on the overall team performance, positive impacts were observed at the level of teamwork and team dynamics such as: better alignment on vision and strategy, greater awareness and acknowledgement of individual strengths and contributions to the team, more efficient task allocation, better understanding of each other's role in the team, shared leadership, as well as a greater ability to anticipate and manage conflicts and divergences. This encouraged continued efforts to this end to bring out the best in BeX academicpreneurs as individuals and teams.

6 Conclusion and Future Outlook

The key learnings and findings from this research-action project are presented here. They will be shared with university faculties and other relevant partners to develop and implement a comprehensive strategy to further enhance and enrich academicpreneurs' learning experience. We trust this will contribute to enriching the reflections and strategies of the various players involved in education.

Acad field, geographical origin, type of study	ID	Gender	Belbin Top Role 1	Belbin Top Role 2	Belbin Top Role 3
Tourism, Valais, full-time study	CM	F	Resource Investigator	Shaper	Teamworker
Life technologies, Valais, full-time study	GB	M	Implementer	Monitor Evaluator	Specialist
Business admin, Geneva, part-time	MA	F	Shaper	Resource Investigator	Completer Finisher
Business admin, Valais, full-time study	CM	M	Specialist	Completer Finisher	Implementer
Business admin, Valais, part-time	ND	M	Shaper	Resource Investigator	Plant
Tourism, Valais, full-time study	CL	M	Plant	Resource Investigator	Teamworker
Life technologies, Valais, full-time study	SB	F	Implementer	Completer Finisher	Shaper
Business admin, Geneva, part-time	LJ	M	Teamworker	Coordinator	Completer Finisher
Business admin, Valais, part-time	VL	F	Implementer	Teamworker	Completer Finisher
Business admin, Valais, full-time study	GM	M	Monitor Evaluator	Specialist	Teamworker
Tourism, Valais, full-time study	CD	F	Specialist	Teamworker	Coordinator
Systems Engineering, Valais, full-time study	AK	M	Completer Finisher	Plant	Shaper
Business admin, Geneva, part-time	PJ	M	Completer Finisher	Implementer	Teamworker
Business admin, Valais, part-time	Pdi	M	Resource Investigator	Monitor Evaluator	Teamworker
Business admin, Valais, full-time study	LM	M	Monitor Evaluator	Resource Investigator	Shaper
Tourism, Valais, full-time study	CS	M	Resource Investigator	Plant	Teamworker
Life technologies, Valais, full-time study	NJ	M	Completer Finisher	Teamworker	Implementer
Computer science, Valais, full-time study	BA	M	Specialist	Resource Investigator	Shaper
Business admin, Valais, part-time	MC	F	Implementer	Completer Finisher	Shaper
Business admin, Valais, part-time	MA	M	Plant	Resource Investigator	Shaper
Business admin, Valais, full-time study	PA	M	Completer Finisher	Teamworker	Monitor Evaluator

Acad field, geographical origin, type of study	ID	Gender	Belbin Top Role 1	Belbin Top Role 2	Belbin Top Role 3
Tourism, Valais, full-time study	GO	F	Implementer	Completer Finisher	Teamworker
Systems Engineering, Valais, full-time study	TF	M	Specialist	Monitor Evaluator	Resource Investigator
Business admin, Geneva, part-time	KB	M	Resource Investigator	Plant	Shaper
Business admin, Valais, part-time	VM	M	Implementer	Completer Finisher	Shaper
Business admin, Valais, full-time study	HJ	M	Shaper	Resource Investigator	Implementer
Tourism, Valais, full-time study	IS	F	Shaper	Implementer	Completer Finisher
Life technologies, Valais, full-time study	TL	M	Plant	Resource Investigator	Specialist
Business admin, Geneva, part-time	CL	F	Shaper	Resource Investigator	Teamworker
Business admin, Valais, part-time	FQ	M	Implementer	Shaper	Monitor Evaluator
Business admin, Valais, full-time study	FF	M	Coordinator	Teamworker	Implementer
Tourism, Valais, full-time study	KK	M	Resource Investigator	Shaper	Completer Finisher
Life technologies, Valais, full-time study	BT	M	Specialist	Monitor Evaluator	Shaper
Business admin, Valais, part-time	GC	F	Completer Finisher	Implementer	Coordinator
Computer science, Valais, full-time study	WL	M	Monitor Evaluator	Implementer	Plant
Business admin, Valais, full-time study	GM	M	Shaper	Resource Investigator	Plant
Tourism, Valais, full-time study	MD	M	Teamworker	Plant	Resource Investigator
Life technologies, Valais, full-time study	CL	F	Implementer	Specialist	Shaper
Business admin, Valais, part-time	BC	F	Plant	Implementer	Resource Investigator
Business admin, Vaud, full-time study	DS	M	Monitor Evaluator	Coordinator	Shaper
Business admin, Valais, full-time study	CT	M	Coordinator	Implementer	Shaper
Computer science, Valais, full-time study	GA	M	Implementer	Coordinator	Teamworker

Thinking roles (PL, ME, SP) · Social roles (RI, TW, CO) · Action roles (IMP, CF, SH)

Fig. 2 BeX 2020–21 team composition (source: authors' own creation)

The main elements we would like to highlight are the following:

- As evidenced by Belbin, individuals and teams have their own specific mix of team roles and consequently each team has a unique entrepreneurial team culture and climate. What the teams do have in common, is that the team members may all benefit from knowing each other's team roles and the effect of their own behavioral style on the teamwork. Belbin methodology can be used efficiently to compose balanced teams and accelerate teamwork. As a result, academics can define ways in their specific contexts to achieve teamwork that is focused on achieving the purpose of their entrepreneurial teams.
- It is recommended that entrepreneurial teams be set up in such a way that roles from all categories (thought, people/social, action) converge and that the full creative potential of these and all participants are used. Gaining the perspective of people with different backgrounds or cultural thinking is at the heart of creating something new and innovative which is the very essence of academic entrepreneurship.
- Diverse teams are necessary in academic entrepreneurship, but if educators just walk away after they have it, they may not get the outcomes they want. Diverse teams must be accompanied, grown, and managed to meet the challenges ahead, develop and sustain.

7 Summary

This chapter focused on academic entrepreneurship at HES-SO through the case of the Business eXperience program. The study demonstrated that academic entrepreneurship produced positive impact on research commercialization and university knowledge transfer. It also provided evidence of the appropriateness of using the seven aspects of the holistic entrepreneurship framework to measure the influence of the internal and external environments in stimulating academic entrepreneurship and the importance of teamwork for achieving sustainable success.

Questions

Question 1. How would you qualify the importance of teamwork in academic entrepreneurship? What are the benefits of teamwork?

Question 2. Is there lack of diversity in the startup world?

Question 3. Why do you think some people are reluctant to add diversity to a team?

Question 4. Do heterogenous teams outperform homogenous ones?

References

Boh, W. F., De-Haan, U., & Strom, R. (2016). University technology transfer through entrepreneurship: Faculty and students in spinoffs. *Journal of Technology Transfer*. https://doi.org/10.1007/s10961-015-9399-6

Bosma, N., et al. (2020). *GEM global report 2019/2020.* Retrieved from http://www.gemconsortium.org/report

Casson, M. (1982). *The entrepreneur.* Barnes and Noble Books.

Cherwitz, R. A., & Sullivan, C. A. (2002). Intellectual entrepreneurship *a vision for graduate education. Change: The Magazine of Higher Learning, 34*(6), 22–27.

Christensen, P. S., Madsen, O. O., & Peterson, R. (1989). *Opportunity identification: The contribution of entrepreneurship to strategic management.* Aarhus University Institute of Management.

Cutcliffe, J. R. (2003). Reconsidering reflexivity: Introducing the case for intellectual entrepreneurship. *Qualitative Health Research, 13*(1), 136–148.

Hayter, C. S. (2013). Harnessing university entrepreneurship for economic growth: Factors of success among university spin-offs. *Economic Development Quarterly, 27*(1), 17–27.

Hayter, C. S. (2015). Social networks and the success of university spinoffs: Toward an agenda for regional growth. *Economic Development Quarterly, 29*, 3–13.

Hayter, C. S. (2016). Constraining entrepreneurial development: A knowledge-based view of social networks among academic entrepreneurs. *Research Policy, 45*, 475–490.

Hayter, C. S., Lubynsky, R., & Maroulis, S. (2017). Who is the academic entrepreneur? The role of graduate students in the development of university spinoffs. *The Journal of Technology Transfer, 42*, 1237–1254.

Hoegl, M., & Gemuenden, H. G. (2001). Teamwork quality and the success of innovative projects: A theoretical concept and empirical evidence. *Organization Science, 12*(4), 435–449.

Hunt, V., Yee, L., Prince, S., & Dixon-Fyle, S. (2018). *Delivering through diversity report 2018.* Retrieved from https://www.mckinsey.com/business-functions/organization/our-insights/delivering-through-diversity

Leonardo 345. https://leonardo345.com/en/home-2/

Lubynsky, R. (2012). *Critical challenges to nascent academic entrepreneurs: From lab bench to innovation.* University of Maryland, unpublished dissertation.

Pittaway, L., & Cope, J. (2007). Entrepreneurship education: A systematic review of the evidence. *International Small Business Journal, 25*(5), 479–510.

Rasmussen, E., & Sorheim, R. (2006). Action-based entrepreneurship education. *Technovation, 26*, 185–194.

Reynolds, P. D., Camp, S. M., Bygrave, W. D., Autio, E., & Hay, M. (2001). *Global entrepreneurship monitor: 2001 executive report.* Kauffman Center for Entrepreneurial Leadership.

Rock, D., & Grant, H. (2016). Why diverse teams are smarter. *Harvard Business Review.* Retrieved April 6, 2021.

Schumpeter, J. (1934). *Capitalism, socialism, and democracy.* Harper & Row.

Shah, S. K., & Pahnke, E. C. (2014). Parting the ivory curtain: Understanding how universities support a diverse set of startups. *Journal of Technology Transfer, 39*, 780–792.

Stanford Encyclopedia of Philosophy. (n.d.). *The capability approach.* Retrieved from plato.stanford.eu: https://plato.stanford.edu/entries/capability-approach/

Thurik, R., & Dejardin, M. (2011, January-February). The impact of culture on entrepreneurship. *The European Business Review*, 57–59. http://www.europeanbusinessreview.com/?p=3380

Line Pillet is a professor in systems thinking and sustainable team leadership at the University of Applied Sciences and Arts Western Switzerland (HES-SO) and leads the Institute of Entrepreneurship and Management (IEM) at HES-SO Valais-Wallis. She holds a Master of Arts degree from the University of Geneva with a specialization in Philosophy of Management (CAS) from the University of Fribourg and Agile Governance (CAS) from HEIG-VD. In addition to her academic activities, she is very active in economic networks as a founding member of the Swiss Cercle of Women Administrators, president of the Association of Women SME leaders in Western Switzerland, and member of several advisory boards and juries. Her research focuses on governance and Complex Systems Dynamics.

Vincent Grèzes, Ph.D., is an Associate Professor of Management, specializing in Strategic Management, International Management, and Open Innovation, at the University of Applied Science and Arts Western Switzerland (HES-SO) in Sierre, Valais. He holds a Ph.D. in Competitive and Strategic Intelligence and leads the Competitive Intelligence module of the HES-SO Innokick Master in Lausanne, Switzerland. His research interests are focused on Business and Open Innovation, Competitive Intelligence, aimed at private and public decision-makers, the Creation of Shared Values, and Pedagogical Innovation. He has been working in the fields of Strategic and Business Intelligence and Market research.

Sherine Seppey completed her bachelor's degree in business administration at the HES-SO Valais-Wallis in Sierre, and Sherine joined the Entrepreneurship and Management Institute (IEM). She has been working there as a research assistant since October 2019 and has since carried out various projects with different work teams concerning different topics. She is currently working mainly in the innovation lab and in parallel she has decided to continue her education by doing a master's degree in Information Systems Management in Lausanne (MScBA MSI), which she will finish in autumn 2022.

Blaise Crettol has been a professor at the HES-SO Valais since September 2005. After obtaining his degree in microtechnology at EPFL in June 1996, he worked for 3 years in an engineering company specialized in industrial automation. He then joined forces with his boss to create a startup active in the field of embedded computing, at the crossroads of mobile internet and smartphones. Today, his areas of research and teaching focus on innovation, business creation and management, particularly through the option he runs, www.businessexperience.ch, offered to final-year students in various fields of study at the HES-SO.

Fierce Academy in the Interstices of Bureaucracy: Academic Entrepreneurship as Cultural Navigator

Carolyn Colleen

1 Introduction

In this chapter, I consider my experiences of academicpreneurship from the perspective of the socio-cultural contexts having a bearing on the term: the academic, and the commercial/industrial. I consider the differences between these two socio-cultural contexts to clarify my own experience of forms of activity that are required to straddle the two, such as in entrepreneurial activity that draws on or operates in academic areas. This is then supplemented by an analysis of the historical forces that have shaped these contexts, primarily modernity, and the bureaucratic mode of social organization by which it is characterized. A consideration of the purpose and nature of bureaucracy clarifies the value and function of entrepreneurial activity in such contexts, with a specific focus on academicpreneurialism. I draw on my own experience and research to explain my understanding of academicpreneur as a "navigator" operating in interstitial "third spaces" (Bhabha, 2012) between established domains; and identify the abilities, attitudes, and approaches that are of value in facilitating such activity. Given my emphasis on the discipline- and domain-traversing nature of academicpreneurship, my own discussion similarly draws on a variety of theoretical and empirical bases in advancing its argument. I conclude with insights of practical value to academicpreneur. This perspective confirms the value and accuracy of Eklund and Wanzeried's Holistic Framework in accounting for the phenomenon. The relevant aspects of the holistic framework are considered in connection with the discussion throughout. To begin with, however, I provide an insight into the personal circumstances of significance in having developed these perspectives, and competences.

C. Colleen (✉)
Fierce Foundation, La Crosse, WI, USA

M. Aldogan Eklund, G. Wanzenried (eds.), *Academic and Educational Entrepreneurship*, Springer Texts in Business and Economics,
https://doi.org/10.1007/978-3-031-10952-2_16

2 My Entrepreneurial Path

My whole life, I have had to navigate zones and spaces in ways that made clear the power dynamics at work in them, and the implications of these power dynamics for those who need to find a way through them. It was this experience that led me to founding the F.I.E.R.C.E. Academy and the F.I.E.R.C.E. Network, as well as Acton Midwest, a STEM school focused on promoting the dispositions and skills of entrepreneurship in young learners. The foundational idea of these initiatives comes from my book *F.I.E.R.C.E.: Transform your life in the face of adversity, 5 minutes at a time!*, which is in turn derived from my own experience of overcoming disadvantage to achieve my professional and personal goals. I applied my own experiences and insights to formulate an approach that will help others succeed in the way I have done. The F.I.E.R.C.E. Academy focuses on providing training and mentorship for leaders and entrepreneurs, to help them optimize their strategies and hone their skills to ensure that they are achieving the best results they can. The F.I.E.R.C.E. approach focuses on all seven domains of the holistic framework to help entrepreneurs develop a balanced, sustainable, well-rounded approach to their endeavors, promoting a model of entrepreneurship that has been shown to produce beneficial outcomes. I have extensive experience of entrepreneurship, both from own pursuits and those of the many entrepreneurs I have coached. The longer I am active in this area, the more convinced I become of the value of the holistic framework of entrepreneurship. It aligns perfectly with my own perceptions and experience, and dovetails with the interpretations of these phenomena that I have arrived at myself.

I've been coaching people on resilience and how to break free from their adversity for 12 years and have founded a school that teaches entrepreneurship. I read 30 books a year. I'm a PhD. But I've realized that we can all continue to evolve and continue to navigate uncharted waters. We can continue to challenge our definition of self-love. Through doing that, I invested in myself, challenging my self-worth, realizing I am worthy. I became an international speaker, have continued to expand my areas of competence, continue to identify areas where I can make a difference. My path has been marked by a number of exceptional circumstances, but I have come to see that it captures something fundamental about entrepreneurship generally, and academicpreneurship specifically. Just as my path has been characterized by a constant movement among and between power structures in the pursuit of my own good, the entrepreneur takes existing arrangement and seeks to identify what value they preclude or obscure, to find a way among and between them to a better solution. I can see, in hindsight, that this has been crucial to the way I have approached my career and professional experience. In this chapter, I explore the links between my own experience, the holistic framework, and the context in which academicpreneurship operates.

3 A Revaluation of the Idea of Value

My experience and qualifications equip me relatively well for academicpreneurialism. For a start, I commenced my PhD research only after lengthy experience of working in a range of roles in the private sector, in a range of fields, including healthcare, financial services, software development, and more. This rich and varied experience has given me deep insight into the imperatives of the private sector, which a career trajectory that has occurred entirely within academia would be unlikely to have provided. One of the primary challenges I've encountered in my academicpreneurial endeavors has had to do with the variations between culture in academia and industry. It seems likely that my professional experience and abilities have played a role in this. In my professional life, I have always gravitated toward roles that have involved communication, collaboration, and interaction. I love being able to bring agents together to achieve something greater than any would be able to achieve on their own and seeing the creative potential of harnessing such synergies in action is frequently inspiring. My own experience has shown me the extent to which innovation and value addition depend on such alignment of contrasting approaches and priorities, to bring together the competencies that are required to achieve complex and challenging objectives. This supports the basic premise of the holistic framework, which is that an encompassing understanding of all factors needs to be drawn on to account for the phenomenon in question, including intellectual, technological, individual and contextual, cultural, political/economic, financial, and social/environmental.

This emphasis has similarly been expressed in my own research, which focuses on the organizational and individual outcomes of leadership. I am primarily drawn to authentic leadership theory (Avolio & Gardner, 2005), insofar as it articulates a vision of leadership that resonates deeply with my own experiences of organizational synergies as arising from alignment of priorities and values. That is, authentic leadership theory holds that organizational leadership is ultimately a function of ethical commitment, fundamental values, and qualities such as integrity, honesty, and authenticity (Avolio & Gardner, 2005). Indeed, this emphasis is written into the very basis of the approach: it was formulated in the late 1990s, in response to perceptions of the deterioration in the probity of the private sector as evidenced by events such as the Enron collapse and associated events (Avolio & Gardner, 2005). This accounts to a large extent for the focus of authentic leadership theory on

> a pattern of leader behavior that draws upon and promotes both positive psychological capacities and a positive ethical climate, to foster greater self-awareness, an internalized moral perspective, balanced processing of information, and relational transparency on the part of leaders working with followers, fostering positive self-development. (Walumbwa et al., 2008, p. 94)

My own research has focused on the effectiveness of such a model of leadership in bringing about positive organizational outcomes, as well as individual benefits such as personal wellbeing and productivity. Like the holistic framework, authentic leadership theory emphasizes the interdependence of the social, economic, organizational, and all other components of entrepreneurial business activity. It is this holistic perspective that provides the enhanced explanatory power offered by such an approach, and in turn, promotes more efficient functioning.

Authentic leadership theory is part of a broader revaluation, in a range of disciplines and areas, of fundamental ideas of value and productivity. For example, authentic leadership theory was formulated in response to a series of assumptions about organizational culture and performance that prioritized profit and relatively abstracted performance metrics above the more amorphous qualities of ethics and organizational wellbeing. A similar shift can be seen in phenomena such as transformational leadership theory (Bass, 1999), organizational learning theory (Argote, 2013), and the application of complexity theory to organizational contexts (Brodbeck, 2002). Beneath the diversity of focuses and approaches of such recent intellectual innovations, they are united by a common perception. This is that models of performance, growth, and development that fail to take account of ecological conditions such as culture, ethics, and systems will necessarily provide a dangerously limited and simplistic conceptual scheme via which to approach the question of value—what it is, how it can be achieved, and how it can be maintained. In the field of entrepreneurship, the holistic framework provides a similar revaluation: it is the interlocking of a range of elements and functions, rather than the emphasis on any single one, that plays the fundamental role in the creation of value.

A point that needs emphasizing in this context is that such approaches are not arguing that we need to sacrifice performance for some non-instrumental alternative ends, such as social good or personal wellbeing. The argument, as I understand it, is that sustainable performance and development is best achieved by adopting a more nuanced and ramified understanding of value itself, one that takes account of factors such as culture and ethics. While it is more difficult to establish and delineate a clear line between organizational ethics and productivity than it is between, for example, compensation schemes and performance, the quantitative tractability of the latter does not necessarily imply that it is therefore some more fundamental relationship, or a more important one. It is this insight that leads me to characterize this theoretical shift as a revaluation of values. The theory has moved from a stance in which method determined content, to one in which content is shaping new methods and approaches with which to explore it, and in the process, fundamental conceptions of value are being updated and enhanced. There's the joke about the economist, who asks, "That's all very well in practice, but will it work in theory?" The shift I'm identifying is one in which the theory is finally being subsumed to the practical requirements, rather than vice versa.

4 Culture as Organizational Software

My own career path equips me well to appreciate the implications of this theoretical realignment for both theory and practice. My professional experience has largely been focused on facilitating the interaction between parts of organizations, operating

Table 1 Cultural differences between academia and industry (Salmelin, 2015)

Parameter	Academia	Industry
Responsibility	Social responsibilities	Shareholders' responsibilities
Research type	Basic research	Applied research
Output	New knowledge	New product
Research orientation	Curiosity-driven research	Problem-solver driven
Openness	Publication and openness	Ownership and confidentiality
Cultural mindset	Sharing	Control
Research strategy	Scientific freedom	Technology roadmaps
Time horizon	Long-term	Short-term

in the interstices between stakeholders, departments, responsibilities, and objectives. Professionally, I've operated not primarily in any of the seven dimensions of the holistic framework, but in roles that involve achieving interaction and mediation between them. I've therefore had first-hand experience of the importance of the "software" that determines how such areas operate. The metaphor of software is taken from Hofstede et al.'s (2005) seminal work on culture and its organizational implications. Hofstede sees culture as a set of attitudes and assumptions that determine the approaches of people in a given group to issues such as conflict resolution and the mediation of disagreement, social hierarchies and the distribution of power, and other such aspects. Importantly, culture is implicit. Organizational rules and policies lay down the letter of the law, but culture is its spirit. No policy can cover every conceivable social interaction, and especially in gray areas where areas of responsibility and authority overlap, and it is here that culture, ethics, and similar implicit systems become of value.

This becomes a topic of great importance in situations of interface between academia and industry. Given the sharp contrasts in the objectives, norms, and processes between academia and industry, there is great potential for challenges to arise from these (Braunerhjelm, 2007). Table 1 below shows some of the fundamental organizational cultural divergences between academia and industry. As the table shows, these encompass some fundamental and crucial aspects, with the attendant possibility of significant misunderstanding. Academicpreneurship accordingly has to operate in the gray zone of overlap between these sharply contrasting cultures, seeking to achieve synergies through the alignment of purpose and approach, and identifying where these can most fruitfully be propagated. It therefore inherently requires a holistic approach, that understands the whole as something greater than the sum of its parts.

In my experience, academicpreneurial activity involves consistent transitioning between these two contrasting cultural schemes. They touch on all seven aspects of the holistic framework. This can pose great challenges to communication, collaboration, and co-operation. For example, assumptions about all aspects of projects and processes can diverge in important ways, without the various parties even being entirely aware of the fact that they hold these assumptions. And of course, if you're not aware that you're operating on the basis of some specific assumption, it's impossible to evaluate that assumption, compare it to those of your interlocutors, and achieve compromise and consensus. In this sense again, Hofstede's metaphor of culture as the software on which our cognitive programs run is instructive (Hofstede et al., 2005). It's easy to see the output of the software, much harder to evaluate the software itself.

One prominent and important example of these differences hinges on the question of openness, as identified in Table 1 above (an important aspect of the "Cultural" dimension of the holistic framework). The purpose of commercial/industrial activity is to obtain competitive advantages, so the products of intellectual innovation are treated as proprietary assets, to be exploited for profit. In contrast, academia has historically been structured around an ideal of the value of shared knowledge and insights (Davies, 2019). The industrial agent seeks to maximize profit, the academic agent to maximize connectivity within their own disciplinary networks (Wowk et al., 2017). Of course, this is changing, as contemporary corporate models are increasingly applied to the management and activity of academia, but the values and assumptions with which the differing models resonate remain a strong element in the way the individuals on whom these organizations depend approach their work and understand their roles. Academicpreneur is therefore required to remain constantly aware of the way these differences inform attitudes and approaches in the contrasting contexts in which they operate, and to translate them to each other where necessary (Braunerhjelm, 2007). It is in this respect that the holistic framework is of significant value.

5 Academicpreneur as Cultural Navigator

A context such as this presents significant opportunities for entrepreneurial activity. One understanding of entrepreneurship emphasizes the way in which it functions by exploiting market inefficiencies (Herron et al., 1992). The entrepreneur identifies opportunities that have not yet been taken account of by the market, and profits from the market inefficiencies created by these differences in insight and understanding. First-mover advantage is therefore a significant weapon in the entrepreneur's arsenal, insofar as a great deal of entrepreneurial success arises from the speed with which opportunities can be identified and exploited. Traversing the domains of academia and industry gives the entrepreneur a great many opportunities to identify potential synergies between approaches or methods, ideas that could be adapted for other contexts, innovative developments of techniques already in use, and other such interventions to produce value from previously unacknowledged or unidentified opportunities.

The kinds of innovations I have in mind are illustrated by the intervention of patient navigation, which I have researched in some detail from an academic perspective. Patient navigation was created as a means of improving healthcare outcomes for groups identified to be under-served by the healthcare system (Freeman & Rodriguez, 2011). To do so, it doesn't add anything to the healthcare system, but simply seeks to enhance interactions and alignment between its various parts. For example, a patient receiving treatment for cancer needs to see a range of different departments of a hospital, and all of these departments need to communicate and coordinate care in order to achieve the optimal outcome for the patient. The founder of patient navigation, Harold P. Freeman, had the idea that simply improving this communication and coordination would bring about better outcomes for patients. To do so, he trained nurses to help patients "navigate" the healthcare system: explaining to them the way the different departments and functions interrelated, helping them find the information they needed, showing them where to get the relevant treatments, and so on. Patient navigation has been shown to be highly effective. It improves health outcomes for high-risk patient groups, enhances patient satisfaction with treatment, reduces inefficiencies in treatment (and therefore lowers costs), promotes communication and collaboration between parts of the system, and achieves a range of other beneficial outcomes (Freeman & Rodriguez, 2011). It must be emphasized, again, that this is all achieved without the addition of any specific functions or assets to the organization. Instead, it relies simply on training individuals to play this navigator role between domains, to enhance interaction. It depends on a holistic approach to the context, seeing the whole as a complex interacting system, rather than a set of discrete functions.

"Navigation" is thus also a helpful metaphor for academicpreneur's activity. Academicpreneur needs to find ways of navigating between contrasting socio-cultural domains, improving lines of access between them and thereby creating innovative synergies and alignments. This perspective clarifies the importance of creativity to academicpreneurship. Of course, it's by no means a new claim to suggest that creativity is a crucial component of entrepreneurial activity. As early as the 1990s the importance of "vision" to entrepreneurial activity had been identified (Nyström, 1993), and subsequent research has consistently underscored the relevance of this link (Carayannis, 2013; Fillis & Rentschler, 2010; Ward, 2004). It does seem a new perspective, however, to link such concerns with creativity with socio-cultural considerations, rather than seeing them in purely cognitive terms. That is, the emphasis in previous research into creativity and entrepreneurship has tended to predominate in subjectivity-focused approaches to the phenomenon, and to focus on the entrepreneur's ability to conceive of innovative products or services to meet pre-established needs. My idea of entrepreneurship as navigation implies, instead, a much more profoundly social activity, whereby creative activity is directed toward achieving greater socio-cultural cohesion, and in this way producing value from greater efficiencies. This aligns with the holistic framework's vision of the phenomenon, which emphasizes the importance of the coherence of the various components. In this respect, it overlaps with the more sociological theories of entrepreneurship, but goes beyond these by demonstrating how the sociological context is the beginning of the explanation, not the end: the sociological context provides the origin, but the entrepreneur's activity, in order to be successful, must extend into new, unforeseen constellations and conjunctions (Mäkinen & Esko, 2022).

One way of approaching this intersection of creativity with socio-cultural frameworks is via Homi K. Bhabha's (2012) idea of the "third space." Bhabha, a postcolonial theorist, argued that the space in which previously colonized societies can develop from the colonial situation is neither by returning to the pre-colonial past (the first space), nor by acceding to the colonial order imposed from without (the second space). Instead, the space in which creative development and innovative self-expression can occur is in a "third space" in the fluid intersection between these two, where socio-cultural frameworks have not yet solidified and there is therefore extensive potential for innovative adaptation of forms and methods to the unforeseen requirements of the present (Peters & Besley, 2008). Bhabha, and the thinkers influenced by him, therefore place emphasis on the importance of "interstitial" socio-cultural zones: spaces between established domains and regimes, where the intersection and overlap between conceptual schemes and systems of order creates the possibility of dynamic new responses and solutions. Bhabha acknowledges that colonialism represents a social crisis, but he emphasizes that there is no possibility of reversing it, and going back to some point prior to the crisis—some "first space" untouched by the disruptions of colonialism and modernity. The only way open is forward, through the open-ended, creative adaptation of the accidents of history.

My view of academicpreneur's activity falls in line with such a view. As argued above, entrepreneurship generally, and academicpreneurship in particular, takes place in the interstitial spaces between established socio-cultural domains. Academia has a relatively established culture governing processes, communication, problem-solving, and so on, and commercial industry has its equivalent. The challenges and opportunity for academicpreneurship are to operate in the third space where these overlap, and identify possibilities for creative, innovative adaptation and development arising from them (Mäkinen & Esko, 2022; Peters & Besley, 2008). The analogy is not simply accidental, insofar as the forms of social organization that create such overlaps are structurally identical to the social context to which Bhabha (2012) was responding. Bhabha was responding to the colonial situation whereby a socio-cultural order is imposed from without, creating such misalignments. Historically, this is itself a sub-component of Western modernity, characterized by bureaucratic modes of organization that, by their very structure, create such third spaces.

6 Bureaucracy and its Interstices

Bureaucracy is the structural innovation that defines modern industry, and indeed modern society as a whole. Bureaucracy impacts on all seven domains considered in the holistic framework, insofar as it is a structural principle that influences all of these aspects of life and society. It is an organizational principle that makes possible enormous expansions in the scope and productivity of organizations, allowing them to operate at levels of far higher complexity by compartmentalizing and distributing responsibilities and authority. In this way, it simplifies individuals' tasks, by limiting them to one specific area of operation. Just as the factory production line enhanced efficiency by limiting individual workers to one specific task, which they could master completely and therefore perform more quickly and efficiently, bureaucracy slices organizational activity up into discrete units, each of which can be carried out largely independently of all others.

But like colonialism, the bureaucratic society represents a form of crisis. Bureaucracy atomizes social functions and roles, breaking up social bonds that serve to ensure coherence and alignment of different parts and functions of the whole. This produces alienation and estrangement. The art and literature of early modernity is full of vivid examples of how the people living through these organizational innovations experienced them. Nikolai Gogol's and Franz Kafka's novels and stories capture the sense of helplessness and alienation of individuals having to function in bureaucratic systems, while the images of artists such as Edward Hopper and L. S. Lowry depict the atomization of social bonds and a sense of connection that seemed so salient a characteristic of the historical moment. This seems unavoidable: if the organizational principle depends on splitting things up, connections are going to be severed. And so, in the midst of the social rationalization represented by the bureaucratization of society and social functions, an increasing range of interstitial "third spaces" were created, between the official domains of organizational structure, in the areas that such top-down organization failed to account for.

Historically, entrepreneurship becomes of increasing importance at the same time as bureaucratic modes of social organization become increasingly prevalent and entrenched. Given the way I have characterized my own experience of entrepreneurship earlier in this chapter, the nature and effects of bureaucracy discussed above demonstrate why this would be so. As bureaucracy atomizes social and organizational structures, functions and roles more and more, there is increasing scope for the entrepreneurial function of operating in the interstices between these realms, aligning areas that have been separated and profiting from the efficiencies to be achieved by doing so. As bureaucracy atomizes society, the need for a countervailing holistic vision and approach becomes increasingly important. While bureaucratic modes of organization have been highly effective in a range of ways, they have also undoubtedly created significant inefficiencies in others. This is being acknowledged in academia itself (Wowk et al., 2017). Researchers increasingly realize that the division of research into specific disciplines and areas means that important ideas are not communicated as widely as they could be, thus stunting development. For example, findings in chemistry with the potential to solve longstanding problems in biology do not get transferred, because there is insufficient interaction and collaboration between areas. It is this insight that has led to the current emphasis on the value of interdisciplinarity in research.

Bureaucracy also has specific implications for creative, innovative thought and activity. Without even trying to be tendentious, one could argue that the purpose of bureaucracy is to stifle creativity—or at least independent initiative. Here again, the purpose and goal of bureaucracy helps clarify why this would be so. As noted above, among the primary aims of bureaucracy is the distribution of responsibility and authority (Birds, 2015). This is the key to its success. No organization of any significant size could function if every decision needed to be made by the person ultimately responsible, and so bureaucratic organization distributes such authority among numerous members of the organization. This enables organizations to become larger and more complex, and to achieve more, as they can delegate responsibility more extensively (Mäkinen & Esko, 2022). But to ensure that such delegation does not generate inconsistency, randomness, and self-contradictory outcomes, it is necessary to systematize and formalize processes and protocols. If an organization were to delegate decision-making authority to an agent without constraining the limits of the available options, it would have no way of knowing how the agent might act in a range of circumstances. Therefore, constraints on such action are established to control this—thereby shutting off the possibility for the exercise of independent initiative and creativity.

This exclusion of creativity from the social and organizational models characterized by bureaucracy therefore in and of itself creates the conditions for entrepreneurial agents to thrive (Birds, 2015). Precluding creativity from within, the bureaucratic model establishes the opportunities for it to be exploited from without, in the person of actors such as entrepreneurs who are free to identify and act on the potentials available in the context. It must be emphasized, here, that such a dichotomous split is a crude simplification of the practical reality. Contemporary corporate structures include measures to foster creativity within and between individuals, departments, and functions, and one can of course by no means claim that no creative outcomes can be achieved within bureaucratic forms of organization (Birds, 2015). Nevertheless, it does hold that bureaucratic modes of organization do inherently need to impose constraints on the free action of the individuals who operate within them, and these constraints must, perhaps necessarily, create gaps in the scope of available responses to contemporary challenges and opportunities. It is within these gaps that the entrepreneur can excel.

7 Academia and Bureaucracy

Academia is, in its current form, one of the pinnacles of this modern bureaucratic approach to the delegation and apportioning of tasks and activities. The university takes the sum total of possible knowledge and splits it up into discrete areas, which are separated out and delegated to various departments. Within these departments, these areas are again sub-divided and compartmentalized, splitting the focus up further, all the way down to the individual researcher. The structure of research outputs demonstrates the ideal underpinning this: research articles clearly delimit one specific topic or question, which they seek to answer unambiguously by drawing on a tradition of methodological work that establishes the validity and reliability of a variety of approaches to various objects of enquiry. It's a modularized enterprise, each paper a unitary brick of information, added to a wall in the edifice of knowledge.

Indeed, the academy has not simply been shaped thoroughly by bureaucracy, but it was itself one of the primary forces in the creation of the organizational approach itself. As William Davies (2019) demonstrates, it was the enterprise of recordkeeping in its various forms that made possible these social structures characteristic of Western modernity—censuses, accounting, scientific experimental reporting, and other forms of data-gathering about people, things, and activities. Data on populations made bureaucratic social organization possible, which in turn made data easier to gather, making bureaucracy more effective. Clear, reliable data on scientific experiments made it possible to formalize the approach to the development of a body of knowledge about the physical world, enabling science to be a systematized into a coherent endeavor with established norms and processes. In all these ways, the abstraction of forms of social organization into bureaucratic structures depends on the kind of abstract data on phenomena that it is the business of the academy to process, analyze, and produce. The academy can therefore be seen to be in an especially close relationship with, and especially deeply invested in, these tendencies that run contrary to entrepreneurial activity—but which, as I've argued above, therefore also make entrepreneurial activity possible.

This makes academicpreneurialism an interesting situation. Given the particularly bureaucratic rationality of the academy discussed above, it is some ways highly antithetical to entrepreneurial approaches. For example, an organizational culture that prioritizes dependability, adherence to established methods and processes, and long-term perspectives is often inimical to the opportunistic, disruptive, rapidly responding approaches characteristic of entrepreneurial activity. As noted above, however, the gaps inherent in bureaucratic modes themselves create entrepreneurial opportunities, and the academy is no exception in this regard (Mäkinen & Esko, 2022). That is, the compartmentalizing rationality characteristic of much of the structural organization of the academy presents opportunities for entrepreneurs to achieve efficiencies and innovations by establishing alignments and synergies between these disconnected areas of activity. Like the work of translation and navigation described above, academicpreneur operates in the gray space between established domains, identifying the gaps such approaches create and ways in which they can be remedied. Academicpreneur operates by applying a holistic framework in an atomized landscape and exploiting the efficiencies this creates.

8 Conclusion: What This Means for Academicpreneur

Academicpreneurship therefore benefits from a specific set of attitudes, aptitudes, and approaches. Breadth of learning is a benefit. Academia generally emphasizes depth of learning, whereby level of mastery over some specific area is prioritized over the number of areas one may have some degree of competence over. However, for academicpreneur, operating between and among various domains of specialization, some interdisciplinary ability is important, to be able to translate concepts and applications from their context of origin to novel situations where they can be adapted and developed. An awareness of the arbitrary nature of disciplinary boundaries and bureaucratic compartmentalization of functions is also important, to enable academicpreneur to be able to see continuities of thought between areas usually considered distinct. As with all forms of entrepreneurship, disruptive creativity is also an asset—an ability to see limitations where others see business as usual, and from these to formulate solutions to problems others are not even aware of yet. And as I have discovered in my own career, strong abilities relating to communication, collaboration, and co-operation—fundamental social skills—equip one excellently to carry out the work of disciplinary, departmental, and domain-based navigation that is crucial to the value academicpreneurship is able to generate from the realms it operates in.

9 Summary

This academic entrepreneurial case is driven by the life story of Carolyn Colleen. Dr. Colleen started up FIERCE academy based on her life and academic experiences. It is an interesting and didactic case for nascent academic entrepreneurs.

Questions

Question 1. Why and how have bureaucratic modes of social organization resulted in atomization of roles, functions, and capacities?

Question 2. What opportunities does such atomization present for academicpreneur?

Question 3. How is a holistic perspective of value to academicpreneur?

References

Argote, L. (2013). Organization learning: A theoretical framework. In *Organizational learning* (pp. 31–56). Springer.

Avolio, B. J., & Gardner, W. L. (2005). Authentic leadership development: Getting to the root of positive forms of leadership. *The Leadership Quarterly, 16*(3), 315–338.

Bass, B. M. (1999). Two decades of research and development in transformational leadership. *European Journal of Work and Organizational Psychology, 8*(1), 9–32.

Bhabha, H. K. (2012). *The location of culture*. Routledge.

Birds, R. (2015). Redefining roles and identities in higher education: The liminal experiences of a university spinout company. *Journal of Higher Education Policy and Management, 37*(6), 633–645.

Braunerhjelm, P. (2007). Academic entrepreneurship: Social norms, university culture and policies. *Science and Public Policy, 34*(9), 619–631.

Brodbeck, P. W. (2002). Complexity theory and organization procedure design. *Business Process Management Journal, 8*(4), 377–402.

Carayannis, E. G. (2013). *Encyclopedia of creativity, invention, innovation and entrepreneurship* (pp. 36–47). Springer.

Davies, W. (2019). *Nervous states: Democracy and the decline of reason*. W. W. Norton & Company.

Fillis, I., & Rentschler, R. (2010). The role of creativity in entrepreneurship. *Journal of Enterprising Culture, 18*(01), 49–81.

Freeman, H. P., & Rodriguez, R. L. (2011). History and principles of patient navigation. *Cancer, 117*(S15), 3537–3540.

Herron, L., Sapienza, H. J., & Smith-Cook, D. (1992). Entrepreneurship theory from an interdisciplinary perspective: Volume II. *Entrepreneurship Theory and Practice, 16*(3), 5–12.

Hofstede, G., Hofstede, G. J., & Minkov, M. (2005). *Cultures and organizations: Software of the mind* (Vol. 2). McGraw-Hill.

Mäkinen, E. I., & Esko, T. (2022). Nascent academic entrepreneurs and identity work at the boundaries of professional domains. *The International Journal of Entrepreneurship and Innovation*. https://doi.org/10.1177/14657503211063896

Nyström, H. (1993). Creativity and entrepreneurship. *Creativity and Innovation Management, 2*(4), 237–242.

Peters, M. A., & Besley, T. (2008). Academic entrepreneurship and the creative economy. *Thesis Eleven, 94*(1), 88–105.

Salmelin, B. (2015). *Open innovation 2.0: Yearbook 2015*. European Commission.

Walumbwa, F. O., Avolio, B. J., Gardner, W. L., Wernsing, T. S., & Peterson, S. J. (2008). Authentic leadership: Development and validation of a theory-based measure. *Journal of Management, 34*(1), 89–126.

Ward, T. B. (2004). Cognition, creativity, and entrepreneurship. *Journal of Business Venturing, 19*(2), 173–188.

Wowk, K., McKinney, L., Muller-Karger, F., Moll, R., Avery, S., Escobar-Briones, E., et al. (2017). Evolving academic culture to meet societal needs. *Palgrave Communications, 3*(1), 1–7.

Carolyn Colleen is a fierce mother of three children, author, international speaker, entrepreneur, and business strategist focused on helping others achieve their goals. Carolyn is the founder of the FIERCE Academy, an online program that helps women create life strategies that enable them to have the life they dream of—without sacrificing their families, careers, or lifestyles. She is also the author of F.I.E.R.C.E.: Transform Your Life in the Face of Adversity, 5 Mins at a Time! Carolyn is the owner of Acton Midwest private schools, where the philosophy is clear thinking which leads to good decisions, Good decisions lead to the right habits, The right habits lead to character and Character becomes destiny, a consultant and thought leader for Case Western Reserve University as a leader within the Xchange approach, an initiative built upon a scientifically based, multi-disciplinary approach for leading and managing teams. In addition, she is currently publishing a second book focused on academic entrepreneurism and is the Executive Director of 1Life Fully Lived, a nonprofit organization that provides people of all backgrounds the tools to achieve success. With a soon-to-be Ph.D. in Organizational Leadership and Behavior, an MBA, and a BA in Business, Carolyn understands the importance of traditional education. She is passionate about uniting as a human race to elevate each other, remain positive through challenges, and raise above the noise to build stronger communities. As a dynamic and innovative workplace leader, Carolyn has worked as a Program Manager and Business Development Consultant at Gundersen Health System, Associate Professor at the University of Wisconsin-La Crosse, Account Management Executive for Gensler, and a Client Service Executive at UBS Financial Services. She knows how to transition people and processes to achieve the next level of success while also aligning with organizational objectives.

Academic Entrepreneurship in a Traditional Multigenerational Family Business

Corinne Mühlebach

1 Introduction

I was exposed to entrepreneurship long before I became interested in academic study of entrepreneurship. This chapter is a personal reflection of my entrepreneurial and academic journey. It follows chronologically the stages of my curriculum vitae from childhood, education, and doctorate to entrepreneurial engagement in our multigenerational family business and my academic activities at university. Along the way, I address the intellectual and entrepreneurial challenges and opportunities I have faced. The chapter concludes with lessons learned and questions for further discussion.

This textbook is based on a holistic conceptual framework of Academic Entrepreneurship. Drawing on my personal example, I would like to illustrate the role of the individual and contextual aspects, and above all, their interaction:

- Entrepreneurship and academic research are influenced by the respective international and cultural, political, economic, and technological context. Which challenges and opportunities we recognize, be it as a researcher or as an entrepreneur, also depends on the environmental context. At the same time, entrepreneurs and researchers seek to shape their environment by coming up with new solutions and new or better answers to existing and new questions.
- In this sense, I understand academic knowledge and entrepreneurial action as a kind of toolbox, which we can use and from which we can draw depending on the issue at hand. Just as entrepreneurial approaches and entrepreneurial action are not limited to the corporate world, scientific approaches are not limited to the

C. Mühlebach (✉)
FHNW School of Business, University of Applied Sciences and Arts Northwestern Switzerland, Windisch, Switzerland
e-mail: corinne.muehlebach@fhnw.ch

M. Aldogan Eklund, G. Wanzenried (eds.), *Academic and Educational Entrepreneurship*, Springer Texts in Business and Economics,
https://doi.org/10.1007/978-3-031-10952-2_17

academic context of research and universities. Instead, innovation and value added often arise where knowledge from different contexts is combined in new ways.

- I am convinced that the fact that I was exposed to an entrepreneurial mindset from an early age has influenced the way I have approached academic issues. Likewise, I am convinced that my academic training and my work at the university have changed and broadened the way I approach entrepreneurial challenges. I believe the combination of entrepreneurial and academic knowledge has helped me to break new ground in a traditional, less academic industry.

2 Early Childhood

I am trying in vain to concentrate on my work. My five-year-old nephew is sitting at the opposite desk, holding up his drawing and interrupting me with questions. He makes me smile. Forty years ago, I was the five-year-old sitting across. I remember the endless laps I took on the office chair while impatiently waiting for my mother to end her phone calls with customers or suppliers.

My mother was responsible for household, parenting, and the administration of the milling business the family ran together. In my childhood in the 1980s, there were about 160 flourmills in Switzerland. They were virtually without exception family businesses, among them many small mills like ours. My great-great-grandfather had acquired the mill and the corresponding farm in 1878. My grandparents used to live and work in the mill, as did the previous generations. In fact, the family's main income stemmed from farming until the 1950s.

My brother and me grew up living right next to the mill. The company was always present in our everyday lives. Over lunch with our parents and grandparents, conversation turned sooner or later to business issues. As kids we did not bother. We loved to play hide-and-seek in and around the mill and to accompany our grandfather in the truck on his way to bakery customers.

My nephew's questions take me back to the present. Meanwhile, he and his brother, the sixth generation, are playing hide-and-seek around the mill. We decide to go on a site visit together. The oldest building of our mill dates from 1657, the last one has been added in 2011. Today, the building dating from 1657 houses our special products line and our offices. Recently we have deconstructed my grandparents' kitchen, where we used to play as children. My nephew obviously enjoys running around in the shell of the building, which will make room for the extension of our mill laboratory. I have always experienced my parents' and grandparents' entrepreneurial activity as something positive. From an early age, we felt emotionally attached to the business. My parents' work was often intense, their free time scarce, but everyone worked with conviction and commitment towards a common goal. Success was shared and setbacks overcome together; nothing unites a family more. I hope that this spirit will also inspire my little nephews, wherever their path may lead them in the future.

3 Education

In the 1980s and 1990s, my father and grandfather continuously expanded the company. A milestone was set at the beginning of the 1990s with the commissioning of a new wheat mill. The processing capacity increased from 15 to 80 tons of grain per day. The company had earned its reputation as a high-quality supplier and counted both artisanal and industrial bakeries among its customers.

My brother and me earned our first money with cleaning work in production and supporting activities in the office. While my brother knew early on that he wanted to follow the example of our father and grandfather and learn the miller's trade, I decided to go to high school and university. My decision to study business administration was influenced by the discussions we had at home. They regularly revolved around economics, politics, and business management and thus sparked my interest.

I moved to St. Gallen for my university studies, made new friends and became excited about international exchange. As an exchange student, I spent several months in Paris and Madrid. An internship took me to an international airline in New York. As much as I enjoyed urban life in Paris, Madrid, and New York, my internship at a listed company in New York gave me doubts about starting a career in a large corporation. Part of my job was to compile monthly statistics for the head office. Since my supervisor considered the statistics pointless, interns like me filled them with meaningless content. In all those weeks, I hardly ever talked to or even met a customer. In the family business, I had mainly carried out routine office work, not requiring a degree. However, I had never doubted the meaning and usefulness of my job. In the few weeks of my internship, I witnessed inefficient processes, bureaucracy, lack of competence, and micro-politics. I had imagined working in a corporation differently.

Back at university, I took courses in entrepreneurship. I remember class discussions on individual and contextual aspects of entrepreneurship like personality traits and characteristics of successful entrepreneurs. There was no mention of female entrepreneurs. Charisma, leadership skills, self-assertion, resilience, motivational capability, strategic thinking, negotiation skills, risk-taking—the list of required entrepreneurial traits seemed endless to me. What was I supposed to do? The image of large corporations had lost its appeal after my internship in New York. At the same time, I was doubting my abilities and whether I would ever have what it takes to be an entrepreneur.

I first came across the family business literature while working on my master's thesis. For the first time, I saw the reality and experiences that had shaped me since childhood reflected in academic literature. Although the majority of businesses worldwide is controlled and managed by families (Zellweger 2017), family entrepreneurship was not covered in my lectures and textbooks. There was no chair on the subject at my university, and no more than a dozen in Europe. In stark contrast to their economic impact, research on family businesses was completely underdeveloped and underrepresented in European business schools at the beginning of the millennium. I was determined this had to change. Still doubting on where and how to start my professional career, I was convinced I had found an intellectual opportunity. I decided to enroll as an external doctoral student at the University of St. Gallen.

4 Doctoral Studies

During my doctoral studies, I felt a bit like an exotic. First, there was no institutionalized research on family entrepreneurship in St. Gallen. I lacked opportunities for dialogue with other researchers and had the impression of being alienated from the field. Second, I continued to work in our family business with six employees at the time. My fellow PhD students, on the other hand, worked either at university or in large corporations.

Fortunately, I soon discovered and registered for the only international scientific family business conference in Europe. The conference turned out to be a stroke of luck. The research area was still small and the number of participants moderate. It was easy to establish contacts with professors and the few other PhD students. Because there was no established research on family business in St. Gallen, I was completely free to choose whatever thematic and theoretical approach seemed appropriate to me. Without regard to established opinions, I was able to bring up aspects that, in my view, had previously received little attention in literature. Only later did I realize that full academic freedom is not always self-evident. Just as a certain industry logic and business model can become dominant in a sector, theories and constructs can become entrenched in social science with the risk of hardly being questioned anymore.

After 2 years, I presented the progress of my work at a small academic conference. Reactions ranged from scathing comments (at least that is how I perceived them) to the effusive statement the work would win an award 1 day (it did). After the initial shock, I remembered my doctoral advisor's comment as an experienced editor: "If a paper is polarizing, you know it's interesting." Taking into consideration the critical comments, I decided that his statement also applied to my work and that I should pursue my ideas.

I found the deficit orientation of much of the family business literature irritating. Convinced that family entrepreneurship deserves more attention in research, I decided to focus on how entrepreneurial families influence the resources and capabilities in a business, either positively and/or negatively. I developed a concept assisting family businesses in analyzing the idiosyncratic influence of the owner family to build competitive advantages based on their strengths (Mühlebach 2005). Thereby the applicability of the results in practice has always been of key importance to me.

Working on my dissertation, I learned to ask critical questions, adopt different perspectives, and look for alternative models and solutions. In this approach, I see a commonality between researchers and entrepreneurs. Both are looking for opportunities. Entrepreneurs look for gaps in the market to satisfy unmet customer needs or create new ones, researchers look for research gaps to generate new knowledge and new research questions.

5 Joining the Family Business

My entry into the company was not planned. I assumed it would be a temporary phase benefitting both sides. I was able to gain management experience, had interesting and varied tasks, and enough time and flexibility to push my dissertation ahead on the side.

During my studies, I had become familiar with Michael Porter's industry structure analysis (Porter 1980). Based on the principles of industrial economics, he had developed a model to determine the potential profitability and attractiveness of an industry. According to Porter, the potential profitability of an industry is higher the lower the competitive rivalry among existing firms, the weaker the bargaining power of customers and suppliers, and the less likely the entry of new competitors or the substitution by other products. My analysis of the Swiss milling industry at the beginning of the millennium showed the following picture (see Fig. 1):

- *Competitive Rivalry*: Of the 160 grain milling companies active in Switzerland in the 1980s, about 70 were still on the market at the beginning of the millennium. The market was characterized by overcapacity and intense predatory competition. An end of the structural change was not in sight.
- *Bargaining Power of Suppliers*: The flour price is largely dependent on the raw material which makes up for 70% of the costs. To protect domestic agriculture,

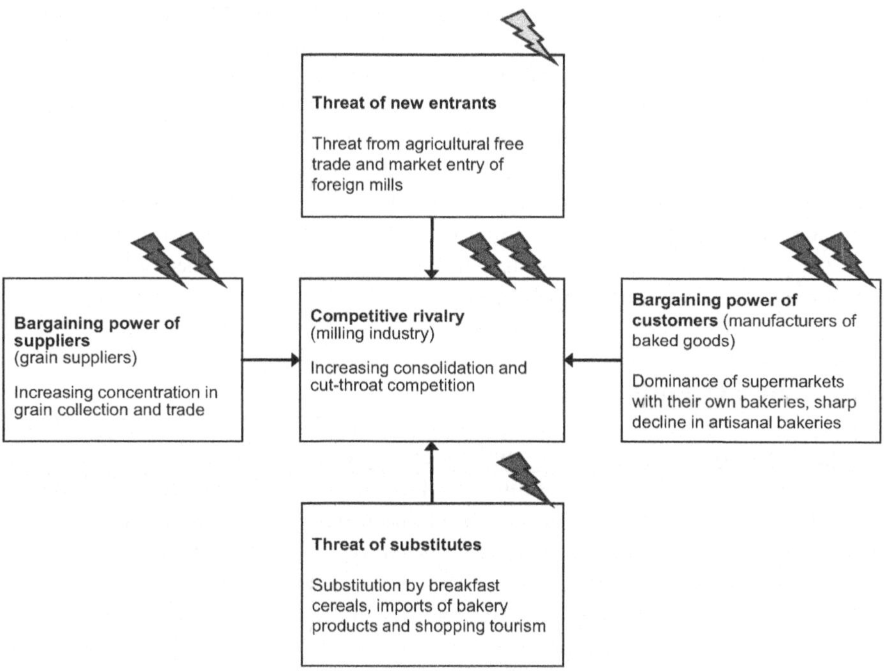

Fig. 1 Industry analysis of the Swiss milling industry (Adapted from Porter 1980)

imports of wheat are subject to tariffs and limited in quantity. In Switzerland, cooperative cereal collection centers control about 80% of grain intake and trade. Bargaining power of smaller mills is limited.

- *Bargaining power of Customers*: The two largest retailers in Switzerland operate their own bread factories and in-store bakeries. They accounted for two-thirds of the baked goods market. Artisanal bakeries accounted for a collective market share of about 30%, with a declining trend. Market concentration on the customer side was already very high.
- *Threat of Substitutes*: Switzerland had benefited for years from strong immigration and a growing population. However, bread consumption was stagnating. Changing eating habits and shopping tourism, the inexpensive purchase of foodstuffs in neighboring countries, limited the sales of flour. There were no growth impulses in sight.
- *Threat of New Entrants*: Switzerland's small-scale agriculture is one of the most highly subsidized worldwide. To support agricultural production, the state grants direct payments to farmers. The European Union (EU) is Switzerland's most important agricultural trading partner. At the time, a potential agreement on agricultural free trade between Switzerland and the EU was on the political agenda. Proponents expected better export opportunities. Opponents feared that Switzerland would be flooded with cheap food imports forcing many farmers out of the market.

Michael Porter concluded companies should locate in attractive industries as they promise higher returns. My analysis based on his model was clear: the competitive environment was difficult and the competitive outlook anything but promising.

Regardless of the competitive outlook, I joined the family business in 2000, full of optimism and drive. I felt no pressure and external expectation to remain in the company as a successor. It was open where my professional and private life would lead me after the dissertation project. I was convinced that I could contribute to the company. I was further convinced that profitability and viability of a company are not solely dependent on industry structure and sector attractiveness, but as much on idiosyncratic resources and capabilities.

6 Red Oceans

As part of my dissertation, I studied strategic management intensively. The challenges our company was facing were typical of mature markets: overcapacity, crowding out, and intense price competition. Kim and Mauborgne (Kim & Mauborgne 2005) would later describe such markets as "red oceans." In "red oceans," firms follow a prevailing industry logic and try to capture higher market share at the expense of competitors. Strategies in an industry become increasingly similar. The more competition intensifies, the more opportunities for profit and growth decrease. Products are interchangeable, and markets are increasingly constricted.

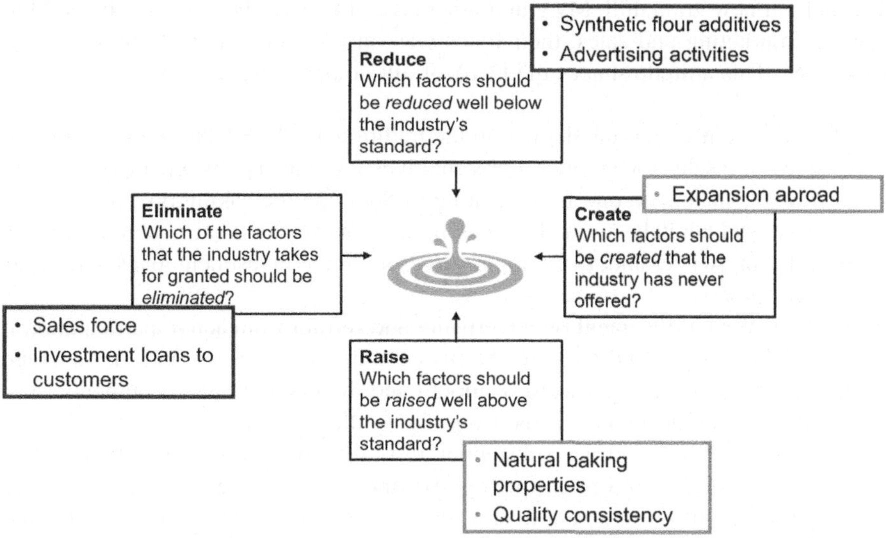

Fig. 2 How to escape the Red Ocean? (Adapted from Kim & Mauborgne 2005)

Successful companies succeed in swimming out into a "blue ocean." They tap new markets and new demand by critically questioning the dominant industry logic and finding answers to four central questions (see Fig. 2):

1. Which of the factors that the industry takes for granted should be *eliminated*?
2. Which factors should be *reduced well below* the industry's standard?
3. Which factors should be *raised well above* the industry's standard?
4. Which factors should be *created* that the industry has never offered? (Kim & Mauborgne 2005)

As an entrepreneurial family, we were having intense discussions about the future of our business. How could our company defend its market position in the long run? What would be the impact of a potential agricultural free trade agreement with the EU? What growth opportunities offered the domestic market, increasingly dominated by a few large corporations? Were my brother and me to take over as successors, what plans would we have for the company?

Though our company was small, it was well positioned and competitive. In a highly automated and capital-intensive industry, we had managed to keep investment costs low. For the construction of the new mill in the 1990s, my father and grandfather had dismantled a complete flour milling plant near London. The equipment was as good as new. The durum mill near London had been running for only 2 years before being shut down. My father reimported the machinery, originally manufactured by Swiss global market leader Bühler, to Switzerland. My brother and me were schoolchildren at the time. I remember how we awaited the trucks with the equipment from the UK full of enthusiasm and fascination. They were to form the heart of our new grain mill. My grandfather and father were both technophiles. More than on marketing and sales, their focus was on product quality, technology, and processes. This attitude shapes the DNA of our company to this day:

- *Eliminate:* An important element in the traditional value chain of a grain milling business is a sales force. Sales representatives visit bakery customers, take orders, and advise bakers on questions relating to flour and the baking process. To date, we have deliberately not had a sales force. Contrary to what is common in the industry in Switzerland, our company does not grant investment loans to bakeries and customers.
- *Reduce:* We hardly spend on advertising and refrain from active participation in trade fairs. Our expenditures in advertising and sales are below industry average. Instead, we capitalize on word-of-mouth and the naturalness and authenticity of our products. Our flours are free from any synthetic additives.
- *Increase:* We concentrate substantial resources on procurement to purchase wheat lots of above-average quality. To find such lots we make extensive use of grain analytics. We do not treat wheat as a commodity but as a top winemaker treats his grapes. Careful selection of raw materials, combined with technical expertise, creates the basis for flours with consistently excellent baking properties.
- *Create:* We were determined to hold on to our success factors. However, how could we escape the red ocean? Would we succeed in creating something new together?

How could we escape the red ocean? It is the question that continues to haunt us to this day. During the long evenings that I spent racking my brain over my dissertation, I often doubted the sense and usefulness of my academic endeavor. Looking back, I think that my dissertation journey has helped me to sharpen my analytical skills and to raise new questions. New questions can be a first but crucial step on the way to new answers. These answers do not have to be groundbreaking or world firsts. What matters is that they are new for the company or the industry and that they offer customers added value.

7 Market Entry Germany

From the terrace of our 42-meter-high grain silo, you have a beautiful panoramic view up to the hills of the Black Forest. Our business is located only 10 km from the Swiss-German border. At the beginning of the millennium, we saw hardly any growth opportunities in Switzerland. If the tariffs for wheat and flour were abolished 1 day, we feared being overrun by competitors from Germany and other EU-countries producing at much lower costs.

We were not the only ones to look across the border. So did the largest Swiss supermarket chain, one of our customers. In 2002, they were planning the opening of a new supermarket with in-house bakery in Freiburg in Breisgau, Germany. The media reported on the company's growth strategy in Germany. The CEO stated within 10 years the company aimed at opening about 20 supermarkets including in-house bakeries in Germany. We had thought about expanding abroad before and always rejected ideas and contacts after brief consideration. Whatever market we looked at, even with local partners, the language and cultural barriers seemed too high and financial risks unpredictable. It was different with our customer's project. We were familiar with the requirements and needs of our customer, and Freiburg in Breisgau is only 100 kilometers away. Our customer was already operating two bakeries in Germany. The purchasing department regularly reported on the difficulties of finding a qualified flour supplier in Germany. They had even considered importing flour from Switzerland and rejected the idea due to excessive costs. We came up with a different proposal. We were ready to take the entrepreneurial risk to set up a flour production in Germany and to supply the customer's new bakery in Freiburg according to Swiss standards.

We wrote a business plan based on the assumptions that within 10 years our customer would open another 20 bakeries in Germany and that Switzerland might conclude an agricultural free trade agreement with the EU. We were still facing a major problem: We had won a customer, though we had no production site. Placing box number advertisements in German trade journals, seeking a grain mill to lease or rent did not bring the desired results.

My father suddenly remembered one of our family trips to the French-German border area. In Kappel-Grafenhausen, a small German town on the border with Alsace, we had once passed by a grain mill. Such coincidences happened surprisingly often on our family trips. As children, we found it exciting to stroll around foreign mills. Would a dog immediately chase us off the grounds or would a hospitable miller's family even invite us for a spontaneous site visit? The opening date of the supermarket in the fall of 2002 was set. We were in urgent need of a production plant. My father took the trip again. He bought a round of beers at the local pub to learn that the small mill had ceased operations 2 years ago. The owner was planning to set up a mill museum in the disused production facility. After negotiations he agreed to postpone his museum project and lease the production.

It was challenging to prepare for the timely start of production in Germany, especially since my father unexpectedly fell ill. He signed the contracts for the foundation of our German subsidiary on his way to hospital. Due to surgery and subsequent rehabilitation, he had to withdraw from the business for several weeks.

Within 3 months, we have founded a company, rented a production plant, and refurbished it to assure food safety and the quality requirements of our customer. My brother, still a university student, took care of the commissioning of the plant, while I was responsible for legal and organizational aspects and setting up quality management. The opening of the bakery was an immediate success. As it turned out, the paper bags for the typical Swiss style bread were too small. The naturally stronger flour quality gave the bread a higher volume. The bakery urgently had to order larger bread bags.

The start of production with minimal investment and manageable financial risk was successful. Based on our resources—who we are, what we know, and whom we know, we had considered what we were willing to invest—in terms of time, money, and relationships. Sarasvathy calls this the principle of affordable loss [Sarasvathy 2008]. We had proven technical and milling expertise, solid market knowledge, and a customer relationship with growth potential. We gave ourselves 5 years to enter the market. Either we could gain a foothold in the market within this time, or we would have to pull down our tents again. Thanks to a modest rent and without local employees, we kept our fixed costs low. We were operating the mill by sending a miller from Switzerland to Germany for about 2 days every 3 weeks. We invested what was necessary to ensure food safety. After a short time, our customer increased the number of jobs in the bakery and looked for more suitable supermarket locations. How could we keep pace? It was undeniable that our production plant was not suited for growth. The building was in poor condition, the machinery outdated, and the plant not automated. The location in the middle of a residential area was unfavorable for a grain mill. Furthermore, we were dependent on a single customer.

Two years after we had entered the German market, the opportunity to acquire a mill unexpectedly turned up. A nearby grain mill had filed for bankruptcy. Rebuilt in 1990 after a devastating fire, the company had never recovered from the financial setback. The plant was modern, automated, and suitable in size and location. Within 10 days, we had worked out a new business plan including financing. We won the bid and were able to reopen the business 2 months after the original bankruptcy. The previous employees, a team of five, stayed on board. We abandoned production in the rented mill and moved it to our own mill with a capacity of 40 tons of grain per day. Gradually, we managed to regain the trust of former customers and suppliers. We remained true to our quality philosophy, which increasingly allowed us to win new customers too.

Eighteen years have passed since our start in Germany. Though academically sound, none of the assumptions in our business plan has come true. There is no agricultural free trade agreement between Switzerland and the EU. The national border cuts across our geographically contiguous delivery area. Quite a few of our German bakery customers are located closer to our Swiss than to our German plant. However, due to the different cost structures and the custom duties between Switzerland and Germany, they are supplied by the German plant. The Swiss supermarket chain, our first customer in Germany, has not realized its growth plan. The company eventually operated four supermarkets with in-house bakeries in Germany. In 2013, they sold their German business to a supermarket chain in Germany, which has since become one of our customers.

Since our beginnings in a rented mill with a single customer, we have established ourselves as a niche supplier for demanding artisanal bakeries. We have continuously expanded both our customer base and our production. It has been a long road, fraught with obstacles, challenges, and setbacks. Along the way, we have been able to rely on our strengths as a family business: Thanks to our independence, we were capable of action and quick when it came to making key decisions. We had the technical and professional expertise to produce flours with above-average baking properties, initially on an old plant. Academic knowledge was crucial in analyzing the initial strategic situation and preparing for market entry. To take the plunge into a foreign market, however, you also need an entrepreneurial mindset. This includes the willingness to take calculated risks and to make long-term investments. Despite the best preparation and careful analysis, there are always unforeseen opportunities and challenges. In unforeseen situations, entrepreneurial skills have proved particularly valuable.

8 Company and University

I submitted my dissertation in 2004, shortly before we had the opportunity to acquire the mill in Germany. Our business was developing dynamically. The company was at the beginning of the transition from one generation to the next. My brother already had an ownership stake in the company. My father and him invited me to continue working in the company. My father set one condition: I was to acquire technical and milling-specific knowledge too. He had seen many business families struggling with conflict because family members had either technical or business expertise, but not both. As they would not understand each other, they were unable to come up with joint decisions. My brother and him had both a technical and a business degree. After my doctorate, I therefore enrolled for a five-month intensive study program at the Swiss School of Milling, one of the world's prime institutions for training technical and management staff in the grain milling industry. For the first time in the history of the school, two women, my Lebanese colleague and me, were enrolled simultaneously.

My dissertation had been published in the meantime and had received some attention thanks to the award from the International Family Enterprise Research Academy (IFERA). During my doctoral studies, I had given my first presentations at scientific conferences. Now, I happily accepted the opportunity to guest lecture at the University of St. Gallen and to present my work in executive education programs both inside and outside the university. Shortly after completing my doctorate, the University of St. Gallen founded its Center for Family Business. Timing was ideal. I was invited to join the Center for Family Business as a Research Fellow which allowed me to be involved in an international research project on multigenerational family businesses (Zellweger, Sieger, Mühlebach, 2010).

It was enriching to continue commuting between the academic world and entrepreneurial practice, especially since milling has hardly been academic to this day. Both my family and my academic mentors encouraged me to combine both worlds. My focus has always been on practice-oriented studies and application-oriented research. This is how I learned about a project on succession planning in SMEs and got hired as a part-time researcher and lecturer at the University of Applied Sciences and Arts Northwestern Switzerland. I have been teaching for 15 years in undergraduate, graduate, and executive education programs. I carry out my own consulting and research projects with companies and get to know many exciting firms.

The methodological knowledge I have acquired in my academic training is also useful in an entrepreneurial context. As part of an Innosuisse-funded pilot project with the University of Applied Sciences for Agronomy, we have developed a quality payment and quality feedback system for organic farmers that has since become the industry standard. The combination of economic and agronomic knowledge, the scientifically sound collection and evaluation of data and, at the same time, the personal discussion and interaction with producers have allowed us to help innovations achieve a breakthrough against initial resistance. In science as in the business world, new ideas are often first ridiculed, then fought against, until they finally gain widespread acceptance. It took both to help our model make a breakthrough in practice—scientific expertise, because at the beginning of the project we simply lacked solid empirical data and models—and entrepreneurial action, tenacity, persuasiveness, and negotiating skills to convince suppliers and partners to follow a new path.

9 Lessons Learned

When I joined the family business at the age of 25, I thought my involvement would be temporary. Twenty years have passed since then. Eight years ago, I took on the role of CEO and became co-owner with my brother. My responsibilities have changed over the 20 years. The company and responsibilities have grown. I continue to lecture and value the interaction with students and colleagues. It is both a challenge and a privilege to keep up with current developments in research and teaching. Therefore, I would like to summarize my experience using the slightly adapted framework for Academicpreneurship developed by Eklund and Wanzenried (2022) (see Fig. 3).

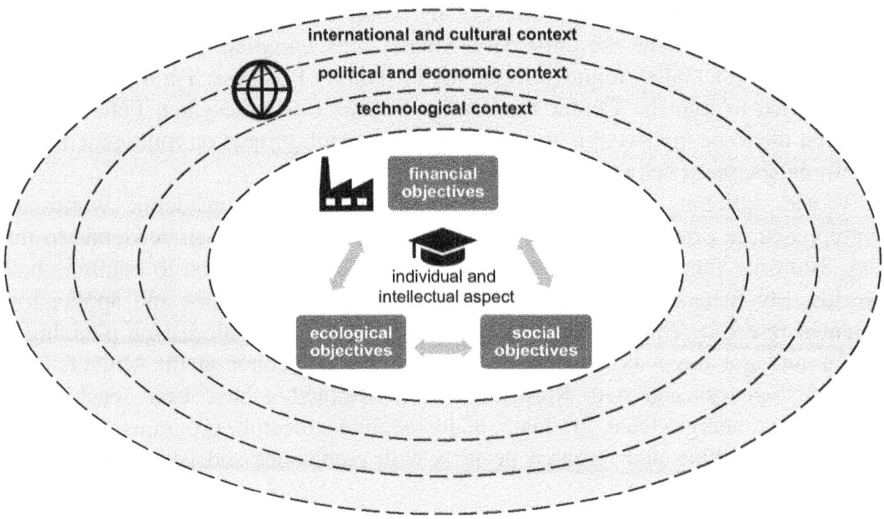

Fig. 3 Academicpreneurship. The holistic conceptual framework (adapted from Eklund & Wanzenried 2022)

Environmental Context Based on a systematic analysis of the business environment, we decided 20 years ago to venture abroad. In retrospect, important assumptions of our business plan did not come true. Our first customer in Germany withdrew from the market without realizing his expansion plans. There is no agricultural free trade between Switzerland and the EU *(political aspect)*. On the other hand, the structural change that was already apparent at the time has become more accentuated. In the meantime, there are still 30 mills in Switzerland *(economic aspect)*. To date, we are the only Swiss grain mill with production abroad. As a family business, we see ourselves as a niche player in our markets, adaptable and agile *(international and cultural aspect)*. We mastered the milling technology and were convinced that our quality policy would allow us to be successful in a foreign market too. Technology has allowed us to develop this quality policy innovatively, to provide farmers with more accurate feedback and thus to influence quality already at the cultivation stage *(technological aspect)*.

Concepts, strategies, and plans are important and valuable. But even the best strategy can never fully reflect the complex reality. Sooner or later, something happens that we did not expect. What benefits can we derive from unexpected positive or negative events in our political, economic, technological, and cultural environment? We have not regretted entering the market. It has undoubtedly presented us with numerous and unexpected challenges, from which we have learned a great deal. But above all, it has opened new business opportunities and changed our entrepreneurial starting position. Doing beats planning. Not everything that is ventured succeeds. But everything that succeeds was once dared. Academic entrepreneurs are characterized by the fact that they combine vision with action. I see this combination of vision and action as one of the most important synergies of academic education and entrepreneurship.

Corporate Context For companies to be successful in the long term, they must generate financial as well as social and ecological value. I see this as one of the potential strengths of family businesses. They tend to have a long-term orientation and have often been rooted in a region for generations. Our company offers qualified jobs and apprenticeships in rural areas. Some of our most important employees have already completed their training in our company *(social aspect)*. Together with our partners, we have initiated research projects and put the results into practice to promote the spread and quality of organic farming. Located in the middle of the quality cultivation area, we are an important partner for local agriculture. At the same time, we are close to the densely populated centers, which allows short distances and regional added value *(ecological aspect)*. We invest continuously in our operations and take financial and entrepreneurial risks in a capital-intensive industry. When investing under high uncertainty, we are guided less by uncertain future profits than by the principle of affordable loss *(financial aspect)*.

New knowledge often emerges at the interfaces between fields of knowledge. I attribute the success of our research project in organic cereal production largely to the interdisciplinary collaboration of agronomists, economists, and farmers. Among other things, this collaboration allowed us to collect data empirically—on farm—

instead of only on experimental plots at a research institute. Ultimately, the decisive factor for the sustainable success of a project is whether the results can be applied in practice. In addition to academic competence and personal persuasiveness, this requires entrepreneurial tenacity and the ability to forge alliances. Today, we can say that our idea of quality payment has prevailed despite initially fierce resistance and is now standard in Swiss grain farming.

Individual and Intellectual Context I am grateful to be able to fall back on my training in everyday business life *(intellectual aspect)*. In addition to my education, my childhood and youth in a multigenerational entrepreneurial family have been formative for my path *(individual and familial aspect)*. Both my family of origin and my academic education have opened professional opportunities I would not have had under other circumstances. However, I consider an academic education neither a necessary nor a sufficient prerequisite for personal and professional success. The decisive factor is always what we make of the circumstances and opportunities we find and how we actively shape them *(individual aspect)*.

In this respect, I find the research encouraging that understands entrepreneurship as a set of methods that are particularly useful when making decisions under great uncertainty (Sarasvathy 2008). This is good news for entrepreneurs and anyone who wants to become one, because methods can be taught and learned. We can acquire them, constantly perfect them, and pass them on to others. It is these tasks, both in the company and at university, which challenge me every day.

It is the combination of different resources, competencies, and experience backgrounds that moves our company and our society forward. We need technical and business, practical and academic knowledge. We need the skills of men and women, the experience of younger and older, natives and foreigners. The decisive factor is the ability to work together and how a person brings his or her competencies and skills into a team, not how they were acquired.

Intellectual, individual, and contextual aspects are central cornerstones of the holistic conceptual framework of academic and educational entrepreneurship discussed in this textbook. Although it is not explicitly mentioned, the family aspect also seems significant to me.

- *Individual and Collective:* The family of origin as well as the social and cultural context are formative for the development of an individual. The individual is inconceivable without the collective.
- *Family and Entrepreneurship:* Families play an important role in most of the companies worldwide, be it as venture capitalists, investors, on boards of directors and/or in the management of start-ups and family-owned companies. Families can also play an important role in the context of academic and educational entrepreneurship.
- *Family and Intellectual Capital:* Intellectual and social capital is passed on significantly within families from one generation to the next, in the form of tacit and explicit knowledge, know-how, networks, and relationships. State education at public schools, universities and in vocational training is therefore

central to equal opportunities in society and the competitiveness of a national economy.

10 Summary

This academic entrepreneurial case is driven by the story of Corinne Mühlebach. Dr. Mühlebach has illustrated how her academic experience at the University of St. Gallen in Switzerland has shaped her multigenerational family business as an academic entrepreneur.

Questions

Question 1. What makes companies entrepreneurial? Is ensuring the continued existence of a company an entrepreneurial achievement? Is it enough to survive in a stagnating market characterized by consolidation and cut-throat competition? What does it take to open up new markets and new demand?

Question 2. What distinguishes family businesses from non-family businesses? What advantages do family businesses have? What weaknesses do they have? How do the developments of family and business, of individual and collective, influence each other? What roles do women play in family businesses, how have these roles changed?

Question 3. Can you learn entrepreneurial thinking and action? Is it a question of personality? What role does education play? What role do coincidences play? What influences entrepreneurial success?

Question 4. Why are companies active in markets considered unattractive according to economic criteria? Would you enter such a company as an entrepreneur/successor/manager, why or why not?

References

Eklund, M., & Wanzenried, G. (2022). *Academic and educational entrepreneurship: Foundations in theory and lessons from practice*. Springer.

Kim, W., & Mauborgne, R. (2005). *Blue Ocean strategy: How to create uncontested market space and make the competition irrelevant*. Harvard Business School Press.

Mühlebach, C. (2005). *Familyness as a competitive advantage*. Haupt.

Porter, M. (1980). *Competitive strategy*. Free Press.

Sarasvathy, S. (2008). *Effectuation: Elements of entrepreneurial expertise*. Edward Elgar.

Zellweger, T. (2017). *Managing the family business: Theory and practice*. Edward Elgar.

Zellweger, T., Sieger, P., & Mühlebach, C. (2010). How much and what kind of entrepreneurial orientation is needed for family business continuity? In M. Nordqvist & T. Zellweger (Eds.), *Transgenerational entrepreneurship: Exploring growth and performance of family firms across generations*. Edward Elgar.

Corinne Mühlebach is an entrepreneur and lecturer at the University of Applied Sciences and Arts Northwestern Switzerland, teaching strategy and entrepreneurship. She is co-owner and CEO of Mühlebach AG, a Swiss multigenerational family business, and serves on various corporate and foundation boards. Corinne holds a Ph.D. from the University of St. Gallen, Switzerland.

An Academic Route to Transnational Entrepreneurship: A Scandinavian-Tanzanian Experience

Pontus Engström, Neema Mori, Trond Randøy, and Siri Terjesen

1 Introduction

Business schools in the USA and Europe are enrolling an increasing number of foreign students (AACSB, 2011; Friga et al., 2003; Mitchell, 2007). This is helping to internationalize classroom learning and extracurricular experiences (Rienties et al., 2015) and foreign students provide valuable income as they commonly pay full tuition (Hall & Sung, 2009), for example in the UK and Australia. In this chapter, we highlight how foreign students, PhD students in particular, need to prepare for the reality of a complex employment situation when they return to their country of origin. Most business scholars in low-income countries cannot rely solely on a university salary for their income. Furthermore, it is a common expectation in low-income countries' universities that faculty members will be extensively involved in providing public services, such as serving on the board of a state-owned firm. With this chapter, we take this further by addressing business scholars' involvement in entrepreneurship, and we discuss such involvement in light of the Holistic Conceptual Framework of Edupreneurship.

P. Engström
Stockholm School of Economics, Stockholm, Sweden
e-mail: pontus.engstrom@hhs.se

N. Mori
University of Dar es Salaam, Dar es Salaam, Tanzania
e-mail: mori.neema@udsm.ac.tz

T. Randøy (✉)
Copenhagen Business School, Copenhagen, Denmark
e-mail: tra.ccg@cbs.dk

S. Terjesen
Florida Atlantic University, Boca Raton, FL, USA
e-mail: sterjesen@fau.edu

M. Aldogan Eklund, G. Wanzenried (eds.), *Academic and Educational Entrepreneurship*, Springer Texts in Business and Economics,
https://doi.org/10.1007/978-3-031-10952-2_18

Research on foreign business students tends to focus on the comparatively larger populations of bachelor's and Master's students, for example how to foster their inclusion in business schools (Zhang et al., 2016). On the other hand, recent research has addressed how professors and their foreign students can co-create knowledge and produce publications (Corner & Pio, 2017), and we take this one step further by highlighting how such academic ideas can help students to examine and pursue potential new business opportunities or social ventures. This is in line with the Holistic Framework's emphasis on edupreneurship as a means to achieving social and environmental sustainability. Nobel Laureate Muhammad Yunus, with a PhD from Vanderbilt University, is an example of such phenomena, as he founded and built the Grameen Foundation based on academic ideas regarding financial market imperfections. We see a lack of theory building around these phenomena, and also underutilized potential for business schools to stay socially relevant to key stakeholders such as international students and sponsoring governments.

In this chapter, we introduce a new concept, academic transnational entrepreneurship, as an extension of academic entrepreneurship. Such entrepreneurial activity involves the development of sustainable business enterprises based on long-standing cross-country interactions between academics and their former and/or current students. We see the greatest potential for such transnational activities linked to professors based in high-income countries and students who come from emerging markets. Based on an outlined Tanzanian-Scandinavian case story, we theorize on how such academic transnational entrepreneurial activities can be created, in line with the Holistic Conceptual Framework of Edupreneurship and its focus on financial and economic aspects.

Academic transnational entrepreneurship can generate sustainable value for both society at large and individual students and faculty members. This concept comes at the intersection of academic entrepreneurship, which focuses mostly on university spin-offs and technology transfer (Shane, 2004), and transnational entrepreneurship, which is defined as "*individuals that migrate from one country to another, concurrently maintaining business-related linkages with their former country of origin, and currently adopted countries and communities*" (Drori et al., 2009, p. 1001). Academic entrepreneurship literature has thus far neglected the relationships cultivated between students (doctoral students in our study) and professors in terms of their operation across wide geographies. The emerging transnational entrepreneurship literature (e.g., Carmichael et al., 2010) focuses mostly on business immigrants (e.g., Portes et al., 2002) and their business experiences. The somewhat-related returnee entrepreneur literature sometimes includes transnational entrepreneurs, but rarely considers these entrepreneurs' academic ties. Although many immigrant and transnational entrepreneurs initially arrived in their host countries for educational reasons (Wadhwa et al., 2007), there is limited understanding of how foreign students' educational experiences might eventually lead to new transnational entrepreneurial activity. The above arguments are in line with the Holistic Framework's focus on international and cultural aspects of academic entrepreneurship.

We believe that academic transnational entrepreneurship is also a desirable way for business schools to show greater social impact and become more relevant to their communities. Interestingly, Muhammad Yunus' (2012, p. 1) motivation to start a microfinance initiative stemmed from his disappointment with the disconnect between research and social impact: "*I began my career as an economics professor but became frustrated because the economic theories I taught in the classroom didn't have any meaning in the lives of poor people I saw all around me.*" Business school initiatives such as the United Nations' PRME (Principles for Responsible Management Education) seek to fill this gap, as illustrated by the first principle: "*We will develop the capabilities of students to be future generators of sustainable value for business and society at large and to work for an inclusive and sustainable global economy*" (PRME, 2015). Some business schools struggle to operationalize such demands and develop sustainable and impactful business models (Blasco, 2012), whereas others, such as the University of Western Australia, Stanford University, Tecnologico de Monterrey, Haas School of Business, and Copenhagen Business School, to mention a few, are better at promoting such activities.[1] What we outline provides an avenue for operationalizing such social business models of academic entrepreneurship.

Academic transnational entrepreneurship is particularly attractive due to the employability challenges of recent graduates, which can be seen as a paradox given the high growth of emerging markets. As one example, Sub-Saharan African countries' real GDP has grown by 6–8% over the last decade (IMF, 2017); however, these markets face huge institutional challenges related to corruption (Transparency International, 2017),[2] institutional impediments to private equity and venture capital investments (Hearn et al., 2018), and shortages of talent and business skills (World Bank, 2014). Despite these challenges, foreign investors in Africa transfer significant funding—over US$80 billion in 2014 as foreign direct investment and US$8 billion annually in private equity (Economist, 2015). We see returning business scholars, originally from emerging markets, as potential bridge-builders for such foreign investments.

2 Methods

This study focuses on the conceptual development of transnational academic entrepreneurship. Given the early phase of our conceptual development, the practical case experience plays a significant part in the initial conceptual development.

To develop the proposed framework and the corresponding propositions, we first examine the evolution of one such transnational business venture. Given that the case involves three of the researchers, as subjects of their own study, it demands a

[1] https://bestbizschools.aacsb.edu/blog/2016/october/business-schools-creating-social-entrepreneurs.

[2] One major area of corruption relates to employment.

high level of critical reflexivity. This is consistent with narrative methods and reflexivity in social science (Cree, 2012; Elliot, 2005) and is furthermore based on the legitimacy of creation-practice-based knowledge (Van de Ven & Johnson, 2006). The latter is an approach that has previously been applied in management research (Cunliffe, 2004), and in relation to the interaction between professors and PhD students (Corner & Pio, 2017; Robinson-Pant, 2009).

We acknowledge several limitations of our study. First, the uniqueness of the persons involved might make the concept less general than proposed. We clearly understand that not every business professor is a potential co-founder and entrepreneur; however, we commonly observe that professors are extensively involved in entrepreneurial activities such as the creation of new study programs (Kolb & Kolb, 2005). Second, the lack of parallel cases limits the generalizability of this case. However, we use the case experience to make propositions that future research can test.

2.1 MTI: Turning Academic Entrepreneurship into Practice

The foundation case for this study is a Scandinavian investment company, MTI Investment SE (www.mti-investment.com), which has, since its start-up in 2014, achieved significant ownership shares (20–70%) in four Tanzanian firms. At the end of 2021, the company conducted an initial public offering (IPO) and was listed on the Nasdaq First North Growth market in Stockholm. The start-up of the business illustrates how a Western-based university environment can enhance business development based on academic transnational entrepreneurship. Academic transnational entrepreneurship was instrumental in the definition of the business model and corporate governance structure.

Table 1 summarizes the multi-year process that eventually led to the start of the investment company. The table highlights how the key actors who collaborated as part of a PhD program took part in the multi-year process. In 2008, two Tanzanian nationals went to a Scandinavian university to undertake a PhD in International Management. Both students had university educations and business experience in Tanzania. Before going to Scandinavia for their studies, the two students were not only members of faculty at their university but also ran businesses, sat on corporate boards, and conducted various consultancy projects. Upon arrival in Scandinavia, they met their PhD advisor, who was keen to work with them due to his experience with emerging markets. The supervisor had served for over a decade as a board member of a Scandinavian-based NGO working in the area of microfinance and had thereby gained familiarity with East Africa. In 2012, a third PhD student, Pontus Engström of Sweden, who also had some experience of microfinance in Tanzania, joined the PhD program and became part of the team, having the same supervisor as the Tanzanian students. The research question the third PhD student was investigating was the degree to which microenterprise performance, among other things, was enhanced by microfinance (Engström & McKelvie, 2017). The insights from this study, in addition to the professor's experience in microfinance, and

Table 1 Evolution of the professor–student relationship: the empirical basis

	Pre-venture and supervision phase (before 2008): important preconditions	Supervisory phase (2008–2012)	Entrepreneurial discovery phase (2010–2013)	Business start-up and operating phase (2013 and beyond) with the assignment of formal roles
Scandinavian professor	Experience as a co-founder of several business in Scandinavia and the USA Ten years of exposure to East Africa as a board member of a microfinance NGO	Ongoing supervisory relationship with the three students Visits to students' home countries (Tanzania and other Scandinavian)	The visit to Tanzania revealed big opportunities, but also great business challenges Development of business model Interaction with potential funds providers in Scandinavia	Board chair MTI investment AS, and board member of one of the subsidiaries. Raising funds
Tanzanian PhD student 1 (2008–2012)	Experience as university teacher and consultant, with a focus on microfinance, in East Africa Four years of experience of running a small business	Ongoing supervisory relationship	A business-exploring visit to Tanzania in 2010 From 2012 on, started to systematically look for investment opportunities Re-familiarizing herself with the business environment in Tanzania	Initially CEO of local subsidiary in Tanzania, later changed to board member Familiarization with legal, regulatory, and tax environment for businesses Identifying businesses and conducting initial due diligence
Tanzanian PhD student 2 (2008–2013)	Experience as controller in a large internationally owned firm in Tanzania Six years of experience as an auditor in one of the four largest global auditing firms	Ongoing supervisory relationship	From 2013, systematically looked for investment opportunities	CFO of X investment ltd., Tanzania, and later more reduced involvement as advisor Due diligence of prospects Financial management support to partner firms
Scandinavian PhD student (2012–2016)	Experience as a portfolio manager in Sweden and	Attracted to a Scandinavian university focusing on	Visits and interaction with advisors and co-investors in	CEO of MTI investment AS, board chair of one of the

(continued)

Table 1 (continued)

	Pre-venture and supervision phase (before 2008): important preconditions	Supervisory phase (2008–2012)	Entrepreneurial discovery phase (2010–2013)	Business start-up and operating phase (2013 and beyond) with the assignment of formal roles
	investment banking in the UK Experience as a CFO of an NGO investing in microfinance in Africa	research in microfinance and emerging-market finance	Norway and Sweden, in 2013 and beyond	subsidiaries, and board member of three others Developing the business model in cooperation with team Raising funds

Source: Created by Authors

insights from the Tanzanian students, laid the foundation for the realization that a new business model was needed for financing growth in emerging markets.

3 Pre-Venture and Pre-Supervision Phase

The first phase of the venture creation was based on the unique competencies that the professor, as well as the PhD students, possessed prior to entering into the professor–student relationship. Both Tanzanian students had business and entrepreneurship knowledge. They also had experience of owning and running small businesses in Tanzania. The third PhD student had extensive experience in financial management and portfolio management. All these skillsets and types of experience made it easier for them to engage in discussions pertaining to the establishment of MTI Investment.

3.1 Doctoral Supervision Phase

The supervisory phase of the focal professor–student relationship started in 2008. A common interest in economic development and entrepreneurship, especially in the context of East Africa, was instrumental in bringing the professor and the PhD students closer together. This issue fits well with the Holistic Conceptual Framework's emphasis on individual and contextual as well as intellectual aspects. The close social relationship between professor and students was evident in the numerous visits made by the two Tanzanian students, together with their children, to the professor's home for informal dinners. The friendly, close relationship led them to plan a joint trip to Tanzania in 2011, in which the professor's wife and children took part. The visit to Tanzania included personal (visiting the PhD students' parents and family members), academic (visiting and guest lecturing at the University of Dar es Salaam), and business (visiting entrepreneurs and financial institutions) elements.

Based on the experience of this visit, the professor and students agreed to explore the possibility of developing a shared investment activity—thus shifting the purely advisory relationship into one that ultimately included entrepreneurial discovery and a business partnership. In 2012, the third PhD student, the Swedish national, who had extensive pre-PhD experience as a CFO and portfolio manager, helped the team to access capital providers in the Scandinavian market. The student had also previously visited Tanzania, including looking at the practice of microfinance in Tanzania, and had a similar research interest to the Scandinavian professor and the two Tanzanian PhD students.

3.2 Entrepreneurial Discovery Phase

This phase was finalized in early 2014, when the professor, the two Tanzanian PhD students (the first one graduating in November 2012 and the second in January 2014), and the new Swedish PhD student decided to establish MTI Investment. Together, they came up with a name that would have a special meaning in Swahili, symbolizing the company's focus on investing in growing companies with the potential to bear fruit as a result of long-term investment, coaching, mentoring, and monitoring. Furthermore, the company's logo symbolizes its environmentally friendly and sustainable investment approach. It was decided that the choice of portfolio companies should be based first on the networks of the partners, especially that of one of the local Tanzanians, and also on firms whose founders and managers were highly educated and had a genuine interest in cooperation.

3.3 Business Assessment Phase

The business assessment phase (from 2010–2013) revealed a number of investment opportunities, but also a number of institutional impediments, such as the cost of establishing a company in East Africa, and uncertainty about legal issues and the secure transfer of money. MTI Investment's business mission is to provide capital and mentoring to East African SMEs. Specifically, MTI seeks well-run SMEs willing to allow a foreign investor to become a co-owner, and with the potential to become national champions in their respective industries. During the first year of establishment, early investments were made in a dairy firm and a loan was provided to a meat-processing company. Both firms were profitable at the time of MTI's provision of funds but needed to increase their working capital so as to expand into larger national markets. The loan to the meat factory remained a loan only. MTI's second and third equity investments were made in the fall of 2015, in a waste treatment company and a cosmetics retailer. The latter two companies both had Swedish-born entrepreneurs and were founded in Tanzania in 2010 and 2012, respectively. The Swedish-Tanzanian connection was instrumental in developing the interest and trust that led MTI to be willing to partner with these firms. The fourth investment was made in early 2017, in a construction company that uses new technology in CAD (Computer Aided Design)-based production to put up homes and schools more efficiently than existing players.

MTI's business model utilizes local staff (including the original PhD students from Tanzania) and focuses on long-term value creation, thus applying some element of the cost effectiveness of microfinance to the investment market. Prior to US$three million IPO at the end of 2021, MTI had raised approximately US$five million. MTI's capital commitment is typically US$100,000 to US$one million for each investment, which is considerably less than that of private equity firms, whose investments commonly start at US$3–five million per transaction, but which prefer deals of at least US$ten million (World Bank, 2014). MTI typically invests through a combination of loans, equity, and convertible loans (an equity option), which reduces risk exposure and enables partnerships with the local firms to develop before larger equity positions are taken (Table 2).

3.4 Operational Phase

It is now 7 years since the business venture was established and all of the investee firms are still operational. Two of them are growing quickly, and two somewhat more slowly. The original business idea is still driving the business, but the focus and structure have changed. In particular, MTI has become more focused on generating synergy between the invested-in subsidiaries and promoting the professional leadership of these subsidiaries (legally considered subsidiaries when the foreign ownership has passed 50%). Almost two years after the start-up of MTI, in 2015, a new political, fifth regime came into position, which brought in a new president in Tanzania, a new ministry cabinet, and a lot of changes in the country, which resulted in a more demanding business environment.[3] This impacted almost all businesses in Tanzania negatively, and made it more challenging to operate a firm with foreign founders, as employing foreign workers became more difficult. The regime changes also impacted exchange rates, with an approximate 40% drop in the Shilling/US$ exchange rate within a three-year period, even with a domestic yearly inflation rate of 5–6%. The outcome was that the two Scandinavian-based founders of two of the five investee firms left the country and their companies, making MTI's local-based academic co-founders and Scandinavian-based CEO (one of the founding PhDs) even more important. With great effort, MTI was able to stabilize the two Scandinavian-founded businesses after their founders left. As of 2021, a new sixth regime has come into power, with the first Tanzanian female president, Samia Hassan Suluhu. The new leadership has reverted to a more normalized form, vouching for greater economic and political stability. However, the world has also been affected by the Covid pandemic, which has had a negative impact on local businesses.

[3] https://www.economist.com/middle-east-and-africa/2018/03/15/tanzanias-rogue-president.

Table 2 Evolution of the professor–student relationship: the conceptual foundation

	Pre-venture phase (before 2008): important preconditions	Building of professor–student relationship (2008–2012)	Entrepreneurial discovery phase (2010–2013)	Business start-up and operating phase (2014 and beyond)
Scandinavian professor	**Transnational competencies** in business and academia relevant to East Africa	Simultaneous building of enablers: **Transnational competencies** and **transnational social** capital (student-professor) illustrated by informal building of friendship between professor and students	**Entrepreneurial discovery**: The business model was developed in close interaction with the PhD students	Capitalizes on **reduced transaction costs** of resource transfers, as well as **alleviated agency cost of monitoring** investments Capitalizes on social capital to raise capital
Tanzanian PhD student 1 (2008–2012)	**Transnational competencies** in entrepreneurship and academia relevant to East Africa and **local social capital** from lifelong relations	Simultaneous building of enablers: **Transnational competencies** and **transnational social capital** (student-professor)	**Entrepreneurial discovery**: The business model was being developed in close cooperation with the professor	Capitalizes on **reduced transaction costs** of resource transfers, as well as **alleviated agency cost of monitoring** investments
Tanzanian PhD student 2 (2008–2013)	**Transnational competencies** in business relevant to East Africa and **local social capital** from lifelong relations	Simultaneous building of enablers: **Transnational competencies** and **transnational social** capital (student-professor)	**Entrepreneurial discovery**: The business model was being developed in close cooperation with the professor	Capitalizes on **reduced transaction costs** of resource transfers, as well as **alleviated agency cost of monitoring** investments
Scandinavian PhD student (2012–2016)	**Transnational competencies** in business and finance—Relevant when gaining access to funding	Simultaneous building of enablers: **Transnational competencies** and **transnational**	Recruited after the initial entrepreneurial discovery phase, and was instrumental in developing the	Capitalizes on **alleviated agency cost of monitoring** and attracting investments, as well as on social

(continued)

Table 2 (continued)

	Pre-venture phase (before 2008): important preconditions	Building of professor–student relationship (2008–2012)	Entrepreneurial discovery phase (2010–2013)	Business start-up and operating phase (2014 and beyond)
		social capital (student-professor)	business concept from an equity fund to an investment company and micro private equity	capital to raise capital

Source: Created by Authors

Looking back on its 7 years of operation, we can observe that MTI's unique approach, capitalizing on the professor to doctoral student relationship, was critical as a start-up strategy but has become less important as the investment firm has professionalized. However, the founder would emphasize that the investment in the firm with the strongest ties to the founders' personal networks, namely the engineering firm, has been the most successful so far. In future investments, MTI sees an even greater need to capitalize on its networks and recognizes the importance of utilizing the social capital built up by, and competencies connected with, MTI. These observations fit well with the Holistic Framework's emphasis on individual and cultural aspects of academic entrepreneurship. By being university-based, MTI's founders argue that they are able to be at the forefront of knowledge creation in East Africa, in line with the Holistic Framework's emphasis on technology.

3.5 Evolution of the Professor to Doctoral Student Relationship

The conceptual foundation for the evolution of the professor to doctoral student relationship and the subsequent establishment of MTI Investment hinged on specific skills. Specifically, we highlight one enabler that was in place prior to the establishment of the firm: *transnational competencies* in business and academia relevant to East Africa. We argue that this enabler was present before the professor–student relationship was established (prior to 2008), but that these competencies were significantly strengthened during the doctoral studies of 2008–2013.

The second enabler is *transnational social capital* that facilitates the efficient transfer of knowledge—or capital. The professor worked closely with the two Tanzanian students, who successfully defended their PhDs in 2012 and 2014, respectively. The professor and the doctoral students developed rich social capital, and subsequently co-authored several academic articles, on the basis of this close cooperation. In the case of MTI, the ability to transfer large (but relatively small in investment terms) amounts (to individuals) without a well-developed corporate

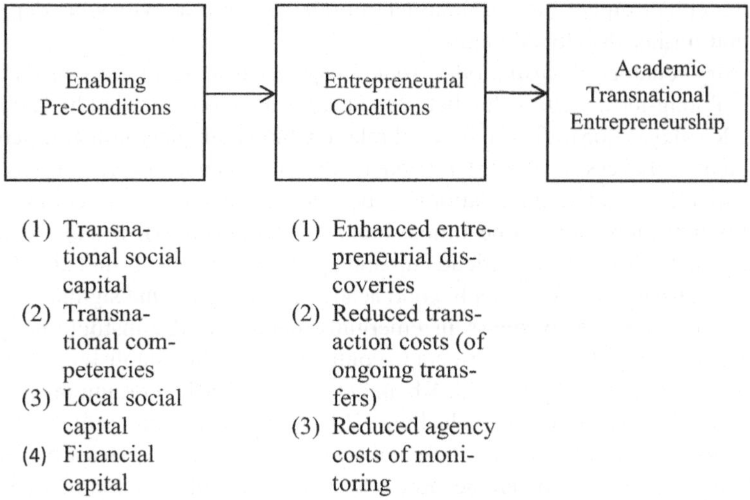

Fig. 1 Enabling preconditions and entrepreneurial conditions that foster academic transnational entrepreneurship, Source: Created by Authors

infrastructure provides the company with a low-cost solution. The two former PhD students, now professors in Tanzania, had in-depth knowledge of the local financial market, which is the third enabler—access to *local social capital*. Local social capital is vital and complements the legal contracts signed with businesses. Without this enabler, we argue that international businesses run a larger risk of failure.

Thanks to the social network and trust that exist between the former PhD students and their local business network, MTI is able to quickly identify and assess unique investment opportunities in Tanzania, supporting the financial aspect of the Holistic Framework. We observe that the student–professor relationship was instrumental in making entrepreneurial discoveries in Tanzania but has become less important as the company has developed its own in-house capabilities.

4 Discussion

Based on participative observation of MTI (in both Scandinavia and Tanzania), we explore how the cross-country professor to doctoral student relationships produced four unique enablers of academic entrepreneurial activities—or what we can label edupreneurial activities: (1) transnational social capital, (2) transnational competencies in bridging across international environments, (3) local social capital, and (4) access to developed countries' financial capital. We argue that, over time, these four enablers facilitate three effects: (1) enhanced entrepreneurial discoveries, (2) reduced transaction costs (of ongoing transfers), and (3) alleviated agency costs of monitoring investments. These three effects can be formulated as propositions about the enhancement of transnational entrepreneurship activities, as depicted in Fig. 1 and further developed below.

The first enabler, *transnational social capital*, is a natural by-product of a successful long-term relationship between an advisor (professor) and his/her student (Ives & Rowley, 2005). This individual relationship is uniquely non-competitive as the student's success is closely related to the professor's success. In fact, it is commonly observed that the relationship between an advising professor and his/her student is multiplex and can become a lifelong relationship (Bowman et al., 1995; Cadman, 2010). Such mutual friendship and appreciation is the foundation for other kinds of trust-based transactions beyond academic advising. One significant impediment to cross-country business in emerging markets is the institutionally weak environment, particularly with respect to contracting and the establishing of business relations (Khanna & Palepu, 2000; Khanna & Rivkin, 2001). Foreign investors face the "liability of foreignness" (Nachum, 2010); however, the professor–student relationship can help by substituting for weak institutions with trust-based social capital, such as access to unique networks and powerful decision-makers across cultural and international barriers. The professor to doctoral student relationship produces two kinds of social capital effects: the *transfer* of resources and capabilities between two countries and *access* to already established social capital in the emerging country. Based on the above, we therefore propose the following proposition:

Proposition 1 Academic transnational entrepreneurship provides more transnational social capital than traditional transnational entrepreneurship. This social capital (a) enhances entrepreneurial discovery, (b) reduces the transaction costs of knowledge and capital transfers, and (c) reduces the agency cost of monitoring, post investment.

The second enabler, *transnational competencies*, relates to the trans-territorial nature of the entrepreneurial ventures and emphasizes how transnational entrepreneurs have the unique ability to bridge across countries in order to access business opportunities (Özden & Schiff, 2005). Given that "*transnational entrepreneurs rely on diverse sets of resources—economic, social, cultural, and symbolic capital—to navigate multiple environments*" (Terjesen & Elam, 2009, p. 1093), we expect the same underlying resources that enable new ventures to *navigate multiple environments* (Drori et al., 2009) to be present in the professor–student transnational relationship. Koehn and Rosenau (2002, p. 109) propose that transnational competencies include four key skills: analytical, emotional, creative/imaginative, and behavioral. Transnational analytic skills include the ability to analyze and comprehend different cultural behaviors, and the reliance on emotional skills in order to be genuinely interested and open to different behaviors. An academic transnational entrepreneur's creative skills bridge various cultural differences to arrive at mutually beneficial agreements. Lastly, the behavioral part involves both the communicative part of speaking the native language, and the functional part of maintaining and developing strong interpersonal relationships. Based on the above, we therefore propose the following proposition:

Proposition 2 Academic transnational entrepreneurship provides more transnational competencies than traditional transnational entrepreneurship. This social capital (a) enhances entrepreneurial discovery, (b) reduces the transaction costs of knowledge and capital transfers, and (c) reduces the agency cost of monitoring, post investment.

The third enabler is the existence of *local social capital* in both countries, since the transnational entrepreneurial effort involves bridging the two countries' business environments. Through this enabler, entrepreneurial ventures can access a resourceful network of family, friends, and businesses. Based on the above, we therefore propose:

Proposition 3 Academic transnational entrepreneurship provides more local (i.e., in a foreign country) social capital than traditional transnational entrepreneurship. This social capital (a) enhances entrepreneurial discovery, (b) reduces the transaction costs of knowledge and capital transfers, and (c) reduces the agency cost of monitoring, post investment.

The fourth enabler is financial capital, in which the emerging-market scholars are seldom well-endowed. The same is commonly true for business professors based in developed countries; however, they have much easier access to wealthy individuals or interested funding institutions that might support such activity.

These four enablers produce a number of preconditions that can increase the *potential* for transnational entrepreneurship. Specifically, we argue that many returning students experience an entrepreneurial alertness—a state of mind that enhances their ability to recognize, develop, and evaluate entrepreneurial opportunities. In addition, due to their exposure to a different and advanced environment, they are easily able to identify and utilize the opportunities they see in their home countries. This phenomenon is a special case of the theory of entrepreneurial opportunity identification and development (Ardichvili et al., 2003). We argue that this state of mind, of increased entrepreneurial awareness, occurs for multiple reasons. First, returning students often face a reverse culture shock when they return home (Adler, 1981; Ward & Kennedy, 1993). This shock is similar to that felt by the returning Odysseus who did not recognize his homeland Ithaca after being away for many years, expressed as "*among what manner of people am I fallen*" (Homer, 1900). A returnee experiences a culture shock different to that of a newcomer or stranger, which may result in academic problems, cultural identity conflicts, social withdrawal, depression, anxiety, and interpersonal difficulties (Gaw, 2000; Robinson-Pant, 2009). Second, while the culture shock may be associated with negative emotions, it also implies that students will see their home country differently. For instance, returnee graduated students might discover under-served product markets and successful business models that are *not* being explored in their home country. These graduated doctoral students have been primed to see opportunities by being exposed to different business models in their host country. Returnee doctoral students will have witnessed these models firsthand, in learning new ways of working and living in a new country, but also through classroom teaching about business models, and sometimes also through qualitative research into businesses.

Third, in their academic endeavors with their advisors, PhD students will have developed means of identifying "new" areas of the literature in which to make contributions through their research. This capability, which will differ from person to person, implies a new way of approaching problems and opportunities (Ardichvili et al., 2003). The PhD education process enhances these students' critical and analytical skills, and therefore we argue that they will become better at perceiving new and unique business opportunities. However, when doctoral students enter an academic life with stable but low economic compensation, their ability to act on these opportunities will be severely hampered by constraints on resources such as time, financial capital, and "hands on" business experience, implying that the entrepreneurial alertness that has been developed will require continued support, or it will be lost.

One of the global drivers of foreign direct investment is the apparent transaction cost involved when firms transfer resources between countries (Dunning, 2003). Hierarchical relations of multinational companies, such as those between a parent company and its host-country subsidiary, reduce these transaction costs. In our model, we view the professor–student relationship as a potential vehicle for business activities that will reduce transnational transaction costs. These reduced transaction costs are due to the closer supervision and strong bonds that develop between a doctoral student and his/her advisor, which will significantly lower the asymmetric information in a business formation setting. The close bonds between a PhD student and his/her supervising professor are often seen in the opening acknowledgements of PhD dissertations, which frequently thank the faculty advisor(s) for providing substantial professional but also personal guidance, sometimes using language related to their being a co-pilot on an academic journey, for example. We argue that this creates a condition for the efficient transfer of ideas, capital, and competencies (as opposed to transfers in larger MNEs). In fact, this phenomenon is observed in the globalization of business education: "*. . .globalization of management education is a key enabler of globalization in many other fields. Increased connectivity across countries has facilitated the transfer of ideas and collaborative development of innovations in fields*" (AACSB 2011, p. 5).

In this study, we link entrepreneurial discovery and reduced transaction costs by highlighting the "*connectivity*" that transcends the transfer of *ideas* and *capital*. However, cross-country business activity is not only based on the ongoing transfer of resources but is also about developing routines and creating well-functioning interactions, including frequent visits, e-mail exchanges, and Skype conversations, especially because of the long distances involved. Importantly, it also concerns the creation of routines to monitor existing investments and evaluate new ones. The monitoring of such assets is commonly very expensive, as the legal and institutional environment will be unfamiliar to capital providers from developed economies. We argue that the trust-based relationship between professor and student provides an excellent basis for reduced agency costs of monitoring such investments. Another attractive feature of the professor–student relationship is the general lack of fixed costs. Furthermore, the professor and student will have well-developed routines for working through problems and resolving them in an efficient and productive matter. When a multinational company or foreign-based fund/investor seeks to invest in unfamiliar environments, this will commonly involve a significant minimum amount of activity, such as a full-time expatriate employee and a permanent office. In the professor–student relationship, the investment can be based on domestic wages, and could also involve part-time employment.

5 Conclusion

This paper outlines one route to academic transnational entrepreneurship, specifically the unique relationship between emerging-market PhD student(s) and their high-income-country-based professor(s). We argue that this has been the foundation for the establishment of MTI Investment SE, a Scandinavian-Tanzanian investment company.

We argue that three factors enabled the cross-country professor–student team to establish a viable emerging-market business: (1) competencies that helped to bridge two very different business environments, (2) access to transnational social capital, both within the host country and between the home and host country, and (3) local social capital within the business community. The access to transnational social capital was based on the lifelong relationships that the PhD students had gained through extended family, friendships, fellow students, and former business relations. These arguments fit well with the Holistic Conceptual Framework of Edupreneurship and its emphasis on individual, contextual, international, cultural, and intellectual aspects.

Our longitudinal study of the entrepreneurial process, leading up to the establishment of MTI and its first investment, illustrates how the multi-year (2008–2021) student–professor relationship facilitated the entrepreneurial discovery of the student–professor team. Their long-term relationship made it possible for them to actively develop and discover entrepreneurial opportunities, at the same time limit significant expenditures, and then implement the business idea fully in 2014. This low-cost approach to transnational entrepreneurship makes *academic transnational entrepreneurship* a particularly attractive and feasible business model, emphasizing how it can fit with the financial aspects of the Holistic Framework of Edupreneurship.

The ability to transfer competencies and capital between Scandinavia and Tanzania was particularly facilitated by the fact that the Tanzanian PhD students had experience with developed economies' business models, and that they could help to implement and adapt such ideas in Tanzania. The unique trust-based networks within Tanzania, and between Tanzania and the parent company in Scandinavia, facilitated lower transaction costs of the transfer of capital than would occur in a typical arm's-length transaction. This was particularly important for establishing a relatively small-sized investment actor, since the variable and fixed costs of such start-ups must be kept to a minimum. Given the relatively small equity investments involved (between US$200,000 and US$one million), it was also important to keep ongoing monitoring costs to a minimum. This organizational set-up allowed the agency costs to be kept lower than in a typical private equity firm, as the use of local staff members (including the former PhD students) as board members in the investee firms lowered the monitoring costs, while still involving highly competent individuals.

We acknowledge that professor–student transnational entrepreneurship appears to be rare; however, we see two avenues for stimulating such activities. We view the greatest potential for academic transnational entrepreneurship to reside in student-to-student-based ventures, which could be stimulated by business schools through cross-cultural teams of students exploring real-life business cases in emerging markets. It is highly possible that successful project-case collaborations might even lead to new start-ups following graduation. Business schools could also stimulate such activities by facilitating access to funds—for example through business venture competitions in which outside investors could be invited to evaluate and potentially invest in companies. We believe that business school alumni could take great interest in such activities, as could development agencies, thus supporting sustainability aspects of edupreneurship.

Before concluding, we would like to acknowledge some limitations of our study. First, we use only one case to illustrate academic transnational entrepreneurship, and this experience might not be generalizable to other institutional environments without considerable adaptation. Although there is great potential for *academic transnational entrepreneurship* (given the number of PhD students from emerging economies), the willingness to take part in such entrepreneurship, and the interest in doing so, might be limited on both the student and the professor side. Second, although action research is important, we must consider the role that we played in our research, as three of the co-authors were actively involved in establishing MTI Investment. We argue that this research shows that *it is possible* to conduct *academic transnational entrepreneurship*, just as going to the moon proves that it is possible to do so, but the explanations for the relationships we propose might not be valid in other cases.

Around the world, there is growing appreciation for the role that entrepreneurship plays in stimulating economic growth and development. The introduced concept of academic transnational entrepreneurship, and the Scandinavian-Tanzanian venture, illustrate how faculty and doctoral students can create sustainable enterprises that cross national borders.

In this study, we argue that academic transnational entrepreneurship can take place in many industries, but it may be particularly appropriate when there is potential for substantial changes in an industry (and thus the demand for a high degree of intellectual and analytical capacity). This study presents a parallel between the global microfinance industry and the new "Nordic" industrial investment model. Nobel Laureate Muhammad Yunus was an economics professor who developed an alternative banking model that enabled banking for the poor. In a parallel fashion, MTI's concept of SME investment aims to combine the trust-based business model of microfinance with the monitoring, mentoring, and resource provision of private equity, and highlights those academic networks provide a good vehicle for such an alternative business model.

We believe that the phenomenon of an *academic* route to transnational entrepreneurship, or international edupreneurship, is ripe for future research, and we offer five general directions for future researchers. First, we highlight that the expanded social mission of business schools around the world should push business researchers to address how academia can enhance entrepreneurship—at all levels of education (not only with respect to PhDs as is the focus of this study). Second, we see a need for more research on how academic influence can transform industries, such as the private equity industry in emerging markets. Third, we see a need for further research into the investment processes of various investment vehicles (e.g., private equity funds, government support schemes) and investment companies. Fourth, we see a need for research into the extent and drivers of cross-country academic networks as vehicles for the transfer of ideas—typically between professors at universities in developed countries and their counterparts in emerging markets. Fifth, following the developments in African business education (see Nkomo, 2015), researchers could examine how academic transnational entrepreneurship on the part of returnee faculty results in other outcomes in African business schools, such as experiential learning and new student-led start-ups, closer ties to industry, and the possible inspiration of other business faculty members with different doctoral experiences.

6 Summary

Can business school student–professor cooperation be leveraged to produce successful transnational business ventures? We investigate how business schools can improve their social mission performance by promoting academic transnational entrepreneurship—that is, the development of sustainable business enterprises based on long-standing cross-country interactions between professors and their students. We explore the phenomena of academic transnational entrepreneurship through the lens of a longitudinal case study involving a team comprising a Scandinavian business school professor and three graduated PhD students—two from Tanzania and one from Sweden. We describe the multi-year entrepreneurial discovery process leading up to the founding of the enterprise and the subsequent operational phase in which the Scandinavian investment company which invests takes substantial ownership stakes in high-growth Tanzanian firms. We develop a theoretical foundation for transnational professor and student cooperation by presenting four enabling preconditions that make such ventures possible: an entrepreneurially supported academic environment, transnational social capital, transnational competencies, local social capital, and access to financial capital. We identify how student–professor cooperation can promote academic transnational entrepreneurship: through enhanced entrepreneurial discoveries, reduced transaction costs of ongoing transfers, and reduced agency costs of monitoring.

Questions

Question 1. Why should business schools engage in transnational entrepreneurship?

Question 2. What are the strengths and weakness of *academic* transnational entrepreneurship, versus other forms of transnational entrepreneurship? How do they relate to one of more of the seven aspects of holistic edupreneurship?

Question 3. What are some of the skills that need to be present, in both student(s) and professor(s), in order for them to succeed in *academic* transnational entrepreneurship?

References

AACSB (2011). Globalization of management education: Changing international structures, adaptive strategies, and the impact on institutions. Retrieved December 2, 2021, from https://www.aacsb.edu/-/media/publications/research-reports/aacsb-globalization-of-management-education-task-force-report-2011.pdf?la=en

Adler, N. J. (1981). Re-entry: Managing cross-cultural transitions. *Group & Organization Management, 6*(3), 341–356. https://doi.org/10.1177/105960118100600310

Ardichvili, A., Cardozo, R., & Ray, S. (2003). A theory of entrepreneurial opportunity identification and development. *Journal of Business Venturing, 18*(1), 105–123. https://doi.org/10.1016/S0883-9026(01)00068-4

Blasco, M. (2012). Aligning the hidden curriculum of management education with PRME: An inquiry-based framework. *Journal of Management Education, 36*(3), 364–388. https://doi.org/10.1177/1052562911420213

Bowman, V. E., Hatley, L. D., & Bowman, R. L. (1995). Faculty-student relationships: The dual role controversy. *Counselor Education and Supervision, 34*(3), 232–242. https://doi.org/10.1002/j.1556-6978.1995.tb00245.x

Cadman, K. (2010). 'Voices in the air': Evaluations of the learning experiences of international postgraduates and their supervisors. *Teaching in Higher Education, 5*(4), 475–491. https://doi.org/10.1080/713699170

Carmichael, B. A., Drori, I., & Honig, B. (Eds.). (2010). *Transnational and immigrant entrepreneurship in a globalized world.* University of Toronto Press.

Corner, P. D., & Pio, E. (2017). Supervising international students' theses and dissertations. *Academy of Management Learning & Education, 16*(1), 23–38. https://doi.org/10.5465/amle.2015.0054

Cree, V. (2012). 'I'd like to call you my mother': Reflections on supervising international PhD students in social work. *Social Work Education, 31*, 241–464. https://doi.org/10.1080/02615479.2011.562287

Cunliffe, A. (2004). On becoming a critically reflexive practitioner. *Journal of Management Education, 28*, 407–428. https://doi.org/10.1177/1052562904264440

Drori, I., Honig, B., & Wright, M. (2009). Transnational entrepreneurship: An emergent field of study. *Entrepreneurship Theory & Practice, 33*(5), 1001–1022. https://doi.org/10.1111/j.1540-6520.2009.00332.x

Dunning, J. H. (2003). Some antecedents of internalization theory. *Journal of International Business Studies, 34*(2), 108–115.

Economist. (2015, January 24). Private equity in Africa. Unblocking the pipes. Retrieved December 14, 2021, from https://www.economist.com/leaders/2015/01/22/unblocking-the-pipes

Elliot, J. (2005). *Using narrative in social research: Qualitative and quantitative approaches*. Sage.

Engström, P., & McKelvie, A. (2017). Financial literacy, role models, and micro-enterprise performance in the informal economy. *International Small Business Journal, 35*(7), 855–875. https://doi.org/10.1177/0266242617717159

Friga, P., Bettis, R., & Sullivan, R. (2003). Changes in graduate management education and new business school strategies for the 21st century. *Academy of Management Learning and Education, 2*, 233–249. https://doi.org/10.5465/amle.2003.10932123

Gaw, K. F. (2000). Reverse culture shock in students returning from overseas. *International Journal of Intercultural Relations, 24*(1), 83–104. https://doi.org/10.1016/S0147-1767(99)00024-3

Hall, G., & Sung, T. W.-C. (2009). Mind the gap? A case-study of the differing perceptions of international students and their lecturers on postgraduate business programmes. *International Journal of Management Education, 8*(1), 53–62. https://doi.org/10.3794/ijme.81.261

Hearn, B., Oxelheim, L., & Randøy, T. (2018). The institutional determinants of private equity involvement in business groups: The case of Africa. *Journal of World Business, 53*, 118–133. https://doi.org/10.1016/j.jwb.2016.02.002

Homer. (translated 1900). *The odyssey*. Translated by Samuel Butler. Retrieved ecember 3, 2021, from http://sacred-texts.com/cla/homer/ody/index.htm

IMF. (2017). World economic outlook. Washington, DC. Retrieved from https://www.imf.org/en/Publications/WEO/Issues/2017/09/19/world-economic-outlook-october-2017

Ives, G., & Rowley, G. (2005). Supervisor selection or allocation and continuity of supervision: PhD students' progress and outcomes. *Studies in Higher Education, 30*(5), 535–555. https://doi.org/10.1080/03075070500249161

Khanna, T., & Palepu, K. (2000). Is group affiliation profitable in emerging markets? An analysis of diversified Indian business groups. *Journal of Finance, 55*(2), 867–891. https://doi.org/10.1111/0022-1082.00229

Khanna, T., & Rivkin, J. W. (2001). Estimating the performance effects of business groups in emerging markets. *Strategic Management Journal, 22*(1), 45–74. https://doi.org/10.1002/1097-0266(200101)22:1<45::AID-SMJ147>3.0.CO;2-F

Koehn, P. H., & Rosenau, J. N. (2002). Transnational competence in an emergent epoch. *International Studies Perspectives, 3*(2), 105–127.

Kolb, A. Y., & Kolb, D. A. (2005). Learning styles and learning spaces: Enhancing experiential learning in higher education. *Academy of Management Learning & Education, 4*(2), 193–212.

Mitchell, T. (2007). The academic life: Realistic changes needed for business school students and faculty. *Academy of Management Learning & Education, 6*(2), 236–251. https://doi.org/10.5465/amle.2007.25223462

Nachum, L. (2010). When is foreignness an asset or a liability? Explaining the performance differential between foreign and local firms. *Journal of Management, 36*(3), 714–739. https://doi.org/10.1177/0149206309338522

Nkomo, S. M. (2015). Challenges for management and business education in a "developmental" state: The case of South Africa. *Academy of Management Learning & Education, 14*(2), 242–258. https://doi.org/10.5465/amle.2014.0323

Özden, Ç., & Schiff, M. (2005). *International migration, remittances and the brain drain*. The World Bank.

Portes, A., Guarnizo, L. E., & Haller, W. J. (2002). Transnational entrepreneurs: An alternative form of immigrant economic adaptation. *American Sociological Review, 67*(2), 278–298. https://doi.org/10.2307/3088896

Principles for Responsible Management Education (PRME). (2015). http://www.unprme.org/about-prme/the-six-principles.php

Rienties, B., Johan, N., & Jindal-Snape, D. (2015). Bridge building potential in cross-cultural learning: A mixed method study. *Asia Pacific Education Review, 16*, 37–48. https://doi.org/10.1007/s12564-014-9352-7

Robinson-Pant, A. (2009). Changing academies: Exploring international PhD students' perspectives on 'host' and 'home' universities. *Higher Education Research & Development, 28*(4), 417–429.

Shane, S. A. (2004). *Academic entrepreneurship: University spinoffs and wealth creation*. Edward Elgar.

Terjesen, S., & Elam, A. (2009). Transnational entrepreneurs' venture internationalization strategies: A practice theory approach. *Entrepreneurship Theory and Practice, 33*(5), 1093–1120. https://doi.org/10.1111/j.1540-6520.2009.00336.x

Transparency International. (2017). Corruption perception index. http://www.transparency.org/research/cpi/

Van de Ven, A., & Johnson, P. (2006). Knowledge for theory and practice. *Academy of Management Review, 31*(4), 802–821. https://doi.org/10.5465/amr.2006.22527385

Wadhwa, V., Saxenian, A., Rissing, B. A., & Gereffi, G. (2007). America's new immigrant entrepreneurs: Part I. *Duke Science, Technology & Innovation Paper No., 23*. https://doi.org/10.2139/ssrn.990152

Ward, C., & Kennedy, A. (1993). Psychological and socio-cultural adjustment during cross-cultural transitions: A comparison of secondary students overseas and at home. International Journal of Psychology, 28(2), 129–147. https://doi.org/https://doi.org/10.1080/00207599308247181

World Bank. (2014). Meeting Africa's demand for skills: The role of regional centers of excellence (English). Report #85806.

Yunus, M. (2012). *A global conversation to join*. Huffington Post. http://www.huffingtonpost.com/muhammad-yunus/a-global-conversation-to-_b_1951292.html

Zhang, M. M., Xia, J., Fan, D., & Zhu, J. C. (2016). Managing student diversity in business education: Incorporating campus diversity into the curriculum to foster inclusion and academic success of international students. *Academy of Management Learning & Education, 15*(2), 366–380. https://doi.org/10.5465/amle.2014.0023

Pontus Engström received a Ph.D. at the University of Agder, Norway. He is co-founder and CEO of MTI Investment SE, now listed on Nasdaq First North in Stockholm. He is also an Affiliated Researcher at the Stockholm School of Economics. He has 20 years of industry experience from firms like the Boston Consulting Group, Credit Suisse, and DnB Asset Management. He has co-founded businesses in Norway, Sweden, and Tanzania, and currently serves on four firms engaged in East Africa.

Neema Mori is an Associate Professor at the Department of Finance, of the University of Dar es Salaam Business School. She holds a Ph.D. in International Business from the University of Agder, Norway; MBA and BCom from the University of Dar es Salaam, Tanzania. She has over 15 years of experience in teaching, researching, and consulting in areas of corporate finance, small business finance, corporate governance, microfinance, and entrepreneurship. She has attended a number of competency-based courses and international conferences on entrepreneurship, microfinance, corporate governance, women entrepreneurship, international strategy, business planning, consultancy skills, adult training, and project management. In addition, she has participated and managed research and consulting assignments for various local and international agencies. Prof. Mori has also published academic papers in international refereed journals such as Small Business Economics Journal, Journal of Management and Governance, Journal of Emerging Market Finance, and Journal of African Business. Currently, she is on the editorial board of the African Journal of Economic and Management Studies and Journal of African Business.

Trond Randøy is a Professor of Corporate Governance at Copenhagen Business School, and part-time affiliated with the University of Agder. He has published more than 50 scholarly articles in journals such as Journal of International Business Studies, Journal of Business Venturing, Entrepreneurship Theory and Practice, Journal of Business Ethics, and Journal of Banking and Finance. He is currently an editor with Corporate Governance: An International Review. Randøy values the interaction with business practice, and he is currently serving on five corporate boards, two as chairman, of which two firms are publicly listed (MTI Investment SE and Sparebanken Sør) and three are private.

Siri Terjesen, Dr., is Associate Dean, Research & External Relations and Phil Smith Professor of Entrepreneurship at Florida Atlantic University (FAU) in Boca Raton, Florida, and Professor 0.2 at the Norwegian School of Economics (Norges Handelshøyskole: NHH) in Bergen, Norway. Siri received her undergraduate education at the University of Richmond, her Master's at NHH in Norway (2002) as a U.S. Fulbright Scholar, Ph.D. at Cranfield University in the UK (2006), and post-doc at the Queensland University of Technology in Brisbane, Australia. Siri is an internationally recognized expert in entrepreneurship, strategy, and corporate governance, with over 80 academic articles and 2 books, and $5.3 m as PI in research grants and gifts. She won teaching recognition from The Economist, Alpha Kappa Psi, and her universities, and is Associate Editor of Academy of Management Perspectives, Small Business Economics, and three other journals. Before academia, Siri was a management consultant with Accenture, and a competitive marathon and ultradistance runner, representing the United States in the World Championships, and winning individual bronze at the World 50 K (2006) and over 40 marathons around the world.

Part III

Practical Insight and Cases on Educational Entrepreneurship

CapSource: A Case Study of Educational Entrepreneurship

Jordan Levy

1 The Origins of CapSource

J. Levy (✉)
CapSource, Tucson, AZ, USA
e-mail: jordan@capsource.io

M. Aldogan Eklund, G. Wanzenried (eds.), *Academic and Educational Entrepreneurship*, Springer Texts in Business and Economics,
https://doi.org/10.1007/978-3-031-10952-2_19

Serial edupreneur and Forbes 30 Under 30 recipient Jordan Levy has been committed to expanding experiential learning within the higher education ecosystem since he was a student at Lehigh University. As an undergraduate enrolled in Lehigh's College of Business program, Jordan spent the first 3 years of his undergraduate tenure learning principles of finance, accounting, and entrepreneurship. It wasn't until the summer after his junior year, during his internship at a large accounting firm, that Jordan realized working in accounting had little in common with what he was studying in the classroom.

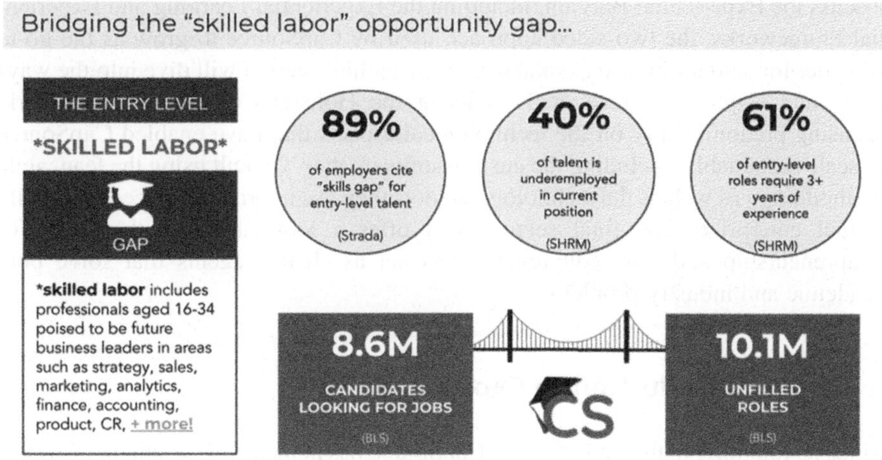

Fig. 1 The skills gap as defined by CapSource (Auter & Francis, 2013; Maurer, 2021; U.S. Bureau of Labor Statistics, 2021)

While Jordan's classes relied on textbooks and case studies to teach students about business theory, they lacked a critical component: a connection to "the real world." Jordan was disappointed with the lack of industry engagement in his curriculum: in order to obtain industry experience, students relied on internships, which are difficult to find and not always useful learning experiences. Even in a top-tier undergraduate business program, the lack of exposure to different types of organizations and different job roles like marketing and data analytics meant that Jordan and students like him were poorly prepared to enter the workforce and able to make informed career decisions (commonly known as the "skills" or "opportunity" gap) (Fig. 1).

In an attempt to solve this problem, Jordan worked with professors and peers at Lehigh to launch his first edtech startup in 2014. The startup, called Real Time Cases, offered prepackaged video-based experiential learning materials that were designed to integrate real-world business challenges into business school classrooms. Real Time Cases was acquired by Curator Solutions in 2019 and has since shifted towards corporate training and development. Still dedicated to bridging the gap between education and work, Jordan decided to use his knowledge, expertise, and network to create CapSource, a new startup focused on using a project-based experiential learning approach that directly connects students with industry professionals through meaningful collaboration. CapSource was created as a way to provide educators with more flexibility and customizability when it came to integrating companies directly into the education process through hands-on applied learning collaborations.

Throughout this case, we will explore how CapSource has evolved from a bootstrapped startup into a leader in experiential learning and hiring. The first section will provide an overview of CapSource and its mission. The second section will discuss the Experiential Bargain, including the Experiential Learning and Experiential Frameworks, the two-sided approach used by CapSource to grow as the go-to provider for student-industry collaboration. The third section will dive into the ways Levy and CapSource have evolved using the Holistic Conceptual Framework, focusing predominantly on the technological aspects that have enabled CapSource to scale sustainably, including the custom software they've built using the lean, agile methodology as well as the technological tools they use in order to succeed as a fully virtual enterprise. The final section will offer a look ahead at the future of edupreneurship and how edupreneurs can act as change agents that solve both academic and industry problems.

2 An Introduction to CapSource

Since its founding in the Fall of 2017, CapSource has helped 100+ academic partners bridge the skills gap for their students by integrating real companies and their challenges directly into the education process through project-based experiential learning programs. CapSource uses technology to attract companies that are interested in partnering with students on research-oriented collaborations, then develops projects that carefully define the goals, timeline, and skills students can develop while participating. This project documentation ensures alignment between industry partners, educators, and students, which is the essential foundation for a positive collaboration and meaningful outcomes.

Like consultants in the workforce, students who undertake CapSource experiential learning projects work to solve real business challenges on behalf of their industry partner. Common business challenges include the assembling financial statements and projections, creating and refining new products, and preparing a go-to-market strategy, all of which require students to dive deep on relevant products, markets, and business models. Given the interdisciplinary nature of many of these business challenges, students who engage in CapSource experiential learning programs are typically exposed to leaders across multiple departments within a business, giving them a holistic view of how a professional organization really works.

Unlike textbooks and stagnant case studies, the CapSource model involves real stakeholders from real organizations, including startups, small businesses, nonprofits, and large corporations. For startups, small businesses, and nonprofits in particular, the projects that students complete can have a significant impact on company growth and direction. Larger organizations use these engagements as a way to attract and vet top-talent for entry-level employment opportunities. No matter the partner or project, students are always able to walk away with "reference-worthy experience," the key foundation to successfully launching a career (Fig. 2).

A crucial piece of the experiential learning process involves educators as academic mentors. "Experiential Educators," as CapSource calls them, serve as a "guide on the side" for students throughout the experiential learning process, emphasizing the direct connection between theories learned in the classroom and applicability to

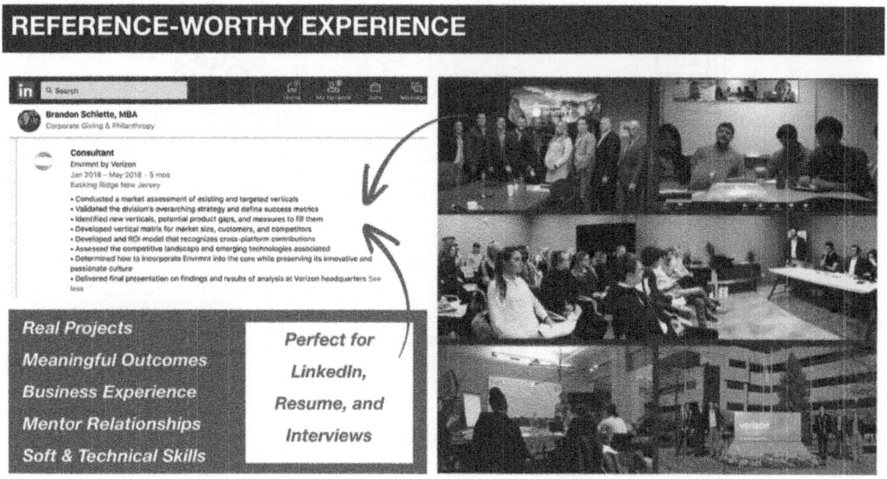

Fig. 2 Brandon Schlette, a Ramapo College MBA student that participated in a CapSource Program with Envrmnt, a Verizon company, gained "reference-worthy" experience that he details on his LinkedIn profile

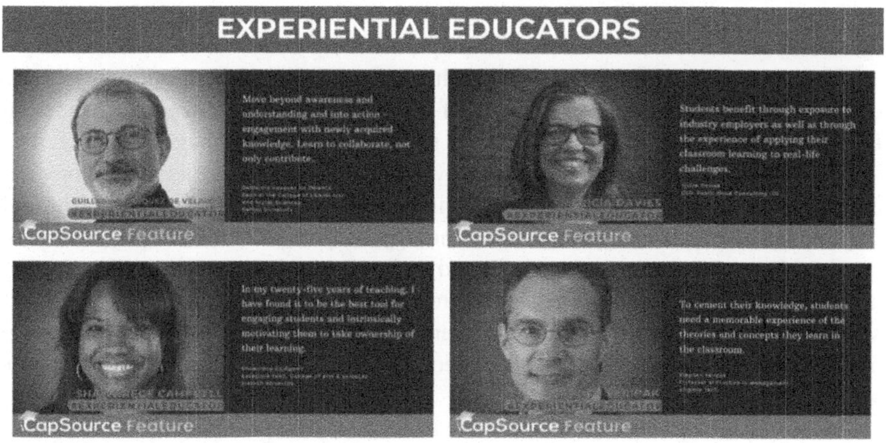

Fig. 3 Experiential educator profiles highlight methods and tactics

the workforce. Furthermore, academic mentors serve as crucial coaches, providing inspiration and feedback before students present their findings to their industry mentors and key project stakeholders. This iterative and reflective process is crucial to making experiential learning work for everyone (Fig. 3).

In order to make experiential programs scalable, CapSource has codified three main engagement formats:

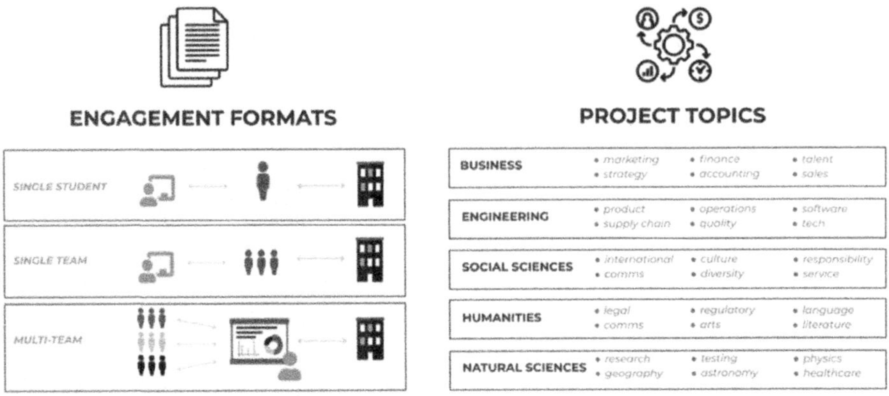

Fig. 4 CapSource's engagement formats and project topics

- *single student* (e.g., micro-internships, co-ops or independent studies).
- *single team* (e.g., capstones or field studies).
- *multi-team* (e.g., live cases or case competition/hackathons).

These three formats provide educators and industry partners with flexibility and customizability in order to meet their unique teaching goals.

To further align industry projects with academic disciplines, CapSource breaks down all projects into one or more of 20 relevant topic categories, including marketing, product development, growth strategy, and data management (Fig. 4).

The future of CapSource relies heavily on its ability to scale its technology and enable others to build unique, high-impact experiential programs. Through CapSource's Software as a Service technology, CapSource CONNECT, enterprise customers are able to customize and brand their experiential ecosystem. Whether it's academic institutions offering capstone programs, governments building apprenticeship programs, or employers offering internship programs, CapSource's technology attracts and aligns stakeholders on projects that benefit all parties—especially the students (Fig. 5).

As of 2021, CapSource has been able to reach 4000 students at 100 educational institutions with the help of 200 unique industry partners around the world. Some of CapSource's university clients include Harvard University, The University of Richmond, and the University of Notre Dame (Fig. 6).

3 The Experiential Bargain

The experiential bargain highlights the tradeoff that occurs between students engaged in "experiential learning" and the industry partners that host them, which CapSource refers to as "flipped" or "experiential hiring." For the experiential bargain to work, students need to walk away with new skills, professional connections, and

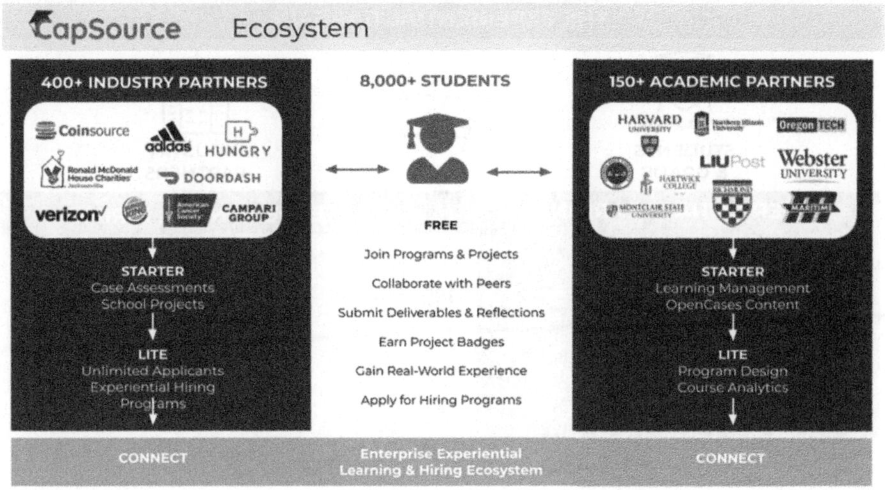

Fig. 5 CapSource's free, premium, and enterprise offerings to its ecosystem of students, industry partners, and academic partners

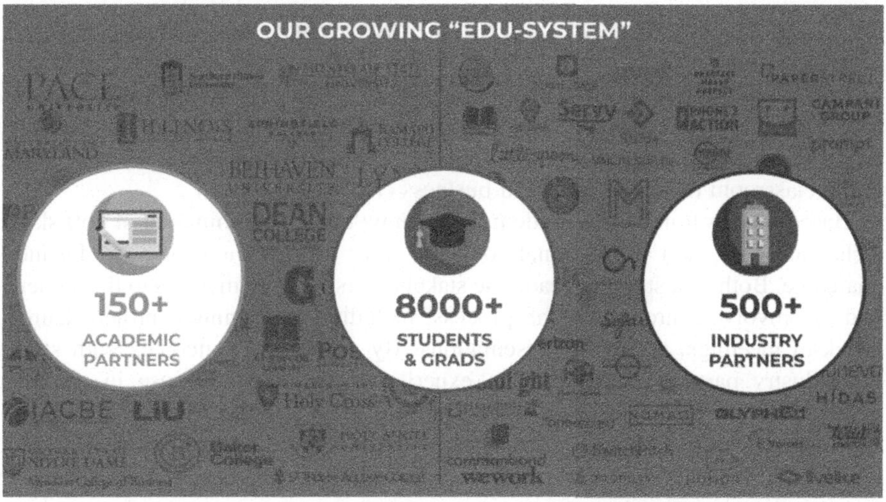

Fig. 6 CapSource highlighting their network across industry and academia

reference-worthy experience working on real projects for real business stakeholders. In exchange, companies need to derive useful, unique insights from the emerging young professionals while getting a chance to on-board, train, and hire top performers. This powerful bargain, if orchestrated and managed correctly, is a win-win for both learners and employers (Fig. 7).

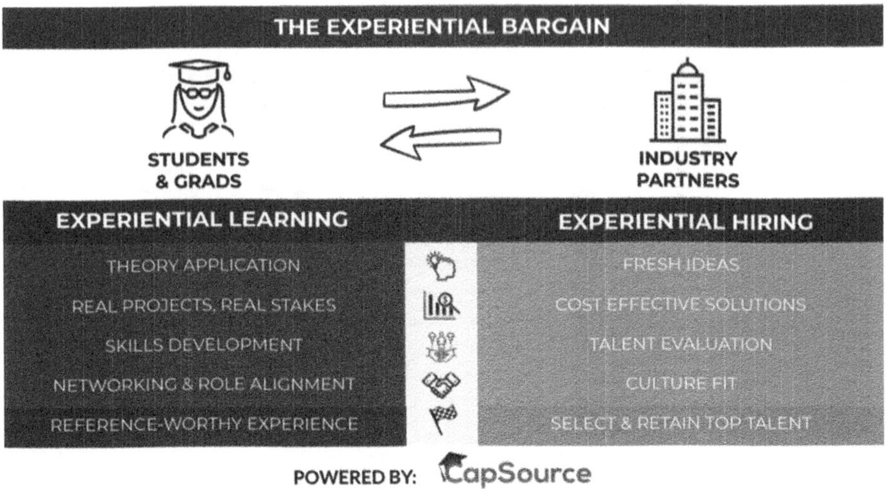

Fig. 7 How the experiential bargain works

4 The Experiential Learning Framework

The CapSource mission is to prepare young professionals for the future of work. To do this, CapSource's pedagogy is guided by their experiential learning framework, a hands-on approach to education that enables students to apply what they're learning in the classroom to solve real-world business challenges (Fig. 8).

Based on this framework, students must draw upon a combination of soft skills, technical skills, and professional tools in order to solve a real-world business challenge. Both industry and academic stakeholders serve as mentors to the students and are involved throughout the process, including at the initial project launch, check-in meetings, and final presentations. By developing outcomes with stakes for industry partners, students gain experiences that they can use in resumes, networking, and job interviews.

Some of the most crucial transferable skills for young professionals revolve around the "4 C's" that CapSource highlights in their experiential learning framework:

- *Communication*: The ability to understand and transmit information quickly through written, oral, or visual formats. According to the 2018 Jobs Outlook Survey from the National Association of Colleges and Employers, only 41% of employers ranked recent grads as proficient in Oral/Written Communications (Eismann et al., 2017).
- *Collaboration:* The ability to work well with others. A 2015 survey from the Association of American Colleges and Universities found that more than 80 percent of midsize or large employers look for collaboration skills in new hires, but

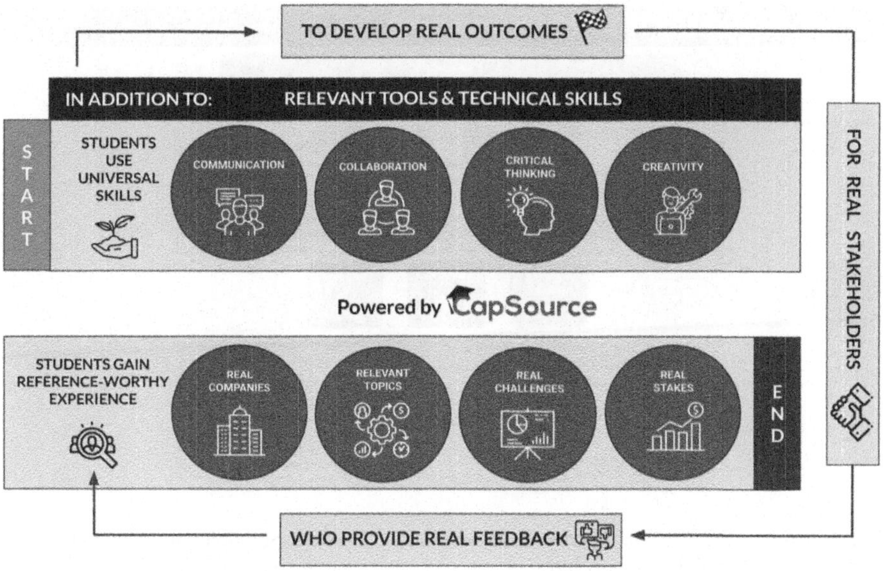

Fig. 8 The experiential learning framework benefits both students and companies

fewer than 40 percent of them believe that recent college graduates are prepared to work in teams (Hart Research Associates, 2015).

- *Critical Thinking*: The ability to analyze information in order to solve problems and formulate decisions. The 2018 Jobs Outlook Survey from the National Association of Colleges and Employers found that only 55.8% of employers believed recent graduates are proficient in critical thinking (Eismann et al., 2017).
- *Creativity*: The ability to innovate and focus on developing entirely new, unique ideas. According to a 2019 study by Adobe, 50% of job postings listed creativity as an important skill, second only to communication (Adobe, 2019).

In addition, students who undertake CapSource projects build proficiencies in widely used business software, including Microsoft Excel, Tableau, AutoCAD, Wordpress, JavaScript, Asana, Amazon Web Services, Google Analytics, and many more. Using these tools while still in college makes students more qualified and competitive in the job market after graduation (CapSource, 2020).

5 The Experiential Hiring Framework

In addition to optimizing student experiential learning and professional development, CapSource also focuses on helping industry partners adopt and utilize an experiential hiring method, which enables industry leaders to assess and hire top-talent using a case-based, project-based, and team-based assessments. By allowing young students and graduates to network and learn more about the

Fig. 9 Experiential hiring produces creative and strategic business solutions and talent that's ready to hit the ground running as new hires

organization, industry, and job roles that exist, employers can know with confidence the candidate has real interest in a position before choosing to employ him or her full time. Employers can also qualify candidates by empowering them to showcase their skills through meaningful collaboration and the creation of highly valuable work products (Fig. 9).

5.1 Edupreneurship and the Holistic Conceptual Framework

CapSource has evolved as a business model utilizing several key aspects of the Holistic Conceptual Framework. Like all growing social impact organizations, CapSource exemplifies each of the seven points within the framework. As an edtech company focused on preparing students for the workforce, we'll focus on the technological, political, and economic aspects of the framework that have enabled CapSource to grow methodically and sustainably.

5.1.1 Technological Aspect

CapSource has created specialized technology to ensure the success of its experiential engagements. The CapSource Ecosystem includes four main user roles: Students, Academic Mentors, Industry Mentors, and Enterprise System Administrators. These users interact through CapSource forms and templates to create custom experiential programs. Through its ecosystem built on Wordpress, CapSource manages an up-to-date online directory of industry partners interested in engaging with students and graduates through experiential hiring engagements. CapSource also manages a network of academic partners who regularly build

Fig. 10 The landing page for SUNY Potsdam's experiential learning ecosystem using CapSource CONNECT

experiential learning programs with companies. CapSource also manages an archive on completed projects and actively creates case content that can be used as hiring assessments or classroom "OpenCases" content.

In 2019, CapSource secured its first enterprise customer in order to meet the needs of one of their clients in the State University of New York (SUNY) system. For SUNY Potsdam, CapSource "white-labeled" their original web application as a Software as a Service (SaaS) environment called CapSource CONNECT. This enterprise software is a comprehensive, centralized experiential learning management system that allows academic partners to on-board students, educators, and industry partners for experiential engagements. CONNECT empowers faculty and administrators to match with partners to design projects while also allowing them to on-board students in order to monitor and track project progress in order to measure learning outcomes. CONNECT draws upon the core value proposition of CapSource's experiential learning and hiring framework, offering enterprise customers a self-service approach so that experiential learning and hiring can be scaled more easily. After the successful launch of Potsdam CONNECT, CapSource made their enterprise software available to all, and has since been adopted by several clients, including the University of Montana and the University of Notre Dame (Fig. 10).

5.1.2 Political and Economic Aspects

As a company that connects industry and academic partners, CapSource navigates a variety of political and economic factors in its work. By developing college and graduate students' professional skills, the company directly supports workforce development. According to research conducted by Strada and Gallup, only 11% of business leaders believe that college graduates are prepared for the workforce

(Auter & Francis, 2013). CapSource aims to solve this economic problem by more closely integrating the workforce into the learning experience.

CapSource also uses its platform and projects to assist in economic development for innovation centers and underserved communities. In 2020, CapSource partnered with the Institute for Urban Policy Research & Analysis (IUPRA) to develop resources on why skill-building can help low-income communities (CapSource and IUPRA (The Institute for Urban Policy Research and Analysis), 2020). They found that skill-building through programs offered by companies like CapSource broaden socioeconomic opportunities because individuals can gain access to more education, higher pay, and expanded professional networks, all of which are factors in upward mobility.

5.1.3 Financial Aspect

CapSource was launched out of NYU's StartEd EdTech Incubator in Brooklyn, New York. Beyond the office and mentorship resources received as part of the startup incubator, CapSource relied on a lean, bootstrapped business model development approach. The company focused on selling the first iteration of its service to universities like Fordham University and the University of Maryland to learn more about the customer and earn some funds in order to establish a technology product based on feedback from educators and industry partners. In order to acquire its first academic clients, CapSource offered discounted pricing for universities, as well as free trials in exchange for case studies and testimonials that could be used in marketing.

One of the biggest financial challenges CapSource faced was finding a way to scale their business model, which was built on developing customized experiential learning engagements for universities. CapSource needed to develop a business model that had the benefits of a high-touch, personalized approach to designing experiential learning projects, with the scalability of a prepackaged case study. By working on multiple experiential learning engagements for university clients, CapSource recognized that the matchmaking and program designing process was something that could be productized and provided as a set of tools to customers. This was the impetus for creating the SaaS platform CapSource CONNECT, which the company offers in addition to custom program design services.

5.1.4 Individual and Contextual Aspects

CapSource was created because its founder discovered a fundamental problem that needed to be solved. This opportunity revolves around bridging the gap between the experience students gain at universities and skills they need to thrive in the workforce. To ensure alignment with the changing needs of academia and industry, CapSource solicits feedback from a Board of Advisors with deep experience working within universities, as well as a dedicated group of Experiential Educators who are top-of-the-class when it comes to integrating project-based learning opportunities into the classroom. CapSource knows no movement can be built without community support. Building an intricate three-sided marketplace is tough, exhausting work for the founding team, but their fully virtual culture allows team members to wake up energized and excited to make a meaningful change in the way workforce education is designed and delivered to thousands of students each year.

5.1.5 Intellectual, International, Cultural, and Sustainable Aspects

CapSource encourages companies to see our next generation as an asset and invest in their professional growth and continued learning. By encouraging deeper collaborations between industry and education, CapSource proposes a solution to the skills gap and promotes a more educated, equal citizenry.

CapSource's team is based around the United States and Asia, and even as a young company, it has a global presence with both academic and industry partners. One of the main benefits of experiential learning is that it translates easily into a virtual learning experience where borders and time zones are more of a feature than a barrier. As of 2020, CapSource's network of industry and academic partners spans North America (Most of the USA and Canada), South America (Peru, Colombia), the Middle East (Dubai, Afghanistan, Israel), Europe (Germany, Greece, UK, Prague), and Asia (India, China).

CapSource has also partnered with international organizations such as the International Accreditation Council for Business Education (IACBE), with which it hosts live case competitions as part of an annual conference (IACBE, 2020).

The businesses of tomorrow will no longer be able to thrive without social and community consciousness, exhibited through a double or triple bottom line. Making profits while harming the environment or employees is the wrong way to build a business, especially with the relentless transparency that exists in the twenty-first century. Not only does CapSource believe in these core principles, it also supports industry and academic partners that feel the same way.

5.1.6 The Future of Edupreneurship

Education may be about "chasing curiosity," but entrepreneurship is about monetizing it. Like the students undertaking CapSource projects, edupreneurs are tasked with seeing challenges within a complex, multifaceted, global education ecosystem so that they can reinvent that system through innovative models and products that ensure more pervasive access to high quality learning experiences for all. Educational products are intellectual products; although they're impossible to feel and touch, they provide the foundation for experience and reflection, which leads to meaningful learning outcomes. As the needs of educational institutions continue to evolve, and as technology continues to change the way we live, learn, and work, edupreneurs like Levy and his team at CapSource will be tasked with adapting their business models and offerings to rise to the occasion.

6 Summary

CapSource serves as a leader in experiential learning by helping colleges and universities bridge the skills gap for students. It integrates real companies and their challenges directly into the education process through carefully designed, project-based experiences. It also promotes experiential hiring by empowering industry leaders and human resources professionals to qualify and hire top entry-level talent using their case-based and team-based assessments. Through a holistic approach to edupreneurship, CapSource helps students become better prepared for the work-force, companies to hire qualified candidates, and universities to diversify their course offerings.

Questions

Question 1. What was the problem that edupreneur Jordan Levy discovered while he was an undergraduate?

Question 2. What is experiential learning?

Question 3. What is the experiential learning framework, and what are some of the skills it helps students to develop?

Question 4. How does CapSource aim to bridge the skills gap for students through their technology?

Question 5. Why is workforce education important for students? How about for schools and industry partners?

References

Adobe (2019). Get hired: The importance of creativity and soft skills. Resource document. Adobe. Retrieved December 19, 2020, from https://cdn2.hubspot.net/hubfs/7381490/Adobe_April20/HED/Assets/Adobe_Get_Hired_Research_for_HED_Nov2019.pdf?__hssc=190225780.1.1608406664363&__hstc=190225780.682c0f0c3fede27ed5c87952dc7b249c.1608406664362.1608406664362.1608406664362.1&__hsfp=2686683400&hsCtaTracking=b969dc42-17a6-46e5-adbd-007b2721556a%7C85173093-d2cc-4ae8-b49c-b1181664761b

Auter, Z., Francis, A. (2013). 3 ways to realign higher education with today's workforce. Retrieved January 15, 2021, from https://www.gallup.com/education/231740/ways-realign-higher-education-today-workforce.aspx

CapSource (2020). Tech Resources. Retrieved December 19, 2020, from https://capsource.io/tech-resources/

CapSource and IUPRA (The Institute for Urban Policy Research & Analysis). (2020). 10 reasons skill-building leads to social mobility. Retrieved December 19, 2020, from https://capsource.io/10-reasons-skill-building-leads-to-social-mobility/

Eismann, L., Koc, E. W., Koncz, A.J, Longenberger, A. (2017). Job outlook 2018. Resource document. National Association Of Colleges And Employers. Retrieved December 19, 2020, from https://www.lander.edu/sites/lander/files/Documents/student_life/2018-nace-job-outlook.pdf

Hart Research Associates. (2015). Falling short? College learning and career success selected findings from online surveys of employers and college students conducted on behalf of the Association of American Colleges & Universities. Resource document. Association of American Colleges & Universities. Retrieved December 19, 2020, from https://www.aacu.org/sites/default/files/files/LEAP/2015employerstudentsurvey.pdf
IACBE (2020). Student Case Study Competition. Retrieved December 19, 2020, from https://iacbe.org/events/student-case-study-competition/
Maurer, R. (2021). Entry-Level-Experience Requirements Could Be Hurting Your Hiring. Retrieved January 15, 2021, from https://www.shrm.org/resourcesandtools/hr-topics/talent-acquisition/pages/entry-level-experience-requirements-hurting-hiring.aspx
U.S. Bureau of Labor Statistics. (2021). Job Openings and Labor Turnover Summary. Retrieved January 15, 2021, from https://www.bls.gov/news.release/jolts.nr0.htm

Further Reading

The Flipped Hiring Revolution. Retrieved from https://www.edsurge.com/news/2018-10-10-the-flipped-hiring-revolution
Education in 2030. The $10 Trillion dollar question. Retrieved from https://www.holoniq.com/2030/
USS University. Retrieved from https://www.profgalloway.com/uss-university
What is experiential learning? Retrieved from https://capsource.io/what-is-el/
The Experiential Hiring Framework. Retrieved from https://capsource.io/experiential-hiring/
There's no losing in experiential education, just winning and learning. Retrieved from https://capsource.io/theres-no-losing-in-experiential-education-just-winning-and-learning/
All-Star-Students - Project Samples. Retrieved from https://capsource.io/all-star-students/

Jordan Levy has started two EdTech companies that are helping students transition from education to work. His method is to integrate real companies into the learning process through hands-on collaborations that expose learners to new industries and job roles by working on real projects with real stakeholders and stakes. CapSource makes it easy for schools and companies to build scalable experiential learning and experiential hiring programs. Through free, premium, and enterprise software solutions, CapSource helps educators and companies coordinate, manage, and scale high-impact case-based and project-based programs designed to help next-gen talent learn, network, and get hired. Since 2017, CapSource has helped 500+ different industry partners like DoorDash, True Religion, and the American Cancer Society collaborate with 10,000+ young professionals from over 150 global institutions including the University of Notre Dame, Harvard, and the SUNY System. Jordan started his first education technology company, Real Time Cases (acquired), which raised over $2000.000 in venture funding while an undergraduate at Lehigh University studying Accounting, Finance, and Entrepreneurship. Outside of work, Jordan is passionate about cooking, hiking, traveling, sailing, tennis, public speaking, photography, mixology, and coaching/connecting fellow entrepreneurs.

The Case of Sabancı University: Educational Entrepreneurship

Berna Beyhan and Timothy S. Kiessling

1 Introduction

Entrepreneurs identify marketplace opportunities and then implement business plans to be successful. One marketplace that entrepreneurs are active globally is in the field of education which is termed Edupreneurship. Edupreneurship is the establishment of a school regardless of existing resources, current capacity, or national pressures in order to create new educational opportunities. Edupreneurs establish new schools either for financial gain or for social causes due to a need in the marketplace to create improvements in the education system (Papadopoulos et al., 2017; Smith & Petersen, 2006). Edupreneurs are innovators effecting the education system who leverage their business experience to the education environment in the hopes of improving educational productivity, efficiency, and quality (Springer, 2019; Cuban, 2006).

The education system in Turkey illustrated a huge social opportunity for edupreneurs. There were approximately only 28 Universities when the first non-profit foundation university was legislatively allowed to be established in 1985 (with a population then of 50 million). Due to the lack of educational university opportunities, the government has since established another 80 public universities while 72 foundation universities have been established. Also of note, is that the public universities are free while students must pay a high tuition for the foundation universities. This illustrates that foundation universities have a distinct value proposition for top students to attend a private education over high-quality education at the public universities.

To compare the education systems in the USA to Turkey, the number of colleges in the USA is shrinking with 20 private Universities closing in the last 5 years in the

B. Beyhan · T. S. Kiessling (✉)
Sabancı University, Istanbul, Turkey
e-mail: berna.beyhan@sabanciuniv.edu; timothy.kiessling@sabanciuniv.edu

M. Aldogan Eklund, G. Wanzenried (eds.), *Academic and Educational Entrepreneurship*, Springer Texts in Business and Economics,
https://doi.org/10.1007/978-3-031-10952-2_20

USA, particularly in the for-profit sector. Edupreneurship opportunity for Turkey is much higher as compared to the ratio of total population to number of colleges/universities: in the USA for every one university in the USA there 44,000 people while in Turkey there are 464,000 people. Focusing on the marketplace need by edupreneur, another key factor for Turkey is the young population desiring to enter college but without the opportunity (median age of Turkey 31; USA 38.4; EU 43; Japan 48.4 as of 2019). The need for globally connected higher education institutes that are designed to provide high-quality education and research environment to students is another drive for edupreneur.

The entrepreneurial process often takes a considerable amount of time in exploration and determination of the resources required and potential success. There are many examples of idea generation then implementation or success, it took 14 years for Amazon to show a profit, Zoom was established in 2011 but only due to the pandemic became successful 9 years later, it took 6 years for Facebook to have a positive cash flow. For Sabancı University the edupreneurial idea was first generated in 1984 and in July 1995 the board of Sabancı Holding decided to establish the university with Guler Sabancı tasked to lead this project. With the participatory design process used, the genesis of Sabancı University can be regarded as an innovation model for higher education (Baburoglu, 2020).

2 Sabancı Holding

Sabancı Holding, headquartered in Istanbul, Turkey is one of the largest industrial and financial conglomerates. The company is still majority owned by the Sabancı family (51.7%) with the rest of the ownership on the Istanbul Stock Exchange (BIST). The holding represents many divisions that operate in 12 different countries such as Europe, the Middle East, Asia, North and South America. The Sabancı Group has seen huge growth over the years due to its many joint ventures and strategic alliances with global Fortune 500 firms, with the resulting side effect assisting in the country's economy. Some of the key business partners include global companies such as Ageas, Aviva, Bridgestone, Carrefour, E.ON, Heidelberg Cement, Marubeni, and Philip Morris. In 2019, Sabancı Group posted combined sales revenue of TL 97.6 billion and consolidated net profit of TL 3.8 billion. The firm is so large that it represents 8.1% of total market capitalization of Turkish equity market.

The company has divisions in the industrial sector: Brisa (joint venture with Bridgestone), Kordsa, Temsa Motorlu Araçlar, Temsa İş Makinaları (joint venture with Marubeni); in Banking: Akbank; in retail: CarrefourSA (joint venture with Carrefour), TeknoSA; in insurance: Aksigorta (joint venture with Ageas), AvivaSA (joint venture with Aviva); in energy: EnerjiSA (joint venture with E.ON), EnerjiSA Üretim; in cement: Akçansa (joint venture with HeidelbergCement), Çimsa; and others: SabancıDX, Philip MorrisSA (joint venture with Philip Morris), Tursa.

3 Guler Sabancı

Ms. Guler was born in 1955 the first granddaughter in the Sabancı family. She received a university degree in business administration and started her professional career at Lassa, the Sabancı-owned tire production company. Later she was promoted to the general manager of KordSA, a position she held for 14 years. Again promoted, she became a member of the board of directors at Sabancı Holding, heading the tires and reinforcement materials group, as well as having responsibility for human resources.

Currently, Ms. Guler is the chairwoman and managing director of Sabancı Holding, the Founding President of the Sabancı University, chairwoman of the Sakip Sabancı Museum, and chairwoman of the board of trustees of the Sabancı Foundation. She is the first and only female member of European Round Table of Industrialists (ERT). She was named second on Fortune's 50 Most Powerful Women in Business (2013) and is listed as the 60th most powerful woman in the world by Forbes. She has always had environmental and social issues prevalent and has received several awards for philanthropy and leadership including the David Rockefeller Bridging Leadership Award, the Clinton Global Citizen Award, a Raymond Georis Innovative Philanthropist Award, and a European School of Management Responsible Leadership Award.

4 Sabancı University

The Sabancı Group established Sabancı University in July 1994, the groundbreaking ceremony for the campus took place on July 31, 1997 and began its first academic year on October 20, 1999. In its short 20 year lifespan the University is ranked 69th in the Times Higher Education (THE) rankings (year 2020), and is considered the top Turkish University by the Times Higher Education rankings, and 521–530 of all universities globally by the 2020 QS Global World Ranking and ranked between 71st and 80th on the QS Top Universities Under 50 years old rankings. Globally, the Executive MBA program is ranked 84th by the Financial Times.

The campus is approximately two million square meters with a dormitory total capacity of 2622 students. There are 440 total faculty members of which 345 are fulltime with 382 administrative staff. There are over 4000 undergraduate students, close to 1000 graduate students with a student/teacher ratio of 18. With only a short 20-year history, there are nearly 13,000 alumni and nearly 70% of all undergraduates receive some sort of scholarship. There are three faculty departments (Faculty of Engineering and Natural Sciences, Faculty of Arts and Social Sciences, and the Sabancı Business School), 13 undergraduate programs, 46 graduate programs, and 15 doctoral programs.

5 Edupreneurship

We use the holistic conceptual framework of the seven aspects of academic and educational entrepreneurship developed by Eklund and Wanzenried (2022) to explore the edupreneurship of Guler Sabancı in establishing Sabancı University in Istanbul, Turkey. The key seven aspects are: (1) Sustainability, (2) financial, (3) political/economic, (4) international/cultural, (5) individual and contextual, (6) technological, and (7) intellectual.

5.1 Sustainability (Societal and Environmental)

Sabancı University was not established as a for-profit institution and has never expected the University to be profitable and a foundation was sponsored by the Sabancı Holding Company to assist in financing the university. The school was established as a social benefit for the Turkish society in general, developing programs that were innovative and reflections of the future. As such, one of the key foci was social responsibility and environmental consciousness which is a corporate mantra for nearly all top firms in the world. One of the principles documented in the philosophy statement of the design process emphasizes the role of university as an integral part of society and its contribution to the progress of the community (Baburoglu, 2020).

When the university was established, it was decided to be a "green" campus. The campus facility had a huge pit in the middle due to a mine that was previously operational on the land. This was turned into a lake in which all rainwater is collected and is reused for irrigation. Other environmental programs established involved the use of solar energy and the campus infrastructure was built by using eco-friendly and recycled materials whenever possible. Even today that message and green culture remains as the most recent building on campus was built as an ecological building. Recycling of metal, plastic, and paper is prominent with disposable bins throughout campus. Current projects include technology advanced solar panel installation, usage, sharing, and even putting back energy into the Turkish electrical grid.

A focus outward towards assisting the society has always been a foundation of Sabancı University. The Istanbul Policy Center (IPM) was established in 2002 and sponsors the Education Reform Initiative (ERG) to assist in developing new innovative educational practices in Turkey and to maintain global standards of world-class quality education. Civic involvement projects by every freshman student is a required class whereby the students must identify key issues that require social or environmental change in the society and to actually attempt to implement their plans. Ms. Guler feels strongly that the responsibility of all citizens towards societal improvement must be impressed on students as early as possible.

Furthering the local community in the immediate area, the Ayvalık-Küçükköy summer school for students between 8–14 years old was established from Ms. Sabancı's own personal funding. An old school was purchased and renovated where cutting-edge classes are taught such as Game Theory, computer coding language training and development, management, etc. In total, one of the key roles of Sabancı University was not only to provide innovative world-class higher education to incoming students, but to provide the society in general with graduates who not only focus on their own career, but to make the world a better place. This focus agrees with the pure definition of edupreneurship where their major goal is not only to educate people but then leverage this knowledge for social good.

5.2 Financial Aspect

As previously noted, the school was not established to be profitable, although needed to be sustainable. Sabancı University was funded by Sabancı Foundation that was established in 1974 by Hacı Ömer Sabancı. In the 1980s, Sabancı Holding had been rapidly growing, making new partnerships with MNCs (Toyota, DuPont, Bridgestone, etc.), and became highly profitable and successful. High growth and financial success drove the holding company/family to increase their social impact. They thought it important on the societal level to leave a legacy, as there was a need for private innovative universities.

However, even at the establishment of the University there were financial problems. For example, when the University concept was presented initially to the family budget was estimated to be 150 million USD, however, to make the University cutting edge, green, and to include all the latest technological infrastructure, laboratories with the latest equipment, the initial final budget reached to 500 million USD, which was a substantial burden. A meeting of the family members about the huge extra cost burden caused conflicts within the family as some family members were not happy with the extra money spent on the university, scholarships, etc. and the entire project was criticized and could have been canceled. The day after the meeting Ms. Guler met with the Chairman of the Board Sakıp Sabancı who stated "we might have mistaken in the planning and budget of the University. However, we will continue. This job is very important and big. . . . We should always keep the big picture in our mind" (Sabancı, 2020, p. 96).

To add to many of the financial burdens, in the second year of operations at Sabancı University (2000) there was a severe nation-wide economic crisis. Two buildings were not yet completed: the sport center and the performance hall. All the budgeted money was gone, and half of Turkish banks went into bankruptcy. Sabancı University could not ask for extra budget to support the university. That year the economy affected all businesses, and the resources were very limited. Family members, brothers, sisters, and cousins supported the university by giving money from their own personal savings/accounts. This was very important; nobody opened it to discussion (Sabancı, 2020).

Since the university was new and needed to enter the market successfully, scholarships were given to nearly all students. Due to this, the university kept the number of students limited so as to not affect the budget, and all the additional funding was secured from the foundation. In the Sabancı family culture they had a principle that comes from their experience in banking: one has to be careful in making commitments. After reviewing the scholarship system in other universities, it was decided to implement a scholarship program where the top students were rewarded. For the first 2 years of inception, in order to attract the most successful students, all students received scholarships along with free notebooks. Starting in the third year, the scholarship to non-scholarship ratio was reduced to 75% and in the following year to 50%.

5.3 Political and Economic Aspect

As like any country, politics played a key role in academia, and more so in Turkey than other countries. There is a governing body (called YÖK) that formulates higher education polices, audits the universities to ascertain compliance, and ensure that all universities follow predefined standards of higher education. However, this system gives universities little leeway to implement new innovative practices. At that time, a student was told what they would study based upon their score on the national test, start and graduate in that department. However, the system designed by Sabancı University had similarities to that of the USA, where students could decide their diploma program, even after 2 years of study. The system was completely innovative in Turkey. The new system was initially approved by YÖK while its president was Prof. Dr. Kemal Gürüz who was one of the scholars who participated in the development of the academic portion of Sabancı University. Unfortunately, the administration of YÖK changed and due to politics, 1 day a call came from the capital (Ankara) on behalf of YÖK: "YÖK doesn't like your program and wants you to change it" (Sabancı, 2020, p. 76). The rector went to the capital in Ankara and had a meeting, but the problem was not resolved. Then an official letter was received from YÖK demanding an immediate change in the academic system. The crisis continued to grow, and representatives of Sabancı University met with the Prime Minister of Turkey (Abdullah Gul) directly to discuss the issue. They were politically successful as Mr. Gul favored Sabancı University's innovative stance, had a meeting with YÖK, and advised YÖK instead of forbidding Sabancı University their innovative educational format, but to give this right to every university and to even make it possible to have different models (Sabancı, 2020).

Although there are some other problems emerging due to the innovative nature of the university's educational design, as an innovator, Sabancı University was constantly pushing the barrier to new and innovative techniques applied around the world and were in contention with this governing body. There were issues of freedom of speech by Professors at Sabancı University on some sensitive problems, issues of women allowed to wear head scarfs, certain classes that YOK makes mandatory, etc. Ms. Guler always took up the challenge, though very time consuming, and was firm in that academics should be free to express their opinions and the university administration need to ensure such a safe environment for academics.

5.4 International and Cultural Aspect

The cultural settings of Turkey hindered edupreneurs 25 years ago but has changed dramatically since. Although university education is one of the most sought-after goals for both parents and students, the traditional standard format was typically preferred. Also, the language of Sabancı University is English, and many students only studied in Turkish. The huge rise of private grade and high schools that teach in English have given the top private universities that all only teach in English a wealth of new students.

Sabancı University wanted to be a world-class University, not just in Turkey, and continues to scan the global academic marketplace to identify new best practices globally. For example, the campus architectural design was prepared by Boston-based Cannon Design. The project was inspired by Ottoman architecture especially Topkapi Palace's inner courtyards with paths. For the external coating of buildings, küfeki stones were selected. Küfeki stones were also used in Topkapı Palace, Süleymaniye Mosque, and many others designed by Mimar Sinan. The design team insisted on using local/traditional materials in buildings.

The Performance Hall was opened by an opera performance prepared by Yekta Kara. The purpose of the Performance Hall is not only for Sabancı University but for the nearby district, which lacks cultural and entertainment facilities. Sabancı University's Sakıp Sabancı Museum (SSM) was established in 1998 exhibiting Sakıp Sabancı's calligraphy collection that had been exhibited in the Metropolitan Museum, Harvard University, and Los Angeles County Museum of Art, as well as in Frankfurt, Berlin, and the Paris Louvre Museum in Europe. One of the most important exhibitions was "Picasso in Istanbul" with 254,000 visitors. It was the highest record for an exhibition. It was a breaking point for Turkey in visual arts. The public relations and communication budget for the exhibition were very high. In Istanbul, posters were everywhere. It was a great contribution to the city's cultural and artistic life and habits. After Picasso, Rodin, Monet, Miro, Rembrandt, Anish Kapoor exhibitions were organized. SSM was the first university museum in Turkey.

Being a first mover and innovative was always important for Sabancı University, as well as being outward focused globally. In 1999 it was decided that the university's advisory board must be composed of globally acclaimed businesspeople and academics. This would be beneficial due to the global knowledge transfer, networking, promotion, and strategic direction. The international partners of Sabancı Holding were invited and Dupont's CEO, Toyota and Bekaert's CEO, Deutsche bank's CEO, with many other influential people such as Lady Barbara Judge (director of the UK's Atomic Energy Authority), Lord Chris Patton (last governor of Hong Kong from 1992 to 1997), and the Chancellor of the University of Oxford holding positions on the advisory board.

Focusing on global edupreneurship Ms. Guler networked with Susan Hockfield (the first woman rector of MIT) and was subsequently invited to the MIT Women in Clean Energy Conference as the opening speaker. Ms. Guler then entered into a five-year agreement with MIT Sloan School of Management to partner with Sabancı University's Executive MBA program, which later partnered with the Columbia

University School of Business. Partnering with Brookings Institute (between 2004 and 2014) Sabancı University held an annual Sakıp Sabancı Conference with the first invited speaker Madeline Albright. Alumni meetings were also organized at dates close to the conference with the first USA alumni meeting having 30–35 alumni attendees with now as many as 150 attendings. All these conferences and alumni meetings increased the reputation and credibility of Sabancı University among think tanks in Washington DC.

5.5 Individual and the Contextual (Edupreneur)

The individual aspect, or their socio-psychological approach, is important when viewing edupreneur. The importance of opportunity recognition and implementation is important for each edupreneur's distinctive human characteristics, personality traits, and entrepreneurial, social, networking, managerial, and technical skills. Our examination of Ms. Guler's background, experience, and views of her edupreneurial experience will be of assistance in analyzing edupreneurs. "To be honest, I was not very much interested in the idea of beginning a university at first. I was working hard for the Turkish Industry and Business Association (TÜSİAD). Everyone was expecting that I would be the first woman president of TÜSİAD" (Sabancı, 2020: p. 13). She later got the offer she had always been hoping for, that to become the president of TÜSİAD but she refused. "I had found a project that I was fully committed to (the development of Sabancı University) and I could not have done anything else" (Sabancı, 2020, p. 29). She didn't want to lose her focus.

Having been born the first grandchild of the largely successful Sabancı Company, she always knew she would work in the family business. However, even though all her uncles were in the textile business, her entrepreneurial streak had already begun to show, as she entered into the automobile tire business contrary to her uncle's focus as she saw a much greater marketplace opportunity. Later, in 1994, her entrepreneurial mentality began to search for other new marketplace opportunities and ventured into the wine production business. At this time, she was influenced by Sakip Sabancı to instead start a university. "At first this project scared me but then little by little I became attracted to the idea. I am not a professor, I am not an academician, but I can be the one who brings them all together" (Sabancı, 2020, p. 16).

Entrepreneurship requires a good team and the ability to manage and listen to experts. "Where will we start? I told everyone. What would an ideal university be? There were various ideas, but I didn't have any idea. I would understand later how useful it was (having no clear idea)" (Sabancı, 2020, p. 19). She convened a conference to advise as to what the university should be, with participants from around the world, top academics at top universities, consultants from top firms, etc. but the participants were far from a consensus. "I realized the conference was an important experience for me. After that conference my role was shaped: mediator and conciliator" (Sabancı, 2020, p. 24).

"I knew that academia is different from business. From the beginning I admitted that I would not be assertive in the intellectual development of the university, I should not. I am a manager in the business realm. I was always cautious about being the person who manages the academic process" (Sabancı, 2020, p. 32). Ms. Guler realized that the terminology and how to speak to academics were very different than that of businesspeople and needed to modify her managerial style to accommodate.

Entrepreneurs are typically passionate about their new focus. "For me, it is very important to feel the same excitement in the people with whom I work. I need to share my excitement and passion. I was lucky I worked with people who had the same level of passion. I never lost my focus, even during negative feedback. I also ensured that nobody lost their focus. I was never afraid to do something that has not yet been done. But I would like to know pros and cons" (Sabancı, 2020, p. 70, 81) She describes her management philosophy as listening well, understanding, making the right prioritization, persuading, and leading the team while being open and transparent (Sabancı, 2020, p. 91).

In developing her university product, she pursued appropriately due diligence, while leaving open innovation, uniqueness, and differentiation of the product. "We searched, analyzed but never blindly copy/imitate good examples" (Sabancı, 2020: p. 71). Her management style focused on input from experts, the cohesiveness of the team, and collaboration "I believe that in the organizations like universities the real success is to make decisions together" (Sabancı, 2020, p. 102). Everyone should have the intention to make a common decision. I spent too much time not only making decisions but also explaining these decisions and persuading others. I spent a lot of attention not to make my words perceived as orders.

The most important challenge for Ms. Guler was the strategic planning for the university. Academics negatively reacted to the preparation of a strategic plan, in fact, they refused to develop one as this was "non-academic." Ms. Guler approach this critical juncture differently "In the first 5 years we didn't use the term "strategic plan", we used instead "focusing" "prioritization". At last, we decided to organize a conference for all the faculties; to develop a common cause, a common direction to be set. I learned that instead of utilizing the term "strategic plan" it was more appropriate to ask "what are our priorities?" which was getting more acceptance. I could resist but I tried to understand them. Now as we are coming to the end of 20th year, our new strategic plan for the next 10 years was completed by the participation of everyone at the university" (Sabancı, 2020, p. 105).

5.6 Technology

When Sabancı University was preparing the budget to start the University they realized that everything will be changing in the twenty-first century. Books were starting to be transformed into digital as well as all the archival periodicals and books. They realized that the concept of a "library" was not sufficient to cover all these new technologies; so the building was named the "Information Center." Every type of document ever incorporated at Sabancı University was received and archived as digital from the very first day. Sabancı University also needed to make the university differentiated from other universities to make it more attractive and modern to students. It was imperative therefore that the latest technological infrastructure all across the campus would be implemented, and provided a wireless network to all faculty and students, which was novel back then. However, it was very expensive, but the university knew it was needed. Sabancı University continues to upgrade and view the world-class practices of other universities and incorporate them whenever it is appropriate. Ms. Guler, from her business background, knew the importance of technology and was focusing on the future, so uniquely started important programs in big data, cybersecurity, the Istanbul Center for Energy and Climate, Artificial Intelligence, Machine Learning, Computer Graphics & Visualization, Computer Networks, Computer Vision & Signal Processing, Data Analytics, High-Performance Computing, Security and Privacy, and Software Engineering, to name a few foci.

To this day Sabancı University continues to be a leader in technology within a university. In 2020, a new campus opened in downtown Istanbul (Altunizade campus) dedicated to classrooms that are fully technologically advanced. Webinars, broadcasting of seminars, interactive classrooms with students not present, recordings, touch screen boards, wireless activities, etc. have all been incorporated specifically to have all the latest world-class technology available for professors and students to utilize.

5.7 Intellectual

Edupreneurs should also be intellectual entrepreneurs with their major goal to educate people who are responsible for their education, leverage their garnished knowledge to add to the global accumulated knowledge, and then leverage this for social good (Cherwitz, 2016). As such, the key question for the first collaborative conference on the development of Sabancı University was "What is the ideal university for the twenty-first century?" As Ms. Guler remembers, "I had heard many ideas in this process, but we could not move forward without consensus" (Sabancı, 2020, p. 21). The ongoing participatory process by discussions of academic and professional businesspeople that occurred during many sessions was without borders or limits and that sought results became the most important strength of Sabancı University.

To develop the intellectual portion of the university, Ms. Guler heavily relied on experts whose global acumen was instrumental in the development of the first curriculum, which is under continuous improvement due to marketplace changes. The variety of participants, who often disagreed but came with compromises and fruitful collaboration, was the cause of Sabancı University's descriptive success. Academics from different disciplines, different backgrounds, and countries were invited to the development conferences: from 22 countries with more than 50 participants. In the development conferences to ascertain an appropriate leading-edge world-class curriculum, the design committees discussed what a world-class university would contain, within the constraints of the conditions and regulations in Turkey. At the end of the conference, the philosophy of the university was shaped: "Creating and improving together." One such approach was the interdisciplinary nature of the departments and how the different departments should not become "silos" as seen in nearly all universities globally. Ms. Guler, from her past business experience, understood that engineering required appropriate management skills, management needed social sciences, etc. and the school was planned to integrate all functions so a student will leave with the necessary skills to work independently.

Development of the programs also focused on the needs and requirements of the local students. After conclusions from the development conferences, market research transpired focusing on future students' manifest and latent needs. A laborious process which included 13 different design committees were formed to develop courses and programs, and the interdisciplinary contexts. As new programs were in the planning stage throughout the history of Sabancı University, preliminary research was performed with a minimum of 5 academics from outside a department to advise and participate in the ultimate product. This outside-in perspective gave any new courses/programs an interdisciplinary construct lacking in many other universities.

Creating together, seeking advice from external experts, and focusing on a common goal of developing intellectual curiosity became the culture of Sabancı University. In accordance with one of Ms. Guler's goals, one of the first actions after the establishment of the university was to publish the statement of academic freedom. Upon the in-depth review and development of the academic programs, it came to light that many universities ignored the business field and the developments outside the university. Sabancı University realized the importance of this relationship and established a center whose sole purpose was to manage research projects and processes. This edupreneurship was so successful, it became a model for all of Turkey, and YÖK entreated all universities in Turkey to establish a similar model. The center was initiated so academics would create projects, which were not only theoretical but can be applied to real-life problems. This model was not only used for engineering, but also in the social sciences. For intellectual creativity, a buzzword had been created "3 T" (Florida, 2002), which represents the combination of technology, talent, and tolerance. Sabancı University has combined them all successfully, and the continued annual increase in the external international rankings illustrates the intellectual prowess of this combination.

6 The Future of Sabancı University

Sabancı University has just completed its strategic plan as of 2020 and follows the key seven aspects of edupreneurship established by Eklund and Wanzenried (2022): (1) Sustainability, (2) financial, (3) political/economic, (4) international/cultural, (5) individual and contextual, (6) technological, and (7) intellectual. The strategy meeting received input from stakeholders such as faculty, the Sabancı family,

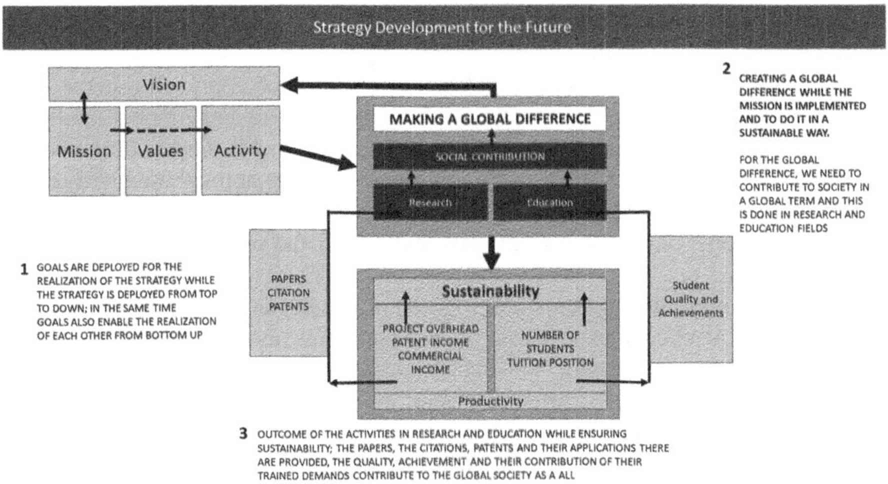

Fig. 1 Strategy Development. Source: Baburoglu (2020)

students, consultants, and academics from globally renowned universities. As Ms. Sabancı stressed 20 years ago, she is not an expert in the field, but is an expert global manager and follows world-class global practices which include obtaining guidance and advice from numerous venues.

The development of Sabancı University's strategy (see chart below) focused on key issues such as a global focus and impact, sustainability, social contribution in both education and research, all aligned with the university's mission, vision, and values (Fig. 1).

After the input from many and varied constituents, Sabancı University developed 14 key goals for continued sustainable success (see chart below). These are in accordance with the seven key aspects of edupreneurship. Sustainability was and will be a key cornerstone of the university with three separate goals (SH1, 2, and 3) with a continued focus on global sustainability programs, educating the students to have a socially responsible mindset, and having research that makes a social impact on society. The financial aspect for any entrepreneur is always on the top of their issues and the new strategic plan included a new and balanced financial structure.

To continue to be a leader in the academic field in Turkey (goal SH9) is the development and application of innovative and online education components. This directly addresses the political/economic issues as this will be implemented with the support and approval of the Turkish regulatory body (YÖK) that can also be encouraged to be utilized in the other local universities. Sabancı University aspires to be one of the top global universities and as such, measures themselves to other top global universities. Their strategic goals include continued growth in these areas through global alliances, improving global visibility and reputation, and a focus on global issues (SH1, 10, and 12).

As with any successful organization, the individual and contextual aspects of human resources, and their improvement drive the success of the university. Sabancı

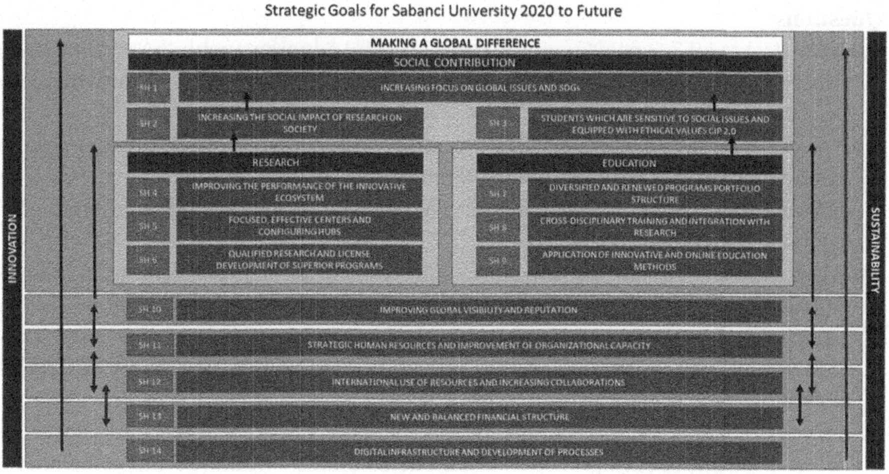

Fig. 2 Strategic Goals. Source: Baburoglu (2020)

University incorporated this component for the future by establishing goals of improving the performance of the innovative ecosystem, reconfiguring cross-disciplinary hubs for research effectiveness, and improvement in organization capability through strategic human resources application (goals SH4, 5,7, 8, and 11). Today's educational and business environment relies on cutting-edge technology and is expected and required by customers and students. Sabancı University's strategic plan addresses this by a continued focus on its digital infrastructure development and through the creation of innovative online teaching methods (goals SH9 and 14). Finally, the development of intellectual curiosity to produce knowledge for the university, society, and the students is at the forefront of the purpose of any university. Sabancı has placed emphasis on addressing this final aspect of edupreneurship to improve the innovative ecosystem, generate cross-disciplinary research, and focus on top research and licensing of intellectual property (goals SH4, 5, 6, and 8) (Fig. 2).

7 Summary

In summary, in Sabancı University's brief history the edupreneur, Guler Sabancı has been successful in terms of long-term sustainability, societal enhancement, and global impact measured by external ratings such as the Financial Times. However, as with any firm or institution, past success does not infer future success, and continuous strategic planning is required as the global marketplace, customers' needs and wants, and their value proposition is constantly changing. The new strategic plan focuses on all the key aspects of edupreneurship with the goal of Sabancı University to be successful for all stakeholders, especially that of global society in total.

Questions

Question 1. Are all 7 aspects required for successful edupreneurship? Are some more important than others? If some are more important, how would you rank these, or are they all equally important? If so, why?

Question 2. Are the marketplace opportunities still available for edupreneurship in mature markets? There is much literature that mature markets have failed to innovate their programs for a century. What type of opportunities are there still available for edupreneurs?

Question 3. Does it make sense to start a university as a for-profit venture in today's global marketplace (consider the competition, subsidies to universities by the government, endowments by alumni, scholarships given to students, huge costs of initial infrastructure and continued upgrade and maintenance, ongoing salaries of professors and administration, etc.)?

Question 4. Do you think there are significant differences between an edupreneur versus a business entrepreneur? What characteristics would be the same/different? What are the most important characteristics of an Edupreneur?

Question 5. How much more innovation can a university do in today's global marketplace? If there are many more opportunities, why have edupreneurs not seized upon this opportunity?

Question 6. Are there significant differences in edupreneurship culturally? Do they vary per country? Can an established university be a successful edupreneur in a different country/marketplace?

Question 7. Do Sabancı University's goals make sense based upon the global marketplace conditions and will align them for success?

References

Baburoglu, O. (2020). The genesis of Sabancı University: The design process of a greenfield site university. In O. Baburoglu (Ed.), *Educational futures: Shifting paradigm of universities & education* (pp. 335–360). Sabancı University Press.

Cherwitz, R. A. (2016). Diversifying graduate education: The promise of intellectual entrepreneurship. *Journal of Hispanic Higher Education, 4*(1), 19–33.

Cuban, L. (2006). Educational Entrepreneurs Redux. In F. M. Hess (Ed.), *Educational entrepreneurship: Realities, challenges, possibilities*. Harvard Education Press.

Eklund, & Wanzenried. (2022). *Academic and Educational Entrepreneurship: Foundations in Theory and Lessons from Practice*. Springer.

Florida. (2002). *The rise of the creative class*. Basic Books.

Papadopoulos, P. M., Burger, R., & Faria, A. (Eds.). (2017). *Innovation and entrepreneurship in education*. Emerald.

Smith, K., & Petersen, J. L. (2006). What is educational entrepreneurship? In F. M. Hess (Ed.), *Educational entrepreneurship: Realities, challenges, possibilities*. Harvard Education Press.

Sabancı, G. (2020). *Bir üniversite var ederken*. Alfa Yayınları.

Springer. (2019). *Classroom Companion*. Business. https://www.springer.com/series/16374

Berna Beyhan is an Associate Professor of Entrepreneurship. She received her BA in Business Administration from Bogazici University and her MA in European Studies of Science, Technology and Society from ITU and the University of Oslo. She completed her Ph.D. in Science and Technology Policy Studies at METU in 2011 and continued her research on innovation and entrepreneurship at the Institute of Innovation and Entrepreneurship at the University of Gothenburg as a post-doc research fellow. Her main research interests are technology entrepreneurship, academic entrepreneurship, acceleration, and incubation programs, and innovation management in emerging technologies. She is the author of the articles published in journals, such as Technovation, Journal of Technology Transfer, Technological Forecasting and Social Change, and Entrepreneurship Research Journal.

Timothy S. Kiessling has over 20 years as a full-time practitioner globally with responsibilities that ranged from strategy development and implementation, Mergers and Acquisitions, computer and organizational systems evaluation and implementation, International Finance, responsible for all operations, strategic global human resource management, etc. Currently, he consults for top management teams in the USA, Australia, and Turkey in strategy, top management team development, international business, etc. and teaches strategy in the Executive MBA program at Sabancı University.

Conclusion to Holistic Academic and Educational Entrepreneurship

Gabrielle Wanzenried

This book deals with the topic of academic and educational entrepreneurship, and it is based upon the holistic conceptual framework developed by Eklund and Wanzenried (2020). It aims to introduce foundational knowledge, concepts, and theories of academic and educational entrepreneurship, and then support it with the practical cases and experiences of academic and educational entrepreneurs. Accordingly, in the first part of the book, the theoretical foundations, including the existing literature and theories related to the topic, are set out. As represented by the holistic conceptual framework developed by/of Eklund and Wanzenried (2020), seven aspects are required to lead an educational and an academic entrepreneur to success, namely, *(1) sustainability, (2) financial, (3) political and economic, (4) international and cultural, (5) individual and contextual, (6) intellectual, and (7) technological aspects*. In the second part, concrete practical cases, first from academic entrepreneurship, and then from educational entrepreneurship, were presented and discussed.

Beginning with the theoretical background of academic and educational entrepreneurship, it is emphasized from the tenet of *resource-based theory, institutional theory, network theory, and human capital, positive, and social cognitive theories*. In the chapter about the *sustainability aspect*, the difficulties, and barriers, as well as the role of values and competencies, for sustainable entrepreneurship are discussed. It also explains how to train entrepreneurs to become sustainable entrepreneurs. The chapter about the *financial aspects* presents the main tools for controlling and forecasting liquidity and future cash needs and discusses the different sources of funding. It also prepares academic and educational entrepreneurs, among other things, to be able to speak with professional investors and to gain an understanding

G. Wanzenried (✉)
University of Applied Sciences and Arts Western Switzerland HES-SO, Yverdon-les-Bains, Switzerland
e-mail: gabrielle.wanzenried@heig-vd.ch

M. Aldogan Eklund, G. Wanzenried (eds.), *Academic and Educational Entrepreneurship*, Springer Texts in Business and Economics,
https://doi.org/10.1007/978-3-031-10952-2_21

of the basic documentation which needs to be provided to them, namely, the business and financial plan, and the cash flow plan. The chapter about the *political and economic aspects* of academic and educational entrepreneurship stresses the role of the "third mission" of universities, with academic and educational entrepreneurship participating in the socio-economic development of local communities, which is an increasingly important reason for the political-economic influence(s) on universities. This chapter also discusses the risks of public policy interventions regarding academic and educational entrepreneurship for higher education institutions, and how concrete policy interventions have to be assessed. Two concrete examples of policy initiatives with an impact on academic and educational entrepreneurship are laid out, namely, the Bayh-Dole Act of 1980 in the United States, and the Bologna reform in Europe in 2011. The chapter about the *international and cultural aspects* of academic and educational entrepreneurship discusses the factors which have to be taken into account to undertake an academic entrepreneurship journey successfully, such as cultural, administrative, geographical, and economic distance. It also deepens the understanding of cultural distance and discusses personal and institutional factors, such as cultural sensitivity, cultural awareness, and the concept of academic learning organizations, which may support or hinder entrepreneurship success. The chapter on the *individual and contextual aspects* elaborates on the impact of personality traits and skills as a success factor for academic and educational entrepreneurs. The chapter on the *technological aspect* of academic and entrepreneurial entrepreneurship first describes the changing landscape of education while emphasizing the characteristics of the new generation. It then introduces the technological tool to help "edupreneurs," before discussing the impact of the Covid-19 pandemic on education, and how different countries responded to the respective challenges. Finally, it suggests recommendations for "edupreneurs" on how to use technology in a new age characterized by changing education requirements. The chapter on the *intellectual aspect* of academic and educational entrepreneurship explains the roots of intellectual entrepreneurship as a philosophy and vision of education and sets out the constituents and purpose of intellectual entrepreneurship. After presenting the intellectual entrepreneurship initiative at the University of Texas, which is a pioneering institution on this topic, and statements by professionals, the challenges and possible solutions for the successful implementation of intellectual entrepreneurship are also put forward.

The *second and third parts of the book present practical insights and specific cases on academic and educational entrepreneurship.* The practice cases contain detailed and rich information on the individual dimensions and the functioning of the corresponding programs and enterprises. The contents are placed in the context of the holistic conceptual framework developed by Eklund and Wanzenried (2020) and provide interesting and instructive real-life cases, with insightful analyses, concrete advice and recommendations for action, and useful documentation of impressive entrepreneurial achievements. It contains the Bø Model at the University of South-Eastern Norway (USN); the case of the Lucerne University of Applied Science and Arts HSLU; the experiences of being an academic and an entrepreneur, and how the entrepreneurial and academic worlds can benefit from a greater diversity of integration; the case of Obermatt, the journey of an academic and entrepreneur who developed a more reliable way to pay executives; the case of Coursera, with the well-known massive online open courses (MOOCs); the case of the University of Applied Sciences and Arts Western Switzerland HES-SO; the Fierce Academy, which provides training and mentorship for leaders and entrepreneurs; the Mühlebach AG, a personal reflection of an entrepreneurial and academic journey; academic route-Scandinavia, an investigation into how business schools can improve their social mission performance by academic transnational entrepreneurship; the case of the Sabanci University; and the case of the CapSource, a high-growth education technology start-up.

Both the theoretical and practical contributions have shown what a multifaceted and correspondingly complex topic academic and educational entrepreneurship is. As is also visible from the structure of the holistic conceptual framework with its different dimensions, this is also a strongly interdisciplinary topic, and the individual and contextual dimensions are, in part, closely interrelated. Accordingly, it is demanding to be a successful educational or academic entrepreneur. Especially, in view of the challenges of our time, on a social, economic, political, and, above all, ecological level, academic entrepreneurship represents a great opportunity.

Academic entrepreneurship is only at the beginning of promising development, and there is still a lot of potential in this direction. More research on the topic is needed, and the contributions of the individual authors have also provided valuable insights. The world clearly needs more academic and educational entrepreneurs, and this book is intended to provide knowledge and experience, and, hopefully, will inspire as many future academic and educational entrepreneurs as possible.

Gabrielle Wanzenried, Dr. rer. pol., MSc Econ LSE is a professor of finance and real estate at the School of Management and Engineering (HEIG-VD) in Yverdon of the University of Applied Sciences and Arts Western Switzerland HES-SO since Sept 2019, where she is the lead of the research group Finance, Governance & Sustainability at the Interdisciplinary Institute of Business development (IIDE). She studied at the University of Bern, the London School of Economics, and UC Berkeley. Before joining the HEIG-VD, she was a professor of corporate finance at the Institute of Financial Services Institute of the Lucerne University of Applied Sciences and Art. Her research and teaching topics are Corporate Finance, Real Estate, Entrepreneurship, and the Ageing Economy. Over the years, she has led several research projects, provided consulting services to practice partners, and written numerous publications on these topics. In addition to her academic work, Gabrielle Wanzenried is co-founder and co-chair of a housing cooperative specializing in retirement homes (www.zuhauseambielersee.ch) and president of the board of the Thiébaud-Frey Foundation (www.laprairiebellmund.ch), a cultural institution that promotes talented young musicians in the field of classical music and organizes concerts for this purpose in its own cultural center in Bellmund near Biel, Switzerland.

The manufacturer's authorised representative in the EU is Springer Nature Customer Service Centre GmbH, Europaplatz 3, 69115 Heidelberg, Germany. If you have any concerns regarding our products, please contact ProductSafety@springernature.com

Printed and bound by CPI Group (UK) Ltd, Croydon, CR0 4YY
30/09/2026
02225234-0009